THERAVADA TRADITIONS

THERAVADA TRADITIONS

Buddhist Ritual Cultures in Contemporary Southeast Asia and Sri Lanka

JOHN CLIFFORD HOLT

University of Hawai'i Press

HONOLULU

Printed in the United States of America
24 23 22 21 20 19   6 5 4 3 2 1

Library of Congress Cataloging-in-Publication Data

Names: Holt, John, author.
Title: Theravada traditions : Buddhist ritual cultures in contemporary
   Southeast Asia and Sri Lanka / John Clifford Holt.
Description: Honolulu : University of Hawai'i Press, [2017] | Includes
   bibliographical references and index.
Identifi ers: LCCN 2016041542 | ISBN 9780824867805 (hardcover ; alk. paper)
Subjects: LCSH: Theravāda Buddhism—Southeast Asia—Rituals. | Theravāda
   Buddhism—Sri Lanka—Rituals. | Buddhism and state—Southeast Asia. |
   Buddhism and state—Sri Lanka.
Classification: LCC BQ408 .H65 2017 | DDC 294.3/910959—dc23
   LC record available at https://lccn.loc.gov/2016041542

ISBN 978-0-8248-6779-9 (pbk.)

For Sarah and Alexis
Joshua and Jacob

Samuel and Neena
and Jasper

Contents

Preface and Acknowledgments

The primary motive for writing this book arose originally out of my teaching experiences over the years at Bowdoin College and while directing the Inter-collegiate Sri Lanka Education (ISLE) Program in Kandy, Sri Lanka (on four separate occasions over a period of twenty-five years). More specifically, in relation to pedagogy, I have become increasingly concerned that my students understand how Buddhism, in particular Theravada Buddhism, is practiced and articulated among the vast majority of its adherents within the contexts of its indigenous Asian ritual cultures, rather than as an abstract system of religious ideas that can be cherry-picked for personal edification. As I have reflected on this problem, it has become increasingly clear to me that theoretical approaches to understanding Buddhism(s) that focus almost entirely on doctrinal and textual concerns run the risk of eclipsing how it is that most Buddhists in Southeast Asia and Sri Lanka actually engage their religious cultures. In my own interactions with Theravada Buddhists over the years, I have found, in general, that most are not overly concerned with philosophy or abstract religious ideas, but instead with attending to matters of ritual and/or matters of ethical observance. Of course there are many Theravadins who are philosophically inclined and for whom ideas count emphatically, especially among the legions of Abhidhamma enthusiasts in Myanmar, but there are far more who understand the religious significance of their religious culture in terms of the importance that is owed to ritual and ethical practice.

Having arrived at this realization over many years of experience in Sri Lanka and Southeast Asia, the task before me then involved determining what rituals within which contexts to focus on when formulating a strategy for this book. I decided to try to identify what were, arguably, the most popular rites most widely observed within the religious cultures of Sri Lanka, Myanmar, Thailand, Laos, and Cambodia. I am perfectly aware that my choices are debatable, but I also know that most Buddhists in these respective national religious cultures would agree that the rites I have selected for discussion are, at least, among the most important and most widely observed.

Methodologically and theoretically, I have been comparative in my approach. What this has meant practically, given the preponderance of my own previous research and living experiences in Southeast and Sri Lanka, is that I often refer comparatively to Sinhala Sri Lankan social, cultural, and historical contexts when discussing rites in other Theravadin ritual milieux. Moreover, I have also tried to recognize how ritual is a social experience, indelibly so, and, as such, cannot be considered completely apart from other social forces (political and economic especially) that are historically in play concomitantly. Finally, I have taken an approach to ritual that recognizes that this form of human activity need not be understood simply as a kind of orchestrated symbolic action reaffirming social and cultural modalities of being, modalities in the process of being transported from the past to the present. Rather, ritual can also constitute a powerful and definitive religious and social (and political and economic) experience in its own right in the present. That is, ritual isn't simply reflective or symbolic. It is also formative, generative.

The research and writing of this book have taken more than six years (from early 2010 deep into 2015 and early 2016) to complete, owing to difficulties in finding the time to observe these rites that are, in each case, celebrated only once a year. My teaching responsibilities made my research agenda logistically difficult; that is, to be present when these rites were being celebrated. Moreover, while I had a solid basis of knowledge to work from in the Sri Lankan and Lao contexts of religious culture, I needed to read widely and collaterally about Buddhist religious culture in Myanmar, Thailand, and Cambodia in order to gain an adequate understanding of the ritual dynamics in play.

The perspectives of many other scholars are footnoted in the discussions that unfold in the following pages, making this work a good example of dependent origination. It is a work that stands on the shoulders of many others who have preceded me. In Sri Lanka, I was also helped much by my good friends and colleagues P. B. Meegaskumbura, Udaya Meddegama, and Tudor Silva, in addition to some fieldwork assistance by Hiranthi Galahitiyawa while observing the *asala perahara*. In Myanmar, the late Myo Myint facilitated my observances of *kathina*, while Juliane Schober and Jason Carbine provided very valuable advice. In Laos, the late Grant Evans provided his wise counsel, and Viengsamay Luangvong assisted me in fieldwork and translations. In Cambodia, Penny Edwards put me in touch with valuable contacts through the Institute for Khmer Studies, where I met Bunnery Chea and Boramy Pong Pheakdey, then graduate students who worked so diligently and intensively with me during the *pchum ben* season. In Thailand, I am grateful for the hospitality and assistance of administrative officers at Wat Phra Dhammakaya, especially the Venerable Pasura who made arrangements for my fieldwork at the temple on two different occasions, and for informative conversations with Nancy Eberhardt, Justin McDaniel, and Patcharin Malairat. Mircea Eliade, Joseph Kitagawa, and especially Frank Reynolds are mentors from the past whose influence is apparent throughout.

I was fortunate to receive a senior research fellowship at the Center for Southeast Asian Studies at Kyoto University in 2010–2011. This is the venue where I began my research and writing on this project. Professor Yoko Hayami was especially instrumental in making my work at CSEAS productive. In particular, she supported an initial field trip to Myanmar during my tenure at CSEAS. I also received a Bowdoin College Kenan Faculty Research Fellowship that freed up time to research and write in Japan and Southeast Asia. Much of chapter 5 appeared in *Southeast Asia* 1 (2012): 1–73.

My spouse, Sree Padma, was a great source of understanding, encouragement, patience, and strength throughout this long process.

I took the photos included in the book. Jennifer Snowe of Bowdoin College made the Cambodia maps, and Samuel Holt produced the map of Sri Lanka and Southeast Asia. Barbara Roos compiled the index. Editor Pamela Kelley professionally nurtured the publication process at the University of Hawai'i Press.

Harpswell, Maine
March 2016

Figure I.01. Map of Southeast Asia

Introduction

The title of this book signals two fundamental questions in play throughout the chapters that follow. First, what do I mean by "Theravada traditions"? Second, what am I referring to by "ritual cultures"?

By "Theravada traditions" I am referring to the Buddhasasana (teaching/legacy of the Buddha) as it has been preserved by a Buddhist monastic lineage whose canonical literature, written in the Pali language (a derivative of Sanskrit), is regarded as a sacred repository of truth, a repository that has been the genesis for an enduring interpretive literary and philosophical "imaginaire"[1] and a repertoire of ritual[2] over many centuries, for perhaps as long as more than two millennia in Sri Lanka and Southeast Asia.

Many Theravadins, on the basis of monastic *vamsa* (or chronicle) literature,[3] would trace this lineage back to the Buddha himself, and aver that this particular lineage of Buddhist teaching is the most original and unadulterated version that has been preserved historically. They would cite the sectarian significance of the first three Great Buddhist Councils (reported in *vamsa*s) that were convened in India during the centuries following the life of the Buddha, councils that are regarded as definitive moments that determined Buddhavacana (the remembered "words of the Buddha"). Buddhavacana includes *dhamma* (the doctrine), as well as the norms of orthopraxy (the monastic code of conduct, *vinaya*). They would then refer to the successful missionary endeavors of Mahinda and Sanghamitta, the son and daughter of the great third-century BCE emperor Asoka, who introduced the *bhikkhusangha* (monastic order of monks) and *bhikkhunisangha* (order of nuns) to Sri Lanka, where the Theravada lineage then thrived for over thirteen centuries before its spread to Southeast Asia.

More critically minded scholars of religious history and textual studies may recognize the summary provided above as the outline of a narrative constructed on the basis of Pali literary texts that were redacted more precisely within the Mahavihara monastery in Anuradhapura (Sri Lanka) during the fourth and fifth centuries CE, and that the particularly distinctive monastic Theravada interpretation of this Pali literature, the interpretive stance that has endured as normative ever since, was framed by the linguistically and intellectually gifted monk, Buddhaghosa, who compiled his authoritative commentary on *sila* (ethical conduct), *panna* (wisdom) and *samadhi* (meditative concentration) within his celebrated *Visuddhimagga* (The Path of Purity).[4]

Other scholars of social and cultural history argue that forms of Buddhism—or Buddhist monastic lineages that eventually became part of the post–eleventh century CE Theravada stream in Southeast Asia— actually antedate the influence of Theravada's Sri Lankan Sinhala-based orthodox foray into Myanmar and northern Thailand by several centuries.[5]

Recently, the very term "Theravada" has come under close and critical scrutiny for the manner in which it has been so uncritically deployed as an anachronistic historical reification. Peter Skilling, and others who have followed his lead, have examined the issue in some detail. Skilling writes:

> I suggest that "Theravada Buddhism" came to be distinguished as a kind of Buddhism or as a "religion"—remembering that "Buddhism" is a modern term and that "religion" is a vexed concept—only in the late colonial and early globalized periods, that is, in the twentieth century. . . . [I]n the pre-modern period, what we call the Theravada Buddhists of Southeast Asia did not seem to use the term at all. It was neither a marker of identity nor a standard of authority in the inscriptions or chronicles of the region. Nor does the term occur in the early European accounts of the religion and society of the region, whether Portuguese, Dutch, French, or English. Simply put, the term was not part of the self-consciousness of the Buddhists of the region. . . . The history of "Theravada" is . . . a history of ordination lineages. It is not a history of "sects" in the sense of broad-based lay groups, as in Reformation Europe. Monks, rulers, and lay supporters were concerned with establishing or restoring pure ordination lineages in order to sustain the life of the *sasana* by activating pure "fields of merit" and ensuring the continuity of ritual. The records show little concern for ideas and philosophy. (2009, 62–64)[6]

What Skilling has pointed out is very compelling indeed. Whenever the term "Theravada" is deployed, it must be done with this caveat in mind: that its current signifying power derived largely from a very modern context. However, one will also search in vain throughout history for a number of other reifications that have also become commonplace in contemporary times. For instance, how old is "Southeast Asia" itself as a concept or as an accepted reference delineating a recognized geopolitical region? Or, for that matter, consider other very relevant recent reifications in this vein, such as "Burma," for instance, a name for a modern country that simply didn't exist before the British colonial intervention, or for that matter, "Thailand" before 1939, or "Sri Lanka" before 1972. Though we are now somehow stuck with using these reifications as conventions, when we do use them we also have to remember there is much more to know about the histories that they seem to encapsulate. That is, these are terms that may also mask or even silence.

The way "Theravada" was used in the early Pali texts, however sparingly, and the way it is used now, are quite different. Of course, "Theravada" is now often used as a collective term, a "mega-category" for the Buddhism of Sri Lanka and Southeast Asia, in juxtaposition to the Mahayana traditions of Tibet, China, Mongolia, Korea, and Japan. That is, "Theravada" has become a mega-category in a manner similar to "Protestant," a very general designation that covers over many important variations, but one that is also united by a general interpretive reading of history, doctrine, and practice that separates specific forms of belief and practice from other forms of Christian religion, chiefly the Roman Catholic and the Orthodox rites.

Todd Perreira (2012) has written a marvelous account in which he traces very specifically the emergence of the term "Theravada" as a general reification signifying the Buddhism of Sri Lanka and Southeast Asia and how its connotations evolved over the past hundred and fifty years, with its triumphal moment of institutional impress at a meeting of the World Fellowship of Buddhists in May 1950, in Kandy, Sri Lanka. By that time, "Theravada" had become the preferred name of the Pali-based traditions of monastic lineage and literature of Sri Lanka and Southeast Asia, a term—given its meaning as "the path of the elders"—that served as a corrective to the impression of inferiority connoted by the term "Hinayana" (little vehicle) that had been coined by early Mahayana polemical apologists in Indian Sanskrit texts such as the *Saddharmapundarika*.

I use the term "Theravada" sparingly and advisedly in the chapters that follow, for Skilling is right to point out that most Buddhists in Sri Lanka and Southeast Asia rarely invoke the term. One is far more likely to hear just "Buddhism" among the English speakers, or Buddhasasana (in Myanmar) or Buddhagama (in Sri Lanka), for instance. Moreover, Sinhala

Buddhism, Burmese Buddhism, Thai Buddhism, Lao Buddhism, and Khmer Buddhism are far more likely the names that one will hear deployed than Theravada. Still, I've chosen "Theravada" for use within the title of this book to flag the general orientation of the study: the Buddhist religious cultures of Sri Lanka, Myanmar, Thailand, Laos, and Cambodia. But I do so simply for conventional reasons, with the knowledge that each of these national traditions are not easily or simply reducible to one source, and that they vary a good deal from one another in terms of substance and emphasis. Indeed, the rites I have selected to study give some sense of their distinctive emphases and the perspective that I deploy in describing and analyzing them is often comparative.

As for "ritual cultures," I can again begin by referring to an observation made by Peter Skilling:

> As a monastic order, Theravada is further defined by its rituals—the performance of *upasampada* and *kammavaca,* and the recitation of *paritta* in Pali. Ritual demarcates physical boundaries (temples, monastic residences, and within them special sanctuaries). Ritual delineates social boundaries and identities—"Buddhist," monk, nun, novice monk, novice nun, *upasaka, upasika,* donor, supporter. Ritual orders time—daily, weekly, monthly, annual rites. Ritual dictates economic imperatives—royal expenditures and the import of precious commodities such as aromatics and precious substances. (2009, 73)

In other words, ritual can often articulate a perspectival order to the world, an order that may be cosmological, metaphysical, social, political, and economic in orientation and whose structure and dynamic will inevitably be hierarchical and yet subject to change. Catherine Bell has described this ordering function of ritual quite precisely:

> [R]itualization not only involves the setting up of oppositions, but through the privileging built into such an exercise it generates hierarchical schemes to produce a loose sense of totality and systematicity. In this sense, ritual dynamics afford an experience of "order" as well as the "fit" between taxonomic order and the real world of experience. (1992, 104)

Ritual not only functions in terms of articulating order, but it also has the power to create or preserve collective identities that may be social, political, national, ethnic, familial, and so on. Ritual is not simply a dramatic expression or enactment of belief systems, though it does seem to function as an effective conveyance of tradition. It is important to understand that ritual can house the participation of a great array of people who ascribe to varying sets of convictions and a multiplicity of perspectives. Symbols and their deployment within ritual are notorious for the variety of meanings that they may signify. In this vein, Bell has argued that symbols

> not only fail to communicate clear and shared understandings, but the obvious ambiguity or overdetermination of much symbolism may even be integral to its efficacy. . . . In addition to the evidence for the fundamental ambiguity of symbols, there is also evidence that religious beliefs are relatively unstable and unsystematic for most people. Instead of well-formulated beliefs, most religions are little more than "collections of notions." . . . [R]itualized activities specifically do *not* promote belief or conviction. On the contrary, ritualized practices afford a great diversity of interpretation in exchange for little more than consent to the form of activities. (1992, 184–186)

In other words, we miss out on the generative aspect of ritual and symbol if we regard them as simply the means by which something else is expressed. Ritual needs to be understood as an event or experience in its own right that constitutes its own realization, a realization that can become definitive for self-understanding, or communal or national identity. In concluding her analysis on ritual and power, Bell advances the following theoretically provocative argument:

> In sum, it is a major reversal of traditional theory to hypothesize that ritual activity is not the "instrument" of more basic purposes, such as power, politics, or social control, which are usually seen as existing before or outside the activities of the rite. *It puts interpretive analysis on a new footing to suggest that ritual practices are themselves the very production and negotiation of power relationships.* (1992, 196; italics mine)[7]

That is, ritual has a "performative" dimension that is concomitantly generative of qualitatively affective experiences. What this means practically for the focus of this book is the assertion that by studying selected rituals of central importance to Theravada Buddhist traditions, we can understand how Buddhists in Sri Lanka and Southeast Asia generate meaning, negotiate power, experience an aesthetic, and embrace identity existentially as individuals, communities, and nations. Ritual is not simply a fossil of the past. At the same time, we must also note that by studying ritual we will not claim to have discovered once-and-finally-fixed truths that are ontologically rooted, only to be realized by various communities in different times and in varying locales. On the contrary, "ritual can change as the conditions of the community change. . . . [T]he same rituals performed over the course of a thousand years can simultaneously affirm long-standing communal values of continuity and authoritative tradition while also allowing people to experience these values with different expectations and needs" (Bell 1997, 252).

Indeed, one of the theoretical maxims underpinning this study is that religious culture stands in reflexive relation to social, economic, and political change. Religious cultures are dynamic rather than static, fluid rather than fixed. How various rites rise and fall in popularity may be accurate indices of social, economic, or political change. Indeed, in this consideration, religion, or religious culture, does not stand apart from social process. Religious culture is part of the mix. This is not the way that religion has often been understood within Euro-American intellectual and academic contexts, nor sometimes in modern transformed Asian contexts either. The importance of ritual as a part of religious culture per se has tended to be downplayed, disrespected, or even ignored by many interpreters (apologists and scholars alike) of religion.

Indeed, since the publication of Heinz Bechert's landmark three-volume study titled *Buddhismus, Staat und Gesellschaft in den Landern des Theravada Buddhismus* in the early 1970s, a primary focus in the study of Theravada Buddhist traditions, in addition to ongoing efforts at textual translations and interpretations of Pali texts, has been concerned with analyzing the salient elements that Bechert identified as characteristic of "Buddhist modernism." Generally, "Buddhist modernism" has been understood as a contemporary reinterpretation of Buddhist thought through a wholly rational perspective, one emphasizing the practice of meditation *and* the inculcation of progressive and politically engaged social awareness. This modern form of Buddhism, also dubbed "Protestant Buddhism" by anthropologist Gananath Obeyesekere[8] and others, has eschewed traditional practices of image veneration, the performance of other forms of traditional public ritual, and has sought to relieve village-oriented "folk" of their reliance on "magical" or supernatural power. Buddhism, it is asserted, is a rational, non-supernaturally oriented religion.[9] The origins of "Buddhist modernism" are at least threefold: from nineteenth-century monastic reforms introduced in Thailand by Bangkok's Western-influenced King Mongkut; from nineteenth- and earlier-twentieth-century theosophically inspired efforts made first by the American Henry Steele Olcott and then later by his disciple, the militant Sinhalese Anagarika Dharmapala in Sri Lanka; and then in the 1920s and 1930s in Cambodia from the efforts of Ecole Francaise d'Extreme Orient luminaries such as Georges Coedes and Suzanne Karpeles, all of whom encouraged a new form of more philosophically inclined and intellectually oriented monastic vocation. In each instance, "Buddhist modernism," though generated by Euro-Americans, was eventually linked to emerging nationalisms aimed at fostering types of political identities that could not only counter the oppressions of European colonial powers, but also provide a pride of place to Buddhist communities throughout Asia. Many aspects of contemporary discussions about postmodernity and globalization within South and Southeast Asian cultural contexts were anticipated by the elements and forces constitutive of "Buddhist modernism."

Other important elements of "Buddhist modernism" came into play in the twentieth century not only in Asia, but in Europe and America as well, where many middle-class spiritual aspirants eagerly embraced this emerging understanding of Buddhism. These included the notion that Buddhism is a nontheistic philosophy (the term "religion" rested uncomfortably), an optimistic "spirituality" (a more comfortable term) of human self-effort that does not rely on supernatural agencies, a scientific perspective arrived at through demythologized interpretations of scripture, a socially engaged activist agenda congruent with democratic principles, and a spirituality best suited to the age of individualism, primarily and essentially concerned with the internal or meditative cultivation of a calmed mind that facilitates mental equanimity. As Gombrich and Obeyesekere summarized the essence of this understanding in their *Buddhism Transformed*, "[R]eligion is privatized and internalized: the truly significant is not what takes place at a public celebration or ritual, but what happens inside one's own mind or soul" (1988, 216). It is precisely this rendering of religion that made its way to become a normative understanding in emergent postcolonial nation-states. In a particularly poignant underscoring of this development, Laurel Kendall, Charles Keyes, and Helen Hardacre, have put the matter in the following way:

> In pursuit of "progress" free from primordial attachments [which is what most experts believed was inhibiting the modernization of Asian nation-states], the rulers of the modern states in East and Southeast Asia all have instituted policies toward religious institutions. These policies have been predicated on the adoption of official definitions of "religion," definitions that again have tended to be derived from the West. Indeed, in most Asian cultures prior to the modern period, there was no indigenous terminology corresponding to ideas of "religion" held by Christians or Jews [and I would add Islam]. Complex dispositions about the nature of religion—the primacy of texts; creeds pledging exclusive allegiance to a single deity, all originating in the theologically unadorned varieties of Protestantism— were brought to Asia by missionaries in the nineteenth century. When these predispositions came to inform official discourse on religion, they were often used to devalue other aspects of religious life such as festival, ritual and communal observances—precisely those aspects that were at the heart of popular religious life in East and Southeast Asia. And as Western

notions about religion were incorporated into law and custom, they also came to exercise a great influence on popular religious life in Asia as well. [. . .] The introduction of modernization, albeit at different times for different Asian states, was inevitably accompanied by direct attacks on those religious practices deemed to be superstitious. (1994, 4–5, 9)

In this project, I emphasize that the Buddhist *sasana* (tradition), as understood by the vast majority of Buddhists in Sri Lanka and Southeast Asia, still bears little resemblance to the largely urban, middle-class, and socially elite articulations of "Buddhist modernism" that have garnered so much attention from scholars and empathetic admirers in the West and in urban Asia. In a now somewhat dated yet still provocative 1983 study titled *Buddhism in Life,* the British anthropologist Martin Southwold warned against the tendencies of academic colleagues who continue to focus on aspects of "Buddhist modernism" that concomitantly have the affect of *colonizing* (not globalizing) Buddhism, on the one hand, and effectively silencing the vast populations of village and rural Theravada Buddhists in Sri Lanka and Southeast Asia on the other. Responding to the critique of "Buddhist modernists" regarding the alleged superstitious character and overreliance on the supernatural within "village Buddhism," Southwold argued instead that what he found to be quintessentially Buddhist about the villagers among whom he lived was the cultivation of an intensely this-worldly oriented ethical consciousness that engendered positive acts of compassion for the welfare of the many. For these villagers, Southwold averred, Buddhism was not primarily concerned with an individual's creedal-centered and *"nibbana*-grabbing quest" (his phrase), but consists, instead, of an ethical imperative to assuage the conditions of *dukkha* (or suffering) in the world.

Scholarly literature focused on Buddhism since Southwold wrote his provocative book, especially the interpretive analytical literature focused on the Theravada traditions of Sri Lanka and Southeast Asia, has ignored, in general, and sometimes ridiculed his warning. Yet other well-known scholars of a seeming kindred perspective had either anticipated or joined Southwold in recognizing the need to reemphasize the more village-based understandings of Buddhism. These include the French scholars Francois Bizot and Marcello Zago who worked in Cambodia for many years, culminating in the 1980s, and Laos for many years, culminating in the 1970s, respectively, in the process producing fascinating studies illustrating how power functions ritually in Khmer and Lao cultures, and S. J. Tambiah's work in Thailand during the 1970s and 1980s, especially his *Buddhism and the Spirit Cults of Northeast Thailand* (1970), which focused on how ritual is the means by which villagers sustain their collective material and spiritual well-being. Nicola Tannenbaum's excellent study of *dhamma* (1992) conceived as power among the Shan Buddhists and Kamala Tiyavanich's (1997) study of the apotropaic practices of hermetic forest monks among the Thai and Lao are also excellent examples of studies that focus on how village-oriented Buddhists attempt to procure power to assuage the condition of *dukkha*. In addition, Peter Masefield's (1986) textual studies of the Pali canon, in which he argued that interpretations of the *dhamma* may have to be "remythologized" in order to arrive at understandings more congruent with most Asian Buddhists, are representative of this minority scholarly vein. My studies in Sri Lanka (1991 and 2004), and more recently in Laos (2009), also emphasize how the religious ritual life of most Theravada Buddhists is concerned with tapping and channeling power that ameliorates the experience of *dukkha*. In each of these studies, the basic object is not an abstract philosophical Buddhism that supports the practice of individually, soteriologically oriented middle-class religion, but rather a dynamic religious culture within which Buddhist ideas and practices are intricately related to the realization of power and well-being.

In the study of ritual traditions that I now present, I follow the trajectories of the analyses cited above, but rather than completely agree with Southwold's claims about the centrality of villagers' ethical awareness, I focus instead on a series of annual rituals performed throughout Sri Lanka and Southeast Asia, rites widely regarded in their respective cultural milieux as perhaps the most important religious festivities held annually. These rites not only generate an ethical awareness and are responsible for the kind of compassionate ethic that Southwold found so compelling among Sinhala villagers, but they are also centrally concerned with generating power and sustaining an orderly (*dhammic*) existence.

As indicated earlier, my understanding of the religious significance of Buddhist rites has been enhanced by theoretical perspectives advanced by Catherine Bell in her compelling essay titled *Ritual Theory, Ritual Practice* (1992). I have been influenced by her theoretical insights to help illuminate the significance of Sri Lanka's *asala perahara*, Thailand's various practices of ordination, Laos' veneration of the Buddha image and its *pi mai* or New Year's rites, Cambodia's *pchum ben* or rites constitutive of caring for the dead, and Myanmar's annual *kathina* rites of monastic robe investiture. As will be seen, these rites comparatively illustrate the dominant this-worldly ethic of lay and monastic Theravada Buddhists. The elucidation of this ethic with the context of intense social, economic, and political change within these contemporary nation-states is the primary aim of this study. But there are other theoretical perspectives regarding the significance of ritual that the reader will also see in play in the chapters that follow. Ritual is usually a performance and, as such, depends upon a narrative that is dramatized through a specifically localized or nationalized aesthetic. In the ritual instances focused on in this book, the reader will gain an understanding of the manner in which the Buddha is venerated, how that veneration has been tied to the emergence of national identities, how the *sangha* is idealized as a virtuous field of merit and a venue for personal transformation, and how Buddhist laity care compassionately for their recently deceased kin.

A secondary aim has been to produce a one-volume study of Theravada Buddhism that is responsible to the manner in which most Asian Buddhists participate religiously within their cultural and societal contexts. My aim here is to give voice to their common ritual experiences. My approach is consciously comparative, thereby necessitating a commentary that ranges across these specific cultures. While what they may share may be housed within a Theravada umbrella, realization is situated, conditioned by the inflecting processes occasioned by the exigencies of time and space. A study such as this can be profitably read to complement other approaches to understanding Theravada tradition, including Asanga Tilakaratne's more philosophically inclined *Theravada Buddhism: The Way of the Elders* (Honolulu: University of Hawai'i Press, 2012), and Kate Crosby's systematic, detailed, comprehensive and often feminist study of the Buddha, *dhamma, sangha,* and society in *Theravada Buddhism: Continuity, Diversity and Identity* (West Sussex, UK: Wiley-Blackwell, 2014).

CHAPTER ONE

Phra Bang

Venerating the Buddha Image
in Lao Religious Culture

A study of early Buddhist material culture in India indicates that visual representations of the Buddha were predominantly aniconic or non-anthropomorphic until perhaps the first century BCE.[1] Before then, sculpted symbols of the Buddha often consisted of depictions of a stupa, the bodhi tree, or a footprint.[2] But in time, the visual center of ritual activity within all Buddhist monastic complexes or temples became the Buddha image hall, within which stylized sculpted images of the Buddha in postures of meditation, preaching, dispelling fear, or reclining at the moment of his final attainment were the focus of religious devotion. The Buddha image remains the symbol par excellence for Buddhist devotional life, for the Buddha is regarded as the paradigmatic teacher and spiritual virtuoso for monks and laity alike. In the Theravada Buddhist religious cultures of Sri Lanka, Myanmar, Thailand, Laos, and Cambodia, the Buddha is also something of a "culture hero," the epitome of what it can mean to be a human being.

While veneration of Buddha images within temple meditation halls is the staple act of spiritual devotion within all religious cultures in Asia where Buddhism has dominated, the nature of the relationship between the Buddha and Buddha image is understood in various ways from one cultural context to the next. In the contemporary Sri Lankan context, for example, most Buddhists realize cognitively that the Buddha, as the *tathagata*, one who has gone beyond to the further shore of *nibbana*, is no longer present in this world as a power to be tapped for immediate benefit. Consequently, Buddha images are usually regarded as reminders, or as markers, of what the Buddha has accomplished (*nibbana*), taught (*dhamma*), or modeled (as the quintessential first monk of the *sangha*). Through these three lenses, the Buddha image is an object of both meditation and devotion. It is very rare for Buddhists, monastic or lay, to regard an image of the Buddha as an active presence, although some ethnographers, in discussing the controversial issue of "presence" or "absence" of the Buddha, have described some isolated instances where the Buddha's power, as embodied within an image, has been solicited by devotees (Gombrich 1971b, 80–143). On the other hand, the question of whether or not power inheres within Buddha images per se is not so subtle in Thailand or Laos, where consecrated Buddha images are almost always assumed to possess a potent presence that invites active petitions. Indeed, many temples gain fame and attract a wide clientele precisely because of the reputed powers ascribed to a Buddha image that has been consecrated within. In this chapter, my focus is on, in particular, the vicissitudes of the famous Phra Bang image of Luang Phrabang, Laos, a Buddha image that functioned historically as the palladium of Lao kingship and, in the process, engendered a perceived political potency for the Lao Kingdom of Lan Xang. It is an image that continues to dominate the contemporary ritual landscape of Luang Phrabang during Laos' annual *pi mai* or New Year's celebrations. In fact, the city takes its name from the image. In this chapter, I examine how Lao Buddhists regard Buddha images, especially the Phra Bang, as powerful animating presences primarily because the conceptuality of received Theravada Buddhist traditions has been interpreted through prisms of the indigenous spirit cults that form the bedrock layer of religious culture throughout much of Southeast Asia.

The first part of this chapter is focused on ferreting out the logic of this prism. The second is more historical, tracing the significance of the Phra Bang image in relation to the parameters and substance of developing Lao political culture. The final section is an ethnographic reprise of the contemporary New Year ritual (*pi mai*) and the central cultic significance of the Phra Bang within that context.

If the spirit cults at the root of Southeast Asian religious cultures are not "timeless" or "primordial" in nature, to use now-controversial and frequently discredited terms, then surely, at least, they must be recognized as archaic and ruggedly persistent. Lao understandings of Buddhism have been conditioned by unique historical experiences and interpreted through Lao cultural assumptions. Marcello Zago, a premier student of Lao religion, once observed that

> the Buddhism practiced by the Lao has through time evolved a distinctive character of its own with deep roots in the general culture and the native

religious substratum. Most apparent at the ritual and administrative level, this Lao character of Theravada Buddhism has also led to the evolution of a view of life and reality [that] is often in conflict with that of the Buddhist canon. (1976, 121)

Zago's comments about how Lao apprehensions of Theravada have been conditioned by "the native religious substratum" are quite salient for the direction of this chapter, especially his subsequent comment (121) that the enduring notions of *phi* (spirit) and *khwan* (vital essence, or soul) are at variance with Buddhist cosmological perceptions and doctrinal assertions.

At the outset, in order to understand how the nature of the Buddha image, in particular the Phra Bang, is comprehended within Lao religious culture, it is helpful to consider the fundamental relationship in play between what theorists of religion refer to as the signifier and the signified. Writing about this relationship as it pertains to Buddha images in a culturally kindred northern Thai context, Don Swearer has noted how power represented by a consecrated Buddha image is construed as an inimitable presence, one that transcends the distinction between signifier and signified, between symbol and reality: "A religious image . . . is not merely a copy of the original; *it is in ontological communion with the original.* Cognitively, aura or presence may be expressed in ontological terms, but at the affective level it is simply felt. It is an emotional as well as a cognitive experience" (2004, 11–12; italics mine).

When I first came to Laos and began to spend time in Luang Phrabang's Buddhist *vat*s (temples), this ontological understanding of the powerful presence of the Buddha contained within iconic images eluded me. My understanding of the significance of Buddha images had been conditioned by my previous years of experience in Sri Lanka, where Buddha images are generally not supplicated for supernatural assistance. But in Laos, Buddha images, especially the Phra Bang, are considered exceptionally powerful presences that, when venerated with a mind of sincerity, can be tapped constructively for worldly benefit. Much of Swearer's study on how and why Buddha images are constructed focuses on elucidating the "theological," or better, "buddhalogical rationales," as well as the complex ritual means, by which Buddha images are consecrated and thereby empowered. Though focused on northern Thai Buddhist contexts, Swearer's discussion has direct relevance for northern Laos as well. In the present discussion, however, I take a complementary approach in analyzing how a specifically Lao understanding of the significance of the Phra Bang image of the Buddha has been inflected through the contours and prisms of spirit cult conceptions. That is, while there is a long tradition of ritually imbuing Buddha images with consecrated power, and legions of stories about their affectively miraculous impacts that can be explained within the discourse of normative doctrinal Buddhist thought per se, I want to highlight how the concomitant presence of the spirit cults in Lao religious culture has contributed indelibly to how the power of the Buddha has been perceived and then deployed in both religious and political contexts.

THE ONTOLOGY OF SPIRIT CULTS

In Lao religious culture, the representation of supernatural spirits, or *phi*, is subtle and almost always aniconic;[3] that is, there are virtually no artistic traditions of sculpting anthropomorphic images of *phi* or portraying their mythic or supernatural exploits in temple mural paintings and the like. While diminutive spirit houses for *phi* are regularly positioned near the boundaries of premises for many commercial establishments (usually hotels and guesthouses in urban areas like Vientiane and Luang Phrabang), the shrines for village guardian *phi* are usually either very humble sheds or ramshackle canopies located in the forest outside of the boundaries of the inhabited village area with little or no symbolic representation; or their presence is indicated simply by a pole or pillar placed at a central location in the village, often in front of the house of the village headman. In either case, whether the *phi* shrine is located in the forest or in the center of the village, *phi ban* (village spirits) are rarely, if ever, anthropomorphized.[4] Some stupas (such as That Dam in central Vientiane) or sacred trees within *vat*s are also regarded as the abode of *phi*. However, there are no freestanding buildings "housing" *phi* within which petitioners can enter to offer their invocations or petitions. Nor will one find full-time administrative or priestly specialists overseeing the well-being of a local village *phi* cult.[5] There is usually an annual or semiannual public ritual in honor of the *phi ban*, but any other interaction with the village guardian spirit is totally dependent on individual, private initiative and the availability of the part-time ritual specialist.

The relative lack of an iconic tradition for the representation of *phi*, the relative lack of social or bureaucratic administration related to the cult, and the relative paucity of public ritual orchestration is, I think, a sure indication of a relative lack of institutionalization of the *phi* cults in general.[6] Yet, there is no doubt that the various cults of *phi* are related intimately to a number of important social institutions: beginning with the family household, and then extending to private or commonly held village fields, the village *vat*, the village itself, collections of villages (*muang*), regional chiefdoms, kingdoms, and even the institution of Theravada Buddhism it-self.[7] Particularly in Laos, *phi* are significantly more nebulous in nature and function than the *devata*s of Sri Lanka, the *nat*s of Myanmar, and the *neak ta* in Cambodia's Khmer religious culture.[8]

In contemporary Laos, spirit houses are often constructed so that they resemble miniature Buddhist *vat*s. This style of spirit houses would, in it-self, seem to indicate the domestication of the *phi* cult within a religious culture now dominated by Theravada Buddhism. Yet, I want to emphasize that there is no image of any kind to be found within the Buddhist-*vat*-inspired-and-styled spirit house. The spirit house usually remains an empty dwelling, precisely because the spiritual force that it symbolically represents refuses, ultimately, to be permanently embodied; for *phi* are ac-tually, within the Lao purview, not essentially embodied personages at all. Rather, they are fundamentally bodiless or "post-embodied" forces, wills, or powers. So, it would appear that the *phi* of Lao religious culture, unlike the *devata*s in Sri Lanka, the *nat*s in Myanmar, and the *neak ta* in Cambodia, have not been subjected, at least not to the same extent, to the powerful processes of "Hinduization" or "Buddhicization" that have con-tributed significantly to the anthropomorphizing of spirits or minor dei-ties in those other nominally Buddhist religious cultures.[9] As such, the *phi* cults have not been subjected to the process of karmic rationalization either, karma being the means of determining why hierarchy exists within supernatural pantheons in various Buddhist religious cultures, especially in Sri Lanka. My sense is that, historically, the *phi* cults of the Lao cultural regions of Laos and northeastern Thailand have remained, in general, rel-atively less encompassed or acculturated ("sanskritized" or "buddhacized"); that is, until recently in Thailand's northeast region of Isan.

Consequently, what one doesn't see in play within Lao religious cul-ture, as one sees very clearly in the Sinhala Buddhist religious culture of Sri Lanka, is a thoroughly Buddhistic rationalization that serves to inter-pret various aspects of popular religion, including the cults of *phi*. In Sri Lanka, one can expect to find a variety of ballads, poems, and mytholo-gies, in written and oral forms, explaining, from a Buddhist perspective, how it is that particular deities or spirits have risen to a current status of power because of how, in the past, they have accumulated vast loads of merit by means of virtuous exploits, thereby earning a special warrant from the Buddha himself to dispense power on behalf of the Dharma to deserving suffering people within a certain region or throughout the country as a whole. It is possible, through a study of this kind of episodic vernacular literature, to chart the veritable "career" of a deity from his or her human origins as a prince, princess, or village or regional headman to his or her apotheosis finally as a Buddhist-sanctioned supernatural being enlisted to assist in the Buddha's bidding to assuage the experience of *dukkha* (suffering, or unsatisfactoriness). In each instance, the trajectory of the deity is framed within an understanding that he or she is on a morally and karmicly empowered dharmic path that will eventually culminate in the experience of *nibbana*. In Laos, I have yet to run across any claim that any *phi* are regarded as advanced candidates for *nibbana*. Their power, while often protective in nature, is also understood to be potentially destructive, if not, at times, downright malevolent, rather than being understood as unambiguously good or morally based. For *phi* can be of many kinds. Rather than begging a comparison to the *devata*s of Sri Lanka, the power of *phi* is more reminiscent of the power of *yaksa*s, a power to be feared because of its ambivalent nature, and less morally informed or engendered. Yet, even then, *yaksa*s are often anthropomorphized and "karmicly" accounted for in Sri Lanka. The power of *phi* in Lao culture, therefore, is less domesticated, less morally guided, less "buddhisticly" channeled, more intrinsic rather than cultivated, and therefore more to be feared because of its ambiguity.

It seems to be the case, therefore, that while Theravada Buddhism in Laos may have become the accepted and authorizing religion of the Lao royal courts beginning in Luang Phrabang perhaps as early as the late fourteenth century CE, and while the monastic *vat* eventually became the veritable hub of the *ban* (village), the popular religious culture of the Lao in the form of *phi* cults was never subjected to the same degree of Buddhist rationalization, or provided with a Buddhistic ontology, to the same extent as the cults of *devata*s and *yaksa*s were in Sinhala Buddhist Sri Lanka. Within Lao cultural regions, Buddhist conceptuality remained more confined and therefore less pervasive in terms of its parameters of influence. Along with the related cult of the *khwan*, the cult of the *phi* seems to have largely maintained its own basic conceptual ontology, relating to and sometimes informing, but at the same time understood apart from, Buddhist conceptuality, or in a complementary relation to it.[10]

Some Western scholars have characterized the relationship between Buddhism and the spirit cults in Lao religious culture as "blended"; still others have used terminology in which Buddhism is seen as "encompassing" or "subordinating." I endeavor to show—and this constitutes one of my major assertions—that rather than a sustained interpretive Buddhist understanding of *phi* and *khwan* based on a Buddhist discourse on karma, the converse is actually more likely to be found among the Lao: Buddhist conceptuality, symbol, and ritual tends to be understood at the popular local level of Lao culture through the lenses of the indigenous religious substratum constituted by the cults of *phi* and *khwan*. Following the French historian of religions Paul Mus, I would also suggest that this archaic ontology resonates with the same kind of indigenous religious culture or substratum out of which Buddhism, itself, within its own native Indian religious milieu, originally emerged.[11]

By making this assertion, I have entered the territory of a long-standing debate that needs to be outlined, at least briefly, before I continue any further. A generation ago, two leading scholars of Southeast Asia, Mabbett and Chandler, framed the debate succinctly:

> It is easy to find traces of profound Indian impact in [Southeast Asian] religion, in script and language, in architecture, in craft, in custom, in popular lore. It is also easy, by a change in focus, to find evidence that indigenous practices in all spheres of life persisted largely uninfluenced, and that apparently Indian forms were really local ones in disguise—local gods with Indian names, local architectural motifs or local legends with Indian top-dressing. (Mabbett and Chandler 1975, viii)

It may seem that I have opened this discussion by siding with proponents of the latter position, those who attempt to document aspects of indigenous religious culture that have been sustained despite centuries of Hindu or Buddhist cultural influence in Southeast Asia. This is not really my complete aim. Rather, what I also find fascinating are those salient instances in which one side of this cultural dynamic has read or interpreted the other side, and how these instances of "reading the other" have been the impetus for yet further reactions articulated through efforts to reform, purify, transform, or, as we shall see, even to eliminate. Thus, when Buddhist ideas and practices have been understood through lenses refracted by the influence of the *khwan* and *phi* cults, some Lao, in various historical epochs, have reacted with efforts to separate Buddhism completely from such (mis)understandings. In studying these instances, it has become apparent to me that the motivation for these delineations may have been more politically, rather than simply religiously (or spiritually), motivated.

S. J. Tambiah's monumental study, *World Conqueror, World Renouncer* (1976), and Clifford Geertz's classic book entitled *Negara* (1981) lay bare the structures of Buddhist and Hindu ideological rationales for the *mandala* political organization of political space in Southeast Asian kingdoms, but Paul Mus' essay, titled "India Seen from the East" (1975), explains *why* this model of political mapping reverberated so powerfully throughout the religio-political cultures of Southeast Asia and became, therefore, such an effective and enduring political device. In Mus' essay, it is possible to clearly understand the dynamic interplay between imported Hindu and

Buddhist conceptuality on the one hand and the indigenous cult of the spirits on the other, or how the presence of the latter rendered the former so powerful. What Mus presented was a daring and grand master theory, the type of which is rarely advanced in contemporary scholarship, owing to our current predilections to contextualize our findings in historically specific moments. While Mus' perspective certainly does not transcend history, he does cross over serious cultural boundaries (between India, China, and Southeast Asia) that since his day have become, perhaps, overly reified in scholarly circles and, as such, resistant to the type of grand theoretical explanation that he envisaged. In his own words,

> [T]he inhabitants of ancient India, Indo-China and southern China believed in spirits, present in all things and in all places—disembodied human souls, spirits of waters and woods, etc., . . . and . . . they also credited certain men with the magic power of conjuring them up or warding them off. [. . .] The two aspects [spirits and their conjuring] go together, and I believe that it is the activity of the sorcerers—their techniques of conjuring them up—which, more than anything else, has peopled the sphere of human life with various spirits: in fact the spirits are seen not at all in isolation but always in relationship with man, embodying in some fashion something that he desires if not something that he fears. Everywhere they are conceived in terms of humanity. The same is also the case with the most important among these spirits . . . , the lord of the soil, who deserves a special place. His cult, and the particular relationship he has with the collectivity which offers him the cult, would characterize, better perhaps than anything else, the form of religion which I believe to have been common at one time to the various parts of monsoon Asia. (1975, 9, 10)[12]

I had some initial grave doubts about Mus' assertion, but try as I might (and I tried very hard indeed) to think of specific contexts of religious cultures on the ground in villages in south India and Sri Lanka (in specific locales with which I am quite familiar) that did not contain the element of a territorial spirituality embodied in the cults of village deities or "gods of the soil," I could not, for the life of me, think of an exception. Certainly, the ubiquitous village goddesses, especially in Hindu south India, match up closely to Mus' "god of the soil," deities whose powers are conjured for reasons of fertility in and protection of the village. In both mythic and ritual contexts, the goddess represents both the protected boundaries and the continuing well-being of the south Indian village. Moreover, almost every predominantly Sinhala village I have visited in rural Sri Lanka over the years, at least every village that has not been white-washed by Christianity or become overly affected by "Buddhist modernism," "middle-class Buddhism," or so-called Protestant Buddhism,[13] contains a shrine for either a village deity or a regional *bandara* (region-specific "chief" deity). In the locales of Sinhala Sri Lanka, there seems to be *always* a deity who is referred to as "the god who is in charge of this place." Finally, from what I had been reading in the anthropological ethnographies of Tai religious culture[14] (or of Khmer and Burmese religious cultures in their own ways as well[15]), there could be no gainsaying the fact that the cult of *phi*, or spirits, is largely centered on a concept of power that is regarded as intrinsic to a specific territory, usually the village, but also relevant to a family's cultivated rice paddy field, a family compound, or to the very sense of a social collectivity, insofar as the deity in question frequently symbolizes the interests of the village or the family. On this, Mus further wrote,

> We are dealing with an entity endowed in some respects with a profoundly impersonal character. Not quite a genie: it is not a superhuman being, but a being to be abstracted from man; invisible, but made in his image, if we could see it. Its basis is rather in *events* than in a human person. At a later stage, the thought came to be endued with anthropomorphism and there was a god [or goddess] of a locality; but at the level we are trying to visualize, the *locality itself is a god*. An impersonal god, defined above all by a localization: *we shall continue to come across vestiges of these conceptions even in the most learned religions*. (1975, 11; italics mine)

What Mus was arguing for in this passage, then, was a notion of power found within or attributed to a given, specific place, a power that accounts for the dynamism of life associated with that locality: its energy or its ethos, depending on either the topographical or social nature of its associated territoriality. While this power is fundamentally impersonal, it is later personalized through the social and psychological experience of events; that is, through its existential realization, it is given a conscious social recognition through embodiment.[16] While many others after Mus, including Mircea Eliade, would write copiously about how "sacred space" is the venue for "hierophany" (the place where the sacred reveals itself),[17] Mus had actually gone beyond (or before) this kind of interpretation in trying to account for the nature of the sacred, or better, the *power* of place. Rather than attributing sacred power to the sacred's own manifestation, what he argued for is a process by which the "power of place" is transformed into an identification of the "power of the group," as a result of the group's experience of the place, of the events that had occurred for the group in relation to it. The power of the place was not, therefore, transcendentally endowed, but rather brought to fruition by its subjective social apprehension by the group.

I also want to underline Mus' comment that "vestiges of these conceptions" are to be found "even in the most learned religions" by noting that it is precisely this sense of territorial sacred power that is attached by the Lao to the Phra Bang Buddha image that became the palladium of their Lan Xang kingdom and from which the city of Luang Phrabang, Lan Xang's capital and ritual center for two centuries, takes its name. How the power of the Phra Bang was conceived as such, then, is a key example of how the conceptuality of spirit cults contributed to a uniquely Lao reading of the Buddha and Buddhism. It also helps us to understand how a Buddha image is thought to be empowered.

Mus was not content with this identification of the religious construction of localized power, however. In a remarkable passage, cited below, he first distinguishes between the religious dynamic he has identified and how Levy-Bruhl's theory-dedicated followers might construe it: as a "childlike primitive mentality" that arises from mistaking the difference between dream and reality. Moreover, and crucial for this discussion, Mus also asserts that the cult of spiritual power associated with locality is actually intrinsic to the manner in which land would be later politically organized and its legal status thereby authorized. And finally, in this same passage, he speculates on how, in some instances, recognition of the "power of place" eventually evolves into an anthropomorphic cult. This passage, therefore, is at the heart of his argument:

> It is not a "primitive mentality" that is reflected by this religious mode. The divinity, collective and without individual personality, seems to me to be implied by the chtonic cults. . . . As we shall see, it is connected with the way in which land is organized and doubtless with something like territorial law; perhaps indeed, impersonal though it is, it is never conceived of except as embodied by the materializations that gave it shape, even those which endow it with a personal form. . . . It is clear that for cults of this type, once they are established, the first problem is to reach the formless deity to make him aware of the needs and desires of the collectivity grouped around him. On the one hand, a god, impalpable by his own nature; on the other, a human group by reference to which he assumes his position as a god. . . . There arises . . . a necessity to endow a local entity that is incorporeal and impalpable . . . with eyes that can see the faithful, ears that can hear their prayers. (1975, 11–12)

Elaborating further on the emergence of this territorial spirit, its relation to community, and its eventual personification, Mus adds,

> It is important to stress that this [place/soil/stone] is not the lodging, the "seat" of the god, but the god himself, consubstantially. Not the stone of the genie, but the stone-genie. In this religious scheme, one must distinguish three terms: the divine position, the human position, and the ritual

position, which mediates between the two others. The stone corresponds to the divinization of the energies of the soil. Over against it stands a human group. Between the two is to be interposed a link in touch with man on the one hand and the god on the other. This link is the temporary personification of the divinity. (1975, 14)

Mus was also not satisfied to describe the metaphysical only in relation to its symbolic ritual embodiment. Perhaps he was too good a student of Indian and Chinese thought, and too influenced by Durkheim in his assumptions, to rest content without parsing out the sociological and political dimension of the religious dynamic that he had uncovered. In yet another pregnant passage, Mus identifies the social and political expression of the religious ontology of the "god of the soil." Specifically, the identification of the "god of the soil" is here modified to include not only the "energy of the soil" (as above), but what also constitutes the "union of the group," and finally, those who have previously invested their own energies in the soil: the ancestors of the group.

> The prestige attributed to the chief certainly did not begin purely with the institution of the chtonic ritual: but all that concerns us is that . . . this prestige is regarded theoretically as *a reflection of the local god in the chief.*
> In this way we can see how the human group finds itself obliged to secure an intermediary, who is its delegate, between the amorphous divinity of its soil and itself. [Through t]he person of the delegate, the earth-god and men commune. But *what better intermediaries could there be to define the union of the group and its soil than the ancestors* of the group, buried in the soil and thus restorers to it? Were not the dead chiefs formerly, in the rites, the land itself made man before their subjects? Now they are linked even more intimately to this land. (1975, 15–16; italics mine)

In light of these rich and compact statements, I will sum up the substance and direction of Mus' argument: (1) the village chief, as the intermediary between the divine and the human, is endowed with the power of the "god of the soil"; (2) thus, the village chief ("the delegate"), as the human social counterpart invested with the power of the "god of the soil," is the means through which the god and the community "commune," or through which power is distributed—the chief is the spiritual pivot; (3) moreover, like the village chief, the ancestors of the village also embody the power or energy of the soil;[18] (4) the village chief, therefore, stands in a relationship of "lineage" to the social past (ancestors) of the given place. What Mus has perceived, therefore, is not only a synchronic linkage between the power of the soil and the socially realized power of the chief, but also a parallel diachronic linkage between the power of the contemporary chief and past ancestors of the village. That is, the linkages are not only made between spiritual and human realms, but through the temporal past and present as well. This is Mus' understanding of the spatial structure and temporal dynamic of the "spiritual" in the "religion of monsoon Asia."

In two subsequent passages, Mus not only clarifies the relationships that he sees between the spiritual power of the land and its social realization, but also asserts that this pattern eventually evolved into the worship of dynastic, regional, national, or royal gods:

> We are concerned not with any stone but with one that is made the center of a clearly defined territory and it is almost a sociological tautology to say that the definition of this territory is at the same time that of a collectivity. So, taken together, these religious conventions would be equivalent to a *spiritual land survey*, the centre of each district being marked by one of the sacred stones. . . . It may be added that the cult of the genie of the soil is associated with that of ancestors, and that the stone which embodies it has already been presented to us as a dynastic or familial contract. (1975, 20; italics mine)

Furthermore,

> [t]o the *genius loci*, the personification of the energies of the earth, was owed the prosperity of the territory occupied by those who united to worship it, and who were defined as a group by this unity. The *yaksa* is everywhere a god of the soil, a cadastral god, a national or at least dynastic god in the city of the king, a community god at the level of village life. (1975, 29)

But this is not all. After establishing how divinity was linked to political territoriality, Mus argues that the principles he has identified were not only also present in the "religious substratum" of southwestern China and India, but that in both instances they were further organized into hierarchy. The result of this hierarchical stratification of power created not only the layers and levels of deities who came to populate supernatural pantheons, but also the hierarchical structure of the sociopolitical order as well. The divine pantheon of the supernatural order was none other than the "double" of the social and political order, the two being but mirror images of each other.[19] In the discussions that follow, it becomes clear that the Buddha, specifically the power inhering in his consecrated image, and the Lao king were indelibly linked in this "doubling" fashion, imagined versions of power operating in tandem at the pivotal intersection of their respective domains. In this manner, the Buddha and royalty were understood to be the veritable powers in charge of the place.

SPIRITUAL AND TEMPORAL POWER IN
THE *BAN, MUANG,* AND *MANDALA*

With the ontology of the spirit cults outlined, how power is specifically realized at various levels of the traditional Lao social hierarchy can be depicted. Each *ban* or Lao village vests authority in its headman, just as each village has its counterpart supernatural *phi ban* (village deity). At the same time, the town or village is regarded as the locus of beauty, virtue, and prestige in contrast to the vagaries and dangerous unpredictability of the forest (Davis 1984, 82).

Transcending the individual *ban* is the *muang,* a nearly untranslatable term, but essentially a cluster of *ban* related not only because of geographic proximity, but for politically defensive reasons as well, with the *ban* that has the most economic means and most politically powerful family, usually meaning the greatest ability to produce rice, serving as its hub in hierarchical relation to the other *ban.*[20] At the hub of the ban at the center of the *muang* is the *chao muang,* or *muang* chieftain, whose own position of power, like the village headman who is empowered by the *phi ban,* is endowed by the power of the *phi muang.* A pole or pillar (*lak muang*) located just outside the *chao muang's* house functions as an axis mundi or vector for the supernatural power that the *chao muang* claims and then distributes throughout the *muang* by his ritually efficacious actions. Aside from its "ritualization,"[21] the power of the *chao muang*[22] is used to muster surplus human resources from the *muang's* various *ban* whenever needed and to coordinate any limited bit of trade or political undertakings between his *muang* and other *muang.* To the *chao muang,* in exchange for his mobilizing role, a measure of tribute is owed. That tribute, in addition to labor, might take the form of surplus food or crafts. The *chao muang* might be, in turn, subordinate to yet another more powerful *chao muang* and pay tribute to his superior by channeling a part of his surplus resources to him: "The degree to which a settlement [*ban* or *muang*] is considered beautiful and civilized corresponds to the level it occupies in the *muang* hierarchy. All beauty and civilization flow from the upper-level *muang* and percolate down into the villages. At each stage in this downward flow, civilization loses some of its luster" (Davis 1984, 83).

While the directional flow of power or "civilization" is quite apparent here, the important point to grasp, however, is that at each level of social and political hierarchy, from family to village, to "district" *muang* (*tasseng*), to larger "regional" *muang,* and finally to the royal capital, these concentric and hierarchically related social units were the basic "political structure characteristic of all Tai peoples, who were remarkably free to conduct their own local affairs in return for allegiance, tribute and manpower in the event of war, contributions sustaining respectively the religio-symbolic, economic military bases of the central power of the *mandala* of which they formed a part" (Stuart-Fox 2002, 3).

I am unsure how far back into Tai-Lao history the larger concept of the political *mandala* can be projected with any degree of certainty, though the dynamics of *mandala* polity seem remarkably anticipated by relations between *ban* and *muang*. *Mandala* conceptuality has been invoked, at least retrospectively, in relation to the specifically Buddhist legitimation of power relative to the very founding of the Lao Lan Xang kingdom. The *mandalic* political structure of Angkor seems to have served as Lan Xang's model, as it did for other emergent Tai states, especially Ayutthaya (in what is now modern Thailand to the south and west).[23] Early-sixteenth-century accounts of the fourteenth-century founding of the kingdom frame a story that casts Lan Xang in the lineage, if not the image of Angkor. While these accounts are clearly written with a motive to legitimate Lan Xang in this particular light, they may also represent a reading of the present (sixteenth-century) ideology into the (fourteenth-century) past. While some scholars have been inclined to believe that the expanding organization of a *mandala* was already in the process of formation with Muang Sua[24] serving as its hub, possibly with the assistance of Mongol support, before the alleged founding declaration of the kingdom of Lan Xang by Fa Ngum in the mid-fourteenth century (Stuart-Fox 1998, 37), it is difficult to discuss Lao *mandala* political structures before entering a historical period when we are more certain that its overtly Indic religious elements (e.g., Buddhist and Hindu conceptions of polity) were actually in play; that is, probably not before the late fifteenth century, and more likely the early sixteenth century in northern Laos. It may indeed be the case that, prior to the establishment of the Lan Xang kingdom by Fa Ngum in the mid-fourteenth century, an emerging confederation of *muang* was in the process of being established, a process that would have yielded Fa Ngum's accomplishment, if indeed it occurred in the manner reported by mythically laced texts a century and a half later, that much more feasible.

This is historically murky territory beyond certitude, but my point here is that the *muang* seems to be a very archaic social conception intrinsic to the Tai people who emigrated out of southwestern China in the latter stages of the second half of the first millennium into what is now the Lao cultural region. While *muang* later became the constituent elements of full-fledged royally centered *mandalas*, and while the *ban* is also a microcosm of the *muang*, and eventually the *muang* a microcosm of the *mandala*, *muang* as localized social structures definitely antedate the emergence of a full-fledged *mandala* polity that later characterized Buddhist-legitimated Lao kingship. What makes the *mandala* distinctive from the *muang* as a means of social and political organization is the fact that principles of power have been recast through the religious language and hierarchical conceptuality of Hinduism and Buddhism. Moreover, at least in the Theravada Buddhist context, the rationale for the political legitimation of *mandala*s was ethicized.[25]

Since *ban* were miniature *muang*s, and *muang*s were miniature *mandalas*, the political *mandala* was the most highly evolved but also the most dependent of the three. In Lao culture, *muang* can be *muang* without *mandalas*, but *mandalas* cannot be *mandalas* without constituent *muang*s. Not only do *muang*s make *mandalas* possible, but it is quite evident that *muang*s historically preceded full-fledged Buddhist kingships governing *mandalas*. Indeed, the relationship between *ban* and *muang* was "the basis for the continuity that carries through those periods when central political authority disappeared. . . . The discontinuity of central political structures [*mandalas*] was overcome by the continuity of political culture based firmly at the village level, anchored in the socio-religious Lao worldview" (Stuart-Fox 2002, 10–11).

In my earlier discussion of Paul Mus' "religion . . . of monsoon Asia," I noted the hierarchical parallelism or mirror imaging that exists between the this-worldly social structures of authority and other-worldly supernatural pantheons of divine power. I have also noted how the element of ancestor veneration came into play in that context as well. These same principles can be seen in relation to "proto-Lao" sociopolitical organization and the degree to which a *muang* could retain its ultimate autonomy in relation to other *muang*. In other words,

> [m]*ueang* identity rested on mythic-historical descent and the marking out of the territory, initially perhaps through the force of arms, but subsequently justified as divinely determined. But relations between *mueang* rested on at least potentially equal claims to autonomy and inclusion, to legitimation through descent and to the potency of regional spirits. Small, less powerful *mueang* still reserved for themselves the right to autonomy, not just in their internal affairs, a right jealously guarded, but in relation to other *mueang* through tribute paid to more than one powerful *mueang*. All Tai were free men: all *mueang* were autonomous polities—at least in theory. (Stuart-Fox 2002, 74)

Despite the fact that most written political history focuses almost exclusively on the expansion and contraction of competing grand *mandalas* administered by or on behalf of royalty, the actual locus of power for most people remained quite localized at the level of the *muang*. Moreover, it was possible for a single *muang* to have cultivated multiple allegiances, or to pay tribute to more than one *mandala*. The powers of *mandala*s would sometimes overlap.

MYTH AND LEGITIMATION OF THE LAN XANG *MANDALA*

The *Nithan Khun Borom,* a chronicle written in the early sixteenth century under the sponsorship of Luang Phrabang Lao royalty, is ontologically bifocal. It contains two narrative cycles that account for Lan Xang's origins: the first is a Tai creation myth still brought to life each year within the context of Luang Phrabang's annual New Year (*pi mai*) rites held in April, a ritual context explored at the conclusion of this chapter; and the second is a quasi-historical account of the kingdom's first ruler, Fa Ngum, which links his power directly to Angkor and to Sri Lanka's Sinhala Theravada Buddhism. The first is a cosmogonic myth clearly designed to link Luang Phrabang's royalty to the cult of the *phi muang,* the putative ancestral spirits of the city; that is, to explain the "divine right" of kings to rule by placing them within a lineage of ancestors traced back to the world's creation by supernatural power. The second scenario attempts to forge a link between Lan Xang's kingship and the lineage of the Buddha; that is, it ties Lan Xang to the wider, universal religious history and cosmology of Theravada tradition. While a century and a half may have lapsed following the founding of Lan Xang, purportedly by Fa Ngum in 1353 CE before these two accounts of origins were knit together within the *Nithan Khun Borom* (1503 CE), and while their simultaneous presence in this text may reflect a compromise between competing loyalties in the royal court, both conceptual orientations represent shafts of legitimation that have remained vital throughout the subsequent history of Lao cultural history.

The cosmogonic myth related to the establishment of Lao kingship is filled with many valorizations, but four related principles stand out: (1) an original primordial unity between the world of the spirits and the world of humanity was ruptured through humanity's refusal to recognize the hierarchy that exists between the power of the spirits and the works of men; (2) the kingdom's ancestors were responsible for the establishment of the economy (cultivation) and society (marriage and morality); (3) the repeated misbehavior of humanity engendered a need for further divine agency in the world, taking the form of divinely descended kingship to sustain order in the economy and society; related to this is the claim that Muang Sua's (Luang Phrabang's) first ruler is none other than the grandson of a supreme spirit; (4) the division of labor (wet and dry rice cultivation) and hierarchical (tributary) relationship between the lowland, river basin based Lao and the upland Kha is established. The message of the narrative is clear: the powers of the land or soil, and therefore the power of the people who live on it, are realized by respecting divine agency and design. Respecting this agency in its tangible form of kingship (Mus' "god of the soil" or "lord of the land") sustains prosperity.

In the mythic narrative here outlined, we can see quite clearly how the ontology of the religious substratum articulated and valorized the power of place through the principle of this-worldly/other-worldly parallelism ("doubling" or "mirroring"). Moreover, it is also clear how ancestor veneration comes into play in relation to kingship and social hierarchy. These, of course, are two crucial ingredients described by Mus as constitutive of the "religion . . . of Monsoon Asia."

BUDDHIST IDEOLOGY OF ROYAL LAO LEGITIMACY

What Theravada Buddhism added to the ideology of the power of place in Luang Phrabang seems almost negligible in structural terms, given the nature of *"muang* metaphysics" already in place before its arrival. But what it did provide in terms of substance was a complementary ethics of power. That is, concomitant to the rationalization of divinely derived kingship, Lao kingship also became heir to specifically Buddhist conceptions of kingship that date back to the third-century BCE reign of the Emperor Asoka in India, conceptions that were further nurtured and refined for a millennium and a half in Buddhist Sri Lanka before they were imported into Southeast Asia. This specifically Buddhist model of righteous rule had been wedded explicitly to overarching organizational principles of the Indic political *mandala* in Angkor before the primordial founding figure of Fa Ngum happened on the scene.

In brief, this Buddhist model of righteous rule was embodied in the mythic figure of the *cakkavattin,* a future universal royal power portrayed in detail in the *Cakkavatti-sihanada-suttanta* of the *Digha Nikaya,* a Pali text of eschatological, apocalyptic, and even millennial significance throughout Theravada history. The *cakkavattin,* because of the vast sums of merit he has generated through his virtuous acts over many lifetimes, not dissimilar from the career of a future Buddha per se, is a universal king who conquers the four quarters of Jambudvipa (Rose-Apple Island, the human abode of men) on a nonviolent pilgrimage throughout the regions of his *mandala.* He succeeds by means of moral conquest, making present wherever he goes the virtues of the *pancasila* (five-fold morality: observing the sanctity of life, truth, honesty, sexual propriety, and purity of mind, i.e., abstaining from intoxicants). Moreover, the *cakkavattin* lays down the foundation of *dhamma*, preparing the world order morally for the appearance of the future Buddha, Metteyya (Maitreya), whose enlightenment and teaching of the *dhamma* will make possible not only untold prosperity for all, but also the consummate experience of *nibbana* as well. The appearance of a *cakkavattin*, therefore, is a harbinger of a wonderful consummating collective future for all who have taken refuge in the Buddha, *dhamma*, and *sangha*. In various biographies of the Buddha, at Gotama's birth, the auspicious signs of his body are interpreted to mean that he will eventually become either a *cakkavattin* or a Buddha. Thus, the image of the *cakkavattin* was a compelling ideal model for Buddhist kings to emulate, if not propagate. It linked them directly to the legacy of conceptions of Buddhist political power.

There was, however, another important dimension to the ideal model of Buddhist kingship that contributes to the power of the Theravada royal legitimation scenario. According to the *jataka*s (the over five hundred "birth stories" of the Buddha that recount his various spiritual perfections, or *paramita*s, over many life times), the Buddha (or, more properly, the *bodhisatta*) was a royal prince not only in his final rebirth, when he renounced the world in search of enlightenment, but in his penultimate rebirth as well. The *jataka* recounting this penultimate birth, the *Vessantara Jataka*, is easily the most popular *jataka* of all among the Lao, and apparently for Lao kingship; the *bodhisatta*-prince who serves as its protagonist perfects the virtue of selfless giving by unconditionally giving away all of his great possessions, including even his loving children and virtuous wife. His actions are so prodigious that they produce unimaginable loads of merit, bringing him to the very threshold of Buddhahood. This ideal model of virtuous kingship, with the implication that a king will eventually become a future Buddha, is added to the *cakkavattin* profile, in addition to a tenfold dharma to observe, to produce a compelling composite image of what a true Buddhist political leader can or should be. The preponderance of moral emphases found within these elements of kingship is why I have referred to the Theravada legitimation scenario as an "ethics of power."

Lao retrospective readings of the establishment of Fa Ngum's new kingdom of Lan Xang emphasize how its establishment paved the way for the fruition of Buddhism and thus connect the new kingdom with the broad universal history of Theravada Buddhism. Though popular lore would have us understand that the Phra Bang image was brought to Luang Phrabang by Fa Ngum, about a century and a half seems to have passed before the Phra Bang was actually installed in Luang Phrabang, an event that quintessentially signals the ascendance of Buddhism as the recognized power and primary ideology of the state. As well, though the ideal image of the Buddhist *cakkavattin* would indeed eventually inform the profile of kingship in Luang Phrabang, this does not seem to have occurred before "the reign of Chakkaphat Phaen Phaeo (1438–1479) . . . the first Laotian monarch to take a Buddhist name. The term *chakkaphat* is a modified Thai/Lao version of the Pali world *cakkavattin*" (Lorrillard 2003, 189). Moreover, the royal construction of Buddhist monasteries, according to Lorrillard's assessment of material culture, did not begin in earnest until "the second half of the fifteenth century [when] . . . Chakkaphat Phaen Phaeo received aid from the kingdom of Lan Na—where Buddhism was flourishing—to repel a Vietnamese invasion" (ibid.). Lorrillard has concluded that much of the substance, especially the styles of material culture that became dominant in Luang Phrabang, owes its origins to Lan Na's influence, rather than to Angkor's. Eventually, the ideal Buddhist image of the *cakkavattin* became undeniably attractive to the Lao royal profile, along with the image of the ideal ruler of dharma articulated in a revamped Lao Buddhist version of the Hindu epic *Ramayana*.

At the beginning, however, at least during the time dominated by Fa Ngum in the fourteenth century, it was probably not the substance of Buddhist and Hindu royal ideal images in play that bolstered his rule, but rather instead the principles of *muang* polity articulated in the ontology of the indigenous Lao religious substratum, the cult of spirits. For, according to Martin Stuart-Fox, this is how the administration of power in the Lan Xang kingdom likely functioned in its early days:

> The kingdom was thus constituted on the *mandala* model, decentralized and segmentary in its political organization. Four principal *meuang*—Xiang Dong Xiang Thong, Xiang Khuang, Viang Chan Viang Kham, and Sikhottabong—formed the core, each with its own dependent, secondary *meuang*. From these the greater part of the army was raised. The frontier *meuang* were responsible for immediately reporting any security threat directly to the capital. What held the kingdom together were the personal loyalties that existed between the king and his *chau meuang*. . . . Every two months, closer *meuang* had to dispatch a messenger to Xiang Dong Xiang Thong [Luang Phrabang] to report to the king. All tributary rulers (*chau meuang*) had also to submit a written annual report on their *meuang* (none of which have survived) and to present their tribute in person every third year. This required them to leave their *meuang* in the first month of the year in what was for many a long and arduous journey by elephant along narrow jungle paths and across swift-flowing rivers in order to arrive at the capital by the third month. There each paid homage to the king, renewed

his oath of obedience, drank the sacred water of allegiance, and offered tribute. Any ruler not so doing would be considered lacking in loyalty, and could be deposed by an armed force sent to exact punishment. A principal requirement was for each *chau meuang* to participate in blood sacrifices to the powerful guardian deities of Xiang Dong Xiang Thong, in accordance with rules laid down by Fa Ngum's forebears. Their presence at these ceremonies presided over by the king symbolically recognized the superiority of the *Phi Thaen,* the ancestral spirits worshipped in the capital over the *phi seua* of regional *meuang.* Such rituals not only established a symbolic unity; they were believed to be essential for the preservation of the power and prosperity of the *mandala,* for only such powerful spirits could prevent malign *phi* from destroying Meuang Lao. (Stuart-Fox 1998, 45)

If this depiction is reasonably accurate, then it confirms the fact that the political and magical ontology of the spirit cults had come to be writ large with the establishment of a grand Lao *mandala.* This portrayal describes quite clearly how Lan Xang's public ritual cult expressed the spiritual principles of "doubling" (this-worldly and other-worldly parallelism), territoriality, ancestral lineage, and hierarchy.[26] We can also see clearly how the centripetal and centrifugal forces between the center and peripheries, what Tambiah has referred to as the "pulsating" effects of "galactic polity," came into play through the ritual comings and goings of *chao muang* who came to the capital to pay tribute and to participate in renewing the excellence of the center. While we have no records of what transpired exactly in terms of the relations at the *ban* and *muang* levels of the *mandala,* or between lesser *muang* and regional *muang,* we are probably not far wrong in assuming that this same administrative and ritual pattern was replicated at those levels too. That is, the renewal of power experienced at the center was ritually confirmed and distributed throughout to the other *muang* subspaces of the *mandala.*

What followed over the next century and a half, however, was the increasing adoption of specifically Theravada Buddhist semiotics of power, not at all different in terms of the dynamics of interplay between the center and periphery, nor in terms of the basic Lao assumptions about the power of place, but different in terms of how power was mythically imagined and ideally acquired. Yet, these Buddhist and Hindu concepts were interpreted and understood, at least in part, through the conceptual categories of the Lao indigenous religious substratum.

The Phra Bang image of the Buddha thus came to represent the powerful center or axis mundi of this *mandala* kingdom. The key to understanding the significance of the Phra Bang in Lang Xang lies in the fact that it was regarded analogically *as if it were a Hindu deity,* at least in terms of the context of its Indic origins at Angkor. But more, in Luang Phrabang, the analogy seems to have been further extended, so that it was also regarded analogically *as if it were the "phi mandala,"* maybe considered as such not so much among the learned monks of the monasteries that were eventually established by royalty in Luang Phrabang and elsewhere in Lan Xang but rather, functionally and structurally, in the mind-set of its many lay devotees, including its chief patron, the king. In other words, the power of the Phra Bang Buddha image was conflated with the basic power infusing the spaces of the grand Lao *mandala.*

Martin Stuart-Fox's account of the foundation of Lan Xang further develops the fundamental point I have just made in the extended discussion above. In describing the central significance of the Phra Bang image of the Buddha, Stuart-Fox has this to say:

> Though the *Phra Bang* itself may be a fine example of Khmer sculpture, the *Pheun Phra Bang* (Story of the Phra Bang) tells how the image was miraculously cast in Sri Lanka, and from there transported to Cambodia before being brought to Laos. Many such popular stories of revered Buddha images were invented to assist in spreading belief in Buddhism through awe of the magical powers these images were believed to possess and their ability to "save humankind from sin."[27] But the association of great Buddhist kings with such images also fulfilled a powerful legitimizing function, for the stories of their miraculous provenance served . . . to anchor Lao culture firmly to its religious and intellectual roots in India and Sri Lanka. Lao history was thus universalized by becoming part of the universal history of Buddhist redemption. (1998, 52)[28]

While I would quibble with some of Stuart-Fox's overly Christian and theologically saturated language,[29] he is quite right in his general assessment of the significance of the Phra Bang image. Though identifying the Phra Bang image with Sri Lankan origins enhances its prestige, since Sri Lanka is regarded as the cradle or cultural mother of Theravada in Southeast Asia, the Phra Bang is definitely not an image of Sinhala origins. That much can be established quite easily on stylistic grounds, let alone the fact that no such similar conceptuality regarding the power of the Buddha image exists in Sinhala religious culture either. We can, however, follow Stuart-Fox's lead by inquiring into how images of the same genre were regarded within the Khmer Angkorian *mandalic* milieu, since the possibility of Sri Lanka being its source is absolutely a dead end historically. Ian Harris' description in this regard is quite helpful:

> The various capitals of the Angkorian kings may be read symbolically as miniature images of the universe. The rivers and the *baraya*s represented

the cosmic ocean; the enclosing walls, the iron-mountain chain (*cakravala*) at the limit of the world's golden disk; and the temples, the central world mountain, Mount Meru. [. . .] Through their construction and accompanying rites, the kingdom was transformed into an ideal realm. At the center of the great city Angkor Thom [City of Dhamma] stands Jayavarman's pantheon, the Bayon, representing Mount Meru; the nearby royal palace is homologized to the residence of Indra; and Neak Pean, to the sacred Lake Anavatapta. We do know that the Siem Reap River, which flows through the city, had been identified with the Ganges sometime previously. . . . *Symbolically then, the Angkorian state has become co-extensive with the entire world.* (Harris 2008 19, 22; italics mine)

It would seem, then, that the eventual "Buddhicization" of the Lan Xang *mandala* not only linked up the history of the kingdom to the universal history of the Theravada Buddhist tradition, but it also contained within it the possibility that Lan Xang would be regarded as a microcosm of the universe that was "co-extensive with the entire world." Thus, the new significance of Lan Xang was not only that it was historically situated within the larger scope of the Buddhasasana, but that it was also now situated in an Indic Buddhist cosmos: that is, it had become a this-worldly center of the *mandalic* cosmos, the linked counterpart to Indra's otherworldly *devaloka*. (Indeed, Phou Si, the scenic hill dominating the Luang Phrabang peninsula, is still identified precisely with Mount Meru, the pivot of the *mandala* and the axis mundi connecting the world of the gods and the world of men.) But to return to the issue at hand, what can we understand specifically regarding the significance of Buddha images within the context of this cosmic symbolism?

Within the Khmer Angkorian cosmology of Cambodia, for centuries, until the Mahayana Buddhist orientation of Jayavarman VII's thirteenth-century reign, the king had projected himself as a *devaraja* (god-king) or as the *devaraja*'s surrogate.[30] The great Khmer temples of the Angkor region built between the ninth and thirteenth centuries were constructed by kings who believed that they were providing "residences" for their deceased parents, in the process consecrating (or "promoting") their royal parents as the divine primordial cosmic couple of Hindu *purana* cosmology, Siva and Uma (or Parvati), thus achieving a Khmer synthesis of indigenous religious practices (e.g., the cults of ancestor veneration and territorial spiritual power) with the cosmology of Saivite Hinduism. The practice of promoting one's parents was based on the following formula: just as the king's parents are equated with the ultimate generative powers of the cosmos, so the king and queen were regarded as their parents' this-worldly counterparts; thus the contemporary royal realm is a "double" of the ultimate heavenly realm where the promoted parents as Siva and Uma now dwell. As the worldly embodiment of this "doubling" phenomenon, the king is therefore *devaraja*, the "god-king," or the "god who is king." Significantly, *devaraja* is also the epithet most commonly ascribed to Sakka (Indra) in Pali Buddhist literature. Its use as an appellation for the king, therefore, in later Theravada post-Angkorian times, signals the "doubling" effect as well.

The cult of the *devaraja* has been the subject of much scholarly attention over the past century, and we need not rehearse much of that discussion here. Harris, however, has made an intriguing point, one that may impinge directly on the manner in which the power of the Phra Bang image was eventually construed in Lan Xang: "Earlier scholars, such as Coedes and Dupont, understood the *devaraja* to be either the deified king himself or a singular image of Siva standing in the king's stead. The matter has not been adequately solved, but it now seems likely that the *devaraja* was a special mobile image (*calanti pratima*) of a protective deity" (Harris 2008, 12). Harris has presented this finding cautiously, but I want to reflect a little further on its possible ramifications for understanding how Lan Xang's Phra Bang, and other Buddha images in the Thai-Lao culture area (a culture area that was so profoundly affected by the religious and political legacy of Angkor) came to be so highly valorized, and thus why the possession of these images became such vital matters for political and military contestation.

In his discussion of the "god of the soil," Mus points out that the spirit is intrinsically the place itself, a "god-soil," or ultimately the "energies of the place" encountered or cultivated in human events. If we apply this understanding in relation to Buddha images such as the Phra Bang, we would then understand that the image itself is not to be divorced from the reality that it is thought to represent, recalling Donald Swearer's observation given at the outset of this chapter. That is, the Phra Bang *is* the presence of Buddha as it has been experienced in the *events* of the place it inhabits. The image is a form of the deity; therefore, it *is* the deity. This is precisely the combination of issues that we meet in the figure of the Phra Bang in early-sixteenth-century Lan Xang, after the image was brought to the newly consecrated Vat Vixun in Luang Phrabang by King Vixun. Indeed, "Phra Bang" literally means "an embodiment (Bang) of the Lord (Phra)." Thus, the Phra Bang is not regarded as simply a symbol, the possession of which was a marker of the king's legitimacy, though, of course, it did function as that kind of signifier too. But within this context of cosmology and power, the Phra Bang constituted the veritable presence of the Buddha. It became the anchoring, centering power of the Lao grand *mandala,* and the king was understood to be its primary caretaker and the dispenser of its power. Therefore, just as the images of Siva and Uma within consecrated "ancestral" temples were to the kings and queens of Angkor, so the Phra Bang image of the Buddha was to Lan Xang kings.

The Phra Bang, however, was not in Luang Phrabang during Fa Ngum's purported reign. Evans (2002, 16) cites a legend about how the Phra Bang refused to go to Luang Phrabang because of premonitions about the moral future of Fa Ngum. This may be related to the tradition that Fa Ngum was deposed in 1374 because of his insistence that he exercise an absolute unfettered share of sexual rights over all the women of the capital.

The Fa Ngum saga also presents a narrative reflecting how religio-political factions of two kinds developed within his court: first, a factionalism between those who represented a "Khmer orientation" and those who sided with the "old aristocracy"; and second, factionalism between those who would support one form of Theravada monasticism over another. The first type of factionalism, ultimately rooted in the politics of power succession, would be enduring and of paramount significance.[31] Implicit in the split between the "Khmer-oriented" faction (symbolized by Fa Ngum himself) and the "old aristocracy" was a philosophical divide between the ideology of Theravada Buddhism on the one hand and the ontology of the spirit cults on the other. The initial impetus for the tension or split was probably occasioned by the growing cultic and social presence of the Buddhist *sangha,* especially in the royal capital but increasingly throughout the river basins and tributaries of the Mekong River.

On the basis of reading the most ancient versions of chronicles written at the end of the fifteenth and beginning of the sixteenth century, Lorrillard (2003, 188) notes that in addition to the Fa Ngum story, there are references to various Theravada monks who came to Luang Phrabang to establish the first monastery, named after Pasaman, a leading monk from Angkor. These were Sinhalese monks from Sri Lanka, apparently, whose first act was to plant a bodhi tree (*Ficus religiosa*) from a cutting originating in Sri Lanka (likely from Sri Mahabodhi in Anuradhapura).[32] Lorrillard further notes that subsequently monasteries were built during virtually every royal reign "in order to preserve the ashes of a deceased member of the royal family. The constructions of *stupa*s are sometimes mentioned. These appear to be funeral monuments" (ibid.). Noting the steady growth and spread of monastic institutions abetted by the support of royalty in the capital and in many important villages, Lorrillard writes in conclusion: "[W]e can however establish with certitude, at a time between the second half of the 14th century and the second half of the 15th century, the emergence [throughout Lan Xang] of a new religious phenomenon" (196).

These findings by Lorrillard are quite suggestive. Given the eventual valorization of the Phra Bang image in the capital, and given that it seems to have been left behind in Vieng Kham rather than ritually established in the center of the new Lan Xang kingdom when the kingdom was being formally declared by Fa Ngum, it is interesting to observe that what the Sinhala monks did bring with them as a marker to indicate the spread of the Buddha's *dhamma* was not a magically empowered Buddha image, but rather a sapling of the bodhi tree, the aniconic symbol par excellence in Sri Lanka signaling the presence of the teaching of the Buddha. These Sinhala monks from Sri Lanka, as orthodox Theravadins, were apparently not participants in the cult of the empowered Buddha image. Instead, they appear to have been learned scholars whose monastic legacy would eventually establish Lan Xang as a center of Theravada in the sixteenth century. Second, the rationale given for the establishment of royal monasteries as venues to "preserve the ashes of a deceased member of the royal family" seems especially reminiscent of royal Khmer motivations for building temples on behalf of deceased parents. The royal proclivity for making merit, for being the primary patron of the Buddhist monastic community, has been merged here with the tradition of royal ancestor veneration. In these two cultic instances then, we see a combination of Sinhala Buddhist Theravada orthopraxy represented by conservative monks on the one hand, and, on the other, a Khmer-influenced royal court motivated to support the growth and spread of Theravada monasticism through motivations rooted not only in Buddhist inspired merit-making consciousness, but also through the persistent and indigenous practice of ancestor veneration, a key element of the ancient spirit cult religious orientation.

Royal support of the Buddhist *sangha* in these early years of Lan Xang would have created tension in the court among the spirit cult–oriented "old aristocracy," as well as among those ritual practitioners, including *chao muang*, who might perceive the spread of monasticism as a rival to the conceptual, ritual, and political bases of their own powers. Indeed, the

[e]stablishment of a powerful and unified monastic order in close reciprocal relationship with monarchical authority came to provide additional weighty legitimation for Lao kings—but powerful social forces had first to be overcome. Opposition was not to Buddhism per se, for its beliefs were known and practised already. Rather it was to the establishment of a Sangha under royal patronage displacing existing animist cults and their powerful priesthoods that was so strongly resisted. (Stuart-Fox 1998, 51–52)

If this was indeed the case, then what caused the tensions between the two factions of the court was not simply a matter of philosophical disagreement, but rather about vested interests in political power structures. With the eventual relative triumph of the *sangha,* signaled by the construction of *vat*s in the center of virtually every significant *ban* and *muang* throughout the *mandala,* a rapprochement between the two rival orientations was eventually forged, though periodically contested.[33]

Within the political *mandala*s of Southeast Asia, there is no doubt that Buddhism was predominantly an urban phenomenon, and the religion of the aristocratic elite. Moreover, the establishment of *vat*s during this time was limited to those major *ban* or *muang* contexts in which adequate resources could support the ritual and fiscal life of the *vat.* We can also be sure that the non-Tai peoples of the countryside outside of the Lao-settled regions of the Mekong River basin and its tributaries, the Khmu in particular in northern Laos, remained quite outside the orbit of Buddhist institutional life.[34] The point I am making indirectly here by referring to the "non-Lao" population who lived within the orbit of Lan Xang kingdom, but outside of the center's Buddhist ideological persuasion, is that these peoples retained their full embrace of the spirit cults. Insofar as they continued to live so intimately with the lowland "ethnic Lao" and remained "animistic" means that the religious culture of the countryside remained predominantly spirit cult oriented. It is likely that the religion of the rustic countryside Lao did so as well, and the extent to which any "rural Lao" would become Buddhist exclusively seems quite remote, especially when "the continued worship at *ho phi* (spirit shrines) [even] by aristocratic families well into the twentieth century shows that these practices were never obliterated" (Evans 2002, 16). For if the aristocrats at the center of the *mandala* persisted in the worship of spirits, there is even a better reason to assume that the veneration of *phi* remained the rule, rather than the exception, in the rural villages of the Lao. While the religion at the center of the *mandala* became increasingly Buddhist during the reigns of kings Vixun, Phothisarat, and Xetthathirat—those decades during the sixteenth century that constituted the halcyon days politically for the Lan Xang kingdom—the spirit cults were sustained, even though sometimes directly attacked at the center and in the regional *muang* of the *mandala.*

"BUDDHIST-MINDEDNESS" IN SIXTEENTH-CENTURY LAN XANG

Some historians have speculated that the establishment of the specifically Buddhist kingdom of Lan Xang rightly owes its origins to King Vixun, rather than to Fa Ngum. While Fa Ngum may have orchestrated a tribute-based unification of *muang Lao* and endeavored, apparently, to establish a

Buddhist monastic presence in Xieng Dong Xieng Thong (Luang Phra-bang) to legitimate his rule, it was not until the early-sixteenth-century twenty-year (1501–1520) reign of Vixun, followed immediately by the reign of his son Phothisarat, that the symbolism of the royal regalia and the ritual life of a royal *mandala* center became unambiguously Buddhist in symbolic and institutional terms. No new political structures per se were initiated that would alter the pulsating or tributary dynamic constitutive of the *mandala* (Evans 2002, 16), but the discourses of virtually all political and cultural life, at least at the center, were now articulated thoroughly through Indic forms, primarily the Theravada idioms. Vixun's reign marks the ritual establishment of the Phra Bang image in Vat Vixun, a monastery that Vixun built especially for that very purpose. "Before it the lords [of the *muang*] would swear loyalty to their king, and hereafter the capital would be rec-ognised as Luang Phrabang, 'the place of the Buddha Phra Bang'" (ibid.). Note here that veneration of the Phra Bang had replaced the veneration of the ancestral *phi* in the annual supplications of the *chao muang*.

As much as Vixun may have further enhanced his capital as a pivot of the *mandala* and inaugurated a trajectory leading to development of Luang Phrabang as a seat of learning and flourishing high culture, his son, Pho-thisarat, who assumed the throne at the young age of nineteen and ruled for twenty-seven years, extended and further intensified the efforts initi-ated by his father. From a gleaning of the *Luang Phrabang Chronicle,* Stuart-Fox provides a concise summary of Phothisarat's religious dispositions and policies:

The young king was nineteen and a devout Buddhist, and his first act was to build and dedicate a magnificent monastery to the memory of his father. In 1523, a mission was dispatched to Chiang Mai, capital of Lan Na, to bring back copies of the entire Buddhist Tipitaka and other texts, and to invite learned monks to a great monastic council.[35] Two years later the king himself was inducted into the Sangha by its Supreme Patriarch, Maha Sichantho, abbot of Vat Vixun, who personally presided over the king's religious education during his traditional three-month retreat. The king's devoted orthodoxy made him intolerant of the widespread popular worship of spirits, or *phi*, some associated with ancestral cults, other with significant natural phenomena, and others still believed responsible for causing all kinds of accidents and sickness. In 1527 Phothisarat issued a famous decree proscribing the worship of *phi* as groundless superstition, and ordering their shrines to be destroyed and their altars thrown into the river. . . . [Moreover] Phothisarat was so far as we know the first Lao king to record his gifts to the Sangha in stone in his own lifetime, such meritorious deeds were proof of his divine status as a *bodhisattva*, or Buddha-to-be. (1998, 74–75)

Michel Lorrillard (2003, 144) confirms that Phothisarat was the first Lao king to record his pious actions in support of the *sangha* within inscriptions and that he, according to the Lan Na *Jinakalamali*, received a full set of the Pali texts composing the canonical *Tipitaka* from the king of Chiang Mai in 1523.

In addition, we also know that, in his zeal to suppress the veneration of *phi*, Phothisarat specifically ordered that the old shrine of the ancestral guardian deities of Luang Phrabang, the former axis mundi of the pre-Buddhist *muang*, should be destroyed. On the very same site of the old guardian *phi* shrine, next to the *vat* his father had constructed for the enshrinement of the Phra Bang, Phothisarat constructed Vat Aham, another temple of continuing historical importance. On this site, the oldest stele inscription surviving in Luang Phrabang refers to the Phothisarat's acts of establishing this *vat*, the purification of its boundaries (*sima*), and proclaims a litany of prescriptions incumbent on monks to follow, similar in kind to the royal *katikavata*s issued by Sri Lankan kings to ensure discipline within the *sangha*.[36] That the efforts of Phothisarat to establish Luang Phrabang as a seat of orthodoxy had gained some international renown is noted by Harris, who mentions that "[s]igns of Buddhist regeneration [in Cambodia] are . . . shown by the significant numbers of Cambodian monks who traveled to Luang Prabang to study Theravada Buddhism, particularly during the reigns of King Phothisarat and his son Setthatirath" (2008, 33).

The major aim of this chapter is to ascertain the manner in which Buddhist thought and practice, especially veneration of the Buddha image, have been construed in Lao religious culture through the prisms of the indigenous ontology of the spirit cults. Even though Phothisarat embodies a religious profile that is unabashedly orthodox Theravadin and ostensibly inimical to the indigenous religious substratum, the litany of actions attributed to this pious king contain at least two important traces, or the latent presence, of spirit cult persistence. The first trace is evident in Phothisarat's enshrinement of his royal father's cremated remains within the consecrated grounds of a Buddhist monastery. Vat Aham was built precisely to honor and venerate his deceased royal parent, recapitulating the practice of royal Khmer to promote, in a cosmic and soteriological fashion, the ultimate identity/destiny of royal parents. Phothisarat's cultic actions to enshrine his father's remains (and memory) are clearly a Buddhist transformation of ancestor veneration and thus are echoes of the residual principle of the "god of the soil" or the "spiritual power of the place." Later, votive stupas used to enshrine the remains of important monastic abbots would be understood as venues for worshipping a transformed presence as a *phi vat* (spirit of the temple). In both of these examples, there is evidence of an enduring belief that a powerful person, seen as responsible for founding, structuring, or ordering a particular space, whether kingdom or *vat*, persists as type of spiritual presence within that very space.

Phothisarat's zealous enthusiasm to continue his father's promotion of Buddhist learning on the one hand, and his campaign to eradicate the cult of *phi*, on the other, may have been a by–product of several factors. No doubt Phothisarat personally benefited greatly from Vixun's efforts to create a powerful Buddhist *sangha* and monastic literary culture: he was raised and educated in a very sophisticated, if not religiously conservative, environment. Only a teenager when he ascended the throne, Phothisarat relied heavily on his trusted monastic teachers for advice and counsel, and it is abundantly clear that the *sangha* was one of the chief beneficiaries of his reign. His exposure to the Buddhist literary world was not limited to the three months he spent in rain-retreat (*vassa*), the annual three-month period of reflection when the recitation and study of texts traditionally intensified within the monastic routine. Rather, literary learning had constituted a central focus of his entire education. What seems apparent is that his "Buddhist-mindedness"[37] was not only of learned origins but also a by-product of the relative simplemindedness present in an overly guided or manipulated youth filled with pietistic passion. Whether Phothisarath's piety was the result of his own independent motivation or instilled by others, it was shrewdly politically inclined as well.

I would like to suggest that Phothisarath's campaign to eradicate spirit cults was a reflection of the tension between two recognized theories of power. During his father's (Vixun's) reign, Phothisarat had witnessed a veritable "changing of the guard" with respect to the manner in which the fundamental power at the center of the Lan Xang *mandala* was constituted, represented, and regarded. That "changing of the guard," as it were, refers to how the Phra Bang image had replaced the guardian *phi* of the city as the substance of power recognized at the pivot of the Lan Xang *mandala*. Indeed, the change in nomenclature of the city from Xieng Dong Xieng Thong to Luang Phrabang in the subsequent reign of Phothisarat's son, Xetthathirat, marks this transfer or replacement of identity rather ostensibly. As Evans has noted, Phothisarat had ordered the destruction of the poles or pillars symbolizing the spirit-based (or spiritual) power of the regional *phi muang*, objects of cultic veneration symbolizing the ontological power replicated in politically this-worldly fashion by the *chao muang*. These destructive actions were followed by the constructive emplacement of very strategic *vat*s, Theravada Buddhist monasteries that became, in the place of *lak muang*, new ritual centers of religious *and* political power.[38]

Consequently, the power of the state became completely embedded in the structure of the *sangha*; and the *sangha*, in turn, was vested completely by the power of the state, a truly prodigious development with major historical ramifications for the remainder of Lao political and cultural history. Both state and *sangha* were related in a dynamic of mutual legitimation, now envisaged as excluding the *phi* cults. At the basis of the Buddhist ontology (now royally enthroned) was the authority attributed to the figure of the Buddha, henceforth regarded as Lan Xang's unchallenged "culture hero." From this point in time forward, regional *chao muang* would also have to demonstrate their motivations and abilities to emulate the actions of the king in supporting the *sangha*. That is, they would also have to become chief patrons of the *vats*, in the same manner as the king (as we know through the stone inscriptions he left behind) had postured as the *sangha*'s chief supporter and trumpeter of *dhamma*.

But this account of what amounts to a war of ontological displacement is a bit too tidy. The rationale for the anti–spirit cult campaign may have been, indeed, consciously forged and then rationalized on doctrinal grounds, grounds that conveniently abetted Phothisarat's political motivation to "clear the land" entirely, to abolish any grounds (spiritual-political) for any potential mounting of resistance to his power. Yet, another factor was also at work, though it may not have actually occurred consciously to the protagonists of this history: that is, the way that they understood the significance of the Buddha's presence embodied in the image of the Phra Bang. (This is the second instance of latent traces of the *phi* cult that I want to take note of in relation to Phothisarat's actions.) How was the power of the Phra Bang understood practically *and politically*? Was the Phra Bang simply understood as a symbol of the Buddha's *dhamma* or the monastic ideals of the *sangha*'s *vinaya*?[39] Or was it, as I have suggested earlier, an understanding of the Buddha's powerful presence embodied in an image; that is, an image constituting a powerful presence of the Buddha?

In the *mandala* structure of Lan Xang, consistent with the principles and dynamics rooted in the religious substratum and constitutive of *muang-mandala* polity, the Phra Bang functioned analogically to the ontological power of a *mandala phi* or a *phi muang*. It was regarded as the originating and legitimating power of the past and present located at the pivotal center of political space. It was "the power in charge of this place," symbolic of the other-worldly parallel that infuses the power of the this-worldly king. It was also analogous in function to the *devaraja* image cult in Khmer Angkor. It is still possible, in this scenario, to say that the king is the *cakkavattin* who righteously conquers and orders the world to prepare his realm for the presence of the Buddha without violating these principles of ontology operative in the indigenous religious substratum. Indeed, understood or read in this way, there is no inconsistency between the two.

What I have noted earlier, however, is that what Buddhism brings to the substance of power envisaged at the center is an *ethic*. The king and the "Buddha-presence" of the Phra Bang may have been understood, and perhaps unconsciously so, in terms of the "powers of the place," an understanding ultimately to be found in the manner that Mus has described within the dynamics of the "religion . . . of Monsoon Asia" and "the god of the soil," but the Buddhist king must also rule by righteousness. While there may have been no structural changes to Lao *muang* polity when its center or pivot was "Buddhacized," its quality was modified by a Buddhist ethical discourse. But just how "ethically minded," rather than simply "Buddhist-minded," Phothisarat ruled Lan Xang is a question that others might try to field in the future. Regardless of how that question is answered, it is also clear that Phothisarat was not necessarily a religiously tolerant or inclusive king.

The reign of Phothisarat's son, Xetthathirat, and the subsequent reign of King Surinyavongsa, mark the political and cultural high-water marks of the Lan Xang kingdom. During the latter period of his reign, Phothisarat had spent an increasing amount of time in Vientiane for strategic reasons, owing to the increasing rise of Burmese power to the west. At the time of Phothisarat's death, Xetthathirat was ruling in Chiang Mai, where he had been married into an alliance with a Lan Na princess. Upon his royal consecration as king, Xetthathirat relocated the Lan Xang capital permanently to Vientiane, taking with him two most highly revered Buddha images: the Phra Keo (Emerald Buddha) and the Phra Xaek Kham, both of which originally were consecrated in Chiang Mai. He left behind in Xieng Dong Xieng Thong the Phra Bang image and renamed the former capital Luang Phrabang. Xetthathirat appears to have marshaled enough resources to initiate what amounted to the most ambitious building campaign in support of the *sangha* in Lao history. Not only did he construct several monasteries in Luang Phrabang, including the architectural masterpiece Vat Xieng Thong, but he also erected temples for the Phra Keo while building a new stupa that served as the palladium for Lang Xang in Vientiane, the That Luang. Here, it seems clear that relic veneration (the cult of the stupa) and veneration of Buddha images had been correlated.

With Xetthathirat's death in the 1570s, a period of internecine fighting among potential successors greatly weakened the political and military strength of Lan Xang, a situation then capitalized upon by the Burmese, who succeeded in establishing their own vassals for around half a century before their own power emanating from Pegu atrophied in the 1630s. After more internecine squabbling, Surinyavongsa eventually emerged as a powerful ruler, but nonetheless in a quite isolated cultural context, wherein Buddhist cultural arts flourished.

Surinyavongsa's long seventeenth rule marks the end of Lan Xang as we have known it. The inability of his nephews and grandsons to agree on succession resulted in the parceling out of the kingdom into three much weaker, yet still for the time being autonomous, *mandala*s: Luang Phrabang, Vientiane, and Champasak.

> The ruling family in each regional kingdom legitimized its succession through traditional means: descent from Khun Borom via the ruling dynasty of Lan Xang, reinforced by the magical power of a Buddhist image venerated with the assistance of the local Sangha as the palladium of the kingdom. . . . [But] [l]ess than two decades later, all three had been forced to acknowledge Siamese suzerainty. (Stuart-Fox 1998, 103)

Thus, the unitary structure of the Lao Lan Xang *mandala* was fragmented, never to be assembled again.

Before the segmentation of Lan Xang, the Phra Bang image had been removed from Luang Phrabang to Vientiane in 1705 to shore up the legitimacy of the *mandala* amid royal internecine disputes. After the fragmentation, which Evans (2002, 24) notes was also partly the result of pressure from the Ayutthaya *mandala* to alienate Luang Phrabang from Vientiane, both the Phra Keo (Emerald Buddha) and the Phra Bang ensconced in Vientiane eventually became enticing targets of legitimation to be seized by the rising power of Siam, which is exactly what occurred after the Thai threw off Burmese shackles. The Burmese had reduced all Tai *mandala*s, including Luang Phrabang and Vientiane, to vassal status in the 1760s. Evans describes succinctly what then transpired:

> Through factional alliances, Champasak was brought firmly within the Siamese mandala in 1778; [the Ayutthaya] army then marched on Vientiane and easily conquered it the following year with the assistance of its vassal state, Luang Phrabang. Members of the royal family were taken as hostages, along with their palladiums the Phra Keo and the Phra Bang . . . , while thousands of families were relocated to Saraburi, 120 kilometers northeast of Bangkok, as royal *kha* [slaves]. By the time of the establishment of the Chakri dynasty in Bangkok in 1782, the Siamese kingdom was the undisputed power in the region and Lan Xang had disappeared. (2002, 25)

Indeed, the first Siamese Chakri dynasty king, Rama I, greatly expanded his *mandala* so that it included not only Lan Na, Luang Phrabang,

Vientiane, and Champasak, but also most of what is now Cambodia, the northern Malay Muslim states, and the eastern Shan plateau (now mostly part of Myanmar). Significantly, the prized Phra Keo or Emerald Buddha, originally from Chiang Mai in Lan Na but having been installed during the time of Lan Xang's suzerainty in Vientiane by Xetthathirat, became the new image of Buddhist power, or the palladium of the Bangkok dynasty, where it remains to this day.

Eventually, the son of the former Vientiane king was allowed to return from Bangkok with the Phra Bang image,[40] but there were no pretenses of granting autonomy in that gesture. Meanwhile,

> Bangkok, strategically better situated than Ayutthaya, rapidly developed into a busy cosmopolitan trading center, able to take advantage of increased trade not only with China, but also with the major European powers as trade picked up following the end of the Napoleonic wars. By contrast, the isolated Lao capitals were reduced to regional centers with limited wealth and resources, unable to maintain even comparably lavish courts. This did not, however, reduce the pride of their rulers in their ancient lineages, nor diminish the memories of past glories. The Lao kingdoms stubbornly resisted Siamese inroads in areas they considered theirs. (Stuart-Fox 1998, 115)

"THE LAST GASP": CHAO ANUVONG, THE DISPERSAL OF THE VIENTIANE LAO, AND THE RETURN OF PHRA BANG

The Lao revolt against Siamese hegemony led by Chao Anuvong in the early nineteenth century continues to spark political and nationalist emotion on both sides of the Mekong River even today: in modern Laos, where Chao Anu is still regarded by some as a proto-revolutionary warrior who challenged Thai imperialist and feudalist rule;[41] in the Khorat Plateau of Northeast Thailand, where the Isan people understand the centrality of Chao Anu's role in the memory of their migration; and among the central Thai, where Chao Anu is regarded as a traitor whose forces were thwarted by the intervention of patriotic loyalty and heroic resistance to unwarranted rebellion.[42]

Grant Evans, who has written a detailed account of the Chao Anu revolt (2002, 25–32), refers to Chao Anu as "the last of the warrior kings" and to his revolt as "the last gasp of a dying pre-modern mandala state system" (25). Indeed, his revolt against the Bangkok *mandala* marked the final occasion in which the Lao attempted to free themselves from Siamese hegemony. The history of the event is rich indeed, but suffice to say that it took place within the early-nineteenth-century era when Bangkok, intensely worried about Vietnamese military designs from the east, was simultaneously becoming increasingly wary of European colonial designs on Southeast Asia. By this time, the British had succeeded in wresting southern Burma from its king only two years earlier. Even before then, the Chakri dynasty had engaged in various policies designed to centralize direct power and further limit the power of its periphery vassals. As Evans notes, "The mandala of Siam thus combined, uneasily, elements of a newly emerging absolutist state system and an older system in which power had been more dispersed and had allowed for the emergence of new men of prowess. Clearly this diversive dynamic was at work in Chao Anou" (27).

Once he assumed the "kingship" of Vientiane from his older brother, who had been "appointed" by Bangkok in 1782 (and who had returned with the Phra Bang image because King Rama I had determined that it had brought him "bad luck"), Anu began to test the continued viability of the "older system [that] had allowed for the emergence of men of prowess."[43] He developed a robust agenda to articulate power. The idioms that he chose were unabashedly those of a powerful Buddhist *cakkavattin* king,

> by building a new palace, and then demonstrating his exalted *kamma* by constructing monasteries and Buddhist monuments and presiding over elaborate religious ceremonies, both in Viang Chan [Vientiane] and at such major regional centers as Nakhon Phanom. In 1813, the king summoned a great monastic council, only the third in Lao history. Instructions were given to carve a new jade Buddha image to replace the *Phra Kaeo*, then in Bangkok. In 1816, this image was ceremoniously installed in the refurbished Vat Phra Kaeo in Viang Chan. An outer cloister was added to the That Luang *stupa*, and Anuvong ordered work begun on Vat Sisaket, a gem of Lao architecture and the only building of this period to escape the destruction of 1827–1828. (Stuart-Fox 1998, 117–118)

Such grandiose undertakings were not lost on Bangkok, especially the provocative acts of convening a grand monastic council (that inferred that Anu's kingdom would arbitrate Theravada orthodoxy, at least in the Lao cultural areas over which the Siamese claimed hegemony) and the carving of a new jade (or "emerald") Buddha placed, as it was, in the *vat* that formerly housed the original image, the very one now in Bangkok functioning as the palladium of the Bangkok *mandala*. Clearly, Anu had designs on reestablishing the autonomy of Lan Xang.[44] In this, he had hoped for external support not only from Luang Phrabang and Champasak, but possibly from Vietnam, Burma, and even the British.

In 1826, Anuvong made his military move, entering the Khorat Plateau under the pretext of assisting Bangkok in resisting a possible British incursion.[45] But his forces were soon engaged by a Bangkok army, forced into a northern retreat, while at the same time encouraging many people in the region to join them, attacking those who wouldn't. "The uprising . . . ended in a fiasco. His son [Chao Anu's] was soon captured, and Anu himself forced to flee to Hue in Vietnam" (Evans 2002, 28). The fury of Bangkok, ever more insecure, was unprecedented.

> The devastation of the Lao areas was horrendous. Apart from the dead, thousands fled into the jungle to escape the fighting. According to Siamese reports, only about nine able-bodied men were taken prisoner for every 200 to 300 women and children. Food stocks had been destroyed and no new crops planted. By mid-year, disease and malnutrition had taken a dreadful toll. Tens of thousands of families were forcibly resettled closer to Bangkok, most in the central Chao Phraya basin. After months of mopping up, tracking down families who had fled Viang Chan [Vientiane], ordering the exemplary execution of those who had given them refuge, and organizing the administration of the region, the Siamese general, Chao Phraya Bodin, returned to Bangkok in February 1828 to find Rama III still far from satisfied. Anuvong had not been captured; Viang Chan had not been razed. The Siamese feared Vietnamese intervention. Bodin was ordered to return and complete his task of destruction. . . . This time the city of Viang Chan was totally destroyed and its entire population deported. Nothing remained but huts among the ruins when Doudart de Lagree and Francis Garnier visited the site almost forty years later. It was to be another thirty years before a new city began to be constructed from its ashes to serve as the administrative capital of French Laos. (Stuart-Fox 1998, 125)

The so-called Lao-isation of Northeast Thailand dates back to this monumental moment of total and final devastation of the Vientiane *mandala*. Tens of thousands of Lao families were forcibly evacuated and deported across the Mekong River into a new region where the absolute political power of Bangkok was assured.[46] "The ensuing political stability [of Northeast Thailand] provided by an ever more powerful Bangkok ensured rapid population growth, and over the coming centuries more ethnic Lao come to be found on the Khorat Plateau than in Laos itself" (Evans 2002, 31).

There were no more vestiges of the Lan Xang *mandala* remaining in Vientiane in the aftermath of the Chao Anu revolt, for there was nothing left of Vientiane at all. The Siamese strategy had been this: there will be no competitive "power of place" in Vientiane if there is no place of power in which it can be realized.[47] Before the Chao Anu revolt, Luang Phrabang had remained loyal to Bangkok as its vassal. Siamese soldiers would remain stationed in Luang Phrabang throughout the remainder of the nineteenth century, until Luang Phrabang became, through a series of unlikely events, a French protectorate. Meanwhile, in an act of apparent charity, the Siamese King Mongkut, in 1867, allowed the Phra Bang image, recaptured during the 1827 sacking of Vientiane, to be returned to Luang Phrabang, after an absence of 162 years following its earlier removal to Vientiane in 1705.

From 1827, the Phra Bang remained in Luang Phrabang under the ritual care of Lao royalty, first during the nineteenth-century period when Luang Phrabang was but a tributary to Bangkok's Chakri dynasty, then during the roughly sixty years of the French colonial protectorate until the mid-1950s, and finally during the war-plagued twenty-year period of constitutional monarchy and Lao political independence until the communist Pathet Lao seized power in 1975 and deposed the last of the Lao monarchs. After an initial fifteen-year period or so in which Buddhist institutions were allowed to survive, though in a limited state of atrophy under Pathet Lao governments, a new era of more relaxed tolerance for religious expression began to unfold in the 1990s.[48] During this most recent period, the Phra Bang has become, again, an increasing focus of cultic veneration.

LUANG PHRABANG: THE CONTEMPORARY RITUAL CONTEXT

Luang Phrabang is auspiciously sited. It is built on a narrow kilometer-long peninsula dominated by a picturesque hill (Phou Si). At the end of the peninsula is the scenic confluence of the rivers Mekong and Khan. Verdant, forest-covered mountains can be seen in every direction (except in the "season of smoke" during March and April, when slash and burn agriculture commences). Nature has been kind to this place.

During the period of French intervention, nineteenth- and early-twentieth-century European and "hybrid European-Laotian architecture [were] introduced to Luang Prabang. However, the original town plan was retained and is still apparent today" (UNESCO 2004, 23). Indeed, Luang Phrabang is regarded as one of the best-preserved cities in Southeast Asia. It is essentially a conglomeration of *ban*, each with its own temple at the core, many known specifically for the handicrafts that they produced or the vocations that their residents specialized in. Xieng Thong (at the tip of the peninsula), for example, was known for its puppetry, and other *ban* in Luang Phrabang for silversmithing, woodcarving, blacksmithing, papermaking, weaving, and embroidery. (Basketry was an occupation followed by the Lao Theung Khmu, who lived in hillside villages surrounding Luang Phrabang proper.) Luang Phrabang articulates an ancient settlement pattern "visible in the archaeological ruins of many important Tai cities such as Sri Satchanalai, Kaphaeng Phet and Chiang Saen" (17), but it is the only contemporary Southeast Asian city in which this settlement pattern has not been layered over entirely by modernity. "Luang Prabang's Buddhist temples are known throughout Southeast Asia for their distinctive style: tiered roofs and pillared porticos, embellished with ornamentation of the highest quality, including wood carvings, stucco moulding, dry fresco wall painting, lacquer work, and glass mosaic work" (24). Indeed, the aesthetic beauty of its temples remains, in my view, the town's most endearing and enduring attraction.

As the Pathet Lao–led Lao PDR opened itself up to the world beyond its former socialist partners in the early 1990s, its disposition toward Buddhism shifted markedly to a more accommodating and more politically and economically strategic stance. This shift occurred when the government began to ponder issues of "heritage management." In so doing, the government fostered relationships with international institutions and donor countries in an effort to explore the possibility of creating a tourism industry to benefit its stultified economy.

Two years after Prime Minister Phomvihane Kaysone's death and his remarkable funeral in 1992 that signaled the state's softening stance towards Buddhism, the Lao PDR Ministry of Information and Culture, with encouragement from the French government, hired a French architectural company to assess the quality and scope of the historic buildings in Luang Phrabang. Consequently, the town's thirty-three *vat*s and eleven of its secular buildings were designated as "heritage buildings." The government announced that Luang Phrabang would be regarded, henceforth, as a "national heritage site." "The building inventory was also used as the basis for determining heritage protection zones and formed part of the supporting documentation to UNESCO for world heritage listing" (UNESCO 2004, 40). In 1995, Luang Phrabang was added to UNESCO's list of world heritage sites and officially cited for its "outstanding universal value, representing the harmonious relationship between the built and natural environment, and for the successful fusion of traditional Lao architecture and urban structure with those of the nineteenth and twentieth century French style" (42). A year later, La Maison du Patrimoine (Heritage House) was set up by the Luang Phrabang Provincial Department of Information with support provided "by the French Ministry of Foreign Affairs, the European Union and the UNESCO World Heritage Centre." Under the supervision of Lao Maison du Patrimoine, "[n]o monuments may be destroyed and no restorations undertaken that do not conform to original architectural specifications" (43). In this manner, Luang Phrabang's preservation was initiated with an emphasis on conserving its material culture. The enshrinement of the Phra Bang on the site of the old royal palace (now Luang Phrabang National Museum) remained a chief focus of the city's preserved material culture and the center of ritual and touristic attention until a new image hall was completed near the entrance to the old palace in 2013.

The extensive UNESCO report published in 2004 notes that Luang Phrabang's strategy for its conservation and preservation is based on "the concept of authenticity . . . [that] may be applied to built heritage such as monasteries, palaces, houses, public monuments, and town layout; movable cultural property such as handicrafts; intangible heritage including rituals and traditional performing arts and practices; unique local practices ranging from cooking methods to medical practices to agricultural techniques" (UNESCO 2004, 55). It goes on to assert that "[a]uthenticity is a particularly complex concept as culture is constantly in flux and draws vitality from the ability to adapt to inevitably changing circumstances. However, while being a difficult concept to describe, cultural authenticity is recognizable and is a key defining feature for World Heritage sites" (ibid.). While recognizing that "authenticity" is a "controversial and complex notion," this UNESCO report, however, makes little effort to define authenticity in greater detail or to relate it quite specifically to the culture of Luang Phrabang, other than to cite examples about how the calendrical pattern or dates of certain rituals should not be manipulated for the benefit of the tourist "high season," or that only appropriate materials should be used in restoring old buildings (UNESCO 2004, 53). Rather, the report simply makes the case that "authenticity" is "recognizable"; one knows it when one sees it in specific cases of "built heritage" and "ritual." One question that arises, therefore, within the context of the marketing of Luang Phrabang has to do with identifying the agency for this recognition of authenticity. What is clear is that the French have played the leading role for Paris-based UNESCO in determining what is "authentic" or not in Luang Phrabang. It is only fair, then, to ask, how authentic is it for the French to be the dominant agency determining what is authentically Lao in Luang Phrabang? Moreover, to what extent would it be right to say that in some ways, with regard to its conservation and preservation, contemporary Luang Phrabang has reemerged, at least in terms of its imagined culture, as a new kind of French protectorate? Or, to frame the question a bit more emphatically (as it has been phrased by one contemporary anthropologist of tourism), "Has Luang Phrabang entered a period of 're-colonialization'?"[49] These issues are not unrelated to Buddhism and how it is envisaged within Luang Phrabang. Indeed, some of the harshest critics of Luang

Phrabang's *samanera*s (novices) are French expatriates with decidedly Western understandings of what it means to be Buddhist.

To be fair, the 2004 UNESCO report reflects a high degree of awareness regarding the complicated impact of Luang Phrabang's designation as a world heritage site. It rightly emphasizes that "Luang Prabang faces the dilemma of ascertaining acceptable levels of change and determining its carrying capacity for absorbing and managing tourism. The challenge is how to avoid compromising the natural, built and cultural heritage of Luang Prabang in pursuit of the benefits of tourism" (UNESCO 2004, 53). Yet this very statement captures the irony of the situation now at hand in Luang Phrabang, a situation quite similar to what has occurred at UNESCO world heritage sites in Sri Lanka, such as Anuradhapura and Polonnaruva. Having embarked on an effort ostensibly to conserve and preserve cultural expressions of "universal value," UNESCO, unwittingly or not, has actually functioned as the key catalyst for dramatic cultural and social changes. Recent history records the reality that being deemed a "world heritage site" by UNESCO means immediately becoming a target of development by the international tourist industry. Angkor Wat in neighboring Cambodia may be the best example of this pattern. While the emerging local economy adjoining a world heritage site grows (the hotels, guesthouses, restaurants, bars, internet cafés, massage parlors, travel agencies, souvenir shops, etc.), the local culture becomes "globalized." Or, as soon as the world heritage site's "universal value" is trumpeted, it is opened up to market forces far beyond local, or UNESCO's, control. Indeed, a social and economic transformation of the given locality is set into motion[50] that has not only serious cultural side effects, but critical environmental consequences as well.[51] The changes occurring in Luang Phrabang over the past ten years because of the rampaging growth of tourism are nothing short of breathtaking in their magnitude. An economic momentum has mounted so much inertia that the government and business interests now have too much at stake to mitigate the growth. Indeed, given the number of major construction projects now under way in Luang Phrabang, and given predictions that the number of tourists visiting Luang Phrabang will double in the next four to six years, the pressures now facing the town will only intensify in the future. Officials at UNESCO are aware of the surging tide that they have helped to unleash. After describing some of the social problems that have resulted from the influx of tourism, the UNESCO report states, "[T]he Luang Prabang community must be made aware that if they choose not to follow UNESCO World Heritage guidelines for protecting the essence of the town, one of the consequences may be the delisting of Luang Prabang as a World Heritage site and the loss of

Luang Prabang's attractiveness as a global tourism destination" (2004, 59). From this ominous warning, it is clear that UNESCO not only intends to protect but also has the capacity to punish if it ascertains that local people and their government are unable to cope effectively with the fallout that UNESCO, itself, has helped engender.

Though UNESCO is certainly well intentioned, it seems as if it is also unable to cope with the consequences that it has helped unleash. Philosophically, its rhetoric not only contains echoes of neocolonialism, but its emphases on "authenticity" and "essence" betray, unfortunately, a naiveté about social and cultural historical processes. The concepts of both "authenticity" and "essence" are wedded to a primordialist view that assumes that cultures possess a qualitative "intrinsicality." If there is a blind spot in UNESCO's approach as it has pertained to Luang Phrabang, it is this: while concentrating its "protectorate" on preserving "built heritage" and remaining at least conscious of conserving the ritual calendar, UNESCO has not anticipated the transformation of social processes that it has itself helped engender. Moreover, some of its own efforts aimed at physically improving the city have been somewhat ill-conceived, given the consequent deleterious effects they have occasioned on specific social processes as well.

Be that as it may, it remains clear that the Phra Bang image remains the chief symbol of Luang Phrabang's cultural "authenticity." Not only does it function as the chief focus of attention for the mounting number of international tourists, it remains symbolically at the center of annual public New Year rites that reaffirm Laos' special historical relationship to Theravada tradition.

PI MAI: THE LAO NEW YEAR

In contemporary Luang Phrabang, it is almost impossible for anyone, Lao or foreign tourist, to escape some form of participation in the New Year (*pi mai*) festivities. *Pi mai*, in addition to the mid-November through mid-February "high season," is now a major economic event marketed zealously by Lao government tourist bureaus and the private tourist industry. Still, the collective ritual articulations of the festival affirm the substance and parameters of the entire social and cosmic order as traditionally conceived.

In all three of their detailed studies of Lao Buddhist ritual, Hayashi (2003) Tambiah (1970), and Zago (1972) have indicated that laity and monks do not regard the New Year's rites as a very significant event for the making of merit. Indeed, *pi mai* is not about merit-making at all, but instead focuses on the renewal of order, both social and, at least traditionally, cosmic

Figure 1.01. Phra Bang
during Pi Mai, April 2007

(Zago 1972, 297–306). As in New Year's ceremonies celebrated the world over, the ethos of New Year rituals in Luang Phrabang is now decidedly and almost wholly secular in orientation, with various degrees of sacred vestige only relatively still in play. But it is precisely these vestiges of the sacred that, as a historian of religions, I am primarily interested in considering, particularly the significant role that is played by the Phra Bang image.

The annual *pi mai* celebrations in Luang Phrabang observed in mid-April have been written about in great length by many capable scholars, so I will not recapitulate in any great detail what is already so well analyzed or easily accessed. Instead, I shall present some salient observations to indicate how changes in the political economy and society of Laos are

Figure 1.02. Vat Xieng Thong

clearly reflected in contemporary religious culture. (Readers interested in greater depth, nuance, and detail should consult Trankell's [1999] and Zago's [1972] accounts.)

Earlier, I referenced the creation mythology that still serves as the narrative backdrop for the national New Year's rites celebrated in Luang Phrabang. Currently, the central rites of the New Year's festivities basically consist of the Miss Lao New Year beauty pageant, which concludes on the first day of the festival; the commercialized morning market on the second day, held on the main road in front of the provincial government buildings, followed in the afternoon by the main ritual procession from the beauty pageant grounds (the old football stadium) to Vat Xieng Thong; the construction of sand stupas on the banks of the Mekong and Nam Khan rivers opposite Luang Phrabang and the return ritual procession from Vat Xieng Thong on the third day; and, finally, the centerpiece of the festival, consisting of the ritual lustration of the Phra Bang image on the morning of the fourth and final day of festivities.

In writing about the significance of the Miss Lao New Year beauty pageant, Trankell (1999, 204–205) notes how the event first came about not only as a result of influence from Thailand, where beauty pageants have become a veritable cultural craze, but as a strategically calculated substi-

Figure 1.03. Sand stupa on the banks of the Nam Khan River on second day of Pi Mai

tution for the performance of the *Ramayana,* since in Pathet Lao post-revolutionary times, the *Ramayana* contains too many associations in Luang Phrabang with its now deposed kingship. She notes that "[t]he winner of the contest (*nang sangkhan,* Miss Lao New Year) represents the tutelary spirit of the New Year and is seen as the incarnation of the *sangkhan* (the horastic animal sign of the year). In the New Year procession, she performs in the main parades mounted on the animal of the year, surrounded by her fellow contestants" (ibid.).

Trankell notes that the beauty contest was first introduced in 1973 by the mayor of Luang Phrabang, who had read a story about how a former Lao king had been ceremoniously venerated by his seven daughters. The mayor had found the substance of this story, therefore, quite fitting for celebrating the beginning of the Lao New Year and thought that the holding of a beauty pageant could convey the spirit of the story's motifs. The most significant dimension of Miss Lao's ritual duties, at least as I see it, is that she now performs some of the ritual duties formerly undertaken by

Figure 1.04. Miss Lao (2015) on New Year's horastic animal (boar) in Pi Mai procession

the king, including the most auspicious and symbolically powerful of all, the lustration of the Phra Bang image. In addition, by virtue of the symbolism that she has been accorded, she embodies the welfare of the community for the following year, just as former kings were emblems of the welfare of their kingdoms. I will simply note that the other festivities, including the morning market, the two parades that attempt to symbolize collectively the hierarchical presence of all Luang Phrabang people according to ethnicity (with the tourists bringing up the rear in 2007!), and the building of sand stupas on the banks of the rivers are heavily patronized. But what I want to focus on in particular, given the interests of this discussion, is the symbolism of the Phra Bang within the totality of these proceedings. It remains the most symbolically potent vestige of traditional Lao religious culture that is invoked during the New Year's rites. I want to put this into the context of what I have already written regarding what the Phra Bang had come to symbolize in the old Lan Xang kingdom.[52]

On the morning of the fourth and final day of the New Year festivities, until the new image hall for the Phra Bang image was consecrated in 2013,

Figure 1.05. New image hall dedicated in 2013 for Phra Bang

the Phra Bang was always brought in procession from the old palace (now Luang Phrabang National Museum) to the front courtyard of adjacent Vat Mai. Now it is simply brought from the new image hall. The costumed Luang Phrabang ancestral *phi,* together with their tamed stepchild lion, first worship the image, thereby indicating their recognition of the ultimate power of the Buddha and their subordinated enlistment to his cause.

After the chanting of Pali *suttas* by monks from inside the *sim* (image hall) of Vat Mai, the ancestors are the first to pour water into the throat of a symbolic *naga* (serpent), from which it cascades over the Phra Bang, the lustration symbolically purifying and renewing the power of the Buddha. The ancestral *phi* are then followed by the four most senior abbots of the Buddhist *vats* in Luang Phrabang, representing the *sangha*'s legitimation of the proceedings. In turn, they are followed by a series of government officials: those representing the national government of the Lao PDR, the Luang Phrabang provincial government, the local mayor, and finally the *ban* chief. These government officials, together with Miss Lao and her attendants, are the first laity given the opportunity to worship the image and to offer their lustrations.[53] There is a widely noted tradition that during

Figure 1.06. Costumed ancestral *phi* venerating Phra Bang

the time that the Phra Bang image is publicly venerated, a household member of every family in Luang Phrabang will participate in lustrating the image. But what is most significant in the contemporary context is the insertion of Lao PDR government officials and Miss Lao into the aspersion proceedings. This insertion not only indicates their official endorsements of Buddhism, since their patronage represents the consent of the state, but it also represents their role as replacements for the disestablished royalty of Laos. The hierarchy of the symbolism in this annual rite of purification and renewal is still quite apparent in general, despite the absence of royalty since 1975. As the king protected and purified the power of the Buddha, and in turn was protected and purified *by* the Buddha, so the same relations are symbolically expressed between the government officials and Miss Lao on the one hand and the Buddha in the form of Phra Bang image on the other. Order, virtue, and prosperity are thereby sustained symbolically through this rite of reciprocation.

Frank Reynolds has interpreted the general symbolism of the New Year's rites as they were conducted before the 1975 revolution in the following way:

The rites themselves . . . center around the lustration of the image, an act which seeks to assure the coming of the rains, the renewal of the magical power of the image, and its continued beneficence toward the community. For our purposes it is crucial that these lustrations are performed both by the masked dancers representing the primal ancestors (the *devata luang*) and by the king. Since, in addition to its other functions, the lustration is an act of veneration and commitment, the participation by the ancestors signals the acceptance by the whole community of Laotians, past, present, and future, of the supremacy and authority of the image (and hence of the Buddha whom the image represents). In the same vein the lustration by the king confirms his own acceptance of the Buddha's authority and prepares the way for the ceremony which immediately follows, the oath of loyalty to him (the king) taken by the nobles. (Reynolds 1969, 86)

From this, Reynolds proceeds to unpack the symbolism of the Phra Bang's lustration in relation to other calendrical rites celebrated annually in Luang Phrabang and then ferrets out the specifics of the socio-cosmic hierarchy that all of rituals these affirm in toto:

When one telescopes these various ceremonial episodes which we have discussed—and in fact they are telescoped in a variety of different ways in the ritual context itself—the lineaments of a strongly hierarchical religio-social ideal can be discerned. The three jewels of Buddhism, the Buddha, Dhamma, and Samgha, appear at the peak of the hierarchy, providing the ultimate norms which regulate the structure and circumscribing the cosmos in which it operates. Below the three jewels and within the world which they define stand the *devata luang*, the ancient divinized kings, and the living monarch who is himself at least potentially divine. Under them are ranged, on one side, the lesser spirits and demons which they have "tamed" and drawn into the service of Buddhism and, on the other, the hierarchy of court nobles committed to the ruling king and responsible for the implementation of his rule of Dhamma. Next in the order come the commoners who are organized in socio-territorial units established by the ancestors and given particular segments of the Dhamma which it is their special responsibility to maintain. Finally, at the bottom of this ideal order, but through their original association with the territory still necessary participants in it, are the aborigines of the area, the Kha. (1969, 87–88)

Reynolds' account would seem to have included his reflections upon the two processions that form an important dimension of New Year's rites. For even today, within these processions are found representatives of the various "commoners" and Kha who collectively make up the totality of the Luang Phrabang community.

As I have indicated, the detailed royal aspects of the New Year's proceedings have obviously vanished since the 1975 revolution along with the banishment of the royal family in 1976, but Trankell (1999, 194–195) has examined the royal protocols at the Luang Phrabang National Museum, formerly the royal palace, and has reconstructed the sojourn of the king's annual "cosmological journey" that followed the Phra Bang's lustration. In this "journey" that marks the first movements of the New Year on behalf of the community, Luang Phrabang's ancestors are also venerated and the Buddha's central authoritative presence repeatedly commemorated throughout the kingdom (at least symbolically). These are the first acts undertaken during the New Year, thereby reconfirming the fundamental order of the kingdom within the cosmos as a whole. According to Trankell,

> the king started his cosmological journey, on the day after the reception of the New Year, at the religious center, the Vat Xieng Thong. There he was offered the purifying bath before entering the temple for worship, which included bathing the Buddha image [Phra Man]. During the course of the following days, he first traveled south to the village of Sangalok. Located at the mouth of the Nam Dong River, where, according to legend, the "grandparents" (ancestors) died after killing a dragon monster that had threatened the kingdom. Sangalok is also said to be the first stop of the Prabang upon arrival in the kingdom, as well as being, in more recent times, a Khmer village which supplied the royal guards and policeman. The following day the journey goes north, where the king should make a stop on Don Khun island outside the tributary of Nam Xeuan in order to receive the aspersion, and to enjoy a short rest, as an act of commemoration of the event when the Lord Buddha arrived at this place. The same day the journey continued north, up the river to the sacred caves of Vat Tham Thing just opposite Pak Ou where the bathing ritual was repeated before the king returned to the city.
>
> The important ritual elements in the king's cosmic journey include traveling along the south/north axis and the offering of water of successively higher social and cosmological levels. The journey constitutes the symbolic recreation of the kingdom in connection with the Lao New Year. (1999, 194–195)

From Reynolds' and Trankell's interpretive accounts, it is impossible to miss the fact that the traditional New Year's rites were fundamentally about regenerating cosmic power and hierarchical social order through rites of purification. In light of this interpretation, what can be said about how the New Year's rites have changed since the disestablishment of Lao royalty and the political ascendancy of the Lao PDR? Answering this takes us some distance in generally assessing the conditions of religious culture in northern Laos today.

Grant Evans' observations in his *The Politics of Ritual Memory* provide an excellent starting point in beginning to answer this question:

> Purification rites of the city previously conducted by parades of the king's elephants have disappeared, as have rites connected with minorities. . . . But nothing has taken their place. Thus the direction or change is towards simplification and secularization of the ritual process through the highlighting of the beauty pageant element. The suppression of the role of the king in the ritual was the cause of a rapid and dramatic simplification and secularization of the ritual process. (1998, 137)

Evans extends these observations later on in the same essay to say,

> As we have seen, after 1975 in Luang Prabang the very elaborate traditional New Year rituals contracted drastically. Significantly, this occurred during the term of a Hmong governor who retired in the 1980s, who now tends to be blamed for the excessive rigidity of communist policy in Luang Prabang. The deposed king could play no role in the rituals, and as far as I can ascertain from informants, the *kha* [Khamu] lost their role. Only after 1989 when the government began to open its doors widely to foreign capital and tourism was there an attempt to revive some of the pomp of the traditional New Year rituals. (1998, 147)

And finally:

> The now defunct rituals which gave prominence to the *kha* and which suggested a profound kinship relationship between them and the Lao have not been replaced by any rituals of equivalent depth. Minorities today in Laos, while legally equal, find themselves in a position similar to minorities in many other Asian countries—they simply provide ethnic flavor for the tourist industry. Furthermore, this works for only some "colorful" minorities like the Hmong. The Khamu, however, who played such a crucial role in the rituals of Luang Prabang do not have this color and therefore they are likely to drop completely out of sight. (1998, 151)

Evans' observations can be supplemented with those of my own from 2007 and 2015 to answer the fundamental question that has been posed. In reading Reynolds' and Trankell's accounts, one might get the impression that *pi mai* is celebrated in Luang Phrabang with great solemnity and sacredness because of the grand social and cosmic issues that seem to be at stake. Indeed, it is likely that in the decades and centuries past, the processions and lustrations were conducted with high modicums of sacrality and sobriety. Even today, one can hear some older Lao residents of Luang Phrabang talk about how much the ethos of *pi mai* has changed. Indeed,

Figure 1.07. Water wars in Luang Phrabang

I found enormous changes even between 2007 and 2015. In essence, Evans was right in his account to emphasize that since 1975 there has been a definite movement toward secularization and simplicity. (I would add that I think the direction also includes elements of profanity and ribaldry as well.) Only the formal lustration of the Phra Bang image on the fourth day at Vat Mai is conducted amid any degree of solemnity. And yet, it is conducted amid such a welter of photo-flashing tourists that its sacrality has also been sacrificed, to some extent, at the altar of tourism. Indeed, the previous three days of *pi mai* in 2007 and 2015 were nothing short of a continuous war of water: squads of young Lao fanned out patrolling the streets in pickup trucks thoroughly dousing every and any person in proximity, in turn being attacked by others lining the streets. Indeed, virtually every intersection in town was manned by young men and women armed with buckets of water and sporting menacing grins as they unmercifully attacked whoever attempted to pass by, all in good fun.

The amount of water tossed during these three days is rivaled only by the amount of Beer Lao being consumed. The only other ritual occasion I have seen in the past that comes close to the licensed mayhem I witnessed during these days in Luang Phrabang is the celebration of *holi* in India. In this Lao instance, however, I could not ascertain any elements of ritual reversals, except for the general fact that the normally exceedingly polite and even-minded people of Laos had become temporarily and happily unhinged.

Thus, the ritual processions through the streets of Luang Phrabang referred to above are conducted within the context of this general "war-footing." Indeed, all of the participants in the processions, including members of the *sangha,* Miss Lao New Year and her entourage, the costumed ancestral *phi* or *devata luang,* representatives from each of Luang Phrabang's *ban,* Khmu and Hmong people, and even the quite loud, sodden, and boisterous tourists in 2007, were thoroughly pelted with water and powder as they made their way through the streets of the city in procession. By end of the procession, all participants are soaked to the skin and many colored over completely from the bursts of powder that had peppered their journey. This was no solemn affair reestablishing order and hierarchy, but more of a carnivalesque atmosphere of lighthearted fun. Indeed, many New Year's celebrations throughout the world are comparatively similar in nature. In the West, one needs only to recall social behavior on New Year's Eve to find an apt analogy. The chaos of the end of the year finally gives way to the reestablishment of some semblance of order at the beginning of the new. But in Luang Phrabang, it is not an exaggeration to say that, at least in public, the accent is now on the former (chaos) rather than on the latter (purification and order).

In any case, the public processions in Luang Phrabang deserve further comment, for they are remarkably inclusive. In 2007 the processions were headed—and I have no idea whether this was countenanced by officials or not—by five overtly gay men ("lady boys") who were dressed as women and who sauntered and stumbled in semi–dance steps in front of the costumed ancestral *phi* and their accompanied costumed stepchild lion. These transvestites, of course, bravely received the first blasts of liquids and powder to be hurled at the procession. Following the costumed ancestral *phi* were elderly Lao Loum residents of Luang Phrabang, followed by a large contingent of the *sangha.* None of these were spared a healthy dousing/powdering either. Miss Lao, in an elevated float, followed with her attendants, who in turn were followed by representatives from outlying villages. These villagers carried with them silver stick-character effigies of *phi,* the only anthropomorphic (or semi-anthropomorphic) representations of *phi* that I observed during my nine months of living in northern Laos. And finally, contingents of Khmu, Hmong, and tourists brought up the final sections of the procession.

Figure 1.08. Hmong contingent

In each of the sections, with the exception of the *sangha* and Miss Lao's contingent, a significant percentage of those in the procession had entered into advanced states of inebriation. But what struck me most about the procession in general, apart from its casual and irreverent ethos, was its remarkable inclusivity. While, as Evans has noted, the elements of formal rituals that symbolically emphasized the place of the Kha may have been discarded, there was a place for everyone, including the tourists, in the 2007 New Year processions in Luang Phrabang.

What had changed, and rather dramatically so in 2015, was the sheer size and degrees of extended inclusivity now apparent. While hundreds participated in the 2007 processions, now thousands do. And the procession is much more highly organized, with a young woman in traditional Lao dress introducing each unit of the procession with a sign in Lao marked prominently by a Pepsi-Cola logo.

In addition to what I've described for the 2007 process, in 2015, the abbots of Vat Mai, Vat Xieng Thong, Vat Vixun, and Vat Aham, the most significant historical *vat*s in Luang Phrabang, ride within specially constructed ritual spaces in the back of pickup trucks along with the other

Figure 1.09. Beginning of *pi mai* procession—note Pepsi logo that appeared on all signs designating contingents of the procession

fully ordained monks of each *vat*, who are then followed by the *vats'* sa-maneras.

But even more significant is the inclusion of so many other aspects of contemporary Luang Phrabang society, including local handicraft crafts groups, representatives of nearby tourist sights such as the Kuang Si waterfall and Pak Ou cave, indigenous music ensembles, members of the Ramayana troupe who play several days a week at the National Museum auditorium, representatives of the newly established Souphanavong University, signs celebrating that Luang Phrabang has been declared "the most popular city in the world for 2015," and so on. In addition there were now sections of the parade organized around the presence of important paraphernalia used in traditional rites: "*basi* flowers," the *ou banf* jar, and iron and sand flags, as well as banana leaves. There were even contingents of "traditional Lao-style fighting" and traditional ritual music. As I mentioned earlier, every contingent in the parade was announced by a sign with a Pepsi-Cola emblem. Pepsi is now the most important sponsor of the rite. This exponential growth and the high degree of organization and

Figure 1.10. Abbot of a leading *vat* in Luang Phrabang

commercialization now evident clearly reflects the trajectory noted by Evans more than fifteen years earlier. And what holds especially true about the *pi mai* procession is its remarkable inclusivity of contemporary Luang Phrabang society. It is veritably a ritual statement about what aspects of life are celebrated and promoted in Luang Phrabang.

I would also note that I think any sense of a holistic or synchronized ritual process governing the entirety of the proceedings has been somewhat lost, if it was ever present in the more traditional past. That is, few people seem to attend all of the festivities. The only participants consistently present at all the ritual venues, with the exception of the sand stupa–making, were the ancestral *phi* members of the *sangha* and Miss Lao and her contingent. But it is still worth pondering the contemporary significance of these three elements.

While I agree with Trankell that Miss Lao and her contingent are structural and symbolic replacements of the king and royalty in these proceedings, I also think that Grant Evans' observations about secularization, and my own sense of the ethos of contemporary *pi mai*, need to be emphasized as well. That is, while scholars may suggest a deeply rooted symbolism indicative of a transformation of royal associations, Miss Lao is, obviously, a beauty queen first and foremost in the eyes of the contemporary public. She has been chosen not just because she represents the community in the manner in which kings may have done formerly (which I think is probably not a thought consciously entertained by many in Luang Phrabang today), but also because she is judged to be a talented and beautiful young woman, or the epitome of Lao femininity, at least to the extent that femininity is adjudged by various criteria in contemporary Laos.[54] As much as beauty contests are increasingly viewed with skepticism and criticism in the West, as events that contribute to the exploitation of women purely as sexual objects, in South and Southeast Asia they continue to gain popularity. What I want to point out within the context of the New Year's rites in Luang Phrabang, however, is that after the beauty pageant has ended, Miss Lao's presence at every occasion that follows is complemented by the attendance of the *sangha* and the ancestral *phi*. These are the three elements consistently present for all formally organized occasions constituting the remainder of the festivities. Members of the *sangha*, of course, may be said to represent the epitome of ideals constitutive of Lao masculinity, despite their formal detachment from sex (which no doubt constitutes a paradox). They are, and this is crucial for the analysis at hand, the human embodiments and symbols of what the Phra Bang itself represents: the profile of the Buddha. The ancestral *phi*, one feminine and one masculine, represent the primordial sexuality of the community. I suggest, therefore, that the presence of these ritual actors, even within the context of secularization, continue to symbolize the continuing *vitality* or viability of the Lao community in the past and present, all nominally continuing to be subject to and beneficiaries of the power of the Buddha symbolized by the Phra Bang. Collectively, all four elements (Miss Lao, the *sangha*, the ancestral *phi*, and the Buddha) symbolize the vital powers of the changing place, degrees of secularization notwithstanding.

There is no doubt that the Lao New Year celebrations in Luang Phrabang have been increasingly "commodified" for domestic and tourist consumption. Anyone trying to book a room at a guest house in Luang Phrabang during the four days of festivities might as well be in Bethlehem on Christmas Eve. The increasingly raucous ethos of the occasion reflects a party spirit writ large, consistent with the increasing relaxation of various social prohibitions in contemporary Laos. The current political regime, though still nominally Marxist, can no longer be accused of being "the party of no fun." At the same time, and though perhaps sustained for expedient economic purposes by the government, the traditional symbols of ancestry and the Buddha, the nominal ontological powers of the place, continue to be affirmed in the presence of socially constructed masculine and feminine ideals. This is not to argue that the ideals themselves are not changing substantively. For, it remains an open question in this evolving context as to what the community of Luang Phrabang is about to further become, what the Buddha will mean to it, and what ideals the masculine *sangha* and feminine Miss Lao will truly embody in the future.

CHAPTER TWO

Asala Perahara

Powers of the Buddha's Tooth-Relic in Sri Lanka

The island nation of Sri Lanka, the teardrop-shaped land mass located just off the southern tip of India, has been known by many different names throughout its long history, reflecting the fact that its geographical location has proven historically congenial to the intersection of many different cultures for more than two and half millennia.[1] Before I first visited this physically beautiful and topographically diverse country in the late 1970s, I imagined it as a microcosmic or manageable version of India, its giant neighbor to the north. I was deluded. Sri Lanka was far more complex socially and politically than I had imagined. While Sri Lanka's history records numerous waves of immigrations emanating out of various regions of the South Asian subcontinent, it has witnessed the emergence of Sinhala Buddhist and Tamil Hindu civilizations whose linguistic, religious, and cultural elements originated in India; the arrival and integration of Arab Muslim traders from the eighth century forward; and then the prolonged four and half centuries of colonial interventions by the Christian Portuguese, Dutch, and British from the early sixteenth through the mid-twentieth centuries. All these communities, in addition to the indigenous Veddas, have contributed to the complex evolution of Sri Lanka's society, one that clearly possesses a distinctive ethos of its own. Sri Lanka is not merely a "little India." Nor has it ever been, contrary to what many westerners assume, a political part of India either. It is an island nation unto itself, but one that has been influenced from many directions throughout its long and varied history. It is more complex and pluralistically nuanced than the claim sometimes made by some contemporary Sinhala Buddhist nationalists: "This is Gotama Buddha's country."

Sri Lanka is also an ancient civilization by any comparative standard. Drip ledge caves, with hewn or carved inscriptions written in the archaic Brahmi script and located in what is now the country's North Central Province, indicate that by the third century BCE Buddhist laymen believed that they were earning merit for a better rebirth by providing contemplative Buddhist monks with a refuge to pursue the life of monastic renunciation. Buddhist monastic chronicles assert that during this same period, an emergent royal power, with its chief seat in Anuradhapura—a settlement that was to become eventually a great cosmopolitan city supported by a system of sophisticated irrigation works—converted to Buddhism as a result of missionary efforts led by children of the great third-century BCE Indian emperor Asoka. These remarkable texts, the *Dipavamsa* (Chronicle of the Island) and earlier sections of the *Mahavamsa* (Great Chronicle), were written in the classical *prakrit* language of Pali by monastic incumbents of the Mahavihara fraternity of what much later became known as the Theravada school of Buddhism during the fourth and fifth centuries CE, when Anuradhapura, the ritual and administrative center of the island's chief kings from the third century BCE until the demise of its infrastructure by imperial Cola invaders from Thanjavur, South India, in the early eleventh century CE, was in full cultural bloom. Aside from archaeological information now coming to light, these texts, while definitively sectarian in perspective, still remain our earliest interpretive windows into Sri Lanka's, and allegedly Theravada Buddhism's, far flung past.

For thirteen centuries, Anuradhapura witnessed the efflorescence of a society and culture supported by a robust economy made possible by the control and distribution of water. The most outstanding feature of Anuradhapura society was the symbiotic relationship that obtained between the royal court and Buddhist monasteries. At the time of their construction by the Anuradhapura kings in the early centuries of the first millennium, the massive Ruvanvelisaya, Abhyagiriya, and Jetavana stupas (reliquary monuments) built within the city's major Buddhist monastic complexes were the largest man-made structures in the world, with the exception of the pyramids of Egypt. By means of generous royal support and the ethic of gift-giving leading to merit-making by the laity, the Buddhist monastic *sangha* thrived. The Chinese pilgrim Fa Hien (whose writings about the Dalada, or "tooth-relic," I cite below) mentions some five thousand and three thousand monks in residence, respectively, at the Abhyagiriya and Mahavihara monasteries alone. The Mahavihara monastery, as I have noted, is regarded as the monastic ancestor of Theravada Buddhist lineage. Each of the three major monasteries developed extensive administrative systems that served as the central bureaucracies for the many disparate village temples that constituted their *nikaya*s (chapters or sects). In effect, the *sangha* became the central source of literary and artistic culture and, in many ways, the economic arbiter of capital wealth.[2] In the later centuries of the first millennium, Anuradhapura continued to be a cosmopolitan city. Though its modern legacy for many Sri Lankan Buddhists is nostalgic, in that it represents the pristine purity of a Sinhala Buddhist cultural past, the monasteries of Anuradhapura (especially the Abhyagiriya and Jetavana) were, in fact, quite eclectic in terms of the types of Buddhist thought and practice that they nurtured. Inscriptions and sculptures reveal that, in addition to the Theravada lineage, Mahayana and Vajrayana Buddhist lineages, including the cults of many bodhisattvas, were also well represented. Indeed, twentieth-century archeological finds indicate that the cult of the Bodhisattva Avalokitesvara, the most prominent of all Mahayana bodhisattvas throughout Buddhist Asia, was widespread in many regions of the island, especially along the east coast and its interior, from the eighth through at least the tenth century and beyond.[3]

The *Mahavamsa* records in some detail the political gyrations that eventually led to an invasion from the South Indian Cola empire that was based in Thanjavur (modern Tamilnadu), an invasion that resulted, seemingly, in the almost total demolition of Anuradhapura's civic and monastic infrastructure in the eleventh century. The Colas, whose power was so ubiquitous at this time that the Indian Ocean was regarded as their own lake, established their new power base on the island in Polonnaruva, about 130 kilometers to the southeast of Anuradhapura, ostensibly to better position themselves to fend off any counter attacks from the Sinhalese, who, in seeking refuge, had fled to the southeast quadrant of the island in the vicinity of modern Tissamaharama. The Colas maintained their position of strength at Polonnaruva for many decades into the eleventh century before the Sinhalas captured it and turned it into their own capital. At Polonnaruva, for a century and a half—before another crushing invasion purportedly led by a chieftain named Magha from Kalinga (modern Orissa in India)—a Buddhist-inspired civilization regained its vigor. The *Culavamsa* (the extension of the *Mahavamsa*) extols the great irrigation works (especially the construction of the Parakramabahu *samudra*, or sea) and building achievements (especially the monastic complex Alahena Pirivena, said to have been attended by some ten thousand monks) by Parakramabahu I (r. 1153–1186) and other kings, including the mighty Nissanka Mala (r. 1187–1196). When the monastic *bhikkhusangha* was reconstituted in Polonnaruva, only monks from the Mahavihara lineage (and none from the Abhyagiriya or Jetavana lineages) were ordained and supported, while no *bhikkhunisangha* (order of nuns) was reestablished at all. This composition of monastic Buddhism, one that holds that the Pali *sutta*s (sermons) and *vinaya* (rubrics of behavioral and ritual discipline) alone are the preserved teachings of the Buddha, is still retained in this fashion today in Sri Lanka and in the countries of Southeast Asia where Theravada has come to dominate religious culture.[4]

It is clear from archeological and sculptural remains, however, that the Polonnaruva capital also sustained a Hindu Saivite presence after its capture by the Sinhalese. Even the *Culavamsa*'s account contains numerous references to Saivite practices in the royal court and within the royal family, probably owing to the fact that Sinhala Polonnaruva kings engaged in the practice of marrying queens from South India. It is possible that the later blending of Hindu and Buddhist popular religion in Sri Lanka received its impetus from the social and political realities of the Polonnaruva courts at this time. But Polonnaruva was also the venue for the writing of the first Sinhala literary compositions, especially those by the celebrated writer Garulugomi. These texts in the Sinhala vernacular took Buddhist narratives from Pali sources for their substance and elaborations. The Sinhala rendered was highly "sanskritized" and therefore very sonorous.[5]

The invasion by Magha that occurred in 1215 was a political and economic disaster so thorough that Sinhala kingship abandoned its splendid capital and began to retreat in a southwesterly direction, situating itself in a series of backwater capitals. Magha's invasion was followed by yet another several decades later, this one by Chandrabhanu of Sri Vijaya (modern Malaysia/Sumatra), who purportedly sought possession of the Buddha's Tooth-Relic and thereby the ritual legitimacy to rule over Lanka. Indeed, the entire period between the thirteenth and fifteenth centuries marks a time of great social turbulence and political instability throughout the island and, with it, the increasing political enervation of Sinhala kings. At the same time, this was a period of unprecedented migration of peoples from various regions of South India, many of whom were originally mercenaries enlisted to fight in the ongoing conflicts. Their presence further abetted a Lankan cultural fermentation, the increased mixing of Hindu and Buddhist elements seen, for example, in the architecture and ritual practices of the Gadaladeniya and Lankatilaka temple complexes constructed (near Kandy) during the Gampola period of the fourteenth century, also a time when the Alakesvaras, a powerful merchant family originally from Kerala, literally supervised the rule of the weakened Sinhala kings of the upcountry from their own power base established in Kotte (very near modern Colombo). In the fourteenth century, the establishment of an independent Tamil kingdom on the Jaffna peninsula ruled over by an autonomous *aryacakravarti* takes place, in effect establishing three competing political power centers of the time. After a coup orchestrated by Cheng Ho, the great Chinese admiral of the Ming dynasty, installed Parakramabahu VI on the Sinhala throne at Kotte for a long reign of fifty-five years beginning in 1412, the island was united under one sovereign's rule for a twenty-year period, the only such time of unification between the Polonnaruva era and the disestablishment of Kandyan kingship by the British in 1815. The Kotte period under the rule of Parakramabahu VI was especially rich in the production of new genres of literature and the increasing influence of Hindu culture.

The arrival of the first Portuguese ships in 1505 inaugurated an encounter with Western political powers and cultures that continues to this day, an encounter that has profoundly influenced the historical trajectories of Theravada traditions. From that time until 1948, Sri Lanka was a venue for the designs of European colonization strategies: first by the Portuguese (1505–1658), followed by the Dutch (1658–1796), and finally the British (1796–1948).

Unlike the Buddhist religious cultures analyzed in other chapters of this book, Sri Lanka endured a very extended historical period of European colonization. While the European colonial experience of the Burmese, Lao, and Khmer was about century in length, or less, and Thailand avoided direct colonization entirely, Sri Lanka's colonial experience lasted almost 450 years. In introducing her readers to modern Sri Lanka, the historian Nira Wickramasinghe describes the general impact of European colonialism in the following way:

> The exceptional length—four hundred years—of the colonial impact on Ceylon, particularly in the coastal areas, radically modified social and economic structures of the island. Ceylon encountered modernity gradually and unevenly. In some respects, the colonial impact extroverted the economy, overturned the traditional streams of trade, and distorted links with India, while introducing into society new elements of heterogeneity: Christianity, the languages of the successive conquerors, new communities such as the Burghers and later Indian immigrant plantation workers. It also imposed unifying factors: modern modes of communication, a unified administrative system, a common language of domination, monetarisation of exchanges. However, the depth of the colonial imprint must not be overestimated: family structures, the caste system and Buddhism were maintained, especially in the center of the island where foreign domination was resisted for three centuries. (2006, 43)

It is precisely this last statement that is very prescient for this chapter. In many ways, the celebration of the *asala perahara,* the annual ten nights of public processions every July/August in Kandy, the last of the traditional royal capitals and still a center for traditional culture, articulates a vision of the past that continues to inform the political present.

The dominant direct legacy left behind by the Portuguese was Roman Catholicism, still practiced today by 5 or 6 percent of the county's population, chiefly along the west coast of the island just north and south of Colombo. One can also readily see the Portuguese influence on Sri Lanka's diet (the introduction of bread and chilis, for instance), on music and dance (*baila*), and architecture (Iberian facades and rounded roof tiles). Indirectly, the presence of Catholicism affected the manner in which Buddhism is publicly articulated in the country as well. For example, one can now observe the ubiquitous presence of Buddha images along public thoroughfares, in the same manner as the presentation of statues of Catholic saints, despite the fact that in traditional Sinhala Buddhist culture, Buddha images were only found within the Buddha image halls of *vihara*s (monastic temples). Traveling around the country today, one can see a plethora of giant imposing Buddha images constructed publicly, indicating the way public space, as an indicator of the climate of national political dynamics, is in the process of being reclaimed by Sinhala Buddhist interests. This is a cultural manifestation of the more aggressive posture denoted by Sinhala Buddhist nationalism, a major theme to be explored within the context of the study of the *asala perahara* that follows.

While the Portuguese were interested in spices and in monopolizing their trade, and in destroying the presence of Buddhist material culture wherever they gained a foothold, the appearance of the succeeding Dutch and their single-minded interest in cinnamon was perhaps the first indication that eventually Sri Lanka would become the venue of a predominantly plantation-oriented economy. Dutch economic efficiency and their deployment of Roman Dutch Law, still an important fixture in Sri Lanka's legal code, remain important legacies, along with what remains of the Dutch Burgher community,[6] which has contributed so much to the production of Sri Lankan English literature. Dutch religious activity was largely confined to ministering among their own, but like the Portuguese they laid siege to Kandy and sought to capture the Dalada (Tooth-Relic), the palladium of Lankan royalty.

While Wickramasinghe (2006) has warned against overestimating the impact of the long colonial presence, the legacy of British rule in Sri Lanka is prodigious indeed. Not only is English language its most powerful legacy—a language now spoken in some measure by about a third of the island's population—but the country's educational, political, and transportation systems, not to mention its business and financial communities, owe their substance and structure to the British intervention. As in India, much of Sri Lanka's basic infrastructure was the by-product of British engineering and organization.

From the early 1980s, Sri Lanka endured what amounted to a protracted civil war between its Sinhala majority and elements of its Tamil minority. While some observers have sought the roots of this conflict within the deep recesses of ancient or medieval history, the fundamental causes of the current conflict seem more recent, causes that have more to do with competition for the relatively scarce economic resources in this comparatively poor (per capita income is a little more than US$1,000 per year as of 2013) South Asian nation. Secondarily, however, the causes of Sri Lanka's social and political conflict are also a by-product of awakened modern and nationalistic ethnic identities fostered, ironically to Westerners, by democratic enfranchisement that has led to a majoritarian rule. Buddhist-rationalized nationalism has increased within the climate of competition that democracy encourages.

Observers outside Sri Lanka have often stressed religion as a key divider between Sri Lanka's communities. While Buddhism, Hinduism, Islam, and Christianity are definitely constitutive markers delineating Sri Lanka's various ethnic communities, until recently religion has not often been a primary motivation for discord between peoples. Rather, its significance has more often surfaced within post hoc arguments that rationalize aggressive or defensive political and military strategies and tactics adopted by the majority. Or, as emphasized throughout this book, religious change is reflected in the way public ritual is articulated, mirroring the larger social, economic, and political forces at work. So on the whole, Buddhism has been less a motivation than a rationalization among the Sinhalese. Having said that, however, the role of religion in the country's political dynamic is beginning to change. In 2004, a new Buddhist monastic political party, galvanized by the death of an extremely popular and politically oriented Buddhist monk,[7] was launched and gained nine seats in Sri Lanka's parliament as the result of its success in general elections. This monastic-based political movement equates the well-being of the religion with the well-being of the nation and vice versa. An offshoot of this monastic party, the Bodu Bala Sena (Army of Buddhist Power) has aggressively harassed and on occasion attacked Christian churches and Muslim communities since 2012 with impunity and with, perhaps, the tacit approval of the government, headed by President Mahinda Rajapaksa until the defeat of that government in early 2015. This militant brand of Buddhist nationalism represents the antithesis of what is necessary for an inclusive umbrella formula demanded by a multiethnic population. It is unabashedly for Sinhala Buddhist supremacy in Sri Lanka. Throughout this recent period of contestation, no dominant perspective that transcends the expediency of ethnic appeal stands on Sri Lanka's horizon, pointing a new way forward beyond the straitjacketed perspectives of ethnocentrism. Unfortunately, neither Sinhala nor Tamil leaders have seemed poised for a constructive dialogue leading to a meaningful partnership in the future. Although there are hopeful signs from a newly elected government, as this book goes to press, the island's future, at least a peaceful future where people from all religious communities compete on a level playing field, remains complicated and problematic, at least in terms of a formula surfacing that meets the aspirations of the island's Tamil, Muslim, and Christian minorities. In this political context, while the annual celebration of the *asala perahara* is certainly a cultural pageant indexing the agrarian heritage of traditional Kandyan culture, it also remains a statement about the well-being and sustenance of Buddhist polity, one based on principles of hierarchy and one that equates Buddhist polity per se with Sri Lankan national polity.

When Sri Lanka gained independence from Britain in 1948, it was a relatively prosperous country and regarded as a "model colony" in some quarters. As the Allies' chief source of rubber during World War II, Sri Lanka had stockpiled considerable wealth, and so its public financial situation was advantageous during its early years of independence. During those early years, much of the country's surplus was invested in its burgeoning free public education system and in its national health care system. Consequently, the country's literacy rate remains quite high and its life expectancy quite long (the highest and longest, respectively, in South Asia). As such, despite the ongoing civil conflict, Sri Lanka continues to enjoy the highest quality-of-life index in contemporary South Asia. Moreover, on the eve of independence, Ceylon did not experience the types of political and communal violence that India or Burma endured. Independence came peacefully. In the initial years of its independence, at least until the mid-1950s, a spirit of inclusion, if not political tolerance, seems to have characterized much of the public political life. Because of Sri Lanka's recent circumstances of contestation, war, and poverty, it is difficult to imagine that a government delegation from another emerging independent state, Singapore, visited Ceylon in the early 1950s to see what it might learn about how to effectively manage ethnic diversity and how to allocate public spending responsibly. It is a national political tragedy that the country was not able to sustain the climate and conditions of its auspicious origins. Sociologists Tudor Silva and Siri Hettige describe the ethos of Sri Lanka's multicultural heritage that seems to have been lost in recent decades:

Called a "Hybrid Island" . . . , for the mixed, hybrid and multicultural nature of the island's society and culture throughout its long history, different communities lived side by side without having to face an assimilation or incorporation drive on the part of ruling groups and having enough opportunities to interact and exchange diet, music, customs and ideas with each other. . . . If multiculturalism involves the acceptance of the right of every group to maintain its own cultural traditions and to develop is own cultural life, this has been the situation in Sri Lanka certainly before the rise of nationalist ideologies in the 20th century. (2010, 8)

Some hold the view that antagonisms between the Sinhalas and Tamils were long simmering and erupted only in the aftermath of British colonial control. This perspective derives largely from an anachronistic view of history, though some British policies did certainly contribute to a degree of acrimony between these communities. Throughout twenty-five hundred years of history, numerous wars were fought between various sovereigns identified in modern histories as either Sinhala or Tamil, but nothing of the sort of demarcated national identities now claiming the loyalties of some within these respective communities seems to have existed during earlier epochs. For instance, it is clear that the Sinhala kings of the fifteenth- and sixteenth-century Kotte period, and several Sinhala kings of the sixteenth- through nineteenth-century Kandyan period, were not only inclusive in their public rhetoric and in the cultural life of their courts, but that also the last four kings of the nominally Sinhala Kandyan kingdom were actually ethnic Tamils who ruled over a predominantly Sinhala but ethnically variegated population. One of these Tamil kings, Kirti Sri Rajasimha (r. 1747–1782), was responsible for a veritable renaissance in traditional Sinhala Buddhist culture.[8] He is also the king who reframed the *asala perahara* proceedings into the manner that they are largely observed today.

While it may be true that the chief causes of civil discord are comparatively recent, a consequence of the past several generations rather than past centuries of strife, how Sri Lanka's historical past is now being written in some quarters of the country (and how it is understood within its diaspora populations) abets the contemporary experience of political stress between communities. The Sinhala-speaking majority of Sri Lanka constitutes some 75 percent of the current population. The Tamil community constitutes roughly 18 percent; Muslims form about 8 or 9 percent; and the Christians a little less. Yet, in the postindependence democratic context, both of the Sinhala and Tamil communities would seem to have suffered, at least from a social psychological point of view, from a type of a "minority complex." From a Sinhala perspective, the Sinhalese are a small but ancient people with a language spoken by only about twelve or thirteen million people (within the context of more than one billion, three hundred million people in the South Asian subcontinent), most of whom practice a religion (Buddhism) that became extinct in most parts of India by the thirteenth century CE. They understand themselves as proud survivors of history, having resisted the major religious, political, and cultural trajectories that earlier spread throughout the Indian subcontinent in the forms of a resurgent *bhakti* (devotional) Hinduism and a conquering Sunni Islam (Mughal India). From their point of view, a mostly rural agrarian population suffered relegation to a subservient status during the history of colonialism, especially during British colonization (1796–1948 CE): a two-thousand-year-old line of kingship (which patronized the Buddhist religion) was disestablished; vast tracts of lands were alienated from traditional use and turned into tea, rubber, and coconut plantations benefiting European colonizers; Buddhism was first "betrayed" by the British (who had originally promised to protect it) and then further abused by Protestant Christian missionaries; while the language (Sinhala) was wholly neglected at the expense of English. Rightly or wrongly, there is a perception that the British had privileged the Tamil minority by affording them a disproportionate share of educational opportunities, such that the Tamils eventually came to dominate the colonial civil service and the professions of education, law, and medicine, as well as business. In the mid-1950s, the majority Sinhalese asserted their new democratically derived power on the basis of their demographic predominance by electing politicians who advocated a series of reforms aimed at elevating Buddhism and the Sinhala language to a special national status, while redressing perceived inequities in the educational and government bureaucratic systems through the establishment of quotas. They also launched ambitious colonization schemes, some in regions of the country that had previously been inhabited by primarily Tamil-speaking people. In effect, many Sinhalese believed that they were simply recovering their primordial ownership of the island. The *Mahavamsa's* monastic understanding of history was utilized to articulate a national understanding of history, one in which Lanka was identified as the *dhammadipa* (island of the Buddha's teaching), the country destined to preserve the Buddhist religion in its originally intended guise. To some extent, it can be argued that the annual performance of the *asala perahara* in Kandy is a ritual statement of this Sinhala Buddhist gestalt regarding national ownership.

From a point of view shared by many Tamil people, the Sinhala nationalist political agenda has amounted to a severe disenfranchisement of basic civil rights, by depriving them of an unfettered use of their Tamil language and of equal opportunity on the basis of merit to secure education at the tertiary levels, and also by discrimination by the Sinhala-dominated government in terms of afforded economic opportunities. Moreover, the *Mahavamsa*'s interpretive rendering of the country's raison d'être cast the Tamil community into the role of being the primordial national antagonist. While resistance was periodic and took many forms, the first signs of sustained violent resistance by Tamil militant groups began to surface in the early 1970s and mushroomed spectacularly following the 1983 ethnic pogrom, a watershed in recent Sri Lankan history, when thousands of Tamils living in predominantly southern Sinhala regions of the island were systematically attacked and murdered, while their homes and businesses were looted and torched during a week of mayhem that has become known infamously as "Black July." Four sustained periods of civil war followed, and countless numbers of violent or terrorist attacks from both sides occurred. On the Sinhala side, the most religiously traumatic of these attacks on sites of Buddhist worship included the 1985 Liberation Tigers of Tamil Eelam (LTTE) assault on worshipers, primarily Buddhist nuns, at the Sri Mahabodhi shrine in Anuradhapura that left over 130 people dead, and the truck-bombing of the Dalada Maligava—where the Buddha's Tooth-Relic is ensconced in Kandy—in 1998, leaving eleven dead. These attacks on sites held most sacred to Buddhists were not only traumatic intrinsically, but they were highly strategic as well, insofar that the bodhi tree and the Tooth-Relic are symbolic of Buddhist identity, especially Sinhala Buddhist national identity. Many other despicable attacks occurred during the civil war emanating from both sides of the conflict, which had the effect of severely scarring ethnic relations until a February 2002 Norwegian-brokered cease-fire agreement was reached that remained largely intact until its pivotal deterioration in the summer of 2006. Following the election of Mahinda Rajapaksa, who succeeded Chandrika Kumaratunga in 2005 as president, and the breakdown of the cease-fire ostensibly because of provocative attacks by the Liberation Tigers of Tamil Eelam against the Sri Lanka Army and its leading officers, the Sri Lankan government armed forces waged a relentless military offensive against the LTTE. During the years of the cease-fire, the Sri Lankan government had scored diplomatic successes in a number of Western countries, especially with Canada, that led to the proscription of the LTTE and its international fund-raising capabilities among the Tamil diaspora. At the same time, the government had built up its military forces and supplies of ammunition. When a faction of the LTTE on the east coast of the island broke away from the northern power base of the movement in the mid-2000s, the LTTE suffered another severe setback in its strength. In May 2009, six months after a pivotal with-drawal from the Mannar peninsula on the west coast, the Tigers were deci-sively defeated as a conventional fighting force, and their leadership decimated, close to their last stronghold near Mullaitivu on the northeast coast. The price for defeating the Tigers was very high, however. The United Nations Commission on Human Rights, supported strongly by the United States, the European Union, and Japan, has urged an indepen-dent probe into conduct during the final months of the war because of the staggering numbers of Tamil civilian casualties, estimated to have been in the tens of thousands.

In the years following twenty-six years of civil war, many Sri Lankans would say, "the war is over but peace has yet to arrive." In the several years since the defeat of the Tigers, unfortunately no serious proposals have been put forward by the Sinhala-dominated government to assuage the grievances of the Tamil people, which might bring about a new era of countrywide solidarity, or a return to an embrace of its multicultural ethos. To the contrary, because the Sinhala-dominated government has not taken meaningful political steps to address the grievances of its Tamil minority, it is likely that the conditions of the current situation may exacerbate com-munal relations in the future. A disturbing recent development involves the appearance of extremist reactionary groups led by politically vocifer-ous Buddhist monks harassing and intimidating, indeed even violently attacking, Muslim communities.

Having provided an historical backdrop of the religio-political history of the island, the focus of this chapter will be on the way the ritual ven-eration of the Dalada (Tooth-Relic of the Buddha), within the context of Sinhala Sri Lanka's most celebrated "national" ritual event, the *asala pera-hara,* reflects the pulse of Buddhist militancy and nationalism in the coun-try today. While the immediate reasons for the pogrom of "Black July" and the ensuing long years of civil war may not have been religious in substance or origins, no one would disagree that the years of civil strife, particularly the odious LTTE terrorist attacks perpetrated at Sri Maha-bodhi in Anuradhapura (where the 2,300-year-old scion of the original "tree of enlightenment" is venerated) and at the Dalada Maligava (Temple of the Tooth-Relic) in Kandy, elicited a rise of Sinhala Buddhist nationalist sentiments in response. The Dalada Maligava in Kandy, the last of the traditional royal capitals of Lanka, is not only the ritual seat for venerating the Tooth-Relic, but it is also the venue for the ritual proceedings of the *asala perahara.*

ORIGINS OF THE DALADA

Veneration of the Buddha's relics is one of the most ubiquitous forms of Buddhist worship in the contemporary Theravada world. Indeed, stupas, or Buddhist reliquaries, can be regarded as the chief symbol for the presence of the Buddha and his religion throughout South and Southeast Asia. It may also be said that no Buddhist temple is regarded as duly complete without the presence of a stupa, for the presence of a stupa indicates the presence of the Buddha, in the same manner as the presence of a Buddha image or a bodhi tree. The presence of these three icons, or types of relics, provides for the ritual space and occasions for contemplative meditation and cultic worship by both monks and laity. In Theravada tradition, relics of the Buddha are not simply reminders of the life of the Buddha in the past, but rather, as John Strong has put it, they can be regarded "as expressions and extensions of the Buddha's biographical process" (2004, 5). By that, Strong means that the presence of the relic is a signifier for the way the life of the Buddha continues in its relevance for the religious lives of Buddhists even today. It continues to inspire acts of devotion and the pursuit of the spiritual path through meditation and moral action. In more doctrinal terms, Strong argues specifically that relics of the Buddha are an index to the fundamental existential processes of coming into being and passing away. Even the Buddha was subject to this inexorable dynamic: whatever is subject to uprising is also subject to cessation. In the Pali *Mahaparinibbana Sutta*, the last words attributed to the Buddha as given to his followers are: "All *dhamma*s ('realities') are impermanent. Work out your paths in diligence" (Walshe 1987, 270).[9]

While this understanding beautifully explains the significance of relics within a Buddhist conceptual framework per se, there is a complementary understanding of relics, this one germane specifically to the significance of the Dalada (Tooth-Relic) for Sinhala Buddhists. H. L. Seneviratne, an anthropologist of Sri Lankan origin who has written meticulously and definitively about the rites performed at the Dalada Maligava in Kandy, including the *asala perahara,* has asserted that "the Buddha and Tooth Relic were not identical, and the Tooth Relic, in the state-sponsored cult, was considered more like a god than the Buddha" (1978, 14). He finds this understanding congruent with the pioneering anthropological analysis offered in the 1930s by Victor Goloubew, the renowned French scholar, who had argued that the conception of the Buddha that was in play at the Dalada Maligava articulated a distinction between a "royal aspect" and a "saintly aspect" (Goloubew 1933, 460).[10] Moreover, Seneviratne has documented in great detail how the daily, weekly, and monthly "rituals of maintenance" performed for the Dalada at the Dalada Maligava are conducted precisely as if the Buddha were a Hindu deity (1978, 40). The implication of this understanding, then, is that there is an extraordinary power intrinsic to the Dalada that can be robustly manifest in this world. The relic is a dynamic, sacred, and powerful presence. It is a transcendent power than can be tapped, can be put to use constructively if it is approached properly through established protocols of purity and honored with the highest respect and gratitude commanded. In describing the rites of feeding, bathing, purifying, entertaining, and entreating, Seneviratne has mapped out how the "grammar" of the cult is fully dependent on religious protocols derived from Hindu priestly traditions.

From several literary sources, but chiefly by examining the fourteenth century Pali *Dathavamsa* written in Sri Lanka, John Strong has provided an illuminating summary of the legendary account of the origins of the Dalada. In this account, the spectacular divine-like powers associated with the Dalada are illustrated in sensational fashion though a series of related episodes. What follows is a condensed version of the miraculous story of Dalada's peregrination from the Buddha's funeral pyre to its ensconced lodging with royalty in fourth century CE. Sri Lanka:

> [A] disciple of the Buddha, named Khema, acquired this tooth from the remains of the Blessed One's funeral pyre and gave it to Brahmadatta, the king of Kalinga [modern Orissa in India]. . . . Brahmadatta enshrined it in his capital city, which was appropriately named Dantapura (Toothville) [!], and there it was duly worshiped by the people and several generations of kings. . . . [I]t is in Dantapura that the tooth, after a while, becomes the target of persecution by non-Buddhist Niganthas [likely Jains]. Despite the inclination of the city's inhabitants toward Buddhism, the Niganthas seek to turn first the local king, Guhasiva, and then the Indian emperor, Pandu, against the relic. Pandu, a Hindu devotee of the gods, is not pleased to find that his subjects are worshiping "the bone of a dead man," and he eventually has the tooth brought to the capital of Pataliputra [in modern Bihar]. There he orders its destruction by fire. A big heap of charcoal is lit for this auto-da-fe, but, when the relic is thrown into it, a great lotus blossom emerges from the flames and receives the tooth relic, which is miraculously preserved, unscathed. King Pandu, however, is not about to give up. He quickly orders that the relic be placed on an anvil and smashed with a hammer. This is done, but the tooth, instead of breaking into pieces, merely sinks into the anvil and remains stuck there, half visible, emitting rays of light in all directions. He then puts the relic into a tank of water, but it begins to swim about like a royal swan. He puts in into a pit in the ground and has the place trampled by elephants, but the relic emerges on a lotus blossom. Finally, one last attempt is made to get rid of the tooth, by tossing it into an open moat that is filled with foul, rotting dead bodies.

Instantly, the moat is transformed into a delightful pool in the midst of a beautiful park. Witnessing all this, Pandu at last becomes convinced of the superior merit of the Buddha and his religion, and taking refuge in the Triple Gem, he converts and becomes a doer of good deeds. Fixing the relic on the top of his crown, he then places it on his throne, worships it with great offerings, and builds a temple for it, entrusting it with brilliant jewels. In time, however, he allows the tooth to go back to Dantapura in Kalinga where it is re-enshrined.

[A] few years later, when Dantapura is threatened by an invading army that seeks to capture the relic, the king tells his daughter, Hemamala, and his son-in-law—a handsome young man appropriately named Danta (Tooth)—to flee the city with the relic, and to take it to Sri Lanka, where the king is known to be a friend and ally. Going south, Danta and Hema-mala first stop by the side of a river. They bury the tooth-relic in a pile of sand [stupa], and, dwelling nearby, they go daily to venerate it. Soon, how-ever, a great naga king coming up the river, sees the rays of light emanat-ing from the sand stupa, and, realizing that a buddha relic is buried at the spot, he makes himself invisible and quickly swallows the casket with the tooth relic inside. He then goes and lies down on the slopes of Mt. Meru. When Danta and Hemamala arrive for their regular worship, they find the relic is gone. Distraught, they call on a passing arhat [a Buddhist monk who has completed the spiritual path] for help. He comes to their aid by taking on the form of the divine king of birds, Garuda, arch foe of all na-gas and greatly feared by them. As Garuda, he confronts the naga king and bullies him into delivering up the casket and the relic, and Danta and He-mamala proceed on their way. . . .

When Danta and Hemamala finally arrive in Sri Lanka, they are re-ceived by King Sirimeghavanna (r. 362–409 C.E.) who has an old building in the palace compound refurbished for the tooth and renamed the Dantadhatu-ghara (House of the Tooth Relic). (Strong 2004, 190–205)

In addition to the miraculous powers attributed to the relic, the pious devotion and caretaking activities by the various royal actors of the Dalada in the *Dathavamsa*'s retelling, and especially the manner in which the relic is venerated by kings, there is present a theme that paradigmatically em-phasizes the symbiotic relation between kingship and the Buddha in the centuries that ensue. The *Dathavamsa* has also followed the pattern estab-lished in *Mahavamsa*'s account of the coming of Sri Mahabodhi (the scion of the original "tree of enlightenment") insofar as the Dalada, like the bodhi tree, was allegedly brought to Lanka by the daughter of a pious Indian king. And as the narrative relates, covetous enemies seek to capture the relic and its power, or to destroy it, a theme that persistently surfaces in Sri Lanka's Buddhist literature, especially in the post-Polonnaruva era, when the relic's significance in relation to royal legitimacy had been firmly established. What is suggested or illustrated in this narrative, then, is that possession and veneration of the Dalada is incumbent on royalty. In return, royalty are regarded as legitimate rulers (Seneviratne 1978, 15–16). Indeed, wars would be fought ostensibly over its possession while colonial powers, especially the Portuguese, would seek to destroy the relic in the hopes of delegitimizing the powers of Lankan kings in the eyes of their followers. In the *vamsa* traditions of Buddhist monastic literature, kings of Lanka would be regarded as custodians of the relic, symbolic of the same way that they are regarded as custodians or chief patrons of the *sasana* (dispensation of the Buddhist religion). Indeed, when the Kandyan chiefs of upcountry Lanka abetted the British in disestablishing the last Sri Lankan king in 1815, they agreed to the terms of the Kandyan Convention that included the provision that British King George and his government would protect the "religion of Boodoo." British colonial agents were thereby regarded by the local populace as the new custodians of the Dalada.[11] Moreover, the first *perahara* performance (in 1828) under the British was held in reaction to the demands of local Buddhists in Kandy, who insisted that it was British responsibility, as rulers of the domain, to perform the rite. This calculation, of course, that the British would be responsible custodians of the Dalada, ultimately proved to be a less than shrewd assumption on the part of the Kandyans. Facing Christian opposition, first in Sri Lanka and then in England, to the Crown's patronage of the Dalada, the colonial government transferred custodianship of the relic to the two chief monks of the Asgiriya and Malvatte sects of the Siyam Nikaya, along with the Diyawardana Nilame, the lay custodian of the Dalada Maligava, in 1846. Still, in the minds of many contemporary Buddhists today, it remains a key responsibility of the postcolonial, democratically elected government of Sri Lanka to protect the Buddhist religion and its foremost symbol, the Dalada. For some stalwart Buddhists yet, as a popular adage has it, "the country exists for the sake of the religion." Perhaps it is because of this legacy regarding the relation between Buddhism and kingship, illustrated particularly by the historic relation between royalty and the relic, that while Sri Lanka's current legal constitution recognizes the freedom of individuals to exercise their private choices in matters of religious practice and belief in one of its sections, it also accords Buddhism "the foremost place" among all religions in another. Thus, the state-supported conduct of the annual *asala perahara* in Kandy is at once a modern ritual articulation of a mythically enhanced theme about traditional political power on the one hand *and* a constitutional responsibility for the state on the other.

In addition to the *Dathavamsa*'s account of how the Dalada came to Sri Lanka, and its frequent mention within the *Mahavamsa*'s recounting of royal patronage, there is one non-Pali primary sources dating from a much earlier period that reveals how the Dalada was venerated publicly shortly after—perhaps within decades of—its purported arrival on the island. Fa Hien was a Chinese pilgrim-monk of the fifth century CE who traveled extensively throughout India and Sri Lanka, leaving behind a vivid description of his observations on the state of the religion at that time.[12] Fa-Hien apparently lived in Anuradhapura for some two years. The timing of his description is conventionally dated to the same century that the *Dathavamsa* claims for the arrival of relic and its initial custodianship under King Sirimeghavanna. How and why the Dalada was venerated is evident from Fa Hien's account. Its importance is signaled by the fact that this passage is the centerpiece of Fa Hien's description of religious life in Anuradhapura:

> The tooth of Buddha is always brought forth in the middle of the third month. Ten days beforehand the king grandly caparisons a large elephant, on which he mounts a man who can speak distinctly, and is dressed in royal robes, to beat a large drum, and the following proclamation:—"The Bodhisattva, during three Asankhyeya-kalpas, manifested his activity, and did not spare his own life. He gave up kingdom, city, wife, and son; he plucked out his eyes and gave them to another; he cut off a piece of his flesh to ransom the life of a dove; he cut off his head and gave it as alms; he gave his body to feed a starving tigress; he grudged not his marrow and brains. In many such ways as these did he undergo pain for the sake of all living. And so it was, that, having become Buddha, he continued in the world for forty-five years, preaching his Law, teaching and transforming, so that those who had no rest found rest, and the unconverted were converted. When his connexion with the living was completed, he attained to *parinirvana* (and died). Since that event, for 1497 years, the light of the world has gone out, and all living things have long contained sadness. Behold! Ten days after this, Buddha's tooth will be brought forth, and taken to the Abhayagiri vihara. Let all and each, whether monks or laics, who wish to amass merit for themselves, make the roads smooth and in good condition, grandly adorn the lanes and by-ways, and provide abundant store of flowers and incense to be used as offerings to it.
>
> When this proclamation is over, the king exhibits, so as to line both sides of the road, the five hundred different bodily forms in which the Bodhisattva has in the course of his history appeared:—here as Sudana, there as Sama; now as the king of elephants, and then as a stag or a horse. All these figures are brightly colored and grandly executed, looking as if they were alive. After this the tooth of Buddha is brought forth, and is carried along in the middle of the road. Everywhere on the way offerings are presented to it, and thus it arrives at the hall of Buddha in the Abhayagiri-vihara. There the monks and laics are collected in crowds. They burn incense, light lamps, and perform all the prescribed services, day and night

without ceasing, till ninety days have been completed, when (the tooth) is returned to the vihara within the city. On fast-days the door of that vihara is opened, and the forms of ceremonial reverence are observed according to the rules. (Holt 2011, 44–49)

Fa Hien's passage is notable for several reasons and would seem to contain a number of harbingers. The first, of course, is that Fa-Hien witnesses the public veneration of the Dalada as early as the fifth century CE in a ceremony carried out by Sri Lankan royalty. Second, moments of public veneration, including the year-round worship of the relic on new and full moon days, are noted as a great opportunity for all, monks and laity alike, to make merit. Third, within the context of the processions to and from the Abhayagiriya *vihara,* processions that seem to form the main focus of the three-month rite, the preparation of the city's lanes and the decorating of the city for the Dalada's adoration all seem to anticipate the form that the *asala perahara* eventually undertakes. Finally, insofar as the context for venerating the Dalada begins with a retelling of the life of the Buddha, and that his many rebirths as known through his more than five hundred *jataka* stories are recalled through illustrations that line the path of the procession, all would seem to indicate, as John Strong has averred, that relics can be regarded as extensions of the life of the Buddha. The relic's ritual celebration in this context clearly seems to depict the Buddha's continuing ability to inspire the lives of religieux.

THE DALADA AND KINGSHIP IN MEDIEVAL SRI LANKA

According to the *Dathavamsa,* the Dalada, from the time of its arrival in Sri Lanka, "was housed on 'royal ground,' . . . [though] until about the twelfth century the *Dalada* did not acquire the association with political legitimacy" (Seneviratne 1978, 16–17). That this association had evolved into a full bloom at this time is evident from the intimacy of the relationship between kingship and the Dalada and the alms bowl relic rather dramatically depicted in the *Culavamsa's* account (74, 99–248; 2, 31–43) of how the Parakramabahu I, the great king of Polonnaruva in the twelfth century, went to war to secure the Dalada and the alms bowl relic from rival hands and established a cult for their veneration in the center of the capital city. Perhaps no other account of royalty and relics emphasizes more demonstrably the degree to which Sri Lankan royalty coveted the presence of the Dalada and spared no resource in securing its possession. Without the Dalada and the alms bowl relic, the *Culavamsa* has Parakramabahu declaring that the fortunes of the island would be "desolate," and that his own consecration as king would be incomplete:

> The Ruler of men, Parakkama, the best of far-seeing men, sent to his dig-nitaries who were at that place [Dighavapi], the following message: "Shat-tered in combat the foe is in flight. They have seized the splendid sacred relics of the Alms-bowl and the Tooth and are fain, through fear, to cross the sea. So have I heard. If this is so, then the island of Lanka will be deso-late. For though here on the Sihala island various jewels are found, yet of quite incomparable costliness are the two sacred relics of the Lord of truth, the Tooth and the Alms-bowl. At the cost of much valuable property and by the constant amassing of well-tried and armed warriors, I have freed this superb island of Lanka from every oppression, but all my pains would be fruitless. My head adorned with a costly diadem sparkling with the splen-dour of very precious stones, would only be consecrated by the longed-for contact with the two sacred relics of the Great Master, the Tooth and the Alms-bowl. Therefore . . . , with the same end in view, with army and train and without in any way departing from the orders I give, conquer the hos-tile army and speedily send me the splendid Tooth Relic and the sacred Alms-bowl. (*Culavamsa* 99–110; p. 31)

Following this passage, a long description of war describes how thousands of warriors were sacrificed and killed in pursuit of a recalcitrant enemy that has absconded with the relics to the southeastern quadrant of the is-land. When the enemy was finally subdued, with great joy, the relics were ceremoniously received in Polonnaruva by Parakramabahu, who is then compared in magnificence to the great god Siva (the Hindu god with the moon in his hair) as he adorns his own crown with the Dalada mounted. Parakramabahu holds a grand festival in the Dalada's honor and con-structs a splendid temple, described in meticulous detail, for the relic's constant veneration.

When Parakramabahu mounts the royal elephant with the relics in his hand in a splendid procession for the temple's consecration ceremony, a mighty thunderstorm appears on the horizon. As everyone fears for the pounding of the impending storm, Parakramabahu bravely proceeds forth amidst its fury in full glory. The people proceed to proclaim the king's wondrous courage during an ensuing celebration that lasted for seven days. This particular moment of high drama is often cited to note how the annual public processions of the Dalada are associated with the relic's pur-ported power to cause rain, a very salient belief that I shall return to later in the discussion. For now, it is important to note that the association be-tween kingship and the Dalada has been aggrandized to a new level of formal recognition in this account of the great twelfth-century king. It is not only legitimacy of Lankan kingship that is emphasized here, but prosperity of the kingdom as well. The *Culavamsa*'s account of Parakramabahu's life and activities on behalf of the Buddhasasana is the longest by far (148 pages of translated text) of any king in the *Mahavamsa* and *Culavamsa*, indicating the degrees of the great importance accorded to this king historically. It is not surprising that his desire to possess and adore the relic becomes paradigmatic for kings who follow.

Some two hundred years later, after the sack of Polonnaruva and the proverbial "drift to the southwest" by Lanka's royalty, the Sinhala *Dalada Sirita* reveals a detailed protocol that had been developed in relation to the liturgical veneration of the Tooth-Relic and its safekeeping. The *Dalada Sirita*, like the Sinhala *Bodhivamsa* and the Sinhala *Dathavamsa* of the same time period, was composed in the fourteenth century in the Sinhala vernacular to provide histories of relics to broader and yet more localized audiences. "This preponderance of history writing in a local language suggests that these texts marked attempts to invoke new social and political formations at a time when the older ones were falling apart (Berkwitz 2007, 7, 18). Berkwitz's comment underscores the importance of the Dalada in relationship to the legitimacy of kingship that remained an important understanding during the post-Polonnaruva era, especially during this prolonged period of political threat and atrophy. The *Dalada Sirita*, a significant portion of which I have had translated and have provided in appendix 1, contains a detailed protocol that became the basis for the elaborated ritual veneration of the Dalada toward the end of the Kandyan period several centuries later. Within the *Dalada Sirita*'s account, it is clear that principles of purity and pollution, related conceptions of social hierarchy reflected in the various types of assignments allotted to corresponding families and government personnel, prescriptions for the ritual experience of *darsan*, the continuing intimate relation obtaining between the king and the Dalada, and the first formal articulation of instructions for the holding of a *perahara* in honor of the Dalada are each laid out in some detail in the form of royal commandments issued by Parakramabahu IV (in the early 1300s at Kurunegala). By comparing these details to *brahman*ical temple protocol for the worship of great deities (e.g., Visnu, Siva, etc.), it would seem as if the ritual grammar in play within the *Dalada Sirita* is inspired by principles and practices shared by south Indian Hindu traditions.

The *perahara* was to be held for a period of seven days, after seven previous days of purification rites engaged in by various ritual participants. During the seven days of processions, *pirit* chanting and the sprinkling of magically charged water (charged by means of the *pirit* chanting per se) indicate that the rite also connoted the function of gaining protection.

Moreover, viewing the Dalada, a daily act enjoined on the king, is described, as I have noted above, as an act of *darsan*, the very term used in Hindu *brahmani*cal ritual contexts to refer to how a deity is both seen by his/her devotee and sees his/her devotee. *Darsan* is understood as a relational experience of communion between the divine and human. The *perahara* culminates with the king publicly exhibiting the Dalada to the gathered multitude of the capital, thus making possible a collective *darsan* for all those in public attendance.[13] Here, the king makes possible the appearance of an extraordinary power and, in so doing, is affirmed as the custodian of the supreme power of the realm. He is the chief patron of an economy of merit. Moreover, from this same passage in the *Dalada Sirita*, it is clear that the Dalada's association with the making of rain has been sustained, and that many steps, including the donating of entire villages and lands, have now been taken to economically endow ongoing ritual life of the "tooth relic house." The Dalada has become a virtual landlord, as ritual veneration of the Dalada has been thoroughly institutionalized within the life of the state.

If the *Culavamsa* narrative after the reign Parakramabahu I is followed, it becomes clear that various kings over the next several hundred years in the Dambadeniya (early fourteenth century), Gampola (fourteenth century), Kotte (fifteenth and sixteenth centuries), and Kandy (late sixteenth through early nineteenth century) periods continued to afford the Dalada immense respect and great care. While there occurred many dramatic episodes during these centuries, including claims by the Portuguese in the sixteenth and seventeenth centuries that they had successfully seized its possession and had it pulverized to bits (Strong 2004, 1), a signal moment of concern for our own account in this chapter is how Vimaladharmasurya I, the first king of the Kandy dynasty in the late sixteenth century, established the Dalada in his capital on the very site where it is located today in the Dalada Maligava, "the Palace of the Tooth Relic." How the Dalada was finally brought to its current ritual venue in Kandy involves a fascinating series of moments in history occurring over seventy years of internecine warfare and intrigue.

Following the culturally halcyon days of the long and powerful fifty-five year reign of Parakramabahu VI that ended in 1467 with a united Sri Lanka, a time when Sinhala and Tamil literature and the arts greatly flourished, the Hindu *aryacakravarti* potentate returned from south India to reestablish an autonomous Tamil reign on the northern Jaffna peninsula. Subsequently, in 1474, a renegade chieftain in Kandy, who had earlier administered the upcountry on behalf of and in a tributary position to Parakramabahu VI in Kotte, declared his independence. In 1521, further convulsions occurred that splintered political rule on the island even further: King Vijayabahu VI of Kotte was murdered through the collusion of his three sons, who then proceeded to divide up what was left of the Kotte kingdom. This meant that no less than five royal contenders or self-styled kings were ruling simultaneously in different regions of Sri Lanka. One of the three murderous sons of Vijayabahu I became Bhuvanekabahu VII (r. 1521–1551), who ruled from Kotte; a second (Vidiye Bandara), who is remembered historically for his skirmishes with the Portuguese, died relatively soon thereafter, and his principalities were annexed by the third brother, Mayadunne, who had set up his rule in Sitavaka, located some twenty-five miles to the east and north of Kotte. Mayadunne relentlessly laid Kotte's Bhuvanekabahu to siege for thirty years in a concerted attempt to establish himself as the undisputed Sinhala king. Meanwhile, Kandy was left largely untouched during these years. Into this mix, the Portuguese had arrived in 1505 with designs on conquering the island, in the name of their king, for Roman Catholicism. In 1551, when Kotte's Bhuvanekabahu VII died, he bequeathed his throne to his favorite grandson, Dharmapala, who had been educated by the Portuguese and baptized as a Christian. Upon Dharmapala's consecration, the Dalada was spirited away to Sitavaka, and Mayadunne claimed the allegiance of Sinhala Buddhists. But in 1581, the situation became even murkier when Mayadunne's son and heir, Rajasimha I, apparently converted to Hindu Saivism. When Rajasimha succeeded his father, his first political act was to try to subdue Kandy, for he knew that the Portuguese had conspired with the rebel chieftain of Kandy, the grandson of the original upcountry fifteenth-century rebel, to marry his daughter to Dharmapala, thereby consolidating rule in both Kotte and Kandy under a Roman Catholic king (Dharmapala) who had pledged his loyalty to the king of Portugal. When Rajasimha I attacked Kandy, the Kandyan chief and his family fled to the west coast of the island under Portuguese protection. As fate would have it, the Kandyan chief soon died, but not before his daughter and his nephew were baptized as Dona Catherina and Dom Philip, respectively. When Rajasimha I laid siege to Kotte and Colombo in 1587–1588, the Portuguese sent a diversionary force to Kandy with the idea of establishing Dom Philip on a Kandyan throne. But unfortunately for them, Dom Philip also died unexpectedly, and Konnappu Bandara, who was chief of the Portuguese forces in Kandy serving Dom Philip, declared himself as king and took the name Vimaladharmasurya I in 1592. And, as his name suggests, he declared himself a Buddhist king and inaugurated what became a 220-year-long dynasty. In 1594, he decisively defeated the Portuguese at the famous battle of Dantura and gained a measure of temporary security and prestige as a result.[14]

In Kandy, Vimaladharmasurya I faced a serious predicament. On the one hand, it was to his advantage that, before his consecration, there was no Buddhist king left on an island where the vast majority of inhabitants were Buddhist; he sought to take advantage of that. On the other hand, he was not a royal by birth and therefore suffered from a lack of legitimate credentials. Possession of the Dalada, therefore, became a paramount aim. In addition to securing the Dalada through a subterfuge within the faltering Sitavaka kingdom under Rajasimha I, Vimaladharmasurya imported a fresh Theravada lineage of monks from Burma to reintroduce lines of *upasampada* (full ordination) in order to reestablish the Buddhist monastic *sangha*. With the *sangha* reestablished and the Dalada under his care, he was then able to project himself as the chief patron of the Buddhasasana. He also married Dona Catherina, the daughter of the erstwhile Kandyan chief, who had earlier fled the upcountry but had returned with her cousin, Dom Philip. It was within the context of these extraordinary political machinations that had blurred unequivocal claims to kingship toward the end of the sixteenth century that Vimaladharmasurya seized the opportunity to establish a legitimate Buddhist kingdom in the remote hill country regions of the island.

About six decades later, Rajasimha II (r. 1635–1687), the third of the Kandyan kings and a son of Dona Catherina (who had also married Senarat, Vimaladharmasurya's brother and successor),[15] successfully colluded with the Dutch to drive the Portuguese from the island in 1658. He ruled from Kandy at the time when Robert Knox, a young Englishman, was brought to the upcountry and held hostage for twenty years. Knox's famous account recounting his capture by the king's men after he was shipwrecked with captain (his father) and crew off the east coast of the island near Trincomalee, his further account of imprisonment and gradual domestication to life among the seventeenth-century upcountry Sinhalas, and then the details of his dramatic escape through Anuradhapura to Dutch-controlled Mannar on the west coast almost twenty years later, are supplemented by his lengthy and thorough depictions of Kandyan Sinhala culture and social customs of those times.[16] Historically, Knox's description is an invaluable historical portrait, and the earliest detailed European portrayal of Kandyan Sinhala culture now extant. Remarkably, though laden with the late-medieval worldviews and the language of a common Protestant Christian Englishman, one can still read Knox's observations of seventeenth-century life in Kandy and find many rich and varied resonances with contemporary Sinhala social attitudes, the performance of ritual practices, and the holding of religious beliefs.

In Knox's descriptions of religious practices in Kandy, there are but few references to the Buddha and to the religious practices of Buddhist monks. Perhaps monasticism had become somewhat moribund during his time and did not play a large role in the public ritual life of the people. Otherwise, it would seem strange, given his penchant for detail, that Knox did not provide such descriptions. Since Rajasimha II, unlike Senarat, his father, and Vimaladharmasurya II (r. 1687–1707), his son, does not seem to have been a particularly religious man, it is not so surprising that Knox did not provide descriptions of a public monastic presence in Kandy. What he has to tell us about the Kandyan practice of religion is confined almost entirely to popular lay religious practices centered on seeking protection from deities and warding off the afflictions of *yaksas* (demons).

Knox began his description of religion among the Sinhalas he knew in the following way:

> There are many both Gods and Devils, which they worship, known by particular names which they call them by. They do acknowledge one to be the supreme . . . , which they signifieth the Creator of Heaven and Earth; and it is he also who still ruleth and governeth the same. This great Supreme God, they hold, sends forth other Deities to see his Will and Pleasure executed in the World; and these are the petty and inferior gods. These they say are the Souls of good men, who formerly lived upon the Earth. There are Devils also, who are the Inflicters of Sickness and Misery upon them. And these they hold to be the Souls of evil men. (1982, 72)

No doubt, Knox's description of the Sinhala "Supreme God," who he says was also regarded as "Creator of Heaven and Earth," was articulated in part under the influence of his seventeenth-century lay Christian conceptions of Protestant religion. The language he deploys, of course, is somewhat biblical. Nonetheless, upon a closer read, it would appear that Knox was actually quite perceptive in his understanding of several aspects of Sinhala religion. Indeed, in the passage cited above, he has quite aptly referred to the Sinhala Buddhist understanding of how karma explains rebirth as either a *devata* or as a *yaksa* and how these supernatural forces are perceived to act benevolently or malevolently upon the lives of the folk. But there is some question about the identity of the "Supreme God" that Knox has referred to in this passage. It could be that Visnu, and the deities that he (Visnu) "sends forth . . . to see his Will and Pleasure executed in the World" are a reference to Visnu and his *avataras* (incarnations), very loosely understood. Or, it could be, but I think less likely, that he has identified Dadimunda Devata Bandara (a very popular, though not so cosmologically exalted deity), and those who are "sent forth" could be construed as the *yaksas* nominally understood to be under Dadimunda's command.[17] In any case, the "Supreme God" referred to here is not the Buddha.

In a subsequent passage, one in which he describes the annual *asala perahara* ritual procession that he witnessed in Kandy, Knox has this to say:

> After these comes an Elephant with two Priests on his back: one whereof is the Priest before spoken of, carrying the painted stick on his Shoulder, who represents *Allout neur Dio*, that is, the *God and Maker of Heaven and Earth*. The other sits behind him, holding a round thing, like an Umbrella, over his head, to keep off Sun or Rain. Then within a yard after him on each hand of him follow two other elephants mounted with two other priests, with a priest sitting behind each, holding Umbrella's as the former, one of them represents *Cotteragom Dio*, and the other *Potting Dio*. These three Gods that ride here in Company are accounted of all other the greatest and the chiefest, each one having his residence in several *Pagoda*. Next after the Gods and their Attendance go Some Thousands of Ladies and Gentelwomen, such as are the best sort of Inhabitants of the Land, arrayed in the bravest manner that their Ability can afford, and so go hand in hand three in a row: at which time all the Beauties of Zelone in their Bravery do go to attend upon their gods in their progress about the City. (1984, 79; italics original)

At first reading, it appears that in referring to *"Allout neur Dio,"* Knox was identifying Aluthnuvara Deviyo (aka Devata Bandara or Dadimunda) as the "God and Maker of Heaven and Earth," or the "Supreme God." "[A] Priest . . . carrying the painted stick" could well be, indeed, a reference to Devata Bandara's powerful "golden cane," renowned in literary and cultic contexts as the instrument used by *kapuralas* (shrine priests) to beat *yaksas* possessing devotees into submission. But during Knox's time in the Kandyan region, Visnu's main shrine in the upcountry region was possibly still located in Aluthnuvara, a village and temple complex some eleven miles to the west of Kandy; or possibly, Visnu's chief shrine had just been moved from Aluthnuvara to Kandy around this time.[18] Because Aluthnuvara had been the long-standing seat of the cult of the Sinhala deity Upulvan—whose identity had been conflated with the "Buddhist Visnu" in upcountry Sri Lanka, a cultic venue that could date back to the thirteenth-century reign of Parakramabahu II—it is also quite possible that Visnu was known at this time and in this region as the deity of Aluthnuvara. Often, in Sinhala culture, deities take on the name of the town or village where their main shrine is located, such as at Kataragama where Skanda (aka Murugan, Kumaraswamy, Kartikeya, etc.) has become known throughout the island as Kataragama Deviyo.[19] In further support of Visnu's identity in this instance is a later reference in the *Culavamsa* (see below) to how the *perahara* was celebrated in the mid-eighteenth century as a festival in honor of the "lotus-hued patron god."

But what is more significant to the concerns of this chapter is that nowhere is the Dalada mentioned in Knox's account of the *perahara*. The traditions previously cited from the *Culavamsa* and the *Dalada Sirita* regarding how the *perahara* processions were and should be performed are nowhere apparent. The *perahara* that Knox witnessed seems to have become primarily a matter of honoring the four major deities (*satara varan devi*) of the Kandyan kingdom. That this remained the case for almost the next one hundred years is quite possible, for during the reign of Kirti Sri Rajasimha (r. 1751–1782), the second of the Tamil Nayakkar kings to occupy the throne of Kandy, Buddhist monks from Siam, who had been imported by Kirti Sri to reestablish the *sangha's upasampada* ordination lineage once again, complained bitterly when they observed that the major public ritual of the year was held in honor of these four deities and to the exclusion of the Buddha. The *Culavamsa* records Kirti Sri's ritual response to this situation:

> After a sacrificial festival for the lotus-hued patron god [Visnu] and other deities such as was popularly recognized as bringing luck even in the days of former sovereigns of Lanka, he had for the purpose of military display, the whole town without exception put in order like the city of the gods. He gathered together all of the inhabitants of Lanka and in the town he had the people from individual provinces separated and made them dwell in different places, provided with standards. Then he had the symbols in the temples of the gods placed on the back of an elephant surrounded by divers beaters of drum and the tambourine and by crowds of dancers, . . . by people wearing the Brahman dress, . . . by women and various groups of dignitaries, by people carrying shields, swords, spears and various symbols and banners; by people who had come from various regions and who understood the different tongues, by such as were practiced in the various arts by divers artisans—with such and many other people he had the elephant surrounded, ordering them to go immediately in front or behind. Thereupon the king set forth, like the Prince of the gods, with great and royal splendor and marched round the whole town, his right side turned towards it. Finally, they all arrived again and entered the town according to their rank.
>
> When our king of kings, dowered with faith, wisdom and other virtues, was wont every year to hold the Asalhi [*asala*] festival [*perahara*], he was minded beforehand to celebrate a sacrificial festival for the Buddha. He had a canopy fastened on the back of the royal elephant beautifully ornamented with gold embroidery. Then he had the elephant, whose tusk was as the bright moon, decorated with ornaments and then surrounded with other elephants whose riders held in their hand silver umbrellas and

fly-whisks, and flowers of every kind, by people having in their hands articles of sacrifice and wearing garlands of flowers, by people with various banners and pennons and by such as wore divers garments, by royal dignitaries and by people hither from various regions. Finally, the Lord of men placed the splendid sparkling casket [stupa] of gold in which the bodily relic of the Buddha[20] was contained carefully under the canopy and by the strewing of flowers let a rain of flowers rain upon it. With the shouts of the cries of "Hail"! ["*sadhu sadhu sa!*"], with the sound of the shell trumpets and the cymbals and with the rattle of various drums celebrating high festival, good and pious people with their hearts filled with astonishment and admiration, with hands folded before the brow, paid lasting reverence to the relic. But the Lord of men had the Tooth Relic reverenced with all kinds of costly sacrificial gifts by people who bore lamps on poles and who were festively attired. Then placing at the head of *the relic which holds the first place among all things worthy of reverence* by gods, demons and men, he ordered all the rest, such as the deities [their symbols] and men to follow behind. He himself in royal splendor to the strains of hymns of praise which promise happiness, set forth in majesty of a Great king, with great magnificence showing men how even thus the King of the gods in the city of the gods is wont to celebrate the high festival of the relics. (99, 42–65; 2, 259–261; italics mine)

When the *Culavamsa*'s description of Kirti Sri's reform of the *perahara* is compared to the meticulous account provided by H. L. Seneviratne (1978, 70–88) regarding how the *perahara* was performed in the 1960s, it becomes very clear that Kirti Sri's mid-eighteenth-century reorganization remains the blueprint for what constitutes the substance and dynamics of the *asala perahara* today.

There are two fundamental themes or symbolic orientations that have crystalized in the discussion of the Dalada and the *asala perahara* so far, especially evident in the *Culavamsa* description of the rite as it was performed in Kirti Sri's mid-eighteenth-century time as indicated above and further substantiated in H. L. Seneviratne's recent study. The first is that the *perahara* is a normative statement about the order of the socio-cosmos and the military might necessary to maintain its hierarchical structure. The second is the theme of prosperity connected to the relic's power to make rain for this agrarian based culture. I will address the theme of prosperity first.

THE DALADA AND FERTILITY

The *asala* "festival season" is inaugurated by the *kap* (pole) ceremony that takes place at the Natha Devalaya[21] located directly adjacent to the Dalada Maligava in what is now known as "temple square" in the heart of Kandy

Figure 2.01. Small stupa
adjacent to Natha Deva-
laya containing *kap*

town. In 1984 and 1985, when I was doing ethnographic fieldwork focused
on Natha's *devalaya*s (deity shrines) in the Kandyan upcountry, there was
no *kap* ceremony that was held at this venue. In 2012, not only did the *devalaya* host the ritual, but approximately two thousand to three thousand
lay devotees were present. After planting the *kap* within a small stupa
located adjacent to the *devalaya* on its east side, the *kapurala* (shrine priest),
accompanied by three drummers and a standard-bearer, proceeded to circumambulate the *devalaya* under a canopy with Natha's insignia covered
under a golden cloth.

This little *perahara* unfolded in much the same manner as the one that
H. L. Seneviratne described in his account of the Pattini Devalaya *kap*

Figure 2.02. Natha Deviyo's insignia under gold cloth

ceremony in 1969 (1978, 71–76). I quote extensively from Seneviratne's account at this point because what he has to say about the traditional symbolism of the *kap* ceremony would seem to still hold in relation to how the ritual is now carried out at the Natha Devalaya:

> The Asala Festival is inaugurated by the planting of four poles, known as *kap* (singular: *kapa*) in the premises of the four *devala*. The *kap* once planted remain for the entire duration of the festival, and it is their uprooting that marks its end. The *kap* then are crucially connected with the festival symbolically, and it is relevant to ask what they mean. . . . Erections of the *kapa* in other Sinhalese rituals suggest permanent fixture, an undeniable property of the center. The Ratana Sutta of the Pali canon refers to the Indra Khila, a *kapa* as immovable. The "sensory" meanings of the *kapa* are those of fertility and prosperity. The *kap* are cut from a lactiferous tree. Milk in Sinhalese thought is a symbol of auspiciousness and prosperity. It is also a purifier and is used on certain occasions to bathe the Sacred Bo Tree and the Sacred Dagab. . . .
>
> The most conspicuous act done to the *kapa* after installation is circumambulation around it. By circumambulating it while carrying the sacred insignia, the Kapurala, on behalf of the king who institutes the ritual, with the help of the gods whose insignia are carried in the act of circumambulation,

is capturing what the *kapa* stands for, namely (1) the "center" or capital, symbolic of the kingdom and (2) prosperity and fertility. (71–72)

Seneviratne notes that the Pattini Devalaya was the only one of the four *devalaya*s to hold the *kap* ceremony in 1969. I am unsure when the other *devalaya*s started to hold the ceremony again. But in 2012, there was a lot of media attention given the *kap* ceremony being held at the Natha Devalaya, rightly pointing out that this rite at this venue constitutes the auspicious moment that inaugurates the *perahara* "season."

In fact, the inaugural rite of the *perahara* season, an act that is supposed to take place simultaneously at *all* of the *devalaya*s within the network of Kandyan sacred places during a moment that has been determined to be auspicious by an official at the Dalada Maligava, is the planting of the god Indra's chief symbol, the *kapa* (the Indra *khila*[22]), a pole or post cut out of a branch from a specially chosen *jak* tree, a tree that is highly lactiferous and bears an enormous fruit (weighing up to forty kilos). The *jak* tree is a very apt symbol of fertility and prosperity. Coomaraswamy has translated portions of the *Mayimataya*, a traditional work intended to be use by architects but actually an astrological handbook and guide for the reading of omens, which contains instructions for the felling of the *jak*, the *asala gaha* (July/August tree):

> Know this, O builders, where the *magul* [auspicious] *kapa* is to be felled, you should go to the tree's root and clear it round about, draw the *atamagala* [eight-cornered] diagram, set filled pots in the four [cardinal directional] corners, sprinkle sandal and the next day go and speak as follows: "Thou, Deva, dwelling in this tree, be pleased to leave the tree, if thou doest wish [us] well"; thus praying, break a branch from the tree; clean and order that tree trunk, scatter flowers, betel, sandal and say "I pray thee, Deva, go to this tree and give me thine own." (1956, 125; italics mine)

The text then goes on to describe how to discriminate between male, female, and neuter trees. Female trees, thin at the top, are to be avoided at all costs because within them dwell *yakkhini*s (female demons). Hollow male trees are preferred, and no risk of harm is taken if they are chosen (ibid.). In Kandyan times, the *kap* for all four *devalaya*s of the national guardian deities in Kandy were taken from the very same tree, with the one closest to the root reserved for the Natha Devalaya (indicating the primacy of Natha among the four guardian deities). That the *kap* are taken from the lactiferous *jak* tree (the milk of which is used to bathe Sri Mahabodhi in Anuradhapura and certain stupas on other occasions), and that the *jak* must be virginal and be treated with probationary restrictions to protect its purity, would seem to indicate that the *kapa,* Indra's *khila,* is a symbol of linkage (between heaven and earth), fertility, and prosperity. H. L. Seneviratne has gone so far as to say, "as the *kap* poles are obtained from 'male' trees, they might also be interpreted as phallic symbols, the lactescence being suggestive of semen" (1978, 73–75). Of complementary importance is the circumambulation of the *kapa* by the *kapurala* holding the *ran ayudha* (golden weapon, or insignia of the god), an action that marks off that specific area as being charged with sacral power. In effect, this ritual act symbolically establishes a center, or an axis mundi, from which sacral power will then be distributed throughout the royal domain.

The first five days of the *perahara* processions are known as *kumbal perahara,* before the second five days of *randoli perahara* are observed. Traditionally understood, the first five-day ritual period established the presence and power of sacrality, and consequently fertility and prosperity, while the second five-day period is concerned more specifically with "righteous conquest," although in what follows it will be seen that both motifs are in play throughout. In medieval Kandyan times, the term *randoli* (golden palanquin) referred to the king's chief queen as opposed to *yakada doli* (iron palanquin), used as a reference to other females in the royal harem (Seneviratne 1978, 176n11). In the *perahara* context today, *randoli* refers to the palanquin that carries the vessels, insignia, and powers or "weapons" of the gods. Each *devalaya* maintains a *randoli,* which is locked up in its anteroom during the year and taken out only to become the focus of ritual attention during the last five days of *perahara* processions.

Hence, the name, *randoli perahara.* Because the *randoli* contains the "weapons" of the *devalaya* deity, it is a clear symbol of divine power. However, its original significance seems to have been more directly linked to femininity and fertility. Coomaraswamy, in describing the *randoli* segment of the traditional Kandy *perahara,* remarks that the *randoli*s of each *devalaya* "were accompanied not only by the women of the temple but by the court ladies and wives and daughters of the chiefs" (1956, 39). In Knox's seventeenth-century description above, the prominence of women in the *perahara* in this section of the *perahara* was also underscored. Writing in the early nineteenth century, John Davy (1983, 129–130) also makes a point of stressing the attendance of young women in the *devalaya* contingents of the Kandyan *perahara.* Today, however, a conspicuous contingent of women attends only the Pattini *devalaya*'s section of the procession. The predominant presence of women in the procession therefore would seem to connote an accent upon fertility. But more significantly, the entire complex of

Figure 2.03. Randoli of the Natha Devalaya at the rear of *asala perahera*

fertility-oriented symbols suggests vestiges of an indigenous goddess cult, the type of which is prevalent throughout all of neighboring Dravidian south India and sustained in Sri Lanka, especially within the cult of Pattini.

In the smaller and more intimate Kandyan village *perahara*s that are performed in the month following the observance of the massive, national *perahara* in Kandy, the symbolism associated with fertility is even more pronounced. In several villages where I have observed, the *perahara* processions commence from the grounds of the local *devalaya* (deity shrine) and lead to another ritual venue known as the *rittage*. At the *rittage,* usually a small wooden temple-like structure prominently located near the center of the village, the "golden weapon" of the *devalaya* deity is placed on the *sinhasana* or "lion throne" within the *rittage,* where, during the final night of the *perahara,* it remains for the duration until the following day. In fact, the term *rittage* derives from Sinhala *rtu grha,* which means "season house." By extension, it also derives from Sanskrit *rtviya:* a woman during the favorable period of procreation. If this is so, then the *rittage* is actually the house of the goddess who is now "in season," and the presence of the male deity's "weapon" on the "lion throne" could represent the union of the god with the goddess to create and recreate order and prosperity in the village for the coming year.

Figure 2.04. Female dancing troupe of the Pattini *devalaya*'s contingent

The symbolism of fertility, of course, is also associated with the rain-making power associated with the Dalada and the *asala perahara* itself. Even today, everyone in Kandy expects heavy rains, especially during the afternoons, during the ten days when the processions are observed. In 1990, while I was living in Kandy, a special ten-day exhibition of the Dalada within the Maligava, an exhibition that reportedly attracted more than a tenth of the country's population, drew such large crowds that queues extended in both directions completely around the circumference of Kandy Lake. The downpours of rain that occurred during that time were extraordinary indeed. Godakumbura (1970), in a seminal article in which he discussed the symbolism of the *perahara* at some length, sees the *perahara* procession as essentially a rite that is mimetic in relation to nature: the ubiquitous torches and the cracking of whips indicate the lightning of the storm, and the booming drums its thunder. The king, he argues, is present in the rite as a this-worldly Indra, the proverbial *devaraja* or king of the gods, the deity in the pantheon of gods most clearly identified with the power to make rain in the *Ṛg Veda*. The *perahara*, therefore, is a dramatizing of the supernatural dynamics of heaven, a parallelizing of the heavenly court in action. In the same article, Godakumbura traces the history of Sinhalese rain-making rites back through Parakramabahu I's celebration in Polonnaruva ultimately to the early cult of Sri Mahabodhi in Anuradha-pura, arguing that the Dalada received the transfer of this particularly potent power because kingship and the relic were mobile, while Sri Maha-bodhi was not; for an agrarian society, rain was a sine qua non.

The predominance of fertility and prosperity can also be seen in the other associated annual public rites instituted during the time of the late-medieval Kandyan kings. *Alut sal mangalyaya* (the New Rice festival on Durutu Poya, the full moon in January), *alut avurudda mangalyaya* (the New Year rites commencing on April 12–13 annually), and *karti mangalyaya* (the Festival of Lights, held on Il Poya, the full moon in November) are still significant occasions at selected *devalaya*s in Kandy and in rural villages, but they are not celebrated with the pomp formerly accorded to them. None-theless, their significance in relation to the *asala perahara* is notable, since all of the *basnayake nilame*s (lay custodians) of the important village *de-valaya*s are required to march in the *perahara* processions, taking up their positions reflecting the affiliation of their *devalaya*s in relation to the four *devalaya*s of "temple square."

During the *alut sal, alut avurudda,* and *karti mangalyaya*s, these selected villages in the outlying regions of Kandy function as receptacles for the ceremonial distribution of rice (on *alut sal*), traditional medicines (on *alut avurudda*), and oil for the lighting of lamps (on *karti*). The ceremonial distri-bution of rice, traditional medicine, and consecrated oil is still carried out today in much the same fashion as in late medieval times. In those days, the *devalaya*s and temples that received shares numbered sixty-four. Collec-tively, these *viharaya*s and *devalaya*s received a total of 108 shares. The relative traditional importance or prestige attached to each *devalaya* and *vi-haraya* would seem to be indicated by the quantity of shares it receives. The importance of the four national guardian deities of the Kandyan kingdom (Natha, Visnu, Pattini, and Kataragama) is clearly reflected in the fact that, between them, they receive most of the shares distributed to *devalaya*s.[23]

Ariyapala (1956, 68–84) provides a list and a discussion of the sixty-four royal ornaments that Sinhala kings are described as ceremoniously wear-ing on ritual occasions referred to in the *Pujavaliya, Thupavamsa,* and *Sad-dharamalamkaraya.* These references indicate a tradition of Sinhala kings wearing sixty-four ornaments as symbolic of the totality of their powers, a tradition that goes back to at least the thirteenth century. In the context of traditional Kandyan ritual, it would seem that the same symbolism is at work: the sixty-four ornaments symbolizing the powers of the king cor-respond to powers of the sixty-four sacred places of the Kandyan king-dom, to which the 108 shares of ritual substances were distributed. The symbolic significance of the number 108 is found throughout religious cultures of all of South Asia: it denotes totality. The ceremonial distribution of these substances is obviously meant to be a ritual dynamic performance aiming to empower the prosperity of the kingdom. That the king wore these sixty-four ornaments is symbolic of the popular belief that the king was a microcosm of the kingdom's power sanctioned by the Dalada. Since the king's power in Kandy derived from his possession and protection of the Dalada, it goes almost without saying that the divinely sanctioned power magically distributed through these ritual substances was thought to be vested with the Dalada's "prosperative" and curative powers. Functionally, "temple square" was regarded as the centrifugal pivot from which power was radiated to the sixty-four sacred places of the kingdom and beyond. "Temple square" in Kandy was thus the centrifugal ceremonial center of the ritual life in the kingdom par excellence. This same centrifugal distribution of power is seen in how, following the performance of the *asala perahara* in Kandy's temple square, subsequent *peraharas* are then held in outlying villages of the Kandyan region where significant *devalayas* of the four guardian deities are located, and whose *basnayaka nilames* have participated during the preceding month in the Kandy *perahara*.

The significance of this distribution in relation to the fertility of crops is especially clear. The Dalada Maligava in medieval times maintained an exclusive field (*keta*) in nearby Gurudeniya for the nurture of rice seedlings. Seneviratne notes that the ritual transactions involving the transfer of these seedlings to the officials of the Maligava from the headman (*vidane*) of Gurudeniya "are strangely similar to what happens at a Sinhalese marriage ceremony when the bridegroom's party arrives at the bride's house to take her away. The purpose of the *alut sal* [new rice] ritual was to insure more seeds just as the purpose of a marriage ceremony is have offspring" (1978, 99). As for the distribution of the seedlings to the sacred places of the kingdom,

[i]n this rite the Temple and the *devala* shrines of the kingdom's center magically gained control over the bountiful reproductive power of the *keta* and through the network of the provincial *vihara* [temples] and *devala* [deity shrines] distributed it far and wide in the kingdom, symbolically charging all the fields of the country with similar bountiful reproductive power. The cultivation cycle itself was inaugurated soon afterwards in all parts of the kingdom. (100)

THE DALADA, ORDER AND CONQUEST

While the dynamics of the distribution of power of the old Kandyan ritual system was and still is, at least symbolically, centrifugal, the performance of the grand *perahara* in Kandy is dynamically centripetal. Not only were the *basnayake nilame*s of the *devalaya*s endowed by kings, and thereby, as part of the system of the kingdom's designated sacred places, required to march in the *asala perahara*, but in addition, as the *Culavamsa*'s description of Kirti Sri's *perahara* indicates, so were *disava*s (chiefs) from the various provinces who reported to either the king and his *adigar*s (prime ministers), people proficient in different languages (here, especially, read Tamil), people wearing the *brahman* priestly dress (read Hindu priests), people who knew the various arts and crafts (here read service castes), as well as *kapurala*s (shrine priests) from the various *devalaya*s, along with the insignia of their deities, all made to take up positions in an assigned order. Contingents from various departments of the "government" or court took up their positions as well, according to their ranks, in addition to the various leaders of the military forces—forces that dominated the beginning and ending sections of the procession, protectively enclosing the procession, as it were. Collectively, then, the *perahara* procession articulated a semiotic of hierarchically ranked power, not only of society at large, since every caste was represented, but also of political rankings in the government, with the king positioned at the apex. Even hierarchy of the divine pantheon was articulated in the procession, with the Dalada preeminent with its largest contingent of dancers, drummers, and officials, followed in order by the contingents of the Natha, Visnu, Kataragama, and Pattini *devalaya*s. Therefore, the ordering of participants in the *asala perahara* was a reflection of order in society and in the cosmos, with the principles of purity and power being the defining organizing criteria. In other words, by the mideighteenth-century reign of Kirti Sri, the *perahara* had evolved into a ritual performance reflecting the normative conception of order in society and the cosmos. What seems clear is that the procession was designed to be all-inclusive, comprehensive, and definitive. The *asala perahara* is a classic example of what anthropologists have called "rituals of maintenance."

With regard to the order of the deities and their *devalaya* contingents, there is a corresponding belief in popular Sinhala religious literature that each of the four guardian deities (*satara varan devi*) are on paths to become buddhas in their own rights: Natha is on the verge of becoming the next Buddha Maitreya, Visnu will appear as Rama Buddha, and so on. These four gods are therefore also regarded as bodhisattvas, whose continuing compassionate responses to the entreaties of their faith-filled devotees, facing the travails of *dukkha*, further fuels their own ultimate quests to selflessness and *nibbana*. From another perspective, however, the inclusion of these specific gods also indicates the ways the major trajectories and orientations of religion that arose in South India and Sri Lanka after the rise of early Buddhism were incorporated, albeit subordinated, into Lankan religious culture. Each of these trajectories is represented in the *perahara*: Mahayana Buddhism (Avalokitesvara/Natha), Vaishnava (Visnu), Saiva (Kataragama), and Sakta (Pattini). These religious traditions accompanied waves of migration to the island from the southern reaches of the Indian subcontinent over many centuries, especially from the eighth century forward. What is more, each of these deities, and the religious traditions with which they were nominally identified, has been subordinated to the power of the Buddha and the Buddhasasana. And each has been provided with a Buddhist profile and rendering through the invention and reinterpretation of literature and ritual practice. That is, they have been provided with Buddhist guises. I have previously mentioned how Avalokitesvara became Natha. The career of Visnu, in the context of this discussion, is also very instructive. In the Lankan Buddhist context, Visnu's most important attribute is that he becomes the guardian of the Buddhasasana.

So, the *asala perahara* is not only a rite of fertility and prosperity associated with the Dalada's purported rain-making powers, but it is a statement of social and political order as well. The ability to maintain hierarchical order rests on the perceived powers and positions of the Dalada and the king, respectively. Indeed, there is an analogy ritually enacted in the *perahara* between the Dalada and the king: as the Dalada (Buddha) is to the cosmos and the supernatural pantheon of deities—all of whom in Sinhala lore draw their warrants for action in the world from the Buddha either directly or indirectly—so the king is to society, a society that cedes to him ultimate power and authority.

Seneviratne (1978, 85) has elaborated on these themes in several places in his detailed study. In relation to how the *perahara* is a normative ritually articulated expression of societal hierarchy, he concludes, "The status system of the society based on criteria of office, occupation, caste, and landholding were given expression in the Perahara. . . . This effervescent enactment was a validation of the existing hierarchical order" (112).

I have already noted the significance of the presence of women as part of the discussion about fertility. But what has not been noted so far is that gender was also a category factored into the *perahara* procession. Knox, in particular, mentioned that in his time, women formed the concluding contingent of the procession. Was this not, then, a marker of their public status in a conception of order based on patriarchy?

The *perahara* procession itself actually involves a physical march, a collective circumambulation of the town of Kandy. In a sense, it further extends the symbolism of the center so apparent in the *kap* ceremony that was referred to earlier. In this vein, Seneviratne writes,

By circumambulating the city, the king (who sometimes rode in the Perahara) directly, or through his officials who represented him in the Perahara,
was gaining symbolic control over the city, representing the larger kingdom. In conducting the Sacred Tooth Relic and the insignia of the gods
in the Perahara, the king was summoning the aid of these sacred objects in
his attempt at gaining this symbolic control. He was in a sense "capturing"
the city, with the weapons of the gods assisting him. His own military
departments formed a most conspicuous part of the Perahara, again suggesting the idea of conquest. The king himself was divine, and the city is
compared in numerous instances in both folk and classical literature as a
divine city. . . . The *Culavamsa* indeed refers to the king's ambulation in
the Perahara as similar to the action of the king of the gods in a divine
festival (II: 261). . . . It should also be remembered that circumambulating
the city also means circumambulating the *kap* themselves. The *kap* at one
extreme of meanings symbolized the "center," circumambulation of which
was also a circumambulation of the city. At the other extreme of meanings,
they symbolized fertility and prosperity, and the Perahara was an attempt to "capture" these benefits also. (1978, 85)

The martial symbolism of the *perahara* cannot be missed. Seneviratne remarks that the presence in the *perahara* of the representations of the "armed
services" with their elephants "would have undoubtedly given the Perahara the look of a great military advance" (1978, 111). Indeed, while the
elephant was regarded as the royal *vahana* (vehicle), it was also an important vehicle for conducting war. To some extent, command over hundreds
of elephants was a marker of royal wealth and power.[24]

Moreover, the *perahara* provided the centripetal occasion for the king
to require his representatives in the outlying regions to come to the capital fortress at least once during the year. By annually participating in the
perahara, and by paying tribute to the king and the Dalada, the subordination of their positions to central royal power would be underlined, and
the probability or possibility of seeking autonomy through rebellion
diminished. In that sense, the *perahara* provided a moment of discipline
as well.

In medieval Lanka, the *asala perahara* was, as Clifford Geertz (1981) so
clearly demonstrated within his case study of the Balinese courts, a theat-
rical enactment of "the doctrine of the exemplary center." That is, the traditional Kandy *perahara* held in the capital city articulated and defined the
power of the state in relation to the rest of the kingdom and offered itself
as a model. The grand *perahara* in the capital was ritually and symbolically
paradigmatic for the "satellite" *perahara*s sponsored by village *devalaya*s
that subsequently were performed in the weeks that followed. Quoting
Geertz, the "doctrine of the exemplary center" is

[t]he theory that the court-and-capital is at once a microcosm of the super-natural order—an image of the universe on a smaller scale—and the material embodiment of the political order. It is not just the nucleus or engine, or the pivot of the state; it *is* the state. The equation of the seat of rule with the dominion of rule is more than an accidental metaphor; it is a settlement of a controlling political idea—namely, that by the mere act of providing a model, a paragon, a faultless image of civilized existence, the court shapes the world around it into at least a rough approximation of its own excellence. The ritual of the court, and in fact, the life of the court generally, is thus paradigmatic, not merely reflective, of social order. What it is reflective of, the priests declare, is a supernatural natural order, "the timeless Indian world" of the gods upon which men should, in strict pro-portion to their status, seek to pattern their lives. (1981, 13)

S. J. Tambiah (1976) has shown how this "theory" was also put into prac-tice in the classical medieval Thai Buddhist state. He describes the verti-cal relationship between the microcosm and the macrocosm (other-worldly and this-worldly), on the one hand, and the horizontal center and periph-ery, on the other, as a "pulsating *mandala*" constitutive of "galactic polity." By this means, he characterizes how "satellites" (in this case, the sixty-four sa-cred places of the medieval Kandyan kingdom) were related to the orbits of political power fully established at the capital center. Kandy's Dalada Maligava and the *devalaya*s of "temple square" functioned as an axis mundi during the annual national celebrations of the Kandyan kingdom: ritual substances were consecrated therein before being disseminated or radiated out to the far-flung sacred places of the kingdom. In the villages, where the *devalaya*s are the center of the cultic life, deities such as Natha and Visnu "inherited" much of the symbolism attached to Indra (king of the gods) and to Sinhala kingship and, in the process, became veritable symbols of royal and divine power and presence on the local village level. The *basnayaka nilame* of the local *devalaya* was the deity's and the king's social counterpart in the village hierarchical order of power. Thus, the ritual system of Kandy, especially as it was exemplified in the proceedings of the *asala perahara*, seems to be an orchestration of divinely sanctioned royal power flowing out from the ceremonial political and religious center subsequently to be realized in the local instances of *perahara* processions sponsored by local *devalaya*s in the peripheral villages of the kingdom.

THE CONTEMPORARY *ASALA PERAHARA*

Having lived in Kandy, Sri Lanka, for more than six years between 1979 and 2014, I have observed many *perahara*s: not only the *asala perahara* in

Kandy on many occasions beginning in 1983 (and including no less than six times in 2012 alone), but *peraharas* in Kataragama, Devinuwara, Colombo, Alutgama, and in the Kandyan villages of Wegiriya, Pasgama, Lankatilaka, Dodanwela, and Ambekke as well.[25] Over the years, the impression I have formed is that *peraharas* have increasingly proliferated throughout the Sinhala regions of the country, and that they are being held in an ever-increasing variety of contexts, while the long-established *peraharas* connected to annual festivals at well-known sacred places and pilgrimage sites (Kandy, Kataragama, and Devinuwara) are becoming ever more grand in scale. While I will make some more pointed assertions about the reasons why this is taking place in the final section of this chapter, here my observations will be more historical and descriptive, though they will serve as a springboard for my conclusions.

My impressions about how *peraharas* have proliferated and expanded in scale are no doubt conditioned by my own experiences in 1983 and 1989. In both of these years, the country was under great duress. In 1983, as I noted in the opening of the chapter, a week of civil chaos during "Black July" had involved mass murders and arson against members of the minority Tamil community throughout Sinhala regions of the island. In the aftermath of this pogrom, most people in the country were in a state of shock and dismay. Though much of downtown Kandy was charred and the city not in a position to entertain any tourists (almost all hotels were closed), nor were people from other parts of the country traveling back home to Kandy for family reunions during "the season," the *perahara* was still performed under these depressing circumstances, although in very subdued and somewhat lackluster fashion. In 1989, the conditions in Kandy were actually far worse for going ahead with the performance of the *perahara* on schedule than in 1983. This was a period when a "JVP insurrection" against the government was at its height, when political officers at the American embassy in Colombo had made a point of warning me, on my arrival in the country in July, against going up to Kandy, because they considered the security situation in the upcountry to be unsafe and the political situation unstable. In Kandy, I found, the JVP was being referred to as "the unofficial government." Through its posters, plastered about at night at the busy intersections in town, the JVP had ordered all residents in Kandy and the surrounding area to turn off all lights at night and to stay indoors after sunset. That is, they had ordered a nightly curfew.

The public was gripped at the time by what was referred to as a "fear psychosis," a state of mind beautifully captured in Michael Ondaatje's riveting novel, *Anil's Ghost*.[26] The phrase referred to a kind of paralysis and uncertainty that people felt while engaging socially in public. Not only was no one sure about the direction of the unfolding political situation, but life in public was unpredictable because there was a sense that no one really knew who to trust. It seemed difficult, in public, to know where personal allegiances might fall. Allegiances were divided between the government and the insurrectionists, and usually not divulged for fear of retribution from either side. In the midst of many murders of public officials at all levels of the government, from village headman to the university registrar to clerks working in city hall and the provincial office to policeman and politicians and more, a siege mentality had set in. Police stations were barricaded and sandbagged, and checkpoints were ubiquitous.

The JVP's murderous, guerilla-style tactics exacted an enormous psychological toll. But the extraordinarily harsh responses by the government in the weeks and months that followed were even more severe in comparison, as the net cast in looking for JVP suspects and sympathizers was so broad and blunt that thousands of innocent people eventually "disappeared." To say that the summer of 1989 brought with it a climate of uncertainty and fear is a vast understatement. And yet, the *perahara* was still performed under these very trying circumstances. The fact that the *perahara* was held during the night hours was a direct act of resistance to the JVP's "orders." I observed far greater numbers of police and army soldiers lining the route of the *perahara* than local "civilian" devotees that year (and virtually no tourists), but still the *perahara* was performed, albeit in a decidedly desultory fashion.

In May of 1993, I was also in the country when President Ranasinghe Premadasa was assassinated on May Day by a Tamil Tiger suicide bomber, just days before the annual festival of Vesak, the full moon day in May when the Buddha's birth, enlightenment, and *parinibbanna* are celebrated, usually with wonderful felicity. Vesak celebrations were canceled that year by the government. I was traveling through the countryside at the time, and while a few village homes still sported a lantern or two, no *pandals*[27] were constructed in marketplaces or crossroads, no public performances of *bhakti gee* (devotional song) were staged by young teenaged girls dressed in white half-saris, and no roadside food stands were erected to make merit while supplying the needs of holiday travelers or pilgrims on their ways to sacred places. I thought that the government's cancellation of Vesak was an absolutely extraordinary decree, for I couldn't imagine that a holiday that combines analogously the religious sentiments of the Christmas and Easter seasons could be canceled for political reasons. (While everyone who was alive at the time in the United States seems to still remember where he or she was upon hearing the stunning news of President John Kennedy's assassination on November 22, 1963, they would also know that no thought was ever given in America to the possibility of canceling the national Thanksgiving holiday a few days later.) Here, in the Lankan context, then, a question to keep in mind, as this narrative proceeds—one that might sharpen analytical inquiry—is this: If the celebration of Vesak was canceled in 1993, why were the *asala peraharas* in 1983 and 1989 not cancelled, especially in light of the fact that the threat of public violence was so much more intense at those times?

In any case, my personal initial introduction to *peraharas* included observations of rather subdued or deflated proceedings, and perhaps that has colored my perceptions regarding the increasing scale and scope of *asala peraharas* performed today. And yet, there is no gainsaying the fact that *peraharas*, in general, have become more emphasized as a cultural fashion for expressing Sinhala Buddhist sentiments, if not ethnic patriotism. They have increased in number and scale in tandem with the surging momentum of public articulations of Sinhala Buddhist nationalism. This proliferation and renewed vigor is, in part, a piece of a larger process of religio-political expression in the country today, one that includes the construction of giant public and quite conspicuous Buddha images; the enhancement of Buddhist archaeological sites that, in some cases, have been transformed into religious pilgrimage destinations; the chanting of *pirit* over loudspeaker systems; and constant media coverage of leading politicians of the government engaged in various merit-making acts of support for the Buddhasasana. What Sri Lanka has been witnessing during the past generation is a process whereby public space is becoming increasingly a Buddhist political space. The reinvigoration of the *perahara* is but a reflection of this process at work, perhaps its epitome.

In 2012, the first of the five nights of *kumbal perahara* was far more spectacular and grand than the *randoli peraharas* (the second five nights of the ten-day rite) that I had seen twenty or thirty years ago, and by this I am not referring to those occasions in 1983 and 1989 that were under duress. In those earlier days, Dalada Vidiya, the main street running east and west through Kandy, and the road on which the *perahara* begins its procession (the route that passes alongside the Dalada Maligava), was not fenced off or restricted either. Once the ethnic conflict escalated and descended into a civil war, the protection afforded to the Maligava made it appear more like a fortress under siege than the holiest religious site in the country for Buddhists. It was armed to the teeth. Even though the civil war ended in 2009, security remains extremely high at the time of this writing.

On that first night of *kumbal perahara*, I counted more than twelve hundred dancers, drummers, flag bearers, torch-bearers, and temple officials processing. I can only estimate, but I sense this is at least twice the size of *perahara*s performed a generation ago. Maligava officials told me that there were an estimated two hundred thousand observers that night, and that five thousand police had been placed on duty. I counted forty-four elephants in that first of the nightly processions.

There is no doubt that in recent years the *perahara* has become an increasingly "commodified" cultural event. It is not only promoted internationally for tourist consumption—advertisements in London aimed at the Sinhala expatriate community quote tickets for viewing the *perahara* from the prime seats of the Queen's Hotel as available for purchase at Rs.13,000 (~US$100). Locally, these seats are sold for as much as Rs.8,000.[28] Virtually all businesses along the *perahara* routes in downtown Kandy provide portable plastic seats that are hawked to foreigners and locals alike at hefty prices. This practice has reduced the space for villagers and less affluent locals to view the *perahara*. It is not unusual, especially during the final five days of *randoli perahara*, for some village families to arrive in the morning hours to begin sitting on the sidewalks for the evening processions that start between 6:30 p.m. and 8:30 p.m., depending on the determination of auspicious times. The space between the promenade and what used to be Dalada Vidiya, before it was closed off to traffic and through-pedestrians,[29] is now used for the construction of a canopied grandstand that holds seats for approximately seven thousand guests. Passes for these seats are distributed to many local (Kandy municipality and Central Province) and Sri Lankan government officials, as well as to important ritual performers (*basnayake nilame*s, lead dancers, school principals, etc.). Some of these tickets are actually sold to others who are anxious to attend.

The municipality of Kandy also has major expenses in keeping the streets clean. The elephants are famous for leaving a residue behind, and so the *perahara* season has an identifiable scent of its own. To help fund its expenses, the city has found it necessary to levy expensive fees (Rs.125,000—almost US$1,000) to videographers of the event, and there are fees for other types of privileges as well. Television coverage has boosted the popularity of the *perahara* nationally. It is broadcast during prime time during the final five evenings of *randoli perahara* and also during the final day. A local director told me that the tape he was making would be seen eventually in 160 countries. At least that is what he believed.

Members of the Sri Lanka Army's highly trained Gajaba Regiment were also seen in force throughout the streets and suburbs of Kandy on the first evening of the *perahara*, and also on the final night and day, because the country's president, Mahinda Rajapakse, was in town to be a part of the occasions inaugurating and closing the ten days of public processions. I observed the processions from the designated "media center," having gained

Figure 2.05. Whip-crackers announcing the beginning of *perahara*

professional status through the intercession of a good monastic friend of mine. And that is where I remained for the five nights of *randoli perahara* as well.

I expected some major changes in the performance of the *randoli per-ahara,* given the changes that have occurred in those who led the then-current government and who were from the southern and non-Kandyan regions of the country. *Perahara*s in Kataragama and Devinuvara that I have studied before in the Ruhunu southern region are considerably more "populist" in character, and sometimes go beyond the serious, almost somber, and obviously sacred ethos of the Kandy *asala* performance. At Devinuvara, in the very heart of the south, from where the leaders of the current political regime hail, the *perahara* is more a curious and awkward combination of young schoolchildren participating in a holiday parade, many amusingly costumed *yaksas,* and bare-chested *baila* troupes of musicians and dancers from the *karava* (fisher-folk) caste, often highly inebriated from drinking (even during the procession it-self) far too much arrack and behaving in ways that, unfortunately, have made India and Sri Lanka infamous for the ways women are sometimes sexually harassed in public.[30] But during the five nights of *randoli pera-hara* that I witnessed in Kandy, there was nothing of that sort. Indeed,

Figure 2.06. Fire spinners

Figure 2.07. Buddhist flag bearers

Figure 2.08. Peramuna rala

the five nights of *perahara*s I witnessed remained, in my own mind at the time, quite traditional in their symbolisms, beginning with the performers in the very front of the *perahara* who crack whips to indicate that the procession is near.

In late medieval Kandy, the traditional means that *disava*s or *ratemahatayas* (regional lords and literally "country gentleman" respectively) used to announce their presence in villages to command attention was by the cracking of whips. This seems to remain the function of cracking whips at the head of the *perahara* procession: commanding the attention of the crowd for what is to follow immediately. The sound of the whips, as I noted earlier, is also associated with the crackling of lightning. Immediately following the whip-cracking is a spectacular display of fire, spin-

Figure 2.09. Perahara drummers reflecting fertility of various agricultural tasks

ning circles of torches that Godakumbura argues symbolize the lightning related to the dominant rain-making symbolic function of the rite. The constant cacophony of the dozens of drumming contingents has been said, as earlier, to represent the thunder. Following the fire spinners, two dozen bearers of Buddhist flags[31] process before the *peramuna rala* (lead person) dressed in traditional Kandyan nobility attire and mounted on a magnificent tusker.

These are followed by dancing contingents (and drummers) holding swords, offering betel leaves, holding pots, rice stalks, *chamaras* (fly whisks), scythes, and swords, all symbols associated with the prosperity of the wet season that results in growing rice, and the military side emphasizing discipline and order through the administration of power.

Figure 2.10. Perahara dancers reflecting fertility of various agricultural tasks

Figure 2.11. Perahara dancers reflecting fertility of various agricultural tasks

Finally, the *ves* dancers, musicians, and drummers entertain the Maligava's Diyawardana Nilame, who regally processes in front of three elephants, the middle one of which carries a stupa facsimile that contains a facsimile of the Dalada, the cultic focal point in the *perahara*. But more than that, the *ves* dancers are paying homage to the Dalada, the appearance of which inspires postures of reverence and sighs of veneration, especially from those in the crowd who do not occupy the premium seats.

While the elements of the procession in the Maligava contingent represent the different aspects of cultivation, and the types of people (castes and subcastes) who engage in cultivation, including those who support them as "service castes," the contingents following the Dalada form the

Figure 2.12. Peter Surasena, nationally famous lead *ves* dancer

Figure 2.13. Ves dancers

segments representing the four *devalaya*s of Natha, Visnu, Kataragama, and Pattini. Each of these contingents actually constitutes a *perahara* within the *perahara*, replete with flag bearers, *chamara*s dancers, *ves* dancers, and so on. The order of the contingents, easily noted because of the dominant colors and flags associated with each, is Natha (gold), Visnu (blue), Kataragama (red), and Pattini (white). This order, as mentioned earlier, represents the divine hierarchy of the Sinhala pantheon, with Natha, who, in following the Dalada, is expected to become the next Buddha (Maitreya), followed by Visnu, Kataragama, and Pattini. All dancers were male until the final contingent of the Pattini Devalaya, which contained one small group of a dozen graceful female dancers. (I have provided a detailed mapping out of the entire *randoli perahara* ensemble, noting the types and numbers of those who perform various roles in order of procession, in appendix 2.)[32]

According to Maligava officials and two *basnayake nilame*s, the ritual participants are no longer simply those who are meeting *rajakariya* ("work for the king") duties in exchange for material benefits they traditionally received from *devalaya* or Maligava lands (such as the right to till the soil). In recent years, it has become more difficult, especially for the Kandy *de-*

Figure 2.14. Diyavardana Nilame (lay custodian of the Dalada Maligava)

*valaya*s, to meet the expenses involved in fielding participants for their segments of the *perahara* as the numbers expected to participate has risen. Traditionally, the *devalaya*s relied on rents received from their lands, donation boxes at the *devalaya*s, and *rajakariya* duties, but now they must find other means of hiring and paying dancers and drummers, in addition to hiring out elephants. In some cases, elephants now cost more than Rs.100,000 (US$700) each. Some dancers receive at least Rs.1,000 per night as a fee for their participation. Some of the torch-bearers are prisoners of the local Bogambara prison. In order to surmount expenses, dance troupes from local schools have now been included routinely. Troupes from the more prestigious local Buddhist schools (Dhammaraja, for example) are

Figure 2.15. Dalada caparisoned on center elephant

selected for the Maligava section of the *perahara*. Troupes from less prestigious schools are included in the *devalaya* sections. At least in this year (2012), some auditions were held in order to determine which groups would be part of the Maligava contingent, with locally famous dancers and drummers joining Maligava officials in determining which troupes would be included and to which segment of the *perahara* they would be assigned. The result was quite palpable to observe, in that the dance and drumming troupes performing for the Maligava contingent were, in general, quite superior to those performing for the *devalayas*. Yet, every *devalaya* seemed to have included at least one high-quality contingent of *ves* dancers in their sections, those who dance and drum immediately in front of the *basnayake*

Figure 2.16. Basnayaka Nilame (lay custodian) leading the Vishnu Devalaya contingent

nilame and the elephants carrying the insignias of the deities. These dancers and drummers are highly skilled and talented.

After watching the *perahara* processions for several nights, and reviewing Seneviratne's study of the medieval *perahara,* and rereading relevant sections of the *Culavamsa,* I noticed an absence of reference to dancers within the *perahara. Ves* dancers and their accompanying drummers account for the most spectacular visual displays of cultural expression within the contemporary *perahara.* I decided to interview one of the oldest and most experienced *ves* dancers, who has performed in the *perahara* for the past thirty or forty years.[33]

**Q. What are the fundamental changes that you see in the
perahara since you began dancing with your grandfather?**
A. In terms of rituals there was no visible change. But, in terms of
dancing items there could be seen a great change. Nowadays there
cannot be seen caste-based services. Everything has been commercialized. Kandyan dancing became something about subject and
not caste based. In earlier time periods there were many traditional
dancing traditions like Ihalawela, Molagoda, Malagammana, and
Uduwela. Now these are not performed in the *perahara.* It is a great
loss to the *perahara* to lose traditional skilled performers. In the past,
there were special drumming recitals for when the *perahara* moved
from one certain street to another along the route. Now such drumming recitals cannot be heard, with the absence of the skilled performers from previous generations. Also there is a new trend in the
arrival of new types of dancers and groups to the *perahara.* For instance, there is a newly established "Maligava Dancing Troup." It
was introduced recently and is actually a group of schoolboys. Of
course, it is good to give a chance to the newcomers. But, there is a
problem about the quality of dancing. Increasing numbers of dance
items is another change visible at this time. Some of the dancing
items do not match what the *perahara* is about. It is fine to increase
dancing items to lighten up the event, but they should be relevant
to the event too. The Kandy *perahara* is an event that is Buddhist, so
dancers need to show respect and devotion to the Dalada. Some of
the new dance items that are recently added do not reflect the earlier
culture of the Kandy *perahara.* For instance, Bulath Padaya Dance and
Kothala Padaya Dance are two dancing items of Kohombakankari
Shanthikarmaya tradition. Also the Paddy Reaping Dance is a folk
dance; it does not show the respect or devotion to the Tooth-Relic.
Apart from those dancing items, the Chamara Dance; the dance
with the coconut flowers; Pathuru Dance; the dance with the narrow
drums; the cane dance and sword dance—these do not match up to
the Kandy *perahara* according to my point of view, because they
do not show the proper respect or devotion to the Tooth-Relic or the
Maligava.

When it comes to the costumes of the dancers, especially costumes of Maligava *perahara,* some costumes are donations to the
Maligava and the names of the business donors are quite visible.
For instance, Chandra Industries is one of the donators of costumes
to the *perahara.* They tagged their names obviously to highlight
their donations. Also the amount of rupees paid to a dancer has

been increased. Dancers are categorized into four in terms of their expertise ranging from Rs.1,000 (expert) to Rs.400 (newcomers) per day. No dancer would like to perform for free. Nowadays, dancers do not own property given by the kings (*nindagam*). They expect a financial gain out of this event.

Q. Can you tell me something about the dance awards now given out to *perahara* dancers?
A. Yes, the value of the awards has been increased. As I can remember, in 2005 my group won Rs.5,000 for being the best dance troupe. Now it has increased to Rs.100,000. And also the quality of the prizes and number of prizes under different categories has been increased. This has been done especially in the time period of present Diyavadana Nilame. It is a great encouragement for the dancers.

Q. What are the main differences you see between the Maligava *perahara* and *devalaya peraharas*?
A. In terms of the payment for the dancers, the Maligava pays well compared to the *devalaya*s. Also the Maligava pays dancers for the day *perahara*, but *devalaya*s do not. The Maligava *perahara* has a greater government sponsorship. Therefore, now, there is a great competition among the dancers to get into the Maligava *perahara*. And also dancers think of performing in the Maligava *perahara* as an honor recognizing their skills. Therefore, the competition is high. But this great competition among dancers has created enmity. This can be seen in their performances as well. For instance, in the *ves* dance, there can be seen two lines of dancers headed by an expert. If you see the faces of the dancers of the two lines, you can see clearly the jealously in their faces. They do not smile at other dancers in the front line when they dance. Also drummers do not play well for their opponents in the same dancing event. Though it is against Buddhist values, it happens with this competition.

Several interesting issues arise in this interview. One is the sense that an appeal to popular display, rather than allegiance to more traditional forms of ritual dance, is intruding into the *perahara*. That is, the *perahara* has become, increasingly, a venue for the display of various forms of Kandyan dance. The new additions are, in part, the result of recruiting young boys from the local schools to fill out the increasing ranks of the *perahara* procession. They perform the types of dances that they have been taught in school, and these are not necessarily in line with the traditions of the ritual per se. Throughout the interview, the litmus test for inclusion, as far as this veteran ritual dance specialist was concerned, was whether or not dance articulates devotion and respect to the Dalada. While he says that ritual per se has not changed, dance has changed dramatically. There is a tension noted here that needs to be explored.

In her extensive study of Kandyan ritual, dance, and sociopolitical context, Susan Reed notes how the "*ves* dance" itself was actually extracted from the traditional *kohomba kankariya* context and recontextualized within the *perahara*. She refers to how this recontextualization "is often cited as a decisive turning point in the history of Kandyan dance, the first instance of the dance being performed 'out of context'" (2010, 99). She notes that the conventional historical understanding is that "in 1917, Punchi Banda Nugawela, a Kandyan aristocrat and the chief lay official of the Temple of the Buddha Tooth, introduced the *kankariya* dancers in full *ves* costume into the Kandy Asala Perahara" (ibid.). But in researching the issue thoroughly, Reed found a meticulous description in the London illustrated newspaper, *The Graphic*, describing in detail a private rehearsal of the *perahara* performed for the visiting Prince of Wales in Kandy in 1875. The description is accompanied by two detailed illustrations. "Both show dancers wearing *ves* costumes similar to those worn by dancers today" (101).[34] Moreover, the article she cites notes that the *perahara* "is generally supposed to commemorate some notable event in the life of Vishnu—either his birth or his victory over the Asuras" (cited in ibid.).

Reed's research is interesting and important on two counts here. First, the implication of her finding about the abstraction of the *ves* dance from the *kohomba kankariya* is that none of the dances now performed in the *asala perahara* were intrinsic or inherent to the processional rite. However, the association of *ves* with the *perahara* is earlier than commonly known. The question that arises, in any event, is this: What does the inclusion of the *ves*, and now the other popular forms of dance in the *perahara*, reflect about the changing significance of the rite?

Reed begins her chapter on dance and the nation by quoting Peter Surasena, the most famous of all Kandyan dancers in his generation: "If there is no dance, and no Buddhist temple, then there is no nation" (Reed 2010, 128). Surasena said this during an interview with Sri Lanka Broadcast Corporation in 1987. Reed goes on to say this:

The post independence period in Sri Lanka, particularly the period of the watershed year of 1956, when Sinhala nationalist S.W.R.D. Bandaranaike came to power, saw the development of Kandyan dance as a symbol of Sinhala pride, taking its place as the national dance of Sri Lanka. While in the 1930s and 1940s Kandyan dance had come to symbolize, along with "oriental" and Indian dances, a rather diffuse "indigenous" culture opposite to that of the British and the Anglicized elite, after 1956 Kandyan dance assumed a new role as a symbol of "national culture," that is, the culture of the Sinhalas. (ibid.)

Reed proceeds to describe how, after 1956, the state became the "most influential proponent of Kandyan dance," how it became an established subject within the curriculum of virtually all public and private schools, how it became the focus of fine arts curricula and institutes of aesthetic studies at the tertiary level, and how its performance became synonymous with expressions of "national culture," thus transcending its religio-ethnic origins in public significance. Kandyan dance was a key signified element in the effort promoted by successive Ministries of Cultural Affairs to revitalize "national culture," and that "national culture" essentially meant "Sinhala culture" (2010, 136).[35]

Reed sees a tension of meaning implicit within Sinhala ritual, particularly in relation to the *kohomba kankariya,* but by implication to the *perahara* as well. The tension is between what she explains can be an epistemic experience of ritual, on the one hand, and an ontic experience on the other. That is, she is pointing to the difference between simply viewing or observing ritual as a spectacle to participating or being in the spectacle itself. The difference would also be manifest in how archeological sites can shift in their significance to become pilgrimage sites, for instance.[36] So, what this means for the *perahara,* and I think this is what the old veteran dancer I interviewed was trying to get at, is that the *perahara* has become two different realities, depending on intentions. The epistemic frame concerned with display reflects "commodification," while the ontic reality is its religious substance. The ontic orientation corresponds closely to Bell's (1992) understanding of the existential realizations produced in the performance of ritual. What is most interesting here is that both epistemic and ontic have been co-opted in the rising specter of nationalism. As Reed argues, dance became a symbol of the national culture, and whether or not it is experienced in epistemic or ontic fashion, it has become increasingly an expression of the state's interests and power in contemporary times. Its increased and emphasized presence in this most public of all Sinhala Buddhist rites—so that it now seems to be an exceedingly important constituent element in articulating "national culture"—is consistent, given the history of the Dalada and the *asala perahara* traditionally as ritual microcosmic expressions of Kandyan society and the power of a Buddhist state.

THE *ASALA PERAHARA* AND NATIONALISM

In one of the last chapters in his study of Kandyan rites, Seneviratne focuses on the *perahara* in relation to modernity (as he saw it in the 1960s and early 1970s). He argues that the *perahara* is the "most conspicuous" of "cultural performances selected and elaborated . . . by the political representatives of the nationalist elites," quite typical of a "new nation or new state" that wishes "to show off their culture to themselves and to the rest of the world" (1978, 120). What I am interested in answering is the question, Why are they interested in "showing off"?

Seneviratne begins his conclusion on the contemporary political significance of the Dalada in the 1960s and 1970s with the following remarks:

> Today there is no belief in the Dalada as a direct legitimizer of power: but indirectly the Dalada has clear political meanings. Thus, when a new government is sworn in, their first act is to visit the Temple from where the mass media broadcast the ceremonial proceedings. The function of this act is two-fold. First, it identifies the rulers with the religion and in this sense gives them a kind of legitimacy. Second, the act identifies the government with the culture of the past, the revival of which is promised by all political parties. (1978, 121)

Indeed, usually one of the first diplomatic acts of all foreign ambassadors, after their credentials are received by the president of Sri Lanka, is to come up to Kandy from Colombo and to pay due homage to the Dalada. Many ambassadors will also call on the *mahanayaka*s (chief monastic incumbents) of the Asgiriya and Malwatte chapters of the Siyam Nikaya. In any event, what is important here is that the Maligava, the Dalada, and the Buddhist *sangha* are all recognized as icons of national identity and power, not just for the Sinhalese, but for the entire nation—and perhaps therein lies an important issue.

Seneviratne (1978, 140) also noted in his study that domestic political pressures were being brought to bear on the Maligawa, and even the selection the *diyavadane nilame* had become a significant moment politically. It still is. Writing in the 1970s, he noted the building tension between "low country" and "upcountry elites": the lack of upcountry representation in the modern national bureaucracy on the one hand, and how the *radala* (high caste) upcountry Kandyans use the *perahara*, over which they still had complete control, "to assert themselves in relation to a group of competitors considered by the *radala* as upstarts, namely, the modern national bureaucracy." Moreover, the nationalist elite has been ideologically opposing this exclusive control of the Perahara by the *radala*. By their greater involvement with the common folk, their arts, and their way of life, the nationalist elite feels that they are better aware of the meaning of traditional culture than the *radala*, considered "westernized" and alienated from the people, preserving when they do only the aristocratic aspects of the indigenous culture. Their emphasis on the cultural aspect of the Perahara is a symbolic way of opposing the domination of the Perahara by the *radala*, and in general a way of expressing antagonism to a wealthier and most prestigeful [*sic*] class. (144)

The political rivalry between the so-called low country and the up-country is a historical legacy of the colonial experience. Under the Portuguese and Dutch, Sinhalas and Tamils living in the coastal regions under colonial control were inevitably affected socially and culturally by sustained contact with the Europeans and their ways. The conversion of King Dharmapala to Roman Catholicism in the sixteenth century was a harbinger of a major shift in the orientations of a significant number of "low country" Lankans. Many converted to either Protestant or Roman Catholic forms of Christianity, sometimes in order to be legally married or to legally own land. (Some historians have dubbed these people as "government Christians.") A new racial minority also emerged, the Burghers, the offspring of Euro-Asian marriages or sexual liaisons, who often assumed the middle ranks of the colonial government bureaucracy or positions in business administration and banking. Under the British, with the further establishment of European-styled primary and secondary education, European conceptions about religion, social mores, political power, and the economy were thoroughly implanted, thereby engendering the emergence of a new Western-educated middle class and elite. For this reason, I would quibble a bit with Seneviratne's comparative comments about the *radala* and the elite of the national bureaucracy; for the middle class and elite of the "low country" were far more Anglicized or westernized than the *radala* of Kandy, especially in terms of language and religion. For many of these, English became the primary language, certainly the language of power.

Under the British, some individuals and families gained a measure of upward social mobility, at least theoretically, insofar as their caste status could be transcended by means of education or successful entrepreneurial effort. Indeed, new sects within the Buddhist *sangha* (the Amarapura and Ramanna *nikaya*s) were established to provide for the aspirations of those born into castes that had been excluded from the upcountry, Kandy-based, *goyigama*-only[37] Siyam Nikaya. Thus, the "low country" not only witnessed religious reform within the Buddhist community, but it also was the milieu in which the first spirited backlashes against Christianity took place, publicly inaugurated by the famous Panadura (twenty-five kilometers south of Colombo) debates between Buddhist monks and Protestant missionaries in 1869. The "low country" was also the venue for the incipiency of Sinhala Buddhist nationalism and cultural reform epitomized by the fiery writings and campaigns led by the Anagarika Dharmapala.[38] In contrast, the Kandyans sought to maintain their self-images as the preservers of traditional Sinhala culture that included, of course, the custodianship of the Dalada Maligava by the chief incumbents of the Asgiriya and Malvatte chapters of the Siyam *nikaya*. In ideal terms, the rivalry was based on alternative conceptions of power: the upcountry appealed to the established order of social hierarchy, a vertically based conceptuality, while the low-country appealed to a somewhat more egalitarian vision, one in which caste and ethnic identities were seen in horizontal, albeit competitive, relation. Ironically, the old traditional hierarchy, the one symbolized by the *asala perahara* processions, appears historically to have been more inclusive in nature, while the more ostensibly democratic conception has led to the rise of exclusivity, owing to consequences of religio-ethnic-based majoritarian politics. The *asala perahara* subordinated, but the new politics of religio-ethnicity excluded. Though the "upcountry" and "low country" distinction has abated somewhat in its significance, in part because of Sinhala cohesion brought about by the ethnic conflict that exploded into a civil war after 1983, it continues to reverberate.

The *diyavadane nilame* in 2012 had been elected in 2009 in a controversial election by the relevant college, consisting of senior monks from the Asgiriya and Malwatte Viharas and assistant government agents. Because the *diyavadane nilame* was a businessman (gem trader) from Sabaragamuva Province (and therefore not a Kandyan, nor a *radala goyigama*), and perhaps because he was recognized as a political supporter of the then president of Sri Lanka, rumors swirled about the legitimacy of his election. It was common to hear unsubstantiated *oppadupa* (rumor-mongering) that significant money had changed hands to guarantee his election. With the election of the *diyavadane nilame*, who defeated an incumbent Kandyan and known supporter of the opposition party in parliament, many suspected that the nature or content of the *perahara* might change, with the inclusion of a variety of elements now included in southern *perahara*s. Given that the new *diyavadane nilame* was the first non-Kandyan, historically, to hold the post since its elevated importance after the disestablishment of Kandyan Buddhist kingship in the early nineteenth century, I expected to see some significant changes myself, but I did not. Instead, the recent politics of power over the old Kandyan system of ritual have changed in more subtle ways, and what has changed is not so visible to the discerning public. What it has involved is a thorough intensification of centralization in the service of the political party that is in control at the national level. I came to appreciate this when I visited three of the rural *devalaya*s where I had conducted fieldwork back in the mid-1980s. There, I learned that the manner in which *basnayake nilame*s are elected to be lay custodians of the *devalaya*s has changed, and these rural sites have been drawn further into the orbit of the concerns of the national government's Department of Archeology or its Ministry of Buddhist Affairs. That is, the control of *devalaya*s is becoming far less local.

Facilitating this increasing administrative centralization, there has been a change in how *basnayaka nilame*s are selected within *devalaya*s that are part of the old Kandyan system. They used to be selected by vote of a college of thirteen assistant government agents and thirteen other *basnayaka nilame*s. But now, they are appointed directly by the Sri Lanka government's Ministry of Buddhist Affairs. This new process makes it more likely that the appointments are politically expedient and leverages power for the incumbent political party at important venues of Buddhist heritage. Since the chief perk of prestige lies in the fact that the *basnayaka nilame* marches in the Kandy *perahara*—a national profile coveted by many, especially would-be politicians—the contingent of *basnayaka nilame*s participating in the Kandy *perahara* are necessarily supporters and representatives of the current government in power. The *perahara* has become their stage, adorned by forms of dance equated with national cultural identity.

This pattern is not surprising, given the political scenario in Sri Lanka at the time. The president and his family were southern "low country" people who had taken over power of the group that Seneviratne identified earlier as the "national elites." They constituted a new national elite of their own and had moved into all corners of power. The takeover of the country was so complete that between the president and members of his family, it is said that approximately 80 percent of the national government budget was directly under their purview.

To what extent this centralization of power can or will be resisted at the village level is a good question, given the fact that two very serious rural-based insurrections (in 1971 and 1988–1990) have been mounted in the past forty years against the central government. In returning to three of the *devalaya*s in rural Kandyan villages where I had done fieldwork in 1983–1985, I found that two were thriving but one was not. Their relative prosperity is not the point I want to address here. What was clear in each of these three contexts is that the government is increasingly involved in the administration of each site. Moreover, other patterns observable within these respective villages indicate that each is losing its appeal in general to the present and next generation. For instance, a *kapurala* in one of these villages, who could still remember me thirty years later, says that while the attendance is up during the weekly *kemmura*[39] days, when he performs liturgies for devotees who wish to approach the deity with plaints to address their problems or fears, and more people are attending the annual village *perahara,* the single most difficult problem that he faces is getting people to observe their *rajakariya* duties so that the temple and its rites can function properly. When I asked him what would happen during the next thirty years, he said that *rajakariya* will probably disappear altogether, and he is uncertain about the viability of the *devalaya* because of that. The *devalaya* will have to rely on any monetary donations provided by its regular clientele and perhaps donations in lieu of services from the twenty-four families. The younger generation does not seem to respect these traditional duties. Unlike in the past, when most tried to remain in the village, now most seek employment afar in garment factories (for women) or in trades (carpentry and other construction trades) for men and try to domicile in Kandy or Colombo. The powerful draw to urban areas seems to be accelerating. Moreover, the enrollment at the local school has plummeted from around six hundred in the 1980s to only about sixty now because most people are sending their children to "central schools" in nearby towns. The children don't want to return following their completion of school. So, with the increased presence of the government and its oversight, there is a concomitant decline in local participation in the maintenance of the shrine. It may be that villages will end up forfeiting their "ownership stakes" to the central government out of necessity, in order for the *devalaya*s to be sustained in any ritually functional manner.

In this connection, it is very interesting to note that each of the *devalaya sthalapurana*s (mythic stories of origins) recounts how various kings, on passing through these locales where the *devalaya*s were eventually constructed, were humbled by the power of the deity and had to acknowledge the intrinsic power of the locale before proceeding on their important business.[40] Indeed, each of these *sthalapurana*s claims explicitly that these *devalaya*s were constructed originally by various kings as acknowledgments of that local power. These myths of origin stories are, in fact, expressions of resistance to central, royal power, at least statements about how the center is also dependent on the periphery. From this moment in time, however, it would appear that the fateful destiny of these same *devalaya*s may lie in the hands of the central government regardless of past sentiments mythically expressed.

CONCLUSION

I am now in a position to answer questions posed earlier in the discussion. Given Seneviratne's brilliant and meticulous analysis, what have the elites, both Kandyan and modern national bureaucratic, wanted to "show off" through enthusiastically bolstering the *asala perahara*? They have sought to emphasize that Buddhism is the reason for Sinhala primordial claims to political ownership to the island. They have sought to assert that this claim has an ancient and continuing warrant. Since the pivotal election of 1956, when S.W.R.D. Bandaranaike changed the Sri Lankan political calculus by running on his platform of Sinhala-only as the national language, and Buddhism as the national religion, public politics among the Sinhalas has been dominated by those politicians who can claim to be more Sinhala and more Buddhist than rivals. In addition to this fundamental move in national political culture, the existential tragedies, the economic distortions, the social acrimonies, and the psychological stresses brought about by civil war of the past thirty years have further abetted the increase in ethnic alienation and the reification of social boundaries between the Sinhala Buddhists and various other communities in Sri Lanka.

Reading the *asala perahara,* like Kandyan *ves* dance, as an articulation of "national culture" signals a fundamental problem that Sri Lankan society as a whole faces today, which is this: the rationalized discourse that follows this ritual articulation, while inclusive, is hierarchical and thereby dismissive of egalitarian aspirations. From a Sinhala Buddhist perspective in relation to Hindu communities, it reads, you are a part of the hierarchical mosaic, but you must recognize that you are subordinated to the basic ontology of our claims to power. (In terms of agricultural imagery, the fields are terraced, not leveled, and the power of water distribution comes top-down.) The worldview reflected in the *asala perahara* is rooted in a now-anachronistic ontology that is too narrow to incorporate all aspirations in a multicultural society. It is a ritual expression of the persistence of political Buddhism.[41] The umbrella that is this ideology leaves too many others, the non-Buddhists of Sri Lanka, out in the sun. The *perahara* is certainly a spectacular national treasure, but it cannot be regarded as *the* national treasure that quintessentially articulates a national vision of what constitutes a contemporary multicultural Sri Lanka.

Why was Vesak canceled in 1993 while the *asala perahara*s in 1983 and 1989 were not? Vesak was canceled because the nation of Sinhalas was in mourning for the loss of its political leader. Person after person told me that to celebrate Vesak then "just would not be right." It would not be right because the overriding presence of death is a moment of pollution inimical to the celebration of life. It is a time when religious focus should be on transferring merit to help create more favorable conditions of rebirth for the deceased. And, it goes without saying that a rebirth of the presidency of Sri Lanka was assured. The nation may have been wounded, but there was no question that it would survive without Vesak that year. In the case of the *asala perahara* in 1983 and 1989, decisions were made that the ritual *had* to be performed in the interest of declaring the survival of the nation in moments when its immediate future was being severely called into question. Indeed, the *perahara* articulates a mytho-political vision that is an antithesis to the Marxist-inspired vision of the JVP insurrectionists, or to the separatist aspirations of the LTTE.

One of the fundamental patterns observed with the birth of a new nation following a colonial experience is that its prospective or newly elected leaders reach back into history to retrieve a lost, or partially lost, identity, or an ontology of power, on which to build anew. This pattern of reaching back is also observable when a nation is under great duress. That is why patriotism often surges in times of threat and war. Certainly this was not lost on the enemies of the Sinhala Buddhists when Sri Mahabodhi and the Dalada Maligava were attacked in 1985 and 1997. While ostensibly centers of religious worship, these places are also live symbols of traditional Sinhala Buddhist political power, owing to past direct associations with Lankan kingship, and the substance of political discourse and identity in the present. The rise in the intensity of popularity of the *asala perahara* stands in reflexive relation to the rise of social, economic, and political stress, because it articulates a cohesive vision, an inclusionary model that argues against fragmentation and alienation. But in the world of contemporary identities, it also articulates a vision of the hierarchical past antithetical to egalitarian ideals of the present, and a vision arising from what is now but a part of the demographic whole, which cannot sustain a vision of the future if the minority communities on the island are to be given a rationale for investing in a united Sri Lanka. The now unanswered question for the future, therefore, is, What will "national" come to mean as the nation of Sri Lanka, as a whole, moves forward? Will it be a nation led by and defined only by the machinations of majoritarian politics, congruent with the symbolism intrinsic to the *asala perahara?* Or will that particular vision be transcended to articulate a celebration of diversity, rather than privileging one community's specific claims to primordial conceptions of prosperity and power?

CHAPTER THREE

Upasampada and *Pabbajja*

Ordination in Thai Buddhist Contexts

Transitions from group to group and from one social situation to the
next are looked on as implicit in the very fact of existence, so that a man's
life comes to be made up of a succession of stages with similar ends and
beginnings: birth, social puberty, marriage, fatherhood, advancement to
a higher class, occupational specialization, and death. *For every one of
these events there are ceremonies whose essential purpose is to enable the
individual to pass from one defined position to another which is equally
well-defined.*

—Arnold van Gennep, *The Rites of Passage*

This passage from Arnold van Gennep's classical treatise,[1] *Les rites des passages,* originally published in 1908, was meant as a generalization relevant across societies and cultures, but seems especially germane to the social significance of temporary monastic ordinations (*pabbajja*) into the *sangha,* a practice that has been widely understood as a customary rite of passage for all young Thai Buddhist males, a necessary marker of their ascension, or eventual ascension, to adulthood. As Jane Bunnag noted in her 1970s landmark study, *Buddhist Monk, Buddhist Layman:* "The Thai practice whereby young men enter the *wat* for a short period of time (*chua khrao*) has been rightly regarded as a kind of *rite de passage* by many anthropologists, as to become a monk for even a brief period is thought to transform young men who are immature or 'unripe' (*dip*) into fully adult members of society" (1973, 36). It is true that for most Thai men, becoming a monk is an essential aspect of what it means to be an adult Thai male, a prerequisite for assuming a responsible place within Thai society. However, while this understanding may be still dominant today, it can mask how the rite may also be of great significance in other religious and social ways for other members of the monks' families or communities, a more nuanced discussion about which I am also greatly interested in exploring. There may be no exact figures available to substantiate an accurate percentage, but it is probably not an exaggeration to say that at least 80 percent of all

Thai Buddhist men undergo temporary monastic ordination at some point in their lives. Some of them may ordain on multiple occasions, for reasons we will explore. Aside perhaps from funerals, daily giving of alms to monks, and Bun Phravet (the celebration of the *Vessantara Jataka,* especially as it is observed in the northern and northeastern regions of the country), ordination is likely the most widely observed Buddhist rite in Thai Buddhist religious culture. As such, it provides a very useful lens for understanding the nature of Buddhist ritual in relation to social change.

A second passage from van Gennep's classic theoretical excursus says this:

> For a man to pass from group to group . . . , for a laymen to enter the priest-hood or for a priest to be unfrocked calls for ceremonies, acts of a special kind, derived from a particular feeling and a particular frame of mind. *So great is the incompatibility between the profane and sacred worlds that a man cannot pass from one to the other without going through an intermediate stage.* (1973, 1; italics mine)

What van Gennep is highlighting in this passage corresponds to the social gravity associated with undertaking the *upasampada* full ordination rite in Thai society. Unlike the *pabbajja* novitiate, *upasampada* signals a serious resolve to pursue the path of the Buddha's *dhamma* as a full-fledged monk, to observe the 227 rules of monastic discipline enumerated within the canonical *Vinayapitaka* that constitute the behavioral realization of the *dhamma,* and to become a virtuous refuge for the laity, an object of merit-making that will benefit the laity in their own quests to improve their lives spiritually. *Upasampada* is a gateway into a prescribed mode of living that is set apart from the daily dimensions of lay life, a modus vivendi that is elevated spiritually and separated vocationally. Formally, it is understood as a renunciation. It is not understood as simply a temporary ordination, a customary incumbent transaction marking a rite of passage.

In this chapter, my intention is to ascertain how the vicissitudes of ordination (especially *pabbajja*) within Thai religious culture over the past thirty years mirror fundamental social, economic, and political changes that have swept through Thai society at large. The nature, and in some cases the function, of ordination has also undergone remarkable change. While ordination may be understood as a way that preserves traditional Thai Buddhist culture, it has also become a means for articulating newly embraced values that have accompanied the profound process of modernization that Thailand has recently experienced.

On my very first visit to South and Southeast Asia during the summer months of 1979, I traveled to Sri Lanka, India, and Thailand for the purpose of gathering ethnographic information on ritual practices pertaining to pilgrimage in Hindu and Buddhist cultic contexts. This research agenda took me to remote or rural regions of all three countries. At that time, the socioeconomic differences between Sri Lanka and Thailand in the rural areas of these countries, respectively (not taking Bangkok into account), seemed not at all very significant to me in terms of economic development (or lack thereof) and the establishment of modern infrastructure. In the rural regions of both countries, phones were scarce, roads were winding and difficult to navigate, trains and buses were almost always over-packed and often in rickety condition, agrarian lifestyles were completely dominant, and television had been introduced to Sri Lanka only earlier that same year, and Thai television broadcasts were definitely in a state of infancy. A few years after my first visit, Sri Lanka plunged into what became a protracted civil war that did not end until 2009. Much of its resources were directed into the deleterious effects of waging what seemed like an interminable war. The country's economy, as a result, remained quite stagnant and underdeveloped for the next three decades, energies being directed elsewhere. Infrastructural projects were put on hold, including the massive Mahaweli Development Scheme that had aimed to revitalize Sri Lanka's agricultural production. The quality of education deteriorated without proper investment or maintenance, manufacturing production was often interrupted, and foreign capital for investment was enfeebled.

When I began to frequent Thailand again many years later, beginning in the early 2000s, I was summarily impressed by the swift pace and thorough impact of modernization processes that had transformed almost the entire country, and how the spectacular development of the Thai countryside stood in stark contrast to Sri Lanka's. While some Thais then complained about how the Asian economic crisis of the late 1990s had hurt their consumptive abilities, I found Thailand positively affluent in comparison to Sri Lanka. Within fifteen years, from 1980 to 1995, the Thai economy had experienced a remarkable upsurge. At the beginning of this period, 60 percent of Thailand's exports had been agricultural. Fifteen years later, 80 percent came from manufacturing. In addition, Thailand's urban population had doubled, and so had its per capita income. Consequently, a relatively financially healthy and educated middle class had emerged. The bulk of the newly minted wealth, of course, was concentrated in Bangkok, a city that was in the process of becoming a "first world" cosmopolitan metropolis, a veritable transportation hub for the entirety of the Southeast Asia *mandala*: it was now replete with a state-of-the-art airport; efficient mass transportation facilities, including both elevated train and subway systems; and arterial superhighways that remain unrivaled in quality and extent in South and Southeast Asia. It was a city connected to the international economy, with the presence of many multi-national companies doing a brisk business, while the north and the north-east (Isan) of the country, known for their poverty, had also prospered relatively well. Regional cities, like Chiang Mai, Khon Kaen, Mahasara-kham and Udon Thani, sported sophisticated shopping malls revealing the new purchasing power and material desires of the people. Moreover, the sustained spread of education throughout the country meant that the expectations that accompany middle-class aspirations had been firmly im-planted in the countryside as well as in Bangkok, including, for some, the progressive ideal of equality between the sexes, for some others the ideal of a fair measure of equity in terms of the total distribution of wealth, and for yet another section of the populace, an awareness of the importance of preserving the country's natural environment.

Yet, while the country in general experienced a great increase in mate-rial well-being, and some sections had begun to adopt these progressive social and political ideals, Thailand had also experienced a real decline in some aspects of its quality of life including, unfortunately, an increasing gap between the wealthy and the poor, environmental degradation, and a debasement of culture as a result of intense commercialization (Darling-ton 2013, 120). The tensions between the newly cultivated middle-class ex-pectations and ideals that accompanied the modernization process, on the one hand, and the traditional stakeholders of wealth and power, on the other, were beginning to cause deep fissures in Thai society nationwide. Since 2006, Thailand has been beset by political turmoil, with an emergent, populist, largely rural-based majority on one side (politically labeled as the so-called red shirts) and the entrenched, business-oriented, urban-based powerbrokers who staunchly support the country's royalty and military on the other side (politically labeled as the so-called yellow shirts). Dangerous confrontations in recent years in Bangkok have left the country unsettled, and the military has twice moved in to unseat democratically elected governments who had come to power through popular support rooted chiefly in the north and northeast. At the time of this writing, the second military coup, rationalized as a way to restore civil order, is still in the process of playing itself out with a newly minted yet highly military dominated constitution ratified, and without any firm date set for the re-turn to civilian or democratic rule. Political turmoil can also be the result of rapid modernization. In contemporary Thailand, perhaps, expectations and reality have not exactly squared up.

In this chapter I show how the profundity of these changes and atten-dant expectations are now reflected in the performance of rites of monastic ordination in selected contexts. But first, to ground this analysis in a textual background to establish its religious significance first within a canonical scriptural context, I begin with a brief study of monastic ordination as it can be gleaned from the Pali *Vinayapitaka*. A brief study of how ordination was first conceived in this classic canonical source reveals that ordination was originally understood as a ritual realization of the Buddha's *dhamma* that concomitantly moored the institutional development of the *sangha*, its purpose to sustain a spiritual lineage of the Buddha. As such, ordination recalls and renews the very origins of institutional Buddhism and symbolically renews its raison d'être. Every ordination recalls this origin. This brief textual consideration is followed by analyses of ordination rites in different social and cultural contemporary Thai contexts, examining instances of both *pabbajja* and *upasampada*.

MONASTIC ORDINATION IN THE PALI *MAHAVAGGA* OF THE *VINAYAPITAKA*

In the contemporary context of Theravada Buddhist religious cultures, the life of the Buddha assumes seminal importance in many ritual and literary contexts, especially in relation to ordinations. The Buddha is often regarded as "the first," or the quintessentially paradigmatic, Buddhist monk. Ordained novices (*samaneras*) and full-fledged monks (*bhikkhus*) are often referred to as "sons of the Buddha." In Sri Lanka, for instance, the life of the Buddha is celebrated as a national holiday on the full moon day in May, which simultaneously marks the beginning of the most auspicious month of the year for monastic ordinations into the Siyam Nikaya, the oldest continuing Buddhist monastic fraternity in that country, with its head temples located in Kandy, the last traditional capital of Lankan kings. These ordination ceremonies (*upasampada*) are often major social celebrations for the families and villages of the candidates themselves.[2] Monastic candidates (*samaneras*) for full ordination (*upasampada*) understand that they are about to join a lineage of practice that is traced back to the Buddha's own religious experience, that is, to the very beginnings of the religion. In Thailand, the full moon day in June, Asala Bucha, which initiates the rain-retreat season, recalls the Buddha's first sermon and hence the first ordinations into the *sangha*, or the inception of the monastic community. In both contexts, rites of ordination are linked to celebrations marking the institutional origins of the religion. In both Sri Lanka and Thailand, then, ordination is understood as recalling the origins of the religion on the one hand, and sustaining it into the future on the other.

In the textual study that follows, then, it is not surprising to find how the earliest account of monastic ordination in Buddhist tradition is thoroughly entwined with an account of the *sangha*'s own beginnings, an account that, in turn, forms a very important slice of an ancient biography of the Buddha.[3] I begin with some general comments about the nature of the *Vinaya* text itself, since this text is seminal for understanding the charter for Buddhist monasticism per se and, hence, what it means to be a monk.

The Pali *Vinayapitaka* is divided chiefly into two major divisions of textual organization. The first consists of the *Suttavibhanga*, an exhaustive explication of the 227 rules of monastic discipline first articulated in the *patimokkha*, an ancient biweekly recital on *uposatha* (new and full moon days) that may have constituted the earliest form of Buddhist monastic ritual.[4] The *Suttavibhanga*'s explication of the *patimokkha* disciplinary rules contains stories that provide accounts of monastic behavior criticized by the laity, criticisms that led to the Buddha's purported formulations of specific disciplinary rules, followed by a careful word-for-word parsing of the rules' formulations, which, in turn, are often followed by a plethora of case histories that reflect how the rules sometimes had to be amended or especially interpreted, given unusual happenstances or the clever ways that some recalcitrant monks sought to avoid culpability. Especially within the contextualizing stories about wayward monastic behavior that prompt the Buddha to declare a particular disciplinary rule, the *Vinaya*'s profile of the Buddha is somewhat akin to a very stern elder, or fastidious, meticulously minded judge. Regularly—literally hundreds of times in the *Suttavibhanga*—the following stock formulaic sentences, adjusted to address the specific issue at stake, can be found whenever a matter of improper behavior has been reported to the Buddha: "It is not fitting, monks, in these foolish men, it is not becoming, it is not proper, it is unworthy of a recluse, it is not allowable, it is not to be done. How, monks, can these foolish men . . . [commit to this foolish behavior, etc.]?" Here the Buddha berates, chides, and admonishes, and only after his exasperated expressions of frustration are made clear does he deem it necessary to formulate the disciplinary rule in question. The Buddha's own words, *buddhavacana*, are what lend the monastic disciplinary rules their great authoritative weight. The "judicial Buddha," then, in the *Vinayapitaka*, often comes off as very sober, strict, and unrelenting in disposition while correcting the foibles and follies of wayward monks. Becoming a monastic follower of the Buddha means cultivating a lifestyle conducive to the realization of the Buddha's *dhamma*, a responsibility not to be taken lightly and one that can be realized only with a healthy measure of disciplined diligence.

While the *Suttavibhanga* reflects the earliest instances of Buddhist juris-prudence and is primarily concerned with adjudicating the disciplined behavior of individual *bhikkhus*, the *Mahavagga* and its sister text, the *Cullavagga*, constitute the second major division of the *Vinaya*, which together are referred to as the *Khandhaka* or "chapters." This is the portion of the *Vinayapitaka* that is primarily concerned with specifying how the collec-tively performed ritual practices of the *sangha*, including *upasampada, pabbajja, patimokkha, kathina*, and *pavarana*, are to be properly observed. It also contains lengthy and, frankly, rather pedantic discussions about how ex-act and proper conditions for settling disputes, administering disciplinary probation, determining *sima*s (sacred spatial boundaries for the perfor-mance of the *sangha*'s rituals), and so on are to be established. These dis-cussions reveal a profoundly conservative ethos reflecting a concerted determination to establish and preserve conditions conducive to the main-tenance of *parisuddhi*, or the "collective purity" of the monastic institution.

While earlier generations of scholars came to a consensus that the *Vinayapitaka* was probably framed as a charter document in connection with the convening of, or the conclusions arrived at, the Second Great Buddhist Council, allegedly held about a century after the Buddha's demise in the fourth century CE, most scholars today believe that it is impossible to know with any certainty the timing and context of its exact origins and its redaction into its current form.[5] Again, it goes almost without saying that although we cannot date with precision the *Vinayapitaka* text that has now come down to us, it certainly reflects the manner in which the early Bud-dhist monastic community grappled with the process of how to specify practices and forms of behavior that were consistent with an evolving un-derstanding of the Buddha's *dhamma*. More importantly, there seems to be a theoretical position asserted within the *Vinaya* that understanding pre-cept and engaging in practice are not two separate realizations. One doesn't necessarily proceed from the other. Rather, they stand in reflexive relation. In this light, the perfection of discipline can be regarded as both a means to the realization *dhamma*, on the one hand, and an external behavioral expression of its internal cultivation, on the other.

Twenty-four sections of the first of the ten chapters that make up the *Mahavagga* contain a partial biography of the Buddha. Unlike other biog-raphies of the Buddha, this fragmentary biography does not contain a mi-raculous birth story, nor does it contain an account of the prince's early life in the royal Sakyan palace, nor the story of the four signs (of old age, sick-ness, death, and renunciation), nor of the prince's "great departure" from the royal palace, nor of the years of ascetic practice in the forest under the tutelage of two eminent *sramana*s. Moreover, it does not contain the famous accounts of the Buddha's final three months (as in the *Mahaparinibbana Sutta)*: a controversial lunch in courtesan Ambapali's garden, the Buddha's scolding of Ananda for not asking him to live longer, the (in)famous warning about being silent in the presence of women, the unfortunate pork curry served by Cunda the smith that led to the Buddha's fatal illness, the Buddha's final and climactic *nibbanic* experience, his cremation like a universal king (*cakkavatti*), or the division of his relics among the republican clans, and therefore no intimations of how his "presence" is to be sustained in either the *dhammakaya* ("truth body" of his teachings) or the *rupakaya* ("form body" presence contained in relics). It does not even contain an account of the Buddha's enlightenment experience. It begins, rather, with an account of the last of the several nights that the Buddha had spent under the bodhi tree while contemplating the profundity of his enlightenment experience. According to this biographical fragment in the *Vinaya's* account, during the three watches of this last night, he ponders *paticcasamuppada* (codependent origination, or the process of temporal conditioning), first directly, then in reverse order, and then in both direct and reverse orders, before declaring respectively that he comprehends "thing-with-cause," the "destruction of cause," and thus the ability to "rout the host of Mara"[6] (*Mahavagga* I: 1–7). That is, the *Mahavagga's* account commences immediately after the Buddha's enlightenment experience and focuses on his actions and words articulated immediately thereafter. Every sermon and disciplinary directive that follows in the ensuing compendious *Vinaya* text is therefore understood as being expressive of the Buddha's enlightened mind-in-action. Indeed, the real focus of the *Mahakhandhaka*, the hundred-section-long segment that begins the *Mahavagga* portion of the *Vinaya,* is the establishment of the *sangha,* thereby seen as an accomplishment ultimately derived from the Buddha's own enlightenment experience. Specifically, however, this Buddha biography actually functions more particularly as an extended preface to a text explaining how the rite of ordination first evolved, and therefore how and why it should now be observed. It is fundamentally an account that establishes monastic lineage and its transmission. Its aim is to frame ordination.

In other biographies of the Buddha, seven weeks, or forty-nine days, of meditation and reflection, or gestation, follow his experience of enlightenment before he sets forth to preach his first sermon at Deer Park near Benares. In the *Mahakhandhaka,* however, only five such weeks are indicated. In addition to the first seven days under the bodhi tree that concluded when, on the final night, the Buddha pondered the truth of *paticcasamuppada,* the Buddha spends a second period of seven days under the "goatherds' banyan" before encountering a mantra-muttering *brahman* who asks him to define what it means to be a *brahman,* to which the Buddha replies curtly by declaring that a true *brahman* is one who acts without blemish, is "curbed-of-self," and rightly speaks (*Mahavagga* I: 1–3), short-hand for and consistent with the principles leading to disciplined modes of action that are articulated throughout the *Vinaya* text. In turn, his third week of meditative reflection consists of sheltered protection (from a violent storm) that he receives from the cobra-hooded *naga* Mucalinda, and culminates with the Buddha's declaration that ahimsa (noninjury) in relation to all creatures, and absence of desire that leads to the "crushing of the 'I am' conceit," constitute the supreme realization of happiness in this world (*Mahavagga* III: 1–4). Then, after the Buddha emerges from seven days of meditation under the Rajayatana tree, the merchants Tapussa and Bhallika, inspired by the revelation of a *devata,* approach to make an offering of barley gruel and honey balls, while transcendentally the four great *lokapala* kings provide a crystal bowl for the Buddha to receive this offering of nourishment. By their paradigmatic act of provisioning the Buddha, Tapussa and Bhallika become the Buddha's first two *upasakas* (male lay disciples), taking refuge by means of the "two-word formula," meaning the Buddha and his *dhamma* (*Mahavagga* I: 1–5). Here, the first two of what later becomes the *triratna,* or "triple gem" (three refuges) are established, and the exchange between the Buddha and the merchants foreshadows one of the evolving phases of how devotees will formally declare their intentions to live the religious life. Following the fifth and final week of meditation, while the Buddha muses over the profundity of his *dhamma* and worries that others may not be able to comprehend its subtlety, he is entreated three times by the deity Brahma Sahampati to make his *dhamma* known to the world. After "surveying the world with the eye of awakening," his consequent compassion for beings with greater or lesser capacities for suffering is aroused, and he declares: "Open for those who hear are the doors of deathlessness" (*Mahavagga* I: 1–13). This declaration effectively concludes what seems to be "Act 1" of the biography. The narrative shifts venue from the vicinity of Gaya to Benares, and the promise of how to achieve deathlessness is then revealed.

While it is with this shift that the substance of the Buddha's *dhamma* is revealed, the central focus of the *Mahakhandhaka* also begins to become more apparent. After learning from *devatas* that his former teachers (Alara the Kalama and Uddalaka) had passed away, and after encountering Upaka, a naked ascetic who seems indifferent to the Buddha's declaration that he has attained *nibbana,* the Buddha proceeds to Deer Park to encounter the five ascetics who had attended to him in helpful ways while he had formerly lived the ascetic life (here the narrative seems to assume familiarity with moments of the Buddha biography that are not directly described in the text). These five are initially skeptical of the Buddha's claim, in that, on seeing the figure of the Buddha, they believe that he has given up the life of ascetic renunciation for a life of indulgent abundance. But the Buddha proceeds to introduce his teachings by proclaiming that both the path of asceticism on the one hand and indulgent abundance on the other are "two dead ends"—that the path that he has discovered is a separate middle path. He proceeds to set the *dhamma* wheel into motion by means of preaching his sermon about the four noble truths and the noble eightfold path, the impact of its resounding salience described in this way:

> In . . . that moment, in that second, in that instant, the sound reached as far as the Brahma-world, and the ten thousand-fold world system trembled, quaked, shook violently and a radiance, splendid, measureless, surpassing the *devas*' own glory was manifest in the world. Then the Lord uttered this solemn utterance: "Indeed, Kondanna has understood." (*Mahavagga* I: 6, 31)

Kondanna, one of the five ascetics, "having seen the *dhamma*, attained *dhamma*, known *dhamma*, plunged into *dhamma*," responds by asking the Buddha for both the *pabbajja* (novitiate) and *upasampada* (full ordination) rites, to which the Buddha simply responds: "Ehi [Come] *bhikkhu*," which I. B. Horner (the translator of the *Vinayapitaka* into English), in a note to the passage (*Book of Discipline* 4: 18n10), refers to as "the oldest formula . . . to become a disciple of Gotama's . . . in the *Vinaya*." And so the *sangha* was born. In serial fashion, the Buddha then instructs Vappa and Bhaddiya, for whom "*dhamma*-vision" is also said to have arisen. *Dhamma*-vision is then specified as the awareness that "what is of the nature to uprise, all that is of the nature to stop." In this passage, then, it is clear that those who have understood the *dhamma* have essentially gained the same understanding (of *paticcasamuppada*) that the Buddha had acquired during the three watches of the seventh night during the first week following his enlightenment experience. Moreover, it is also clear that *dhamma*-vision, or grasping the significance of *nirodha* (cessation), at this moment of the narrative, is what leads to the pursuit of the religious life in a condition of homelessness. But before the narrative proceeds to describe the similar experiences of *dhamma*-vision by the two remaining ascetics, the Buddha institutes the practice of seeking alms. The lengthy sixth section of the *Mahakhandhaka* concludes with the famous "Second Utterance" (the sermon of setting the *dhamma* wheel into motion being the "First") with a sermon about how the body is not the self, nor is feeling, perception, or consciousness. All are impermanent[7] (*Mahavagga* VI: 1–47).

The next four sections of the *Mahakhandhaka* (*Mahavagga* I: 7–10) bring the Buddha into encounters with Yasa, a young wealthy merchant, and his family and friends. Yasa's story of conversion, his acquisition of *dhamma*-vision, is significant in a number of ways for understanding the establishment of the *sangha* and the significance of ordination. Yasa's merchant background also signals the beginning of an association between the *sangha* and the urban merchant community that would become socioeconomically important for the history of Buddhism in India and beyond. Moreover, the conversion of Yasa and his friends marks a recognition of a differentiation of caste identities in the *sangha* in this early moment of its development. Those who would join the *sangha* would hail from a wide spectrum of castes and not be drawn exclusively from the priestly *brahman* community. This opening up of the clerical pursuit to different caste ranks signals a significant development in the history of Indian religious culture. Great material wealth, a marker or goal of the merchant life, is also indexed for what needs to be renounced: the life addiction to the senses. The narrative's depiction of Yasa's own dissatisfaction with the life of the senses vividly recalls a scene from other well-known biographies of the Buddha, the scene immediately before his own "great departure." Here is how the narrative describes the attendant women musicians that Yasa sees, having awakened from his sleep in the middle of the night before his own "departure": "one with a lute in the hollow of her arm, one with a tabor at her neck, one with a drum in the hollow of her arm, one with disheveled hair, one with saliva dripping from her mouth, muttering in their sleep, like a cemetery before his very eyes" (*Mahavagga* I: 7, 2).

When the disillusioned Yasa leaves his home and encounters the Buddha in the early morning hours, he hears two sermons. The first is a "talk on giving, talk on moral habit, talk on heaven . . . , the peril, vanity, depravity of pleasures of the senses, the advantage in renouncing them" (*Mahavagga* I: 7, 5). This establishes a pattern for much of the remainder of the *Mahakhandhaka* Buddha biography. If the people addressed by the Buddha are understood to have minds that are "ready, malleable, devoid of hindrances," then the Buddha preaches a second sermon that gives rise to the acquisition of *dhamma*-vision, a sermon that is essentially the four noble truths and noble eightfold path. Those who hear only the first sermon become *upasakas* and *upasikas* (laymen and laywomen), while those who hear the second sermon and acquire *dhamma*-vision become *bhikkhus* (monks). Yasa's parents and his wife, distressed at their son's disappearance, hear only the first sermon and become the first laity to take refuge in the "three-word formula" of the Buddha, *dhamma*, and *sangha*. Their subsequent support for Yasa's decision to join the *sangha* also serves to flag how family, when rightly instructed, can acquire the wisdom necessary to understand the ultimate necessity and nobility of renouncing the life of the householder, another problem of crucial importance to the history of the *sangha,* one that is returned to again in the final section of the biography.

As the narrative continues, four wealthy merchant friends in search of Yasa also arrive, hear both sermons, and ask for *pabbajja* and *upasampada.* These four are followed immediately by fifty more merchant friends who, after hearing the two sermons, ask for *pabbajja* and *upasampada,* thereby expanding the *sangha* to sixty "perfected ones" (*arahant*s) by means of the "Come, O *bhikkhu*" formula. Following this scene of mass conversion, the Buddha declares his famous words of dispensation: "Walk, monks, on tour for the blessing of the many, for the happiness of the many, for the welfare of the many, out of compassion for the world, for the welfare, blessing and happiness of *deva*s and men" (*Mahavagga* I: 11, 1).

Meanwhile, Mara (death incarnate) approaches the Buddha again and scowls that the Buddha cannot escape the bondage of "mind-impressions" that arise from the senses, but then skulks off with a resignation that, indeed, the Buddha understands what causes bondage to the world (*Mahavagga* I: 11, 2). The *Mahakhandhaka* narrative then proceeds to describe how the *sangha* continues to expand as the sixty monks set about bringing more and more people to the Buddha for *pabbajja* and *upasampada.* In a practical response to this situation, the Buddha declares that it is no longer necessary for him to perform every *upasampada,* but that the monks themselves can admit newcomers, who should shave their heads, don yellow robes, sit down on their haunches and salute with joined palms before taking the threefold refuge. What this development indicates is a transmission of the *dhamma* that is no longer dependent on the Buddha's own bodily presence, that the *dhamma,* or better, the *dhammakaya,* can be transmitted from mind to mind within the context of a teacher-student relation independent of the Buddha's physical presence. Thus, the *sangha,* through the Buddha's act of delegation, has now become the preserver and disseminator of the Buddha's *dhamma.*

The *Mahakhandhaka* next incorporates a story also mentioned in the *Jataka*s about "thirty friends of high standing" who were enjoying themselves in a woodland with their wives, except for one who had brought a "woman of low standing" who proceeded to abscond with their belongings. The Buddha encounters the men as they are searching for this woman. When he hears of their predicament, he asks: "What do you think of this, young men? Which is better for you, that you should seek for a woman or that you should seek for the self?" (*Mahavagga* XIV: 2). Affirming the search for the self, all thirty hear the two sermons and receive *pabbajja* and *upasampada*.

This section of the text would seem to bring a coherent unit of narration to conclusion, for the *Mahakhandhaka* then shifts its focus once more to a very different phenomenon. What follows is a series of episodes in which the Buddha displays his miraculous powers (*iddhi*) in various ways in the company of three different groups of five hundred matted-hair ascetics, each led by a different teacher with the name Kassapa: Uruvelakassapa, Gayakassapa, and Neranjerakassapa. Uruvelakassapa is impressed by the Buddha's performance, but after each of the Buddha's miracles, he declares to himself that the "great recluse is not as perfected as I am." Finally, when the Buddha reveals that he has been reading Uruvelakassapa's mind all along, Uruvelakassapa inclines and asks to receive *pabbajja* and *upasampada*. His followers also decide to do the same, and so, in serial fashion, do the other two Kassapas and their followers. This is the only instance in the *Mahakhandhaka* account in which *pabbajja* and *upasampada* is not the result of the teaching on *dhamma*. It is clearly interpolated textual material originally stemming from a different source.

The very next section of the *Mahakhandhaka* (*Mahavagga* XXI) has the Buddha traveling with those same "thousands of monks" to Gaya, where he delivers the famous "Fire Sermon" about the burning of the eye, ear, nose, tongue, body, and mind: "With what is it burning? I say it is burning with the fire of passion, with the fire of hatred, with the fire of stupidity; it is burning because of birth, ageing, dying, because of grief, sorrow, suffering, lamentation and despair" (*Mahavagga* XXI: 3). He concludes with an exhortation to remain detached from these types of conditioned consciousnesses, and the section ends with the mention of how these thousands of newly ordained monks were freed from the effects of the conditioning process on the mind. The "Fire Sermon," of course, also comes from a separate source that has been inserted into the narrative. It replaces the two-sermon formula previously noted and functions rather appropriately in this context, as all of these converts have been living the life of *tapas*, of generating internal heat or burning for the purpose of purification of body and mind. So the Buddha has framed his sermon in such a way to reinterpret the significance of heat: from that which purifies to that which is symbolic of the problematic nature of desire, especially in relation to how consciousness arises conditionally. Heat is not so much a purifier as it is a by-product of desire.

Accompanied now by thousands of new disciples, logistical problems are further begged by the *Mahakhandhaka* account. This challenge is met by relating the story of the Buddha's encounter with King Bimbisara at

Rajagaha, who, after hearing *dhamma* by the Buddha, takes refuge in the triple gem (*triratna*) as an *upasaka* and offers an *aramaya* (a forested park) to the Buddha and the *sangha*. This is a definitive moment of institutionalization for the *sangha*, insofar as the Buddha declares his allowance for the acceptance of parks, an act that recognizes the beginnings of the shift from a wandering to a settled monastic lifestyle, one supported through the patronage of kingship.

The twenty-fourth section of *Mahakhandaka* is the final episode of the *Vinaya Mahavagga* per se, before the focus of the text dramatically shifts to considerations of various types of issues, major and minor, that lead to the formulation of allowances of monastic routine and disqualifications from joining the *sangha*. Indeed, the following seventy-six sections of the *Mahakhandhaka* are exceedingly juridical, technical, and somewhat arid literature that reflect the meticulous complexity involved in organizing an expanding and self-regulating social institution bound by fundamental principles of morality, etiquette, decorum, and legality. It is also bereft of a biographical narration as it proceeds in its formulaic fashions.

The final episode of the biographical account occurs in the twenty-fourth section of the *Mahakhandhaka* and is concerned with the conversions of Sariputta and Moggallana, two followers who are regarded in later Buddhist tradition as the most accomplished of all of the Buddha's disciples, particularly Sariputta, who is regarded as an interlocutor of the *Abhidhamma*, the third basket of the *Tipitaka* (in addition to the *Sutta* and *Vinaya*) that is primarily concerned with identifying states of consciousness. At the time of their conversions, Sariputta and Moggallana were followers of the wanderer Sanjaya. In due course, Sariputta encounters Assaji, the last of the Buddha's original five ascetic converts, who was seeking alms in Rajagaha. Impressed by his appearance, he inquires into his *dhamma*. Assaji says that since he is new to the Buddha's *dhamma* and *vinaya*, he cannot give a full explication. When pressed by Sariputta, Assaji explains that the Buddha has understood how things proceed from a cause and how these things may be stopped. From this brief explication, *dhamma*-vision arises in Sariputta: "[W]hatever is subject to arising is also subject to cessation." Immediately approached by Moggallana, who notices a change in Sariputta, Moggallana asks if Sariputta has attained deathlessness. Convinced of the verity of Sariputta's attainment, the two proceed to Sanjaya and explain their decision to seek out the Buddha as their new teacher. Sanjaya attempts to dissuade them, but the two convince Sanjaya's 250 other followers to join them as well. The Buddha ordains them all, but there is consternation raised in the populace about how Gotama has made so many parents childless and so many wives widows.

This consternation is reported to the Buddha, who asks the question: Who would be jealous of seekers after truth? Moreover, he declares that this matter of concern will subside after seven days, which, at the conclusion of the twenty-fourth section, it does.

What has been accomplished by this slice of biographic narration placed at the *Mahakhandaka*'s beginning of the *Vinaya Mahavagga*? First, the history of the *sangha* has been rooted ultimately in the decision of the Buddha to make known the *dhamma* that was realized in his enlightenment experience. The substance of that experience has been specified as *paticcasamuppada* and *nirodha*, further reprised as *dhamma*-vision experienced by his converts: "[W]hatever is subject to arising is also subject to cessation." The simple inducement, "Come, O *bhikkhu*" has first evolved into taking refuge in the triple gem (Buddha, *dhamma*, and *sangha*) and then further into the elaborate ceremonies that become *pabbajja* and *upasampada*, ceremonies meticulously prescribed in ensuing chapters of the *Vinaya*. Those fully initiated into the *sangha* are provided with a dispensation to ordain others, signaling that the transmission of the *dhamma* will proceed from mind to mind. (Even Sariputta, who becomes an eminent follower, is enlightened through Assaji's simple and curt articulation.) Links to the merchant community are acknowledged as primordial, the superiority of the Buddha's teachings to other *sramana* groups is acclaimed, the paradigmatic relationship between royalty and the *sangha* is established, the settled form of monastic life in one place affirmed, and the radical nature of going forth into homelessness from family life is legitimated. In short, the beginnings of Buddhistic monasticism are chartered in the articulation of the Buddha's enlightenment experience. In the *Vinaya*, the Buddha is not only the legal-minded embodiment of incipient Buddhist jurisprudence, he is also the original monastic progenitor who institutes the ordination process, and so he is unambiguously the primordial disseminator of *dhamma* and *vinaya* as well. The gateway into the Buddha's religious world is through taking refuge, formally observed through the performance of ordination rites.

ETHNOGRAPHIC BACKGROUND ON THAI BUDDHIST MONASTIC ORDINATIONS

Though every Theravada Buddhist religious culture recognizes the scriptural and ritual authority of the Pali *Vinaya*, including the account just surveyed in the *Mahavagga*, variations in *upasampada* and *pabbajja* exist within the cultural orbits of Sinhala, Lao, Khmer, Burmese, and Thai Buddhist monastic practice. Indeed, even within the Thai national context, how these rites are administered and performed in different regions of the country can vary significantly; for example, how they may be observed in sophisticated urban contexts in Bangkok, such as at Wat Phra Dhammakaya, or how they may be observed in rather rustic and rural settings, such as in the extreme northwest in Mae Hong Song, or in the agricultural contexts of the northeast (Isan), often reveal more than simply shades of local cultural nuance and preference. Moreover, in addition to cultural contexts, socioeconomic forces also condition the manner and understanding of their performances. Given Thailand's rapid modernization process over the past thirty years, change sometimes has been dramatic. In other words, a number of variables are in play that include local, regional, and cultural influences, as well as the extent and dynamics of socioeconomic forces.

Kenneth Wells' account of ordination, drawing from observations that he made from the 1930s into the 1950s, is a valuable source basic for understanding *upasampada* and *pabbajja* even today, insofar as he has provided the essential textual sources that are used in the liturgical performance of both rites that he had observed in Bangkok and Chiang Mai. From reading his book, *Thai Buddhism: Its Rites and Activities*,[8] somewhat historically dated as it now may be and, of course, somewhat innocent of the types of theoretical concerns that one finds in later anthropological literature, one nevertheless can grasp the structural outlines of both *upasampada* and *pabbajja*. Indeed, I found the textual sources that Wells quotes extensively from in his account to be fully in play within an *upasampada* rite I observed in Chiang Mai at Wat Phra Singh in 2012. (My observations of that *upasampada* are recorded subsequently in this chapter.) Valuable as it may be, an account like Wells' is bound to remain somewhat wooden, as it exclusively privileges the textual without providing much commentary on the ethnographic setting and its participants. Nonetheless, the ethnographic generalizations that Wells does manage to make in passing are helpful, as they indicate a mid-twentieth-century orientation, before the advent of rapid modernization.

While describing what might be called "pre-*upasamapada*" rites in Chiang Mai, Wells notes the performance of two ceremonies, one widely found throughout north and northeast Thailand as well as in Laos, and another found not only in these regions of Thailand and Laos, but also in Sri Lanka and especially Myanmar. The first of these is what Wells refers to as a "leave-taking ceremony" (1982, 137), but is actually a *basi* ceremony, also known as the *sukhwan* rite. In *sukhwan*, a ritual specialist (not always a *brahman*, as Wells seems to infer), chants a series of invocatory texts to recall the various thirty-two souls that are thought to inhabit disparate regions of the human body, souls that might have strayed away from where they belong to reside externally, to return to their appropriate positions within the body to restore its optimal vitality and strength. *Sukhwan* is a rite of "recentering" or "rebalancing" an individual person before an important moment of transition is to occur, such as a wedding, domestic relocations, extensive travel, the inauguration of any important undertaking, or any other moment that may involve a significant existential encounter with liminality or transition. It is fundamentally a preparatory rite for a moment of passage. But it is also a rite of social solidarity: at the conclusion of the ritual chanting, a white thread that is thought to have harnessed the powers of the invocations is cut and tied around the wrists of all ritual participants as a sign of the protective power that has been conjured through the chanting and "recentering" process.[9] In the context of monastic ordination, it is a way of ensuring that the candidate enters the process of initiation in a condition of maximal strength and composure. It is a corollary to considerations about auspicious timing. But it is fully a domestic or householder rite and is preliminary in nature. No monks are present.

The second ritual follows *sukhwan* either immediately or on the following day. It is also a "leave-taking" ritual of sorts: the candidate leaves home in a regal style reminiscent of Prince Siddhartha's (the Buddha's) own "great departure," with an umbrella (sign of royalty) shading the way. In Sri Lanka, sometimes the candidates are mounted on elephants (the royal animal), but Wells notes in the Thai context that, in the past, a horse was ridden (in emulation of Siddhartha riding his horse Channaka), but these days it is an automobile. It not at all unusual to see these processions all over Thailand and in Myanmar (see figure 3.01).

Two other aspects of Wells' account are salient when compared with the situation in Thailand today. The first is that, during Wells' time, those who intended to become novices had to show themselves proficient in learning the rules and precepts for novices before they were issued certificates by the monastic district[10] head monk (Wells 1982, 135). How extant this formality remains throughout Thailand would be an interesting issue to explore, for it is clear that in many temples *pabbajja* is conducted for many aspirants who may spend as little as three or four days in the temple, and in many cases only a week.[11] Some of these novices are not proficient in terms of their knowledge of monastic rules of discipline and what it means to observe the precepts. In these instances, certificates of ordination are issued only by the local temple, and not by the monastic district office. Bunnag notes that in her time (1960s) and acquaintance, "unless a man is a monk during the entire Lenten season, his name will not appear in the official records of the Religious Department in Bangkok"

Figure 3.01. Village ordination procession

(1973, 37). I found among informants at Wat Phra Singh in Chiang Mai that remaining in the monastery for the entire *vassa* rain-retreat season adds not only prestige to ordination, but also the perception of much greater merit being earned. What has changed during the past generation is that fewer and fewer novices enter the *sangha* for the duration of *vassa,* that temporary ordination is for a much shortened period of time, and consequently that *pabbajja* is becoming more pro forma in nature. In a later discussion focused on ordination at Wat Phra Dhammakaya, it becomes clear that this trajectory is understood as problematic for the future of the *sangha.*

The second remaining aspect of interest here in Wells' commentary is more of a quasi-legal matter. He notes:

> A man who has entered and left the priesthood three times may not enter for the fourth time. If a husband goes to the monastery for seven days only

he retains legal control over his property. If he goes for a longer period, the property he owned at the time of his marriage goes to his wife unless he has made some other provision for the disposal of his goods. If his wife maintains the home while he is in the priesthood and he leaves the Order and goes back to her, then he again becomes the head of the house and the owner of the property. If a government official goes into the priesthood during the three months of the rainy season, this does not constitute a divorce between husband and wife and the government continues the salary of the official during this period. However, only one such period in the priesthood is provided for. (1982, 150)

This last provision specified by the government of Thailand is still a policy today. But Hayashi says, on the basis of his extensive field experience in Isan, that a man can be ordained as a novice "any number of times" (2003, 106). Whether or not there is a limit on how many times a man may ordain, what is clear in the Thai context, and what differentiates it especially from the Sri Lankan monastic context, is that movement between lay society and *sangha* is accomplished quite easily, without any stigma attached. Indeed, *pabbajja* is understood by many Thai to be primarily a merit-making occasion, rather than simply a "coming of age" custom. What this also means is that the number of *pabbajja* rites vastly outnumbers the *upasampada* rites. In this regard, Bunnag rather ironically says that, contrary to a ritual that signals detachment from the social world and the beginning of an other-worldly quest,

[t]he Buddhist value of merit can . . . be regarded as a conservative and stabilizing force in society rather than the reverse. The quest for merit does not mean that one relinquishes all social ties and consequent volitional actions, but rather that one tries if possible to perform meritorious actions which often merely means fulfilling one's social obligations. (1973, 179)

In recognizing Bunnag's observation about the value of merit and the fulfilling of social obligations, the motives that seem to underlie the fundamental rationale for ordination, Hayashi has attempted to sort out further reasons for why the *pabbajja* temporary ordination takes place so frequently in the Isan cultural and regional context and has offered the following typology:

It is possible to classify monks according to their purpose in being ordained. The four basic categories are: temporary ordination in accordance with custom (*buat tom praheni*); ordination as an offering to the deceased at their funeral (*buat na sop, buat chung sop*); ordination as a petition or as a "return gift" (*kae bon*) for recovery from illness, practices which are thought to have been influenced by Chinese customs; and ordination to study at the temple (*buat rian*). From the early to mid-twentieth century, when secular education under the state was not well established, a high percentage of monks belonged to the fourth category. Today, however, the first category is the most common for people to be ordained at a later age and to remain a monk for a shorter period of time. (2003, 106)

In my own interviews in Chiang Mai and Bangkok and in support of Hayashi's observation, I found the spread of education and its impact on the *sangha* and its traditional social function being stressed repeatedly: that the spread of education had made a very significant impact not only on why the *sangha* attracts fewer candidates for *upasampada*, but why more and more opt for a brief temporary ordination. The *sangha* has ceased, largely, to be an educational conduit facilitating upward social mobility in Thailand, though I hasten to add that I found in Laos in 2007 that education remained one of the most-cited rationales for joining the *sangha*.[12] The difference between the Thai and Lao contexts is that a higher quality and more extensive education is now much more readily available throughout Thailand than it is in Laos. Moreover, it is clear that even the timings of most *pabbajja* temporary ordinations throughout Thailand are now determined by the timing of school vacations (the prime season is mid- to late March, when at least a month-long vacation is provided). In any case, if one considers carefully the nature of the first three of the four categories that Hayashi has set forth above, one finds that the motive of merit-making is at the base of each of these. My sense is that, as far as monastic ordination is concerned, this is far more true in Thailand than it is for any other Theravada country. Moreover, the chief recipient of that merit-making is most often one's mother. Hayashi observes,

[T]he amount of merit to be shared also corresponds to the degree of social intimacy. For example, merit from the ordination of P is shared in the order of his parents, close kin, and then anonymous parties who are participants in the ritual. This larger share between the parents goes to his mother because she was confined for many months during pregnancy, gave birth to, and raised her son, for which he is deeply indebted. The degree of her importance is demonstrated by the fact that sharing merit with one's mother is referred to as a "nursing fee" (*kha nomsot:* literally, fee for mother's milk). This expression, which is used to mean repaying benefit (*bunkhun*), is a clear indication of the reciprocal relationship between mother and candidate. Merit transfer to the mother is valued as repayment for raising the initiate and the importance of the ordination ceremony is derived from the fact that it is a manifestation of this common social value. In that sense, the main actors in the ordination ceremony are the candidate and his mother who, as a woman, is excluded from the monkhood. (2003, 143)

It is this particular point about the centrality of the mother that Nancy Eberhardt (2006) stresses in her analysis of *pabbajja* temporary ordination rites in Mae Hong Song, a discussion that I will look into in some depth after an ethnographic description of *upasampada*. But for now, there are two further important issues to note.

The first is that the primary emphasis in the ideology of merit-making within this context has shifted from a focus on the candidate as the primary beneficiary of merit to those with whom the merit is to be shared, primarily the mother. There is, of course, a long history of merit-transfer in Buddhist tradition, an issue dealt with in some depth in chapter 5, in an extensive discussion that focuses on *pchum ben*, the annual Cambodian rite of caring for the dead. Hayashi has noted that sometimes ordinations in Thai contexts are undertaken precisely to transfer merit to the recently deceased.

The second issue that arises has to do with the fourth category that Hayashi has cited with regard to the spread of education in the twentieth century, a phenomenon that reflects the increasing degree of secularization or modernization that is taking place in Thai society. In what Hayashi offers below, its consequent impact on Buddhist religious culture is clearly seen in what he calls "contradictory processes."

> There is a movement towards secularization and personal practice in response to changes in the social foundation of daily life, such as the penetration of the market economy and the dissemination of secular education. The result is two apparently contradictory processes existing side by side. On the one hand, there is partial secularization of religion among young Buddhist monks coupled with the monetary and material expression of merit-making. On the other hand, there is a deepening of the individual's internal faith, particularly among the elderly. Even in the village temple today, ostentatious displays of wealth when making offerings coexist with the solemn gravity of the laity, the majority of whom are elderly women, in the spiritual act of receiving the precepts. (2003, 337)

I find Hayashi's analysis quite insightful insofar as he has highlighted how, within the monastic context of ordination rites, there is an increasing materialization and commodification reflected in the contemporary ritual process. Certainly this is seen very clearly within the context of temporary ordinations as they are conducted within Wat Phra Dhammakaya's *pabbajja* celebrations, a focus of discussion later in the chapter, though his observations are drawn from rural Isan. What Hayashi has also registered is the irony that the more deeply spiritual dimension of the ritual transaction often lies with laywomen (rather than with the young male monks). Women, of course, are regarded as hierarchically socially and spiritually inferior in status to men within the traditional framework of Thai societal assumptions, and the laity are, of course, regarded as spiritually inferior to monks. What I intend to show, with the help of Eberhardt's analysis of *pabbajja*, is why it is the case that women are often, in fact, and very ironically at that, at the very center of importance in these ordination rites for men. In a subsequent discussion in this chapter, I also discuss the controversial issue of women undertaking ordination in Thailand. But first I address the performance of *upasampada* that I observed at Wat Phra Singh in Chiang Mai in 2011, before proceeding to a more detailed consideration of *pabbajja*.

CONTEMPORARY ETHNOGRAPHIC OBSERVATIONS OF *UPASAMPADA*

That Asala Bucha (Sanskrit and Pali: Puja) is held on the full moon day immediately preceding the first day of *phansa* (Pali: *vassa*), the so-called Buddhist Lent, makes a good deal of sense. This Thai national holiday commemorates the *Dhammacakkapavattana Sutta* of the *Digha Nikaya*, the Buddha's first sermon at Deer Park in Sarnath near Varanasi where the Buddha, after spending weeks in contemplation following his night of enlightenment (celebrated on Vesak, or Visakha in Thailand, on the full moon day of May) converted or enlightened his first five monks and thereby established the *sangha*, as we observed in the brief survey of the *Mahakhandhaka* of the Pali *Vinaya Mahavagga*. This is the seminal occasion, as noted, when the Buddha made known his *dhamma* to those who came to constitute the first converts of the *sangha*. Monastic sermons on this day at Thai Buddhist *wat*s to the laity, therefore, stress the beginnings and legacy of the Buddhasasana. Those sermons also typically recall the content of the Buddha's first articulation of *dhamma*: the four noble truths and the noble eightfold path. What is so appropriate about the timing of Asala Bucha is that it immediately precedes the three month period of the religious calendar when, according to the *Vinaya*, monks were required to stay in one place and to cease their eremitical wandering. During this sedentary time frame, monks traditionally intensified their study of the *dhamma* and their practice of meditation. A symbol of this feature of the rain-retreat season is that one of the most common or traditional gifts given by the laity to monks at this time is a very large saffron-colored candle to help illuminate the night so that study of the *dhamma* can be carried on well into the evening hours.

What struck me as different about the celebration of Asala Bucha at Wat Phra Singh in Chiang Mai, in comparison to the many *poya* full moon day rites I have seen over the years in Sri Lanka, was the absence of laity "taking *sil*," the practice of white-dressed *upasaka*s and *upasika*s in the temple for the day vowing to uphold five (*pancasila*) or eight precepts, listening to sermons by the monks, and perhaps engaging in group chanting or meditation, doing all of this while fasting, some for the whole day but others from noon. In contrast, the activities at Wat Phra Singh during the day seemed to be far more monk-oriented, or the stress was on the monks being present in order to play their roles as the objects of virtuous giving on future donative occasions. Indeed, to be sure, there was a morning sermon delivered at Wat Phra Singh, but it was a run-up to the main raison d'être for the laity: to present various types of gifts to the monks in order to earn merit. As I thought about this, the comparison between the contexts reflected two different strategies for merit-making. The former (Sinhala context) was more about the moral pursuit and ascetic effort required to make progress on the path, while the latter (Thai) was more about giving materially as the means of making merit. But while "taking *sil*" constitutes a kind of temporary monastic pursuit in the Sinhala context, temporarily ordaining, the practice that dominates the days immediately following Asala Bucha at the beginning of *phansa* (*vassa*) also stresses literally a temporary monastic pursuit of its own, at least for newly ordained young males who are undertaking *pabbajja*.

Yet, at the evening rite in Wat Phra Singh, a small number of people dressed casually in white, wearing t-shirts and pants, were present with the intention of spending a short night at the temple. After twenty minutes of Pali chanting by the monks (some fifty *samaneras* and ten fully ordained monks, including the young man whose *upasampada* I had recently observed), the head monk delivered a forty-five-minute homily that commenced with a brief outline of the *Dhammacakkapavattana Sutta* before he tailored his comments in Thai about how the Buddhasasana was first established and how it eventually came to Chiang Mai. Following the conclusion of his sermon, the monks led a procession out of the temple and a circumambulation clockwise around the temple three times, each carrying lit incense, a saffron candle, and a lotus bud. This procession ended around 8:30 p.m., leaving those intending to spend the night with about seven or eight hours before a formal meditation session would begin at 4 a.m., followed by another service beginning at 6 a.m., formally commencing *phansa*. And so, the two occasions were blended into each other. But the number of laity who had determined to complete this regimen was but a handful, no more than ten. I came to the conclusion that the practice of "temporary ordination" was observed through *pabbajja* in Thailand because it was somewhat functionally equivalent to "taking *sil*" in Sri Lanka. The results were nearly the same insofar as each respective constituency was exposed to teachings about *dhamma* and the practice of meditation. But what was different in Thailand was that the practice of "temporary monastic life" had been institutionalized into the monkhood per se and understood primarily as a means of merit-making/merit-sharing and as a rite of passage as well.

When I asked the retired principal of Wat Phra Singh's large monastic school and the senior head monk of Wat Phra Singh what had changed the most over the past thirty or forty years with regard to the practice of ordination, the senior monk responded by saying that, while virtually every young man before the age of twenty will take on a temporary *pabbajja* ordination, there are fewer now than there used to be who opt for the *upasampada* and who will then remain in the *sangha*. In his considered view, this was the result of the government having built schools in every remote place of the country, a development that obviated the need to seek an education through joining the *sangha* (confirming one of the main assertions made by Hayashi in his observations cited above). In the past, many younger *samaneras* who had attended monastic schools would choose to remain as monks. The monkhood was a veritable option exercised by many. That is no longer the case. Enrollments at monastic schools are also now dropping precipitously, I was told. What this means is that the *sangha* is now definitely less the conduit for upward social mobility than it used to be.

At the same time, both the senior monk and the retired principal were of the opinion that laypersons of today are far more devout than they used to be, with many beginning to take part in *vipassana* meditation and volunteering to assist as they can at the *wat*. This may be a by-product of an emerging middle class that has more leisure time to spare. Moreover, the senior monk and retired principal said that the number of merit-making occasions seems to have increased in frequency and in expense. This explains why more and more young men become monks temporarily: in order to make merit for their parents. Some join for only three days, others for five, seven, or ten days, or two weeks. What seems to be of enduring importance, according to the retired principal, is that the holding of the performance of the *pabbajja* ceremony itself functions as a type of rite of passage. When I asked him and the senior monk why this was the case, the only answer was that "it is the custom." So, they had iterated the rather conventional understanding about how undertaking *pabbajja* is essential to Thai adult male identity. The retired principal, who had several daughters, said that he would not give consent for his daughter to marry a man unless the man had undertaken *pabbajja*. In spite of Hayashi's conventional proclivities for understanding *pabbajja*, it was clear that his observed parallel processes of monkish secularization and increased piety among the laity within a predominant ethic of merit-making were the primary forces in play.

In the summer of 2011, I observed a full *upasampada* rite at Wat Phra Singh. Just before the rite, an uncle of the candidate commented to me that "this rite was being performed as it should be." It turned out that what he meant referred to two specific aspects. First, Wat Phra Singh is a hallowed sacred place in the history of Chiang Mai. The *wat* was founded in the fourteenth century and its *sima* has remained intact during the entire intervening historical period. The *ubosat* (Pali: *uposatha*) hall is still situated atop the same fifteen *sima* stones that consecrated the ordination hall back in the fifteenth- and sixteenth-century reign of King Phra Muang Kaew (r. 1495–1523), just before Chiang Mai was united for a few years with Luang Phrabang. Inside the ordination hall, a replica of the Emerald Buddha has been installed to emphasize the temple's link to Thai royalty.[13]

The father of the candidate told me that the ordination was taking place on this date, rather than four days later when the rain-retreat season would formally begin and when a host of *pabbajja* ceremonies would be held, because in this way his son could remain a monk for the entire period of *phansa*, and not for just a few days' time. In addition, he would not be ordained amid the welter of *pabbajja* activity that accompanies the rather mass ordinations for those *samaneras* who would be staying in the temple for only a few days. So that was the second aspect of the words that the candidate's uncle had previously offered: both the space (Wat Phra Singh) and the timing of the rite for the duration of the rain-retreat season had been very carefully considered.

As the specific time for the *upasampada* approached, the candidate, dressed in the white color of lay *upasaka* status, carefully studied the words of the impending liturgy that he would recite. Members of his family began to assemble in the *ubosat* hall, about ten in all, including his father, sister, and aunts and uncles. About twelve somewhat junior but fully ordained monks took up seats in four rows of three, two on either side of a senior monk who would provide quiet counsel throughout. Then about five very senior monks, including the candidate's *upajjhaya* (preceptor), joined the other monks in sitting, and the rite commenced.

Figure 3.02. Interior of *ubosath* at Wat Phra Singh, Chiang Mai

After the salutation to the Buddha, *dhamma,* and *sangha,* the candidate begged three times for permission to join the *sangha.* He was instructed to take off the white upper garment and replace it with a saffron one instead. He was then led by some of the junior monks behind the altar of the Emerald Buddha image, out of sight of everyone else, where he donned the full complement of the saffron robe for the first time and returned with his ceremonial begging bowl strapped to his back. It was a big moment for his family to absorb. The formal liturgy of the rite then commenced, with the most senior monk leading the taking of refuge in the Buddha, *dhamma*, and *sangha* in Pali. At this point, the family and other observers were asked to leave the hall while the liturgy concerned with "presenting the candidate" was chanted by the most senior monk. (I was allowed to remain.) Intermittently, the candidate was guided and prompted by the first senior monk on how to respond to the taking of the ten precepts (the *pancasila*, and refraining from dance and music, from adorning the body, from sleeping on a high or wide bed, and from receiving money). After this, the candidate asked the *upajjhaya* for *nissaya*, which basically means accepting the tutelage of the *upajjhaya*. A few minutes later, the candidate appeared on the portico of the ordination hall, where his family and onlookers were waiting. Here, two monks joined him to question him about the twenty "disqualifications."[14] Having answered satisfactorily, the monks and attending family all returned inside the ordination hall. The final acceptance of the candidate into the *sangha* was then ritually processed, first by the silent acceptance of all fully ordained monks present and then by the declaration of acceptance chanted by the most senior monk, who then handed over a decorative certificate of *upasampada*. Following this acceptance, all of the monks turned about, while remaining seated, to face the attending laity. Trays of gifts consisting primarily of a lotus bulb, chopsticks, candles, a small pamphlet, and flashlights were then given to each of the attending monks, while the candidate was given an additional robe, pillow, blanket, mat, and sandals. After the ceremony, the newly minted monk appeared on the portico and tossed handfuls of coins to members of his family as auspicious commemoratives of this merit-making occasion. The monetary outlay for these displays was considerable. The *wat* also expects a generous donation from the monk's family.

I found the straightforwardness of this *upasampada* in great contrast to the ordinations I had previously seen in Sri Lanka and Laos. In the Sri Lankan context, *upasampada* seemed to have involved most members of the candidate's village, who had made their way to Kandy for two full days of festivities. On the first day at the Malwatte Vihara in Kandy during the month of *Vesak* (rather than just before *vassa*), the candidate had been dressed up as if he were Prince Vessantara, Lankan-style, and taken over to and back from the Dalada Maligawa (the revered Temple of the Tooth-Relic) on an elephant, in a "mini-*perahara*" where he enjoyed an hour or so of Kandyan dance performed for him as a "last night" of enjoyment in the company of fellow villagers and family. The next morning, he undertook an oral examination by senior monks in front of all of his well-wishers, an examination that consisted of his ability to recite portions of the *Dhamma-pada*. He did this with four other candidates simultaneously (one who did not pass and would have to wait another year for *upasampada* as a result). The senior monks were quick to correct mistakes and to show their disdain for any ill-preparedness. Then a much more thorough liturgy was performed. I surmise that the relative straightforward character of the Thai version, in comparison to the Lankan, was that Thai *upasampada*s are a much more common affair and do not take on such an aura of finality as the Sri Lankan versions afford. Most fully ordained monks in Sri Lanka have the intention to remain as monks permanently, though attrition rates, particularly among those who attend the university, are nevertheless quite high.

In the Lao context, *upasampada*s are more often than not also held much earlier in the calendar year. An *upasampada* that I witnessed in Luang Phra-bang in 2007 was held immediately following the two-day recitation of the *Vessantara Jataka*, or Bun Phravet. The head monk of Vat Xieng Thong explained to me that this timing was one of the most spiritually fortuitous times of the year, insofar as Bun Phravet is the most auspicious merit-making rite of the year. During that rite, the changing of the robe took place behind a curtain of saffron cloth in front of the *sim* (*dhamma* hall), and water was poured through the mouth of an elongated symbolic *naga* on to the candidate before he donned the saffron robe. Clearly this was a ritual bath of purification meant to symbolize a spiritual rebirth. No such colorful displays were part of the Thai rite. In Laos, *upasampada* also remains a serious and uncommon rite for a young man to undertake, and most monks who undergo it remain in the *sangha* for at least a period of years before contemplating a departure. While the rite is definitely a merit-making occasion for parents, it is also considered a mark of prestige for the monk even if he should decide to revert back to lay status after a few years.

Upasampada rites do not evince the types of changes so evident in how *pabbajja* rites are performed because they remain, on the whole, rather thoroughly monastic rites performed within the *ubosath* (Pali: *uposatha*) halls within the campuses of temple complexes. In Thailand, it is usual that, in addition to the requisite number of monks who attend, only close family members are present, unlike *pabbajja* rites, in which entire villages often participate, or mass ordinations that occur at major temples, where throngs of laity are in attendance. I attended both the *pabbajja* and *upasampada* rites at Wat Phra Dhammakaya in March and July 2015, and this pattern held true there as well. The former, especially the "local" Wat Phra Dhammakaya *pabbajja*, were attended by thousands, while the latter was an intimate affair, and I was seated on the side of the *ubosath* along with no more than six or seven other laypeople for the three monks who were about to become full-fledged *bhikkhu*s.

PABBAJJA IN A VILLAGE CONTEXT

Modernization, of course, is affecting village as well as urban contexts. Yet, very important differences remain between each context, which significantly affect the social and religious experience of ordination. In this section, I refocus on a specific village context to highlight how *pabbajja* is such an important rite not only for the candidate, but especially for the sponsors of the rites and for the community as a whole. To my mind, the most compelling ethnographic observations about *pabbajja* in rural Thailand have been advanced by Nancy Eberhardt, who opens her discussion by noting how novice ordinations by Shan Buddhists in Mae Hong Son in the far northwest have become such a grand spectacle that tourist businesses in Bangkok are now organizing tours for devout lay Thai Buddhists to observe them (2006, 124). The fact that the village that Eberhardt worked in is ethnically Shan and not Thai does not obviate the importance of her study for this chapter for three reasons: (1) that many urban Thai Buddhists flock to Mae Hong Son to witness *pabbajja* ceremonies, like others do to Luang Phrabang in Laos to observe Bun Phravet, indicates that what they hope to see represents something of an ideal vision of Buddhist religious culture as they envisage it;[15] (2) despite the predominance of ethnic Shans, Mae Hong Son is very much a part of Thailand—children are taught to venerate the monarchy, education is conducted in Thai exclusively, and the local *sangha*, like all local Buddhist temples in Thailand, comes under the supervision of the national clerical hierarchy with its regional and national offices; and (3) much of what Eberhardt observes within the context of "her Shan village," might also be found characteristically in some Thai villages in the northern regions of the country.

While Hayashi and Tambiah have determined that annually celebrating the *Vessantara Jataka* (Bun Phravet) and the gift-giving rite of *kathina* are easily the most important annual rites celebrated in the Isan northeast, Eberhardt says that "most Shan would surely rank this ritual as one of their most important and enjoyable customs, a ceremony that is anticipated with great excitement and remembered long afterward with pride and pleasure" (2006, 124). Her analysis of ordination in Thailand is unique, insofar as she focuses on the role of the sponsor instead of on the candidate and thereby emphasizes its merit-making significance, as well as the manner in which it plays out in relation to the articulation of wealth, generosity, and prestige. What Eberhardt finds important within the village context contrasts sharply with what transpires during *pabbajja* ordinations at urban Wat Phra Dhammakaya just outside of Bangkok.

Just as Wells mentioned in his description of the ordination process dating back to the 1930s through the 1950s, the formal ordination procedure in Mae Hong Son is preceded by a *sukhwan* (soul-calling) rite and then the "leave-taking" rite emulating Prince Siddhartha's departure. In this way, the powers intrinsic to the bedrock principles of religious culture, the spirit cults,[16] are marshaled into support for the occasion, before the paradigmatic significance of the "first monk," the Buddha, is invoked. The former rite prepares the candidate to be at "his best" to assume his profile as an imminent "son of the Buddha." I can think of no better instance in Theravada Buddhist Southeast Asian Buddhist religious culture in which the "culture hero" status of the Buddha is so conspicuously articulated. From Eberhardt's point of view, however, the candidate is a rather passive player in the ritual drama that is unfolding, literally just going along for the ride. The catalyst for the entirety of the series of ritual proceedings, and the one for whom merit will most fundamentally accrue, is the sponsor of the *pabbajja*. As Eberhardt says, by becoming a sponsor,

> one is temporarily setting oneself up as a lord (tsao . . . "lord/owner of the ritual" or "master of ceremonies") with those who attend being placed either in the role of the "recipient of offerings" (usually monks and/or temple sleepers[17]) or in the role of helpers and dependents (everyone else). As such, the sponsor takes on all of the usual obligations and privileges inherent in the senior role of any hierarchical relationship for the duration of the ceremony—most notably, to look after and provide for one's dependents while retaining the right to direct their labor. (2006, 125–126)

Becoming a *tsao*, or *chao*, signifies a position of power in the village. The *chao* is normally the village headman, and in the spirit cults that dominate from northern to northeastern Thailand and throughout Laos, it means being the human counterpart or "double" of the village deity, since the traditional political structure of the village (*ban*) and region (*muang*) is replicated in the projected supernatural pantheon. Indeed, after the *sukhwan* and "great departure" ceremonial moments, the next ritual occasion consists of a pre-dawn visit to the village guardian deity shrine to ask for help and protection, to insure that the rite will have good weather and that no fighting will break out for the duration of the festival. By becoming a *chao* temporarily, the sponsor is a social counterpart parallel to the power of the village deity.

While some boys may pester their parents to be ordained, others are recruited by eager sponsors waiting for the opportunity to make merit (Eberhardt 2006, 127). Preparations begin weeks in advance for what becomes three days of festival. Eberhardt says that women talk about these arrangements in the same way that some American mothers of the bride talk about the details and share the excitement of wedding plans (personal communication). She says that without a doubt it is the women who drive the planning, organization, and responsibility for monastic *pabbajja* ordinations in the village. "[W]omen clearly regard it as an anticipated rite of passage for themselves, a 'ritual of maternity' or, even more broadly, a ritual of middle age to which any woman (whether she was literally a mother or not) could aspire" (139). Moreover, there is a

> long-standing inclination to regard novice ordinations as somehow emblematic of Shan culture and because of the increasing tourist traffic in Mae Hong Son Province, which has reinforced this link and made the ritual into an icon of "Shan-ness." Hence, women regard the task of putting on an ordination festival as one that is fraught with significance for the entire group, not just for them personally (as sponsors) or for the boys who are being ordained. (140)

Mae kham (mother-sponsor) is how women sponsors are referred to during the three days of rites, and Eberhardt notes that a woman's reputation is on the line when she decides to be a main sponsor, as if the ritual is really about them. As she notes, "achieving the title of *mae kham* is about as good as it gets" (141).

It is because of these observations about the importance of *mae kham* that Eberhardt questions the traditional interpretation of novice ordinations as genuine rites of passage, at least in modernizing circumstances. First, the young male candidates are increasingly ordained at an earlier age, even as early as ten years old, before they have truly entered into a physical or mental liminality.[18] They still remain within the orbits of their families following the rite. So, Eberhardt wonders, what passage or transition are they really making? Citing several reasons for why the rite has become truly more symbolic than transitional socially for the candidates, she argues (2006, 141–143) that the *pabbajja* ritual is more about "reciprocity" between son and mother, another way in which the mother intensely nurtures the son (even during the short period of novice time, the mothers visit once a day to check on their child's well-being and also arrive with food). Of course, what is eventually expected in return is that the son will care for the mother in old age. In a time of modernization, when women are asserting themselves more progressively, Eberhardt notes with irony, "Adult women will continue to try to use the ceremony for their own ends, in ways that are meaningful to them, but in so doing they risk reinscribing the very categories of gender difference they seek to transcend" (144). In other words, while they exercise power through their sponsorship of what is perhaps one of the most traditional of Thai Buddhist rituals, that power does not necessarily translate into forms of gender equality that some are now hoping to realize in these modern times.

There are two other dimensions in play here that I wish to highlight: (1) how *pabbajja* has become an occasion for reciprocity not just between mother and son, but between families within the village context; and (2) that *pabbajja* is understood very often as an occasion for a village-wide festival and, in so being, reinforces a community identity rooted in Buddhism (a young man becomes a monk) and the local spirit cults (which assures prosperity and goodwill among the villagers).

With regard to reciprocity beyond the mother-son relation, Bunnag (1973, 39) noted that gifts during the *pabbajja* establish reciprocity between families within the village, and a rupture can occur if one side does not reciprocate at an equivalent level. Eberhardt also raises this issue and notes that villagers are very mindful about who has contributed to what particular occasion, so a culture of expectation arises when it is one's own turn to be reciprocated. At the same time, there is a substantial economic risk involved in being the primary sponsor of a *pabbajja* ordination. According to Eberhardt, the generosity that is required or demanded by the occasion fosters a sense of "detachment toward material loss" (2006, 135); "being a sponsor entails some risk. People want to do it—for the merit and for the prestige—but they don't want it to bankrupt them" (133). There can be "major" and "minor" sponsors who are trying to articulate generosity to make merit. Merit, prestige and money are inextricably linked (ibid.). This final point needs to be underscored in light of the rather spectacular materialization and commodification of culture that has occurred during the past generation. As noted, Eberhardt has compared the planning that now occurs among women for a *pabbajja* as similar to how American mothers sometimes get so enthusiastically involved with the planning of a daughter's wedding. I think that is a very apt comparison, insofar as weddings in the United States have become commodified to the extent that a significant industry now caters to aspirations that, like *pabbajja*, are concerned with wealth, status, or prestige of the family. In this Thai Buddhist religious context, the amount of merit earned and distributed is tied to the grandeur achieved during the occasion. *Pabbajja*, while affirming community identity and constituting a rite of passage for the candidate or the sponsor, particularly for *mae kham*, remains basically a merit-making occasion. What is new now within the contemporary scene is that the merit-making occasion has become so materialized. Gifting has become extravagant by traditional standards.

One final point about reciprocity can be raised here. As Eberhardt notes, if the sponsor is not one's own parents or relations and is an eager and more well-to-do member of the community, the candidate "may also end up joining that household and working for them for a while after he completes his stay in the monastery" (2006, 131). In other words, the quid pro quo aspect of the rite can also be extended in terms of relations between the candidate (and his family) and a sponsor. What this clearly indicates is that reciprocity is cashed out within the context of hierarchy, hierarchy determined by relative wealth. In this sense, being a sponsor represents an opportunity not just to contribute to a reaffirmation of community or village identity and solidarity—in the process having contributed to the sustenance of the Buddhasasana and the coming-of-age of a young man— but rather

> ordination festivities signal a suspension of everyday social reality and cast something of a feudal overtone on the event, a romanticized longing for a village ordered by ideal hierarchical relationships that is expressed in people's descriptions and memories of past ordination festivals. In this Camelot-like nostalgic reverie, the wealthy and powerful protect the poor and weak. In this sense, ordinations can be seen as an exercise in utopia building and sponsors are implicitly challenged to meet requirements for being "king" (or "queen") for a day. (Eberhardt 2006, 132)

It is precisely this community-wide and traditional understanding of village life that is completely transcended within the ultramodern context of ritual at Wat Phra Dhammakaya in Bangkok. In that context, there is also a relative eclipse of the importance of the mother and/or primary sponsor that is so amplified in the village context. The focus is trained, rather, upon the candidate himself, as well as upon the temple as a beneficiary of his monkhood.

PABBAJJA AT WAT PHRA DHAMMAKAYA

The rise of Wat Phra Dhammakaya from a branch meditation center affiliated with a minor Bangkok Mahanikai temple in 1970 to Thailand's single largest and most heavily endowed Buddhist institution[19] with at least fifty-seven centers located worldwide in twenty-three countries has been as spectacular as the transformation of Thailand's domestic economy itself. Indeed, the two have arisen in tandem, the former impossible to contemplate without the latter. In part, because of Wat Phra Dhammakaya's emphasis on how wealth is a reflection of successful merit-making and its avowed affirmation of personal and institutional prosperity, the temple has drawn severe criticism from many quarters of Thai society as an institution that fosters the kinds of consumptive values that have corrupted modern Thailand.[20]

For this reason perhaps some readers would be critical of my decision to focus on Wat Phra Dhammakaya in this chapter dedicated to a study of ordination rituals in Thai Buddhism: that Dhammakaya is simply not representative enough of the whole, or that it is an embarrassing representation of Thai Buddhism. That is a fair criticism, one with which I could agree. On the other hand, my theoretical interest in illustrating how religious culture is affected by social, economic, and political changes in Theravada-dominated societies is extremely well illustrated by this particular focus. Wat Phra Dhammakaya is quintessentially modern, and yet it is a modernity that is also articulated in a style that is quintessentially Thai. The *wat*'s very skillful and sleek use of media (beautifully designed books and professionally produced films, as well as slickly produced radio and television programs broadcast on its own platforms of dissemination), its effective proselytization and marketing techniques, its unabashed emphasis on materiality as a sign of sincerely practiced religiosity, its corporate structure and highly disciplined organization (the leading monk, Phra Dhammachayo, has an MBA), the spectacular futuristic and modernist architecture of its sprawling campus just outside of sprawling Bangkok, its international or global outreach and appeal (particularly in the United States, Europe, and Japan, where it has established the vast majority of its centers), and, as I will show, its sophisticated articulation of ritual on a massive scale, are all reflective of the leading edges of contemporary Thai culture and society. Wat Phra Dhammakaya has been likened sometimes to Protestant Christian mega-churches of America and to the contemporary Buddhist Sokka Gakkai movement in Japan, because of its successful use of media in the first instance and its aggressive, this-worldly approach, constitutive of its religious claims, in the second. While some of its teachings, especially at the advanced level of instruction, are no doubt controversial and undoubtedly heterodox, the ritual and social life and aims of the temple remain thoroughly rooted in Theravada, given its emphasis on meditation, merit-making, the manner in which traditionally observed rites are orchestrated, and its concern for sustaining peace in Thailand and in the world at large.

While Wat Phra Dhammakaya is very effective at marketing its brand by means of the latest media technology (film, radio, television, and print), it also relies on the staunch dedication of its *upasaka*s and *upasika*s to recruit new followers to the throngs who are already within its fold. In months preceding the first of two *pabbajja* "seasons," which usually culminates in March when schools are on vacation, squads of laity fan out

Figure 3.03. Mahacedi at Wat Phra Dhammakaya

throughout Thailand to shopping malls and market areas to set up information booths replete with glossy literature for prospective novice candidates. In addition to its "full-court-press" approach through the media and
through personal proselytizing, several advantages for potential novices,
or even full ordination, are emphasized. Perhaps of greatest importance,
in terms of advantages, is that ordination is free. When I asked the temple's
respected director of communications why families would opt for *pabbajja*
observances at Wat Phra Dhammakaya rather than in their home village
or in urban neighborhood temples, his first response was exactly that: the
ritual observance is free. None of the extensive and time-consuming process of logistical planning for a village-wide ceremony is necessary for the
families of the candidates either, nor the great financial outlay entailed in
providing for expensive preparations. All food for the occasion, usually
one of the premium costs for staging a village-wide *pabbajja*, is provided
gratis by the *wat*. Indeed, virtually all the expenses usually involved in
supplying provisions for attendant monks are not necessary either. Moreover, the rites are performed in an elegant and decidedly upscale style, and
on a stage in a venue that is quintessentially modern (or even futuristic),
not to mention sophisticated. Indeed, the scale of the rites is on the massive

side (in July approximately ten thousand candidates were ordained), thereby affording the candidates and their families a sense of belonging to a community that is big and grand, an experience that seems to foster a national, or even international, conceptual horizon.

What may be sacrificed in terms of intimacy on the village level is replaced by what might be called a kind of socially transcendent experience on another. There is no worry about having to sustain an ethic of reciprocity with other villagers either. The focus of the rite is on the merit-making activities of the individual novice. The occasion also remains entirely recognizable as a Buddhist rite. Wat Phra Dhammakaya takes great pains to link itself with the deep traditions of ritual within an imagined Theravada past, but its arc also stretches the experience of its participants into the future. (A description of the ordination rites is provided below to illustrate specifically this important point.)

During my fieldwork stints at Wat Phra Dhammakaya, I was fortunate to gain a two-hour interview with the senior *bhikkhu* responsible for the *wat*'s recruiting efforts,[21] as well as a second interview with the temple's director of communications. The former afforded me with a detailed picture of the overall recruitment strategy deployed by the *wat*, couching its rationale within the present context of modern Thai society. In what follows, I attempt to reproduce, as faithfully as I can, the substance of his remarks.

He began by noting that, while the Thai government still provides a three-month leave for any aspirant publicly employed who wants to ordain into the *samanera* novitiate, private business has not followed suit. Moreover, with the spread of public education in the twentieth century, the traditional function of the *wat* as a provider of education has atrophied (a point previously stressed by Hayashi and the head monk and the retired principal at Wat Phra Singh in Chiang Mai), and the amount of time that can be spent in the *wat* has diminished for school-aged boys, largely restricted to vacation times in the academic year. From the perspective of Wat Phra Dhammakaya, the result of this reduced amount of time available for religious education in the *wat* has meant a lessening of ties to the *sangha*, and a weaker understanding of what it means to be a monk and how the *dhamma* is understood and cultivated within Thai society at large. Wat Phra Dhammakaya monastic leaders believe that social problems have mounted in Thailand because fewer novices are spending enough time in the *sangha* to understand how observance of the *dhamma* can help foster the moral values that preserve a healthy order in society.

With this understanding in mind, Wat Phra Dhammakaya's strategic plan has been to institute two programs that serve as preliminary types

Figure 3.04. Video screen showing ten thousand *pabbajja* candidates at Wat Phra Dhammakaya, July 2015

of experiences that encourage youth to observe its much more substantial *samanera* novitiate, a novitiate that consists of seven full weeks: three weeks in preparation for *pabbajja*, during which time the candidates observe the eight precepts and prepare for the *pabbajja* ritual occasion itself, and then four weeks consisting of a full introduction to monastic life, with an emphasis on meditation. Many other temples in Thailand have reduced the novitiate experience to seven days or even less, he observed. Traditionally, youth entered the *sangha* for a full rain-retreat season that is three months in duration, and this assumption is still in play when the temple holds its *pabbajja* rites at the beginning of *phansa*, usually in July. Because this is proving impractical in the contemporary context, Wat Phra Dhammakaya is attempting to utilize the entire school vacation period, while encouraging its novices to return to the *wat* for further training when more time becomes available to them, possibly during rain-retreat seasons if possible.

In any case, he proceeded to describe two programs that have been rather successfully instituted to recruit would-be *samaneras*, in addition

Figure 3.05. Seated senior ordained monks facing ten thousand *pabbajja* candidates at Wat Phra Dhammakaya, July 2015

to the media campaigns and the personal proselytizing mentioned above. These include the Path of Progress program and the V-Star Project ("V" stands for "virtue"). In the Path of Progress program, copies of the *Mangala Sutta* are distributed widely in the public schools, with children urged to study the text with an aim to writing an essay that competes for a "Dhamma Prize" and a monetary scholarship. Competitions are held in each of the five major regions of the country. Winners receive an inscribed plaque noting the King of Thailand's recognition of their achievement and are thereby admitted into the competition of the World Peace Ethical Contest, which involves a competition with others who have submitted essays from Dhammakaya's extensive number of international centers. The final award is made on Macha Puja. The program was initiated in the mid-1990s and has involved more than ten million youth since its inception. The V-Star Project aims at trying to motivate students to put *dhamma* into practice; that is, to engage in social work for the benefit of society. Students are encouraged to record their efforts in social work in their own record books, a kind of karmic scorecard. This practice is perfectly congruent with the manner in which Wat Phra Dhammakaya stresses the importance of merit-making. Awards for the most significant record of projects are made each December at Wat Phra Dhammakaya, and monetary scholarships are also awarded. A movie about the benefits of heaven and the harrows of hell is shown during the award ceremony. All of this is undertaken to encourage youth to return to the *wat* to see the fruits of their labor being recognized and, more importantly, to return to the temple eventually to undertake the *pabbajja* novitiate.

The monk also said that the temple has also attempted to widen the scope of its participatory rites to encourage more attendance by laity. For instance, a distinct "hair-cutting" rite is now emphasized at the outset of the preliminary *pabbajja* period, to attract more lay followers to the temple for more than one occasion.

The *wat* has also tried to streamline or to eliminate the many ancillary forms of social gatherings that traditionally have accompanied *pabbajja* rites in the village. For instance, no gambling is permitted, nor the killing of buffaloes to feed the expected throngs, nor is there record-keeping of what has been given by respective families in the village on previous occasions, and so on. Instead, the *wat* emphasizes the importance of meditation. Thus, it would seem as if there has been a kind of shearing off of the social dimension of ordination rites, so that the entire side of "popular religious culture," including the *sukhwan* rite, the "great departure" processions, and the invocation of the powers of the village guardian deities have been eliminated from or dissociated from *pabbajja*. In that sense, Wat Phra Dhammakaya's ritual proceedings reflect something of the neo-Orientalist forms of Buddhism that characterize a number of urban *wat*s, a type of Buddhism that seeks to empower the individual, in this case through merit-making rather than seeking to gain power through rites addressed to deities or spirits, or rites that are clearly matters of sympathetic magic. Wat Phra Dhammakaya styles itself and its ritual performances as quintessentially modern. Indeed, at the massive ordination ceremony I observed in March 2015, a well-known monk from one of Bangkok's major temples, who delivered the key sermon, stressed that while it would appear on the surface that participating in the *pabbajja* rite makes one a monk, monks are really made by practicing meditation assiduously in the weeks that follow. As I mentioned earlier, the *wat* strongly emphasizes the practice of meditation, and some of the novices, if they are beyond the school age, may stay on in the temple to study Pali after the conclusion of the post *pabbajja* four-week period. In these cases, the temple might also initiate them into a job-training program for work at the temple. There is a sense that by nurturing the individual novice, the temple as well will eventually benefit.

The head monk of recruitment also mentioned that the *wat* has also instituted a pilot summer program of study and meditation in which 40 percent of the recruits end up staying on in the temple to contribute to its mission. The general figure for *pabbajja* novices staying on in the *wat* is 10 percent. Both figures are far beyond those that obtain for the average *wat*, village or urban. Wat Phra Dhammakaya has also launched a national initiative to ordain one hundred thousand novices over a period of several years. This follows the initiative to ordain over one hundred thousand monks through *upasampada* that was launched several years back. When rites are scheduled they are held en masse, which I think is a key indicator contrasting its ordination rites with how they have traditionally been transacted. Wat Phra Dhammakaya aims to achieve the monumental, not the intimate. It aspires to be an international movement, not only a traditional fixture in the village context. Every initiative undertaken is envisaged on a grand scale. For instance, its so-called *thudong* monks engage in a month-long pilgrimage around Thailand during the month of January, supported by legions of accompanying lay supporters. The point of the pilgrimage is not only to showcase the disciplined asceticism of some of the *wat*'s ordained monks, but it also constitutes an impressive local presence wherever its path leads and indirectly leads to recruitment efforts. While it is focused on the possible repossession of Thailand's approximately 6,500 abandoned temples, it also fosters levels of material support for the *wat*'s many other programs. Wat Phra Dhammakaya has been extremely effective at soliciting financial support from its dedicated laity, especially the elderly, sometimes earning criticism from its vocal detractors in the process.

In addition, there are programs that have been instituted at the *wat* to train *upasika*s, a development that, as far as I know, is unique to Wat Phra Dhammakaya. These programs are basically extensions of traditional meditation retreats. Their aim ostensibly is to bring more women to the same level of understanding of the *dhamma* as men. The head recruiter monk said that this is another example of the *wat*'s overall goal to "change the world," in this case to promote more gender equality in the realization of *dhamma*. Yet, one would not find any *mae ji*s at Wat Phra Dhammakaya, nor has the temple offered any overt support for the movement to establish an order of *bhikkhuni*s in Thailand, despite the fact that the devotee who perfected and then sustained the original meditation regimen of Luang Pho (the controversial founder of Dhammakaya) was Kuhn Yay, a female devotee for whom an impressive modern-styled stupa in the campus has been constructed as a memorial. Kuhn Yay actually relocated her fledgling meditation practice to Pathum Thani, the site where the eventual massive Wat Phra Dhammakaya campus was built under the leadership of Phra Dhammachayo,[22] the longtime entrepreneurial incumbent.

With this extended backdrop, I turn now to my account of the ritual activity constitutive of the *pabbajja* ceremony that I observed in March 2015, during the school vacation at Wat Phra Dhammakaya, and then contrast it with what I observed at the beginning of the rain-retreat season in July.

At 6 a.m., lay dignitaries of the temple, along with candidates for ordination, who were organized according to their ages (meaning that men who appeared to be approaching their seventies were in the lead and young children who were no more than five years old brought up the rear), and family supporters bearing requisite gifts, all lined up collectively in a disciplined orderly procession in front of the Maha Cedi to hear a brief sermon on "finding the light within" and benefiting from the merit that was about to accrue from this auspicious occasion. "Finding the light within" refers to the practice of meditation that focuses on a crystal ball of truth that exists at the seven bases of the mind, the ultimate base in the abdomen area of the body. The crystal ball is emblematic of the *dhammakaya*, or the true self, or the true mind.[23]

While the programs that I have described above yield some recruits, the majority of novices come mostly from Bangkok, but also from all over Thailand, given the national reputation of the *wat* as the country's largest and most "modern." Many have been recruited by lay followers who, as I mentioned earlier, have set up information booths in their hometowns and villages in the weeks preceding *pabbajja*. The temple is so successful that it schedules two dates, two weeks apart, for *pabbajja* ordinations in order to accommodate the number of aspirants. No less than two thousand were ordained on the date I observed, and they were accompanied by at least ten thousand well-wishing relations and friends.

Some candidates were present for a second or third time and had signed up for a more advanced preparatory program, or they were assisting with the training of first-timers. Indeed, laity often recruit these returners as well. Once the brief sermon concluded, recorded chanting issued from the loudspeaker system and an orderly circumambulation of the great stupa commenced. At 8 a.m., the candidates and their parents, along with other merit-sharing well-wishers, took up positions in a massive hall, replete with five large wall-mounted wide flat-screen video monitors.

Here, media technology thoroughly abetted the ritual experience, and what impressed me in this context was the combination of emphasis on

Figure 3.06. Pabbajja candidates venerate Mahacedi before circumambulation, at Wat Phra Dhammakaya, March 2015

Figure 3.07. Circumambulating the Mahacedi

Figure 3.08. Laity bearing robes to be given while circumambulating Mahacedi

meditation and technology that made this experience so unique in comparison to village rites. With the five screens simultaneously featuring scenes within the hall, many candidates had their "moments in the sun," as it were, when they were featured on the big screens. In many ways, this session constituted the central moments for *pabbajja*, wherein the candidates received their robes and bowls from their parents. Each candidate had been carefully assigned a number, and all were neatly organized in long rows to take up their positions just opposite their parents.

The parents and friends were first urged to purify themselves in body, speech, and mind before they prostrated and made their offerings to the soon-to-be novices in a sort of moment of "mini-meditation" shared by all. An impressive sermon followed, by a very well-known Bangkok senior monk who emphasized first how, on this occasion, it was incumbent on the candidates to feel gratitude to their parents. He continued by stressing the importance of cultivating the correct form or etiquette involved in becoming a monk, learning how to move and to posture properly, to become an embodiment of the presence of the *dhamma*. That is, the proper observance

Figure 3.09. Pabbajja candidates take up positions amid families in ordination hall

Figure 3.10. Novices listen to sermon following robe investiture and taking of precepts

of the form that *dhamma* takes is in the details constituting *vinaya* observance of precepts. (Parenthetically, the newly acquired capabilities of novices at Wat Phra Dhammakaya to comport themselves in a composed and graceful manner compared very favorably to other struggling novices I often observed at temples in Bangkok and in Chiang Mai in the days and weeks before and after the *pabbajja* at Wat Phra Dhammakaya. These other novices, obviously, had not benefited from a comparable regimen of training.)

This type of mindful observance, the master monk said, only enhances the merit that will be given to parents. He further emphasized that Wat Phra Dhammakaya ordains monks not merely as a matter of convenience, or simply as a rite of passage, but demands that candidates study the procedures (*vinaya*) and learn how to study and practice meditation, the important ways of discerning *dhamma*. He went on to stress that, unlike other temples that merely provide seven days or less of instruction, Wat Phra Dhammakaya actually provides for a seven-week program, three weeks in preparation for *pabbajja* and then another four weeks of practice. He asserted that it is this depth of training that produces Buddhists who

Figure 3.11. Novices venerated by families

are imbued with *saddha* (faith, confidence) and who can contribute to the preservation of Buddhism and the moral maintenance of Thai society. Insofar as this is the goal of *pabbajja* on the social level, he emphasized that the meditation program emphasizes how *samatha* (calm) and *vipassana* (insight) are the methods of cultivation for the individual to understand *anicca* (change) of the body. The sermon, impressive in terms of substance, was also delivered with an accomplished style that riveted the attention of all who were present.

The monastic saffron robes were then received following the sermon, and the candidates, after donning them, received the ten precepts that they would then observe during the remainder of their time at the temple. They were now observant Buddhist monks. The taking of the precepts was then followed by the reception of alms bowls from parents. Now equipped with the traditional requisites, a session of chanting ensued, during which the transfer of merit to parents was transacted.

The entire ritual procedure seemed to me to involve a push and pull between appeals to the core and "ancient teaching" of Buddhism on the one hand, and an appeal to modernity, technology, and organized discipline on the other.

The sequence of events for the *pabbajja* program was being filmed and then edited for television broadcast on Wat Phra Dhammakaya's international TV channel. There was also available a short but well-illustrated booklet titled *The Ordination* that contains firsthand accounts of the transformative nature of Dhammakaya practice. It contained the following declarative and provocative sentence at its beginning: "The ritual of ordination is a process whereby the individual raises his level of consciousness and transcends from being a follower of the Triple Gem, to becoming a part of the Triple Gem."

There are, of course, great similarities with the *pabbajja* held in July, including the initial early morning circumambulation of the stupa and the monumental efforts made for filming the rite for international consumption. There was also an impressive sermon delivered by a renowned Bangkok monk. But the purported purpose of the July occasion was rationalized in a fundamentally institutionalized way. Over ten thousand candidates, rather than approximately two thousand, were present. Of these, almost one hundred (eighty-seven) came from internationally located affiliated Dhammakaya temples in fourteen countries. They were provided with headsets so that the Thai portions of the ceremony could be translated for them into either Chinese or English. Instead of donning robes in the presence of parents, one hundred fully ordained *bhikkhus* raised the robes of these ten thousand candidates.

Figure 3.12. Robe investiture during July 2015 mass ordination

One of the major differences between the March and July *pabbajja*s was that virtually no family members were present for this latter occasion, and the rhetoric informing the July observance was clearly oriented toward the individual or toward the temple. Moreover, in the July instance, *pabbajja* was clearly being understood as a temporary ordination preceding *upas-ampada*, with the assumption that following *pabbajja*, most of these ordi-nands would return to village contexts to spend the rain-retreat season in intensive study and meditation. So, the July *pabbajja* was a far more serious affair than what had transpired in March and seemed far more directed toward sustaining the expanding fortunes of the temples' corporate body. While almost all of the ten thousand ordinands would be returning to branch or affiliate temples throughout Thailand, the dozens of foreigners would be divided into two separate groups according to their preference for Chinese or English. These groups would pursue specially designed study and meditation routines for the duration of *phansa* in Pathum Thani before returning to their home countries as full-fledged *bhikkhus*.

It would be tempting to assert that, in contrasting village iterations of *pabbajja* with what transpires at Wat Phra Dhammakaya, the latter raises merit-making to almost a soteriological level for the individual, at least, the possibility of its pursuance. Also very contrastive is that its venue consists of an almost futuristic setting, one that has been constructed thanks to a relentless program of institutional solicitation. While, in village contexts, an ethic of reciprocity governs the exchange of material gifts and merit, at Wat Phra Dhammakaya the recipients of benefit are unequivocally the individual on the one hand and the institution on the other. While merit-transfer for parents is also enacted within the ritual context during the March *pabbajja* at Wat Phra Dhammakaya, it is the regimen of learning *dhamma* and becoming a proper monk that is emphasized in all of the temple's ordination ritual contexts. Moreover, it is the corporate institution (Wat Phra Dhammakaya) that will benefit ultimately from this attainment of monkhood and the donations that it receives from grateful parents who have been impressed by the elegance and elaborateness of the ritual proceedings, no doubt at least partially thankful for being excused from the intense set of social obligations that attend to a more traditionally transacted *pabbajja*. The temple has shielded them from the economic and emotional intensity of that experience. Inasmuch as it has provided, the temple has also benefited from, a potential long-term relationship with the novitiate and his family. In the end, as an icon of modernity in the Thai context, Wat Phra Dhammakaya provides convenience, efficiency, rationality, and economy for its aspirants and their families, while stressing the importance of the individual cultivating an awareness of *dhamma* through meditation and disciplined behavior. It has also realized an international or global presence.

THE ORDINATION OF WOMEN

In a previous section of this chapter on the important role played by women as sponsors of *pabbajja* rites, it became quite clear that women are very active players in the ritual processes constitutive of Thai Buddhist religious culture. Nancy Eberhardt has gone so far as to say that *pabbajja* ordinations in "her village" in Mae Hong Son function as kind of rite of passage for middle-aged married women. Moreover, anyone who has lived for some time in Sri Lanka, Myanmar, and Thailand knows the extent to which *dasa sil matas*, *thila shin*, and *mae ji* are now a conspicuous and important presence in many Buddhist temples and pilgrimage sites.

In Sri Lanka, I have participated in a number of *pabbajja* ceremonies for *dasa sil matas* over the years, and have also come to know the way many individual "nuns" are so very highly regarded by sections of the lay Buddhist community. In interviewing a number of laity about why they support the *aramaya*s of *dasa sil mata*s, I have been told consistently that these women earn respect as a consequence of their piety and that becoming a "nun," unlike becoming a monk, has no societal advantages in comparison. There are no special statuses given to "nuns," such as preferences for university admission, a well-heeled lifestyle in a well-endowed Kandy or Colombo monastery, or even a special seat on public buses. Moreover, just a casual notation of the demographic of people who frequent temples regularly, especially on full moon days, or who are the people who prepare or give alms to monks, will indicate that women actually form the backbone of Buddhist cultic life in the religious cultures of Theravada-dominated countries. It should then come as no surprise that some women of piety have aspired to undertake the religious life in a fashion that is as serious as possible. That is, some have sought to revive the tradition of the *bhikkhunisangha*, the order of nuns that thrived in Sri Lanka from the third century BCE to the tenth century CE. While the order died out in Sri Lanka, with the Tamil Cola invasions of Anuradhapura from South India probably its death knell, the tradition was sustained throughout China and to a lesser extent in Korean and Japanese history. A robust lineage of fully ordained Buddhist nuns continues today, especially in Taiwan. Amid great controversy, Sri Lankan *dasa sil mata*s have been ordained recently into this *bhikkhuni* lineage, and a high-profile *bhikkhuni* ordination (discussed below) has occurred in Thailand as well.

As social change accompanying the "modernization process"[24] has affected Thai society in general, the transformation of women's roles in society, in the family, in the workplace, and in education has taken place in various degrees as well. While Thailand remains an overwhelmingly agrarian society, its cities, especially Bangkok, Chiang Mai, Khon Kaen, Udon Thani, and the like have been venues where women have self-consciously stepped out of traditional normative family roles to stake a claim for greater autonomy and self-definition. Some have sought to warrant their new assertions of power and identity within a Theravada Buddhist worldview, the episteme that unquestionably continues to dominate modern Thai society. Nowhere has this been seen more clearly than in the controversy surrounding the ordination of Buddhist women into the *sangha*, an issue that has also become a major focus of attention in Sri Lanka.[25]

Chatsumarn Kabilsingh, a Buddhist studies academic who later was ordained as a *bhikkhuni*, has written about antecedent efforts, beginning in the earlier decades of the twentieth century, aimed at the establishment of *bhikkhuni upasampada* ordinations, efforts that led to the arrest of the young women who dared to defy the prohibitions of the Thai *sangha* and state. She has also detailed the spiritual career of Voramai Kabilsingh who, in 1957, established the first temple in Thailand by and for women. The temple also supported an orphanage and was active in promoting the welfare needs of the local *sangha*. Eventually, in 1971, Voramai was "the first Thai woman to have received full ordination as a *bhikkhuni* in the Dharmagupta subsect of the Theravada tradition" (Kabilsingh 1991, 52). Nonetheless, "[t]o the general public in Thailand, Vorami is still only a mae ji. To the Thai Sangha, her status at best was that of a Mahayana *bhikkhuni*, and she is not considered [to have been a] part of the Theravada tradition. The Thai Sangha believes the Theravada order of *bhikkhuni*s is extinct and cannot be revived from Chinese Mahayana tradition" (ibid.).[26] Kabilsingh also reviewed the founding of the Institute of Thai Mae Jis in the 1960s that was established at Wat Boronives, a royally established and favored Thammayut temple in central Bangkok, where the current king spent two weeks as a novice in the 1950s. The institute was founded for the purpose of uniting and organizing *mae ji*s throughout Thailand—an umbrella organization with many branches throughout the country. The institute regularly holds *dhamma* talks and publishes a quarterly, the *Mae Ji Sarn*. "One of its most important functions is to establish guidelines and monitor the activities of its members, in order to reduce the number of those who create a bad image for the mae ji and the institute. This is especially important for raising the public esteem and support for mae jis" (55). Patronized by the queen of Thailand, the institute has established youth centers, provided teachers for Buddhist Sunday Schools, and helps with refugees on the eastern border with Cambodia as well as with natural disasters. Kabilsingh has also described how the Santi Asoke movement in the 1960s established nunneries and began ordaining nuns who are *sikhamat*, brown-robed renunciants who are ten-precept holders. (Their numbers in the Santi Asoke are restricted to one-fourth of the number of monks.)

In an article that Kabilsingh was asked to write about prostitution in Thailand, a piece that later became a book chapter, she made the following very pointed observation: "It is interesting to note the resemblance in the reasoning of both prostitutes and mae jis for their life choices. Due to 'gratitude' or obligation, some women become prostitutes to repay their parents materially, while others choose to become mae jis to repay their parents spiritually, offering them the merit of their religious activities" (1991, 78). Other researchers have noted that many of the prostitutes in Bangkok and Pattaya come from Isan, the poorest part of the country, and that a good deal of their remunerations, whatever they can afford, are sent back to support their families in rural villages, who remain unaware of the source from which these remittances are derived. What Kabilsingh's comment reveals is the deep sense of obligation that more traditionally oriented Thais continue to feel for the family unit, especially daughters for parents. Kabilsingh's main issue in pointing out the parallel is that merit and money are both understood fundamentally as transferable currencies.

Professor Chatsumarn Kabilsingh was ordained as Bhikkhuni Dhammananda in the spring of 2001, thereby sparking a heated debate within Thai social and monastic circles. The debate was not so much about whether men or women equally have the potential to gain awakening (*bodhi*), but rather about how reestablishing the *bhikkhuni* ordination of women could be accommodated by the *Vinaya* (Seeger 2006, 159). There is no historical evidence to suggest that a female order of *bhikkhuni*s has ever existed in Thailand. The lineage of Taiwanese nuns referred to earlier is of the Dharmaguptaka order, a Sthaviravadin sect that claims to have sustained its lineage back to the time of the Buddha. In fact, the Dharmaguptakas, like the Theravadins, are a subsect of the Sthaviravadins, and not to be mistaken as the same order or lineage. This, however, is not the manner in which Bhikkhuni Dhammananda framed her argument for the legitimation of her ordination.

When, in the 1920s, those two young women described by Kabilsingh attempted to become ordained as nuns in Thailand, the Thai *sangharaja* issued a regulation forbidding monks to ordain women as *samaneri*s (novices) or *bhikkhuni*s. This regulation is still in effect today.

As Seeger has noted,

> According to Bhikkhuni Dhammananda, this *sangha* regulation contradicts the Thai constitution which guarantees equality between men and women . . . [with regard to the] freedom to adhere to and practice any religion. Since, as Bhikkhuni Dhammananda maintains, the constitution is the highest authoritative body of laws in Thailand, the aforementioned *sangha* regulation that contradicts it is, as a matter of course, invalid. . . . At the same time, however, a *bhikkhuni* ordination in Thailand might be rendered judicially precarious by a paragraph in the Thai penal law, according to which a person who is not properly ordained, but wears the robes of clerics, can be sentenced to imprisonment no longer than one year or to a fine of not more than 20,000 Baht, or both. (2006, 160–161)

So, there remains ambiguity about the ordination of women under Thai law.

Some Thai monks have argued consistently that the Chinese lineage in Taiwan from which Bhikkhuni Dhammananda claims legitimacy is "Mahayana aided" and thereby tainted. A further impediment for Thai monks arises when considering how strictly the ritual observance of the ordination act is to be followed. Not only have properly consecrated *sima*s often been a matter of heated contestation within Theravada tradition, but the actual language of the ritual must be in Pali, the language of the Theravada's canonical texts. The Dharmaguptakas do not use Pali in their ritual transactions (Seeger 2006, 163–166), and, of course, there are no Dharmaguptaka temples with consecrated *sima*s in Thailand.

Suwanna Satha-Anand, however, a leading Buddhist studies and philosophy professor at Chulalongkorn University in Bangkok, has argued that the Buddha agreed to ordain women within the context of a patriarchal society, in the process demonstrating the need to realize the nature of ultimate truth as opposed to merely accepting conventional truths. By this, she has meant to argue that both men and women were recognized by the Buddha as capable of realizing ultimate truth, which makes the conventional truths of customary practice but a "cultural constraint." Suwanna Satha-Anand interprets the Buddha's action to ordain women as a matter of adjusting practice beyond social expediency. It also reflects the Buddha's willingness to adjust to compelling spiritual contingencies, and she urges the modern *sangha* to adjust to the social changes that have affected the emergence of women in Thai society as well. Since contemporary Thai society is more open-minded about women's issues, Suwanna demands that the *Vinaya* be changed accordingly. She says that "[t]he principle of truth over convention should serve as a basis for future feminist interpretations of Buddhist scriptures. It should also serve as a basis for institutional decisions of the *sangha* in relation to women's issues. What is at stake is not only the human rights of women, but also the philosophical universality and institutional integrity of Buddhism itself" (Satha-Anand 2001, 290). In response, leading Thai scholar-monks have asserted that to change the *Vinaya* is to risk fragmentation within the *sangha,* an assertion that is not a far-fetched reaction, insofar as, historically, schisms within the *sangha* have occurred not as a matter of doctrinal differences but precisely because of arguments about the rules of discipline, however minor they may appear to the modern mind.

Other feminists have responded to that defense by arguing that the Buddha, the ultimate authority in the tradition, never rescinded his decision to ordain women, and that to deny women ordination now is to contravene authoritative practice as sanctioned by the Buddha. Still others have argued that the order of *mae ji*s should be simply upgraded instead of pursuing the goal of *bhikkhuni* ordination, and that *mae ji*s, because of their commendable efforts in social service, would actually be

more beneficial to Thai society in general than more renunciant oriented *bhikkhuni*s.

However, or if ever, this debate about the ordination of women is resolved, there is little doubt that women are becoming ever more active
and predominant within Thai Buddhist religious culture in general. They
certainly have greater opportunities to study and practice Buddhism within
this era of modernization. It may be that many more women are gaining the
confidence and support from more and more laity, who seem to regard
the spiritual accomplishments of women as if they were fully ordained
and committed *bhikkhuni*s (Seeger 2006, 179).

ORDINATIONS OF TREES

At first sight, the robing of trees may appear to be oxymoronic, especially
to Western observers, given some of their assumptions about the beliefs
and practices constitutive of Buddhism. But within just a decade of the
first tree ordination in 1988, the practice had become an accepted way of
expressing environmental consciousness in Thailand. To be sure, the first
tree ordinations were met with much consternation, as a veritable violation of the *Vinaya* rules, since only human beings can be ordained as
monks. But as Susan Darlington points out,

> While the rituals are not ordinations in a formal sense, the image of sanc-
> tifying trees and the forest through the ritual gained national (and inter-
> national) attention, raising awareness about the difficulties people dependent
> upon the forest face. The shock value of using ritual to highlight social
> problems and challenge social power provided environmental monks with
> an effective tool to meet their goals. (2013, 11)

Darlington goes on to point out that the increasing acceptance of the practice of ritually wrapping a robe, or robe material, around a tree gained full
acceptance when, in 1996, a group of Thai nongovernmental organizations
mounted a campaign to ordain fifty million trees in honor of the Thai
king's fiftieth year of reign. Moreover, in the years that followed, the state
appropriated the practice to its own advantage. Subsequently, one can
see how the practice of enrobing stupas has become a standard practice in
the past fifteen years as well. Even old stupas that are obviously no longer
venerated may be enrobed as matter of course.

But what exactly is the point of a specifically Buddhist environmentalism reflected in the process of "ordaining" trees? Darlington, while discussing the exemplary socially engaged Buddhist views of the well-known

monk Phra Maha Chan, notes that, in general, care for the environment is seen as inextricably bound up with ameliorating the *dukkha* (suffering, unsatisfactoriness) that is a direct consequence of environmental degradation (2013, 13).

Harris has pointed out that an ecological ethic is hardly to be found in the ancient Pali literature, or *buddhavacana,* and that the adoption of such an ethic is a by-product of Buddhists importing elements from a burgeoning and globalized environmental discourse (1997, 378). That may be true, but it is also certainly a part of the modernization process. Darlington argues, that the emergence of the Buddhist ecological ethic, symbolized by the ordination of trees, is simply a reflection of how some progressive monks are "critically examining the tradition in light of contemporary situations and problems" (2013, 14). That is, they root their perspectives within the conceptuality of Buddhism, and how environmental degradation leads to the experience of *dukkha* is the precise rationale that they articulate. Insofar as *dukkha* is the first of the Buddha's four noble truths, it has been argued that assuaging that condition is perhaps the basic fundamental concern of the Buddhist religious path.

What is it that happens during the tree ordination rite per se? Obviously, unlike *upasampada* and *pabbajja,* the tree is not really transformed in its social status; rather, its sanctification is more a matter of its preservation, a recognition of its intrinsic contribution to non-suffering. Unsurprisingly, the texts used in the tree ordination rites are not the same ones used in the ordinations of monks. Rather they are the same texts used by monks to consecrate Buddha images, the celebration of the king's birthday, the protection of houses and businesses, and the like. That is, they are *paritta,* or protective chants, the most famous of which is the *Mangala Sutta.* The intrinsic power of the Pali words constituting the text is ritually transferred into the object being consecrated.[27] That is, the trees are being imbued with the power of *dhamma.*

Darlington reports that villagers have a more literal understanding of tree ordination that is reflected in how they will *wai* before an enrobed tree in the same manner in which they would signal their respect for a monk (2013, 64). I would add that it is a common staple in lay religious culture in northern and northeast Thailand and Laos that trees are often understood to be the abode of spirits, and so the tree's consecration is also understood as a way in which the spiritual force inhabiting the tree is sanctified, controlled, and channeled constructively.[28]

But what tends to get stressed in the sermons preached at tree ordinations is the interdependence between the conditions of the forest and the well-being of villagers' lives. The ordination of trees creates sacred symbols refracting the understanding that being environmentally proactive is a moral position. Protecting the forest is karmicly efficacious, while destroying the forest results in demerit (Darlington 2013, 75).

> Rituals provide a means of negotiating both the political and economic aspects of environmentalism. While rituals are only one tool used by environmental monks, they are a tool available only to the monks, thereby setting them apart from other social agents such as environmentalists and government officials. Rituals also form another bridge for the monks themselves—between a conservative practice of Buddhism and a radical interpretation that promotes social justice, change and nature conservation. (91)

In a similar vein,

> [D]evelopment monks use familiar rituals to integrate their spiritual and economic goals. They recognize the power of ritual for conveying religious values and conferring them on mundane projects, as they publicly display their acceptance of the underlying values and goals the rituals embody. (95)

What these monks have also done is to recast *dana* (giving) in a way that makes giving not so much a matter of giving for the benefit of monks or the temple, but for the general well-being of nature and society, including charity to the poor. Sizemore and Swearer (1990) have argued that a tension between nonattachment and the acquisition of wealth has existed throughout Theravada history. The key to its mediation lies in how the practice of generosity becomes a way of articulating selflessness. This is exactly what "development monks" have attempted to do in their recasting of ritual. They have also demonstrated how ritual need not be simply symbolic in nature, but can function in a truly existential manner for realizing ideals, rather than simply symbolically articulating them.

Once tree ordinations became socially and politically acceptable means of articulating religious values with ecological consequences, they also risked being co-opted by "the very same economic and political structures that they initially criticized" (Darlington 2013, 223). This was clearly the case once the king's Royal Crown Property Bureau became involved.

> Especially after the fifty-million-trees ordination project in honor of the king, the ritual became a symbol of the state and monarchy's efforts to care for the people. While the symbolic power of the king brought additional incentives for people to participate and uphold the goals of the project, the connection with the state simultaneously undermined the moral criticisms of economic development policies. (226)

Environmentally engaged monks have faced real risks from those who benefit from the policies that they criticize. Some have even been murdered. The symbolic capital that the monks have won from much of the public in their struggles to protect the agrarian rural poor from developers is considerable.

> The appropriation of the ritual symbol of the tree ordination and the assassination of environmental and social justice activists together demonstrate that these activists have touched a sensitive spot for those with power. The issues engaged monks are addressing through their rural development and environmental projects are real; people are in debt, often manipulated by those who stand to gain from their debt or cover their land. Tensions surrounding land use and water rights are real. While Buddhism provides only one response to these tensions, the popularity of tree ordination performances shows its effectiveness. Engaged Buddhist monks have influenced, and continue to influence Thai society. They have brought attention to social problems, and offered solutions. (Darlington 2013, 230)

As Tannenbaum has noted, "Tree ordinations, environmentalism, and sustainable development are now part of the rhetoric and practice of the Thai intelligentsia, development workers and politicians. In the past, tree ordinations organized by monks were part of a larger protest against modernization, capitalism, and development that were seen as destroying traditional values and ways of life" (1992, 116–117).

CONCLUSION

The aim of this chapter has been to examine the ways in which ordination rites in Thai religious culture refract the nature of rapid social, economic, and political change in modern Thailand. At least five new developments in what we might see as an "ordination tradition" have immediately stood out in the modern context of change: (1) the manner in which ordination at Wat Phra Dhammakaya, as well as in the village contexts, reflect the increased materialization of Thai society and culture; (2) how the emphasis on the individual, both in terms of the aspirant at Wat Phra Dhammakaya and the sponsor in Mae Hong Son, seem to be indications of the increasing importance of merit-making for individuals, reflecting the specter of a increased realization of individualized self-consciousness; (3) how ordination has become a contested issue with regard to the possibility of women ordaining into the *bhikkhunisangha*, a matter reflecting the rising aspirations of women to experience parity in all walks of life with men; (4) how the ordination of trees indicates the manner in which ritualization is being adapted in a new era of global environmental consciousness as key Buddhist concepts are being deployed in ever new and relevant ways; and (5) how the dynamics of ordination are implicated in contemporary political processes, the issue with which I conclude this chapter. I briefly address this issue with two recent instances.

The first instance involves how, in 2014, the leader of the People's Democratic Reform Committee, Suthep Thaugsuban, quietly became ordained in a famous monastic complex established by the reform-minded monk Buddhadasa. His ordination followed a series of political protests that he had led that ultimately resulted in enough civil strife and instability in Bangkok that the Thai military eventually made a move to disestablish the government of Prime Minister Yingluck Shinawatra in May 2014, a fate she then shared with her populist brother, who was also deposed by the military in 2006. Suthep's relentless campaigns to paralyze the government and jeopardize its hold on power—thereby impeding a good share of the capital's commerce as well—in order to generate support for what became an undemocratic change in government, resulted in loss of life for some and hardship for many others. The *Bangkok Post* speculated that

> Former PDRC spokesman Akanat Phromphan left the monkhood early this month after he had been ordained at Wat Chonprathan Rangsarit in Nonthaburi for 15 days, saying he wanted to make merit for the protesters killed during the PDRC's six-month street protests. It was speculated that Phra Suthep, as PDRC's ex-front-man, may have decided to wear the saffron robe for the same reason.[29]

Ordaining for a variety of expedient reasons, including the political, remains a means by which Thai men articulate a desire to generate power on behalf of others. It is not unusual for a close relative of a deceased, as Hayashi has pointed out, to ordain briefly as a monk in order to transfer merit, thereby assisting the dead in making a transition to the next rebirth. Suthep's action not only makes religious logic in this way, but also articulates his own moral position in paying back his erstwhile political supporters. It helps him claim a moral high ground in the contemporary political discourse.

A second overtly politically expedient use of ordination was evident when many young men ordained in late March and early April 2015, ostensibly with the idea of transferring merit to strengthen Princess Sirindhorn, whose sixtieth birthday was widely celebrated in public throughout Thailand. Pictures of the princess, who is often profiled as a promoter and preserver of Thai cultural arts, were ubiquitous in major cities throughout the country at this time. While the current laws governing succession to the ailing King Bhumibol Adelyaj favor the throne being passed on to his controversial son, the Crown Prince Vajiralongkorn, there has been significant speculation that the princess may ascend to succeed her father when he passes away. The move to mobilize mass ordinations to transfer merit on behalf of the princess was interpreted by some political observers as a move in concert with the "yellow shirts," the conservative Bangkok-based business- and royalty-oriented elite and middle class who have ceded democratic power to the Taksin-based populist movement rooted in the north and northeast, who have been thwarted twice by military coups within eight years. Insofar as the princess seems to be the successor of choice for many interests in the former political faction that seems to have become increasingly reactionary and desperate to maintain its position of dominance in the political economy, the merit made from ordination also becomes a means by which morally derived power can be generated for political cause. Making merit on behalf of the royals is not an unusual phenomenon in Thai society, as many Thais see the royal family as embodying the vitality of the nation, given their perceptions about how much the royalty has accomplished on behalf of the people. Empowering royalty by means of merit transfer generated by ordination is thus understood as a way of empowering the nation, at least this particular vision of the nation.

However *pabbajja* and *upasampada* may be construed within a strictly religious culture as sustaining the Buddhasasana, it is also clear that these rites have been appropriated to sustain social, economic, and political impulses and expectations in the modern contemporary contexts of a changing Thai society. These appropriations index the fact that Buddhism remains a powerful episteme, a congenial frame for articulating power and meaning of great relevance for the variegated interests of an evolving modern Thailand.

CHAPTER FOUR

Kathina

Making Merit in Modern Myanmar

The geographical and political region of Southeast Asia officially known to the world as Myanmar (formerly the Union of Burma) now contains a population of about fifty million people that is about 85 percent Buddhist and, with the exception of mountainous regions making up the country's borderlands, has been a site of predominantly Buddhist religious culture for at least the past thousand years.

Recently, in light of major political and economic reforms initiated in 2012 by the quasi-democratically elected government that was reluctantly put into place constitutionally by a military junta seeking more legitimacy, the country has been experiencing dramatic change. Aung San Suu Kyii and her National League for Democracy swept the elections of 2015 by taking a whopping 80 percent of the national vote and a corresponding number of eligible seats in the upper and lower houses of parliament. High expectations have followed this landslide landmark event as the actual transition to power occurred in March of 2016. Yet, according to the 2008 constitution approved under a questionable vote, the military still controls one quarter of all seats in parliament and the key ministries of defense, home, and borders. The extent to which Myanmar will function as a democracy is still a bit of an open question given the military's strategic control. But change is definitely in the offing.

Yangon (formerly Rangoon), the nation's leading city and former capital, is awash with too many Japanese reconditioned automobiles clogging its dated arterial system of roads. Dozens of new high-rises are under construction, without much regard for zoning. Tourism has multiplied graphically. While this economic growth is championed by some, the country has also been wracked by communal violence, beginning in 2012 between Arakanese Buddhists and Rohingya Muslims in the country's western Rakhine State (historically known as Arakan), and subsequently in other regions of the country, chiefly central Myanmar, where nationalist Buddhist monks have inspired aggressions against other non-Rohingya Muslim communities because they believe that, if left unchecked, the Muslim population will eventually overrun the Buddhists and the country will become another Malaysia or Indonesia. Four "race and religion laws" promoted by more militant members of the Buddhist *sangha* that are aimed at restricting religious, marital, and family planning prerogatives of Myanmar's Muslims have been passed by the country's national (and then rightest) parliament in 2015 before Daw Aung San Suu Kyii and her National League for Democracy came to power. As this book goes to press, it is too early to know exactly what political changes await Myanmar's Buddhists and Muslims, but there is hope that the NLD will prove to be more inclusive than the previous government. An eight person commission headed by former UN General Secretary Kofi Annan will make recommendations about the Buddhist/Muslim problem in the Rakhine State in 2017. Politically, Myanmar remains in a curious state of liminality.

A variety of forms of Buddhist material culture have been created continuously within the cultural space of what is now Myanmar since the beginning of the Common Era.[1] Among its many Buddhist peoples, whether Burmese (Bamar), Shan, Mon, Karen, Arakanese, or other ethnic minorities,[2] the ideology of the economy of merit, that is, the practice of merit-making in the form of giving (*dana*) that assuages conditions of *dukkha* (suffering or "unsatisfactoriness"), seems to seep ubiquitously into everyday patterns of life in sometimes the most inconspicuous and subtle ways. For instance, in urban neighborhoods of Yangon (Rangoon), Mandalay, or Mawlamyine, and also in rural villages throughout the countryside, "earthenware jugs filled with cool water for the benefit of passers-by [are a] means of earning Buddhist merit and lessening the suffering of pedestrians in the hot afternoon" (Seekins 2011, 9). That simple offering of water to those who may be in immediate need poignantly reflects the ubiquity of merit-making acts generated by generosity that permeates social life in Myanmar.

The first of the four noble truths made known by Gautama the Buddha in his original sermon, the Dhammacakkapavatta Sutta (Turning of the Wheel of Truth) in the Pali *Suttapitaka,* is that the experience of human existence is laced with *dukkha* (suffering, or unsatisfactoriness). *Dukkha* may be experienced in many forms: it may be physical, but more significantly for the religious path, it is more a deleterious mental or a psychological condition, an inability to understand that all phenomena in existence are transitory in nature and that desire to contain, control, or possess phenomena is ultimately futile. Pali *suttas* describe in many ways how the Buddha explained the causes of, and the way out of, *dukkha* to the unfettered experience of *nibbana* by means of the "path of purification":[3] that is, by the integrated cultivation of *sila* (ethical behavior), *samadhi* (concentrated mediation), and *panna* (cultivated wisdom) that counteract the conditioning effects on the mind of the *asavas*—passion (*raga*), hatred (*dosa*), and stupidity or delusion (*moha*)—the mental "sores" that can ulcerate the mind through *ahamkara* (self-obsession), which, in turn, engenders the experience of *dukkha*. This formulaic understanding of the conditioning process and the antidotes that may assuage it is quite explicitly articulated repeatedly in stock paragraphs appearing myriad times as a refrain in the *Mahaparinibbana Sutta* (1.12) of the *Digha Nikaya*:

> And then the [Buddha] . . . gave a comprehensive discourse: "This is morality, this is concentration, this is wisdom. Concentration, when imbued with morality, brings great fruit and profit. Wisdom, when imbued with concentration, brings great fruit and profit. The mind imbued with wisdom becomes completely free from the corruptions, that is, from the corruption of sensuality, of becoming, of false views and of ignorance."[4]

Yet, the Buddha's identification of the fundamental problem of existence, its causes and solution, was also framed in more relatively straightforward terms, especially for the laity: the simple assertion that whatever actions are undertaken to assuage the condition of *dukkha*, to arrest the process of suffering, those actions veritably constitute the religious path. As such, merit-making is one of the general means, and certainly the most widely deployed practice, by which *dukkha* is confronted, not only for those who suffer and to whom a gift might be given, but for the giver as well. In this chapter, while the focus of discussion is on the religious quality of ritual giving, especially within the context of the annual robe-giving rite known as *kathina* (or *kathein* in the Bamar or Burmese language), and the positive karmic consequences that are thought to accrue to givers as a result, the nature of power in relation to the cultivation of merit and karma will also be examined within modern and contemporary Myanmar political history. The significance of who gives, and how, why, and to whom they give, is ferreted out in some detail. In Myanmar, in the present as in the past, merit and power are intricately related.

For even a casual visitor to Myanmar, it is staggering to observe just how much of the nation's material wealth, and how much of its citizens' expendable income and voluntary energies, are dedicated to the maintenance, sustenance, and aggrandizement of the Buddhist *sasana* (Bamar: *tatha-thana*), especially to its sacred pagodas.[5] *Kathina*, formally the annual ritual act of giving robes to the *sangha* at the conclusion of *vassa* (the rain-retreat season), is regarded widely throughout the country as the most important merit-making ritual occasion of the calendar year for the laity. The *kathina* rite epitomizes the ethic of gift giving that articulates the basic Buddhist practice of *dana*. It is by giving, by giving selflessly and without attachment to the fruits of the merit that derives from charitable action, that lay (and monastic) followers of the Buddha can hope to make progress on the path to overcoming *dukkha* and experiencing *nibbana*. *Dana* is also understood as the chief means of gaining a more favorable rebirth. In general, virtuous members of the monastic *sangha* are regarded as the most worthy objects of the laity's selfless giving. Generations of Buddhist kings in Burma continuously sought to purify the *sangha*, ostensibly to preserve it as the most virtuous field of merit. Gifts to worthy members of the *sangha* are a potent means of assuaging *dukkha*, either in the immediate context of this life, or in the eventual life-processes of the next.

While gifts that sustain the *sangha* and the *sasana* are the most highly charged in terms of generating merit, there is yet another important related reason as to why the monastic *sangha* is so highly revered in Myanmar:

> [The *sangha*] is the only cultural institution surviving the collapse of the traditional kingdom after the third and final Anglo-Burmese war in 1885. Buddhism has been a rallying point for resistance against the colonial state and its successors since independence in 1948. The sangha has played a critical role in mediating such sentiments. As other-worldly ascetics detached from worldly gains, monks have traditionally enjoyed a position of authority permitting the sangha to speak the "truth" to those in power. Monks agitated against colonial rule in 1886 and again in the 1920s and 1930s. The sangha has also been a steadfast critic of Burmese governments from the democratic administration of U Nu [in the 1950s and early 1960s], to Ne Win's Socialist Program Party [from 1962 until 1988], and its successor regimes [1988 until 2011] under the State Law and Order Restoration Council (SLORC), and most recently, the State Peace and Development Council (SPDC)." (Schober 2007, 55)

It is because the *sangha* is at once such a revered religious institution, and the veritable historical link to the legacy of Buddhist political and cultural traditions of Burmese society as well, that Juliane Schober has made the Gandhian-like statement that "[i]n the Theravada Buddhist world, religion is necessarily at once political and religious" (2010, 140). If this is so, then other questions also arise: How has the *sangha* managed to maintain its lineage of purity while being a politically significant player throughout its prolonged two millennia of history in India, Sri Lanka, and Southeast Asia? Is there a particular strategy or modus vivendi that has made the *sangha* such a venerable, highly respected Theravada tradition? One approach to answering these questions can be derived by considering the nature and function of the *sangha*'s continuing ritual life, especially in relation to *kathina*'s observance.

PATIMOKKHA AND *PAVARANA*

The collective recitation of the *Patimokkha Sutta*, essentially the 227 rules of monastic discipline incumbent upon every *bhikkhu* fully ordained by means of the *upasampada* ordination rite, occurs every new and full moon day of each month, ensuring that it is the most frequently observed of all Buddhist monastic rites. The *patimokkha* is also likely the most ancient of all Buddhist monastic rites.[6] In the religious culture of the Ganges River Valley of ancient India, its performance defined the Buddhist monastic community uniquely in comparison with other orthodox and heterodox religious communities who were thriving at the same time. The *patimokkha* is also the core or root text from which the voluminous *Vinaya-pitaka* (*Book of Discipline*) was then elaborated. The great importance placed on behavioral discipline by the early *sangha* is reflected in the *Vinaya*'s chartering story regarding the origins of the practice of reciting the *Patimokkha Sutta*.[7] Here, King Bimbisara requests the Buddha and his followers, like other religious groups of the time, to make known their *dhamma* (teaching, truth) on *uposatha* (the new and full moon days of the month). Formerly, these specific days had been designated occasions for ritual sacrifice in *brahmani*cal or Vedic observance. But *sramana*s, those religious communities like the Buddhists who were heterodox in their views when compared with the orthodoxy of the priestly *brahmani*cal community, had taken to the practice of making known their teachings in public, their distinctive *dharma*s, on *uposatha* (new and full moon) days instead.

According to the *Vinaya*, initially the Buddha and his followers were silent in response to Bimbisara's request; but when observant laity criticized their silence subsequently, the Buddha instituted the practice of collectively reciting all of the rules of Buddhist monastic discipline on *uposatha* days. At least on that occasion, then, reciting of the disciplinary rules was tantamount to propounding *dhamma*. I have argued elsewhere (Holt 1981) that the Buddha's *vinaya*, or his advocacy of mentally disciplined action, is regarded, at least within the logic of the early Pali Buddhist textual imaginaire,[8] as an affective expression of *dhamma*, the behavioral corollary of truth. Moral discipline is a form of the truth that is behaviorally realized in the same way that a mantra in Vedic texts is a sound-form of the truth when chanted, or a mudra is a gestured form of reality. The difference, however, is that *vinaya* is morally informed; it is *sila* (ethical practice) writ specifically in great detail. Moreover, historically it carries the force of monastic law and constitutes a precedent for virtuous action.

The *patimokkha* also bears a special relationship to the *pavarana* rite that occurs before, in some cases immediately before, the celebration of the "*kathina* season." Before offering a discussion of the celebration of *kathina* in the contemporary Burmese context, I want to discuss the related significance of both the *patimokkha* and the *pavarana* rites, for they really make possible, according to the Buddhist logic quite apparent here, the power of merit produced during *kathina*. While the *pabbajja*, the temporary ordination rite initiating novices (the focus of the previous chapter within the Thai context), is probably the most visible of all monastic rites observed in Myanmar and in all the other Theravada-inclined Buddhist religious cultures, considering that often entire Burmese villages make up the public processions celebrating the grandeur of the occasion (see figure 3.01), the *patimokkha* and *pavarana* rites, which are not now observed in public, are extremely crucial to the maintenance of the qualitative moral corporate religious life of the *sangha*. Indeed, the logic of these two related rites is what makes *kathina* and its associated gift giving a fortuitous affair not only for the lay givers, but for the monks as well.

The recitation of the 227 rules of monastic discipline every two weeks on the new and full moon days by the *sangha* is carefully prescribed in the *Vinaya*. Special rules articulate in great detail those monks who are deemed eligible to participate in the *patimokkha*, the recitation of which culminates in a collective declaration of the local *sangha*'s *parisuddhi*, or continuing "complete purity"[9] in relation to upholding the entirety of the behavioral norm. Monks within the monastic compound who have previously confessed offences of a more serious kind are excluded from the recitation. Nor may others who have been derelict in meeting various communal responsibilities participate. The importance of executing this ritual properly and precisely accounts for the fact that after centuries of recitation in various religious cultural locales across South and Southeast Asia, the Buddhist monastic disciplinary code has remained remarkably similar in its various textual recensions, or better, in its detailed ritual observance. Recitation of the *patimokkha* by virtuous monks who have adhered to its various tenets ostensibly expresses the moral purity of the inward condition of the collective monastic community. The behavior that the disciplinary code requires by observant monks is expressed through the agencies of the body, speech, and thought, the "gates" through which intention is inevitably expressed.

The *Vinaya*'s description of the related *pavarana* rite bears a great functional similarity to the *patimokkha*. In comparing these two rites, I. B. Horner, the pioneering scholarly British woman who laboriously translated from Pali into English the *Vinayapitaka* into six volumes in English as the *Book of Discipline*, has observed that "the recital of the Patimokkha was 'to remove' offences by confessing them during the nine dry months of the year; the Invitation [*pavarana*] was to remove any offences that monks had committed during the three wet months [*vassa*] and would help them to aim at grasping discipline [*vinaya*]." (*Book of Discipline* 4: xvii.) Instead of being held every two weeks, the *pavarana*, like the *kathina* rite, is held annually at the end of *vassa*, the three-month-long rain-retreat season. During the *pavarana* rite, each monk is "invited" to identify transgressions against the disciplinary code. But unlike in the *patimokkha* ritual context, the transgressions referred to in this instance are not their own, but their fellow monks' contraventions instead. So, the *pavarana*, unlike the *patimokkha*, is not an introspective self-examination leading to confession and expiation. Within the *Vinaya* text, it was actually conceived of as a court of law in which a monk might be judged on the basis of what has been seen, heard, or suspected (corresponding to how actions are thought to be expressed through body, speech, and mind) by his monastic colleagues. That is, the *pavarana* is a ritual occasion when monks are invited to examine the behavior of their fellow monks after an intensive period of time in which the monks have been, again ostensibly, focused on making their own positive progress on the religious path. Traditionally, or at least according to Pali textual traditions, the rain-retreat season was a time given over primarily for reflection, meditation, and study, when moving about in villages and in the countryside was deemed inconvenient, even karmicly deleterious,[10] owing to the inclemency of the weather.

In the final analysis, the end of the *vassa* season, the time when the *pavarana* and *kathina* rites are still held today, is the most auspicious season of the year in relation to the putative spiritual condition of monks who make up the contemporary *sangha*. For the preceding three months, monks have not only been engaged ideally in furthering their spiritual pursuits by means of study and meditation, but they have also observed each other's behavior such that, by the conclusion of *vassa*, they can assert their collective *parisuddhi* (complete purity) in relation to the moral norm of the *patimokkha*. They are, as it were, morally pure and, so, spiritually potent.

In Cambodia, *pavarana* is often held at major temples on the night immediately preceding the holding of *kathina*. But in Myanmar, *pavarana* is held a month before the *kathina* observance, on the preceding full moon day. That month in between the two rites has become a season of its own in Myanmar, one of intense donation campaigns throughout the country. Moreover, *pavarana* has also been "informalized" nowadays to the extent that it does not resemble a court of law at all. Rather, in some instances, monks are simply asked on the occasion to provide advice to each other about how they can improve their spiritual pursuits, or whether they have any complaints about each other's distracting social behavior. Ritually, however, the *pavarana* procedure remains a very important marker, insofar as it signals not only the end of the *vassa* rain-retreat, but also the declaration of a collective spiritual condition of purity, a condition that makes the *sangha* a potent object of merit-making for the *kathina* season that immediately follows.

KATHINA: LITERARY AND HISTORICAL PERSPECTIVES

Like the *pavarana* and *patimokkha* rites, *kathina* is an ancient Buddhist monastic ritual that has been sustained within the *sangha's* cultic calendar for more than two millennia. Indeed, detailed concerns for the observance of *kathina* and fastidious rules for the manner in which robes are to be worn and maintained form two full sections of the *Vinaya's Mahavagga*, or nearly one hundred pages of translated text. Each of the two sections contains an opening story of paradigmatic importance about the giving of robes to the *sangha*. The first *Vinaya* story is one that I also heard cited in Myanmar in 2010, when I was conducting fieldwork in Yangon at the Shwedagon Pagoda and at a very large and very well-endowed monastery in Insein township, in the northwestern part of Yangon. It is the story[11] about how thirty "rag-wearing" monks[12] were trying to reach the Buddha's company before the onset of the monsoon season but were caught short in inclement weather and forced to spend the three months by themselves, though they reported to the Buddha that they were well supported and looked after during this stint by the laity. Following the holding of the *pavarana*, these now rag-wearing monks made their way to the Buddha, who observed how unkempt they had become during *vassa*, and so he declared: "I allow you, monks, to make up *kathina*-cloth when monks have completed the rains" (*Book of Discipline* 4: 352). The Buddha then specified that having a *kathina* robe, which in turn seems to indicate that a monk has become presentable, allows monks to go out into the public on alms rounds among the laity and that monks may also receive group meals and be given as many robes as they require, once *kathina* has been observed.

Detailed specifications about allowances and care for robes and their composition that follow in this section of the *Vinaya* are supplemented in the second section referred to earlier and together make for an especially tedious reading of legalistic and seemingly trivial significance. However, how the robe should be worn precisely has been an especially important issue in the history of Buddhist monasticism, disputes over which have led to considerable sectarian wrangling. One of the major issues debated has been whether or not the robe should be worn over one shoulder or two. The principle behind what, on the surface, seems as if it is a trifling concern actually has to do with the matter of how external expression is seen as an indicator of disciplined internal or inward cultivation. This very issue was at the center of a century-long dispute resolved finally in late-eighteenth-century Burma during the reign (1782–1819) of King Badawpaya.[13] An unkempt appearance can be taken as an indicator of an unkempt mental disposition. Indeed, what the Buddha meant by karma is actually well illustrated by this understanding. That is, the cause-and-effect relationship that constitutes karmic efficacy is the relationship that exists between the quality of one's inward volition and the nature of one's external behavioral expression. *Behavioral expression mirrors volition.* That is why during the *pavarana* rite, as I noted earlier, monks are asked to comment on what they have seen, heard, or suspected, based on observations of behavior expressed respectively through body, speech, and thought. The outward reflects the inward. Karma is the causal connection between the two.[14]

The other detailed section of the *Vinaya* concerned with robes opens with an almost epic story about a certain Jivaka Komarabhacca, an orphan born of a courtesan who was found in a reed basket by a prince who then raised him as his own. The prince ensures that the young boy is fully educated, and so he eventually becomes a doctor of great renown whose career, described in several entertaining episodes, then intersects with the Buddha, who happens to become his patient. Jivaka cures the Buddha of a condition of "imbalance of the humors" through a series of thirty "purgatives" and then presents the Buddha with a pair of glorious *siveyakka*[15] robes, which seems to symbolize the first giving of *kathina* robes and thereby reflects the purified condition that the Buddha has attained, both physically and mentally. The story does certainly reflect what becomes one of the main themes of *kathina*: the laity's attempt to honor the worthy and purified character of the *sangha*, here represented by the first monk, the Buddha himself. In so doing, it paradigmatically articulates the lay concern for monastic well-being and the desire to honor religious achievement. The robe, then, actually becomes a symbol of the religious path to *nibbana*. By providing robes, like those provided by Jivaka Komarabhacca, the laity affirms its support for and veneration of this path. While a monk is further along the religious path in terms of progress, laity are also headed in that same direction. Their gifts of robes empower their own journey as well as the monks'.

It is interesting that a number of other sections of this part of the *Vinaya* are also concerned with matters of medicine. In more than one instance, monks who are ill are described as having soiled robes that must be tended to by other monks. There are also issues raised about how robes and bowls belonging to deceased monks should be reallocated to the universal "sangha of the four quarters" (*caturddisasangha*) before being allocated specifically to the monks who have cared for the deceased before their passing away.

Beyond these and many other details, there are references within the *Vinaya* accounts to practices that can still be observed within the *kathina* ceremony today. The spiritual rewards for supporting the *sangha* materially, particularly through providing woven cloth for robes, is summed up by the Buddha who blesses the laywoman Visakha for her support of providing bathing-cloths for nuns in the following way (*Book of Discipline* 4: 419):

> Whatever [woman], much delighted, endowed with virtue,
>   a disciple of the well-farer [*sugata*], food and drink
> Gives—having overcome avarice—the gift is heavenly,
>   dispelling sorrow, bringing happiness; [and]
> She gains a *deva*-like [divine] span owing to the spotless, stainless
>   way,
> She, desiring merit, at ease, healthy, delights long in a
>   heavenly company.

This passage well captures the soteriological consequences of living a life of virtuous giving in the manner in which it is still understood by Buddhists in Myanmar and in other Buddhist cultural regions of Southeast Asia today. While heavenly existence is not *nibbana*, it is a type of rebirth in which *dukkha* is minimized.

More specifically, this section of the *Vinaya* also contains specific details about how many robes may be kept and how *kathina* robes are to be distributed in ways still undertaken today. When I describe the events constitutive of the *kathina* rite I observed in Yangon in 2010, I will mention how robes and other amenities given by the laity were divided up by a lottery system. Consider the following passage, probably written at least 1,500 years ago, or perhaps even centuries earlier, from *Book of Discipline* (4: 404–405): "Then it occurred to the monks who were distributors of robe-material: 'Now, how should a share of the robe-material be given: in the order in which they came in, or according to seniority?' They told this matter to the Lord. He said: 'I allow you, monks, having made good anything lacking, to cast lots with *kusa*-grass.' "

That *kathina* enjoyed a long history specifically in Burma, in ways strikingly similar to how it is celebrated today, is attested by inscriptions and paintings that date as far back as the Pagan period (eleventh through thirteenth centuries), the era that was formative for the widespread establishment of the Theravada in Burma. I will quote from one of these inscriptions verbatim, as it was translated for me into English, and then briefly discuss another two. The first inscription, translated below, is attributed to Daw Oh Kyan Thin, an *upasika* (laywoman). It was found in a field near a brick mound just south of Yengwe village, north of Mahlaing town, in Pagan. It is now located in the "inscription shed" at the Mandalay Palace and dates to the year 1098 CE:

> After Oh Kyaw Thin had built a monastery in the month of Tabaung
>   [twelfth month] in the Mayanmar Era
> of 560 [1098 CE], she offered two robes each to 31 monks,
> one *stupa* made of clay, one wishing tree hung with various articles
>   and one cow,
> in order not to be reborn in hell during her time in *samsara* and
>   so she can attain
> *nirvana* at the end of *samsara*.
> To make her share of merit, she [also] offered
> 4,000 oil lamps when *kathein* was held,
> 40 needles, 201 sprinklers, four p[lates]
> five alms bowls, one bell and 20 threads for needles
> in order to gain the merit she desired.[16]

Here, the ideology of the economy of merit is clearly extended beyond hope for a heavenly rebirth to the eventual and ultimate goal of *nirvana*. In terms of ritual detail, it is interesting that this inscription contains a direct reference not only to the giving of robes, but also to the providing of a wishing tree, the practice of constructing and offering of which has become (or has remained) so prevalent in contemporary Myanmar. Two paintings from Pagan temples dating from the fourteenth century illustrate *kathina* ritual moments.

The second Pagan inscription I refer to dates to 1101 CE and is attributed to a monk, Thingy Nyang Oak. In his inscription, he lists the various sermons he had heard delivered by famous monks of his time that were given throughout his years of attentiveness, sermons that were also witnessed by other "men of wisdom." He notes how he dedicated three slaves

Figure 4.01. Fourteenth-century Pagan painting of Kathina tree

to a certain monastery that, when completed, was the venue for the performance of *kathina*. He also offered food, oil lamps, brown lotuses, and blue flowers as his ritual good deeds, the merit of which was to be shared with his teacher, parents, and grandparents, and also in the hope that he would become an *arahat* when Arimetteyya (Maitreya) becomes the future Buddha. He further desires to share the merit of his actions with his brother, his younger sister, his older and younger sons, his mother, and all of their male and female slaves.[17]

A third and longer inscription, unfortunately not dated but which (according to my knowledgeable translator, Than Saw, a retired archaeological commissioner in Pagan) undoubtedly dates to at least the twelfth or thirteenth century CE, refers to a variety of donations, including the sponsoring of a *kathina* ceremony at the famed Shwezigon Pagoda in Pagan. Uniquely, after announcing that he wants to share his merit with his parents and relations, this layman declares that he first wants to be reborn as either a *cakravartin* or as the king of the *nat*s (divine lords) in *natloka* (the abode of these deities). And beyond that, he aspires to become a buddha.[18] In this inscription, as in so many others that have blanketed the landscape of material culture at Pagan with its 2,700 religious monuments in a five-mile radius, the ideology of making merit, sharing merit, and merit's power to engender a succession of favorable rebirths leading to the ultimate realization or *nibbana* is radically dominant as the determinative focus of religious pursuit. As we shall see, it has certainly not yet been displaced in contemporary Myanmar Buddhist culture and society either.

A CONTEMPORARY OBSERVANCE OF *KATHINA*

I seized an opportunity to observe a complete and formal *kathina* rite in Insein township (in the northwest section of Yangon) in November of 2010.[19] The Insein monastery has a population of about four hundred monks, approximately sixty to seventy of them fully ordained, with the remainder being *samaneras* (novices). Every morning at this monastery, there is a formal *dana* (prepared food donation) given to the monks, sponsored by a selected lay family who provide not only for the late morning meal, but also typically provide a monetary donation of about 1,000 kyat (~US$1.10 at the time) per monk in the monastery. This represents a considerable layout, given that the per capita income of Myanmar in 2011 was about US$700 per year. Obviously, only the economically well off, who seek social status as much as the merit, can afford to be the chief sponsors of this kind of major merit-making occasion.

Before the meal that constitutes the *dana,* many novices have also been out on *pindapata* (alms rounds). They canvas nearby neighborhoods every morning, stopping at appointed houses, apartment dwellings, and businesses, bringing back their rice and curries to the monastery to be shared for the late morning or early morning meals as a supplement to what has been provided by the *dana.* Some of the laity along the alms rounds routes provide food to monks every morning, while others only on selected days of the week. The specific timings of the alms rounds are set, known by both laity and monks in advance. Ritual begging by monks and giving by the laity is routine. Some monks in Myanmar, often from the very discipline-conscious Shwegyin sect or others, will eat only one meal per day. Others, known as *dhutanga* monks, an ancient designation for monks who are especially known for their homelessness and asceticism, also eat only one meal a day. In any case, the more sedentary monastic context is carefully provided for by laity, who have been organized into groups or families on a rotating basis to see to the provisions of the monks' food. And the food is, generally, of excellent quality, with more served than the monks can possibly partake. The leftovers from *dana* and *pindapata* are usually distributed to volunteer laity working in the temple that day, who then distribute it to others in the neighborhood of the monastery as well. In Myanmar, the monastery is often a redistribution point for wealth and excess.

Typically, the morning *dana* liturgy begins with the assistant "abbot," or *uppajhaya,* providing a brief homily on how eating is done to sustain the body and should not be enjoyed simply for pleasure, and how this communal occasion is marked by the process of sharing. Indeed, it is impressive how the entire ritual routine provides a very effective means for the distribution of food. Accordingly, the merit accrued by the giving of the generous laity is also shared by everyone present in an act of *anumodana.* *Anumodana* is one of the key concepts at work in this context. It refers to the ability to share in the joy of giving, or to rejoice in the intrinsic goodness of the act of giving. What it reflects is a conscious recognition of why an action is karmicly fortuitous. By cultivating a disposition of joy in giving, the internal motivation, or corresponding volition for giving selflessly, is registered.

A *kathina* rite can formally take place within a pagoda as soon as the *pavarana* rite has been observed. As I mentioned earlier, in Phnom Penh, Cambodia, *pavarana* is celebrated on the night of the full moon and *kathina* is observed immediately on the following morning. The two rites were explicitly seen in these contexts as completely linked by the monks I interviewed there. Indeed, in the two sermons I observed at Wat Langka and

Wat Unnalom in Phnom Penh (see chapter 5), the chief monks had talked about the importance of the *pavarana* precisely in terms of how the rite makes it possible to transform the *sangha* into a virtuous object of support. This was not exactly the case I encountered in Myanmar. Most *kathina*s are held on the last day possible of the month following *pavarana,* which in effect, as I have mentioned, creates a month-long season for gift-giving campaigns that culminate on *kathina* day proper. The knowledgeable head monk of the large Yangon monastery where I observed *kathina* was surprised when I suggested to him that I thought *pavarana* and *kathina* were necessary linked to one another. This conjunction had not occurred to him before. The confusion arose, I think, because I had described the function of *pavarana* as the conclusion of the purificatory *vassa* season when, in fact, it was clear that he understood *pavarana* as the *beginning* of the *kathina* season. Neither of these positions, I then humbly admitted to the esteemed monk, are necessarily mutually exclusive. And so he graciously agreed.

When I asked monks and laity why *kathina* seems to be the most popular season or ritual occasion in Myanmar's religious calendar, both responded rather routinely by saying that each mutually benefit from the reciprocity of the monk/lay relation. Many asserted that *kathina* is a matter of *sukha* (happiness) that aids each in ultimate quests for the realization of *nibbana.* That the giving aspect of the ritual is highly meritorious, it is enthusiastically stressed, almost goes without saying. In the past, I had understood, on the basis of reading Pali *sutta*s and the *Vinaya,* that merit-making leads to better rebirth, perhaps with the *deva*s, or to a better human rebirth. But for the Burmese laity with whom I now spoke, merit is explicitly the means to *nibbana,* if not in a better rebirth in the human abode, in the time of the Buddha Metteyya's dispensation in the future. This, of course, had been the precise aspiration expressed in Pagan inscriptions many centuries earlier. In that sense, there seemed a deep spiritual kinship between the Buddhists of the distant past in Burma and the laity of the contemporary present.

Campaigns for raising funds for gifts to the *sangha* begin in earnest a month before most rites are celebrated. There are campaigns in one's household or extended family; there are campaigns in urban neighborhoods; there are campaigns in every village; there are campaigns within lay religious associations; and there are campaigns at one's place of employment. It is likely that pious laity will contribute in any number of these contexts. The monastery in which I observed *kathina* was supported not only by various groups of laity, but by the Myanmar government's Home Ministry as well. I was informed, and I later confirmed, that every ministry in the government supports at least one designated Buddhist monastery.

Apparently, it is seen as a proper use of government funds for any leftover surplus from a ministry's budget to be donated to the *sangha*. In other words, *kathina* is such a grand merit-making occasion that one would be hard-pressed to escape giving even if one were an avowed religious skeptic or a practitioner within another religious community.

I was told by one of the senior monks in Yangon that, from the monastic point of view, *kathina* functions as a kind of equalizer in that all monks benefit from the gifts. While gifts of cash, rendered in the shape of a wishing tree, are generally given for the general maintenance of the monastery, the other gifts are distributed in a somewhat equitable fashion. An effort is made to insure that every monk, whether *bhikkhu* or *samanera*, receives at least one new robe during *kathina*. The other gifts, which I describe below, are also equally distributed by a lottery system, the type of which, as I mentioned earlier, is attributed to none other than the Buddha in the *Vinaya* text.

Throughout the month preceding *kathina,* or the month during which *kathina* rites are held, one can observe in the various neighborhoods of Yangon the steady collection of money and goods taking place publicly. Goods, whether they be robes (of which various qualities these days are sold in department stores for the convenience of the laity), towels, clocks, soap, bowls, pots and pans, dishes, umbrellas, plastic buckets, or virtually any household item of convenience (a refrigerator was donated to the monastery where I was closely observing), are left on street corners or at other conspicuous sites in the neighborhood for all to see. This practice of exhibition serves as an inspiration for others to contribute as well, or as a barometer of the levels of charity achieved. These goods, including the money trees, which are made of tens and even hundreds of thousands of *kyat* notes, might be left virtually unguarded overnight in the heart of urban areas without apparent concern for potential pilfering, an extraordinary fact when one considers the various degrees of poverty endemic to contemporary Myanmar. On the morning of *kathina* ceremonies, these gifts can be seen being loaded up into processions of trucks, "tuk tuks," motorcycles, rickshaws, and the like, accompanied by joyful, celebratory music together with reveling laity making their ways through the streets to the destination of temples. In the early 1960s, Nash described a very similar village scene occurring (1965, 133), though what I saw and what he described are separated by forty-five years and the venue I was observing was a very sophisticated urban milieu.

Here follows what I saw formally of the *kathina* rite at the aforementioned Yangon monastery. Once all of the gifts were assembled in the monastery's largest sermon hall during the morning of the *kathina* rite

Figure 4.02. Kathina "money tree"

Figure 4.03. Kathina "gift tree"

proper, the monks were summoned by the beating of drums around nine o'clock in the morning for the beginning of the morning liturgy. The monastery's head monk presided, accompanied by twenty senior monks who flanked him in two rows seated in special chairs. Behind the two rows of special chairs, the remaining *bhikkhus* and *samaneras* filed into the hall according to their hierarchical statuses, rankings determined by when each of them took *upasampada* (full ordination) or *pabbajja* (novitiate) orders.

The service began with the chanting of the eight precepts and the five cardinal moral principles (*pancasila*), plus three other more or less symbolic observances, followed by a chanting of the *Metta Sutta* (the discourse on loving-kindness). The chief monk then delivered the featured homily that emphasized the importance of purity of mind, detachment, and selfless giving. Following the sermon, the chief donor family, a young husband and wife in their late thirties with two young children, presented robes to the chief monk and the twenty senior monks. It was mentioned by the chief monk that the purchase of all the robes for the monks in this monastery had cost some ninety-six lakhs of kyats, or close to US$10,000.[20] Altogether, including other gifts and the preparation of the feast that was then consumed by the nearly five hundred people present, about 155 lakhs, or roughly US$16,000, had been spent for this occasion. This is, of course,

Figure 4.04. Monks at *kathina* meal

Figure 4.05. Monks receive their new *kathina* robes from laity

Figure 4.06. Money (1,000-kyat notes) gifted to monastery in the shape of a fish

a staggeringly huge sum of money in Myanmar. Then followed the distribution by the laity present of new robes to each monk and novice present.

Between the morning and afternoon rites, *samaneras* (novices) were kept busy by cleaning up after the feast, rolling back rugs, sweeping the floors, and taking apart all of the money "wishing trees" or, in one case, a "wishing fish," or fish made out of thousand-kyat notes.

The various gifts that made up other "wishing trees" were taken apart, in turn, and parceled out into about four hundred "shares," distributed into little piles on the floor. Many piles consisted of a new robe only. But since there were not enough second robes to go around for everyone, other piles consisted of a combination of new begging bowls, umbrellas, towels, thermoses, books, fans, flashlights, pens, and so on.

Lottery slips were then written out and attached to each pile. Nash commented on a similar procedure in the village monastery he observed fifty years ago in another part of Myanmar and concluded that the basic point of the lottery was to maintain "the fiction that the corporate group is recipient from an anonymous and grateful body of householders" (1965, 134). He says that this is a fiction because, as he had indicated previously, laity will not support monks that they know are undeserving, and the amounts of donations to particular monks are an accurate barometer of village estimation of their status. Nash also indicated that the wealthiest families in the village he observed also conducted their own private *katheins*

Figure 4.07. Gifts from laity put into piles distributed by lottery

for the monks as a way of generating extra merit (and thus the possibility of *anumodana* for yet others).

At 2 p.m., all the incumbent monks of the monastery were again summoned by drumbeats. The head monk presided again and announced that 560 robes had been given in total and that twenty-four lakhs of kyats (~US$2,600) of cash had also been donated that day for the general maintenance of the monastery. He then proceeded to chant a special liturgy, during which he held up a robe that had been folded into the shape of a flowerpot. Within the "pot" there was a plant. This "flowerpot robe" was then presented as "the *kathina* robe" to the senior-most "teaching *bhikkhu*."[21] The head monk and six senior monks at that point were excused from the main hall and made their way to another small meditation hall located about a hundred yards away. Meanwhile, the chief monk adjourned to his own quarters. The remaining monks chanted special *gatha*s germane to *kathina* while the senior teaching monk was formally awarded the ceremonial *kathina* robe. Following this presentation, the senior monks returned to the large hall where the rest of the monks had waited. The merit-sharing, or *anumodana*, derived by the good efforts put forth by the senior teaching monk, was then shared among all of the monks. Then followed "the lucky draw" lottery to determine who would get what pile of gifts. And with all gifts assigned and distributed, the *kathina* came to a close for the year.

KATHINA ROBE-WEAVING AT SHWEDAGON

Twice a year, the famous Shwedagon Pagoda in Yangon is open for the entire twenty-four hours of the day and night: at the beginning of *vassa* (Burmese: *waso*) and of *kathina*. *Kathina* at the Shwedagon is a much-anticipated event, not only for the tens of thousands of Buddhists who flock to the site, but especially for the forty or fifty lay religious associations who collectively tend to the upkeep of the pagoda throughout the year.

Each association comprises individuals who have signed up, typically, for six-month memberships. During the course of this half year or so, each is expected to perform various chores at the pagoda at least twice a month. Performing these services is regarded as highly meritorious, though the services provided might seem quite menial, such as sweeping the marble platform surrounding the lavishly endowed gold-gilded stupa. It is the lay religious associations that are responsible for the festivities at the Shwedagon during *kathina*. The focal point of *kathina* festivities is the robe-weaving contest.

It is worth a brief digression to describe a bit more the nature of these lay religious associations.[22] While at the Shwedagon robe-weaving ritual,

I was given a pamphlet by a member of the Saythana Thanbarya, the religious association of Kyeemyindaign Township. The group purports to have been first established in 1908 and is formally registered with the government's Department of Religious Affairs. This lay association was celebrating its sixth donation ceremony to the Shwedagon by giving a further eleven pure gold sheets "weighing three ticals" to be added to the facing of the central Shwedagon stupa, along with 13.5 lakhs of kyats (~US$15,000). In addition, they were providing a feast of food open to all comers during the week before *kathina*. Their pamphlet also detailed the total of their previous five donations, which have, all told, consisted of "345 gold sheets weighing thirteen vises and 83 ticals" and fifty-five lakhs of kyats (~US$61,000), plus a donation amounting to an additional 5.5 lakhs (~US$6,100) to help renovate religious buildings destroyed by Cyclone Nargis, which rampaged through lower Myanmar in 2008). They were also inviting one and all to a "feast of sacred food" honoring all donors on the day before *kathina,* when libations are poured and merits shared for their "good deeds and [finally] donations to all the creatures living in the Thirty-one Planes of existence." It seemed quite clear to me that lay religious associations such as this epitomized the culture of religious giving and merit-making in contemporary Myanmar. They are focused primarily on sustaining the material culture of the *sasana.*

It has long been the tradition in Myanmar, and other Buddhist cultures as well, to fabricate *kathina* robes for the *sangha* within a twenty-four-hour period.[23] It was also the custom to adorn important sculpted images of the Buddha with robes during *kathina*. This remains a very popular practice not only at the Shwedagon, but at many other temples throughout Myanmar as well. At the Shwedagon each year, nine teams of weavers compete in a contest to see who can weave a robe to adorn the main Buddha images of the Shwedagon in the quickest possible manner. Each religious association hires at least three professional weavers to contest on their behalf. The competition begins in earnest around 5 p.m. and continues for about nine or ten hours until 2 or 3 a.m. Each team of weavers is supported by an enthusiastic membership of the religious association, who, through cheers and offerings of money, entreat their representatives to try their very best to bring home the first-place prize, the honor of emplacing the just-completed robe onto the bodies of one of the nine central Buddha images at the Shwedagon. When I observed, fourteen teams had initially indicated that they would compete in the contest. Indeed, fourteen different associations began the festivities around 4 p.m. at the Shwedagon by circumambulating the stupa three times before making their way to the staging area for the weaving competition.

The symbolism of the robe is indeed very rich in Theravada-dominated religious cultures. It is quintessentially a symbol of the noble eightfold path per se and, as such, venerated by all who respect the Buddha's teachings. Sometimes it is said that when a layperson worships a monk, he or she is really worshipping the robe. Jordt cites the story of how one day a lay donor piously venerated a monk, but the next day bitterly scolded him for being a scoundrel. When asked about the inconsistency, the layman responded by saying that in the earlier instance he was venerating the robe, in the latter he was remonstrating the man within it (2007, 44). The story emphasizes how donations should be made to the *sangha* in general, symbolized by the robe, rather than to the individual monk. Nevertheless, as I will indicate later, the identification of virtuous monks (in order to make donations fortuitous) is regarded by many as the key to making merit.

In commenting on the significance of the robe to the monk, Spiro put the matter this way: "It is a symbol of his [the monk's] poverty, the badge of monastic office. When a layman gives homage to an impious monk, they say that they are showing respect not for the man—he is merely a 'human in a yellow robe'—but for the robe.[24] Indeed, for the laymen the robe is believed to possess quasi-magical properties: he who wears the robe is immune to attacks by ghosts, witches and so on" (1970, 100). Spiro goes on to talk about the specific significance of the *kathina* robe. Of chief importance in this context is the fact that a monk is not allowed to leave his monastery unless doing so with the *kathina* robe, which, I have noted previously, is one of the most important concerns in the *Vinaya*'s relevant account. Thus, the robe becomes a symbol of the monk's public "homelessness," or his detachment from all contingent objects of the worldly life. It also almost goes without saying that as a garment the robe also disguises or dissolves one's distinctive physical appearance, even one's sexual orientation. Combined with the shaven head, the differences between male and female cloaked in robes can sometimes be difficult to discern at first glance, especially in Sri Lanka, where nuns wear the same color robes as monks. Indeed, as a symbol of monasticism, the robe clearly refracts the "sexlessness"[25] that constitutes the Buddhist monastic ideal. Or, to put the matter in even more general terms, the robe is a symbol of one who has left behind all of the categories of domesticity, all attachments to this world.

THE IDEOLOGY OF MERIT

Virtually all anthropologists who have conducted studies of Theravada-inclined lay Buddhists at the village level in Sri Lanka and in Southeast Asia from the 1960s to more recently[26] have recognized the centrality of merit to the worldviews and value orientations of peoples in these cultures. While Theravada Buddhism is a critical ingredient in the expression of Sinhala, Bamar, Shan, Mon, Karen, Arakanese, Thai, Lao, and Khmer national or ethnic identities, there are some reasons to assume that merit-making and the associated cosmology concomitantly reflected in Pali literature remains rooted at least as firmly, if not more so, in Myanmar among the Burmese, Shan, Arakanese, and Mon, than among any of the other Buddhist cultures mentioned above. This assertion can be advanced for several reasons. Chiefly, the fact that Myanmar has been so sheltered from the social and political world external to its borders during the fifty years between 1962 and 2012 has meant, obviously, that its peoples have been less affected by the various dimensions and processes of "globalization" that now seem so apparent in other Buddhist cultures. Upon spending any amount of time in Myanmar, one can see the ramifications of "isolation" reflected in many different ways. In terms of personal appearance, for instance, men of all classes in society, not just villagers, continue to wear the *lungi* or *sarong* along with sandals, having not yet opted for trousers and shoes, though that is beginning to change a bit in Yangon. Indeed, wearing a *lungi* is something of a nationalist statement in relation to a rejection of the "trouser people." Almost all women still wear *thanaka* paste[27] on their faces rather than western style makeup.

In terms of commerce, credit cards, as of 2012, were not accepted in any retail outlets (except in the very rare instance that the merchant had a connection with a bank outside of Myanmar). More hotels are now accepting credit cards as of 2016. With regard to transport, there are very few private automobiles. Most automobiles in the cities were run-down taxis that date from the 1960s and 1970s. That had changed by 2015—a flood of reconditioned vehicles from Japan had been imported, so many that, in January 2015, limits were reluctantly established. Bicycle rickshaws would still ply the streets in Mandalay in 2010, although one has to admit that the new inexpensive Chinese motorbikes had made significant inroads in finally replacing them, and by 2015 the rickshaws had almost disappeared. One could go on citing various examples that indicate that Myanmar has been relatively isolated from the influence of the outside world, though that has changed, in sometimes dramatic fashion, since the relative opening up of the country, especially to tourism, since 2012.[28] But perhaps the most significant point with regard to the present discussion is that no other more or less comprehensive ideology, such as Marxism with its associated "socialist culture" (read Vietnam, Laos, and intermittently Cambodia and Sri Lanka) or capitalism with its rampant consumerism (read Thailand and Sri Lanka), have competed with or have threatened to displace Buddhism as the system of thought and practice that anchors personal perspective in most people's lives. There was a brief two-decades-long experiment with the "Burmese Way to Socialism" from the 1960s until the early 1980s, after the military strongman Ne Win overthrew the democratically elected government of Prime Minister U Nu, but by the early 1980s, the government was back to patronizing Buddhism in a very public and vigorous way.

I am not arguing that Sri Lanka, Thailand, Laos, and Cambodia are not fundamentally Buddhist societies. They are. But what I am simply noting is that Myanmar's relative isolation and lack of international embrace left its ideology of merit largely intact, without much of any challenge to the way it dominates and governs much economic activity beyond the level of subsistence. Perhaps only "about 5 per cent of the [Rangoon] city's population can be considered wealthy, or at least well-off enough to have sufficient disposable income to participate in the new post-socialist consumer economy. . . . [M]any people must spend more than 80% of their income on food and still suffer from malnutrition" (Seekins 2011, 176). Seekins' comments about the relative lack of distribution of wealth and how this condition affects the manner of giving to the *sangha* also indicates that lavish and ostentatious displays of donations, now quite common in the contemporary "post-socialist" era, are the by-product of very few people relative to the whole population. Indeed, conspicuous giving to the *sangha* has become an important pastime for the urban "new elites." This would, of course, include the lay donors who sponsored the *kathina* rite in Yangon described earlier. What these laity have provided as a gift to the *sangha* is dramatically far beyond the means of almost all other people in Myanmar society. Having said that, virtually all Buddhists in Burma remain merit-conscious, despite the fact that some are in a position to give so much more than others. The ideology of merit continues to orient a sense of value and accomplishment for most. Not only is it a marker of one's mind-set, but one's ability to give is a marker of one's status.

Jordt has described this social reality at some length in her insightful study of lay mass *vipassana* meditation traditions and the politics of giving to the *sasana*. In addition, she introduces the more specifically religious and psychological factors that are in play within the process that constitutes the act of giving:

> In Buddhist Burma, it would be impossible to have high social status *without* participating in sasana-directed donation. . . . [T]he public aspect of donation is important because through it, others may share in the merit making and therein produce within their own minds feelings of metta

(loving-kindness), saddha (faith), and so forth. This emotional facet of mental participation in acts of devotion and generosity is a critical under-pinning to the way in which moral communities emerge out of like-minded participation in collective rituals.

Sincerity in the act of donation is valued because it is the foundation for one's merit base in a system of moral causality in which intentions are the final determinants of what one will reap in the future. The meritori-ousness of the gift (that is, the strength of its "return"), is dependent upon the state of mind of the donor at the time of the donation, the state of mind of the monk recipient, the type of gift, its value or appropriateness to the recipient, and so forth. Intention is the single most important criterion for the evaluation of the cosmic return of the gift. The sangha is popularly viewed as the best field of merit for the laity's offerings, for two reasons. First, monks are exemplars who have renounced their worldly lives and pleasures and are prohibited from owning anything other than bare es-sentials, such as an alms bowl, robes, needle, and umbrella. They therefore embody the ideal of detachment from materiality that the *dana* is intended to induce in the giver. Second, wealth donated to the *sangha* . . . is seen as serving the sustenance and reproduction of the Buddha sasana, or the teachings and dispensation of the Buddha. (2007, 101–102)

In this compact passage, Jordt has provided a concise overview of the various principles underlying the importance of *kathina* for the various players of the rite in the public and private spheres. She has noted that *cetana*, or volition, the dispositional mind-set of the actor, is the key driver in determining the potency of the action. *Cetana* is actually how the Bud-dha is said to have defined karma when prompted.[29] What one wills is what foremost conditions one's behavior. Therefore, the quality of one's disposition to the phenomenal world, the *samsar*ic world of desire, is re-flected in the degree to which one freely gives materially to the *sangha*.[30] "The individual's cultivation of the *dana parami* is directed at training the volitional inclination of the mind toward spontaneous and unprompted thoughts and acts of generosity. The mind should become unhesitating, uncalculating and freed from clinging notions of 'me' and 'mine'" (Jordt 2007, 101).

While volition articulated with genuine sincerity is regarded as the key driver of karmic potency, the condition or quality of the object of one's giv-ing, as Jordt has indicated in her discussion, is also very consequential. And while *kathina* is a ritual that contains a liturgy performed by the monks in which declarations of *purity* are made public, and while this col-lective public declaration follows on the heels of *vassa* and *pavarana*, "[t]he self-evidence of the sangha's purity is not ultimately affirmed by monks but by the laity. . . . Laity are simply the means through which endorsement and validation of the Buddha's teachings are made representationally available, that is, as materially expressed through [support for] institutions, requisites, buildings, lands, ordination, and so forth" (Jordt 2007, 126). That is, giving by the laity is at once the public material response to the *sangha*'s purity on the one hand, and the normative expression of a spiritual disposition in which the ethic of detachment has been inwardly cultivated on the other.[31] It is how *dukkha* is assuaged. What I examine next is the way this ethic of giving to the *sangha* as the most auspicious field of merit has become institutionalized in Myanmar. More specifically, I examine the question of how Burma's notorious military government attempted to articulate its own legitimacy through the very practice of merit-making, thereby profiting as the erstwhile leadership of politically potent Buddhist nationalism.

THE ORGANIZATION OF MERIT

While it is clear that merit-making is the chief means by which most laity articulate their religiousness publicly in Buddhist Myanmar, the context in which they may do so varies according to their economic abilities and their social statuses. When discussing the robe-weaving ritual at the conclusion of *kathina* at the Shwedagon Pagoda in Yangon, the efforts of lay religious associations were noted in passing as one of the means by which individuals pool their efforts to make significant donations for the sustenance of the *sasana*. Jordt and Schober, two perceptive western anthropological observers of public Buddhist religious culture in contemporary Burma, both refer to associations like these as "*dana* cliques." Jordt says that, for women, "*dana* cliques" are frequently the same as business cliques, insofar as the women with whom one shares a "*dana* network" are the same women one would turn to for a loan (2007, 11).

A good deal of merit-making occurs within the context of these "*dana* cliques." Some "cliques" are more formally organized than others. For instance, lay religious organizations that support the ritual life and material maintenance of the Shwedagon function as types of religious clubs that, by virtue of their numbers and collective strength, can accomplish what are perceived as major accomplishments, and hence very fruitful meritorious action for individual members. Membership in one of these associations would seem to be driven by purely religious purposes. What I focus on here, however, is how the Myanmar military government, which suffered from a notorious reputation as being one of the most morally reprehensible regimes in Asia, if not in the world, actually and ironically functions as a catalyst for merit-making. As such, its presence and significance in the public merit-making arena raises some interesting issues about the logic and function of merit, not just as a religious action but, simultaneously, as a political act of economic importance as well. The government often serves as a channel for supporting the *sangha* and *sasana* in a number of ways. And even though the government's monopoly on power has been mitigated since 2012 by reforms that were introduced through a constitution that allows for limited representation determined by direct vote, its leaders, including many military generals, continue to dominate the public merit-making dynamic in contemporary Myanmar.

In the first instance, the government has attempted to serve directly as the chief patron of the *sangha* and *sasana* for the past twenty years or so of Burmese history. It has attempted to do so in conformity with the traditional role ascribed historically to Buddhist kings in Burmese society. It is a familiar role. Jason Carbine has put the matter this way:

> [T]he SPDC [State Peace and Development Council], as with its predecessors, has increasingly turned towards certain forms of Buddhist ritual and devotional activity in an effort to link themselves with pre-colonial conceptions of a good Buddhist ruling order. In this sense, it embraces a political pattern also embraced by the U Nu government [of the 1950s and early 1960s]. This pattern consists of trying to promote political legitimacy and national integration vis a vis the *Sasana*. (2011, 26)

Carbine's comment not only puts the *sasana* front and center into this discussion, but it also puts the military government's efforts into historical perspective. In aligning them with precolonial kingship and the popular and democratically elected government of U Nu that was overthrown by General Ne Win in 1962, Carbine is pointing to how traditional Buddhist cosmology continues to function in Burma's culture as the background and framework for meaningful public ritual activities that are at once religious as well as political, just as Schober has suggested in her interpretive work. Because the Burmese military regime is known for their abuses of human rights, their scandalous conduct of war against a number of Myanmar's minority peoples, their apparent involvement in the drug trade to finance the acquisition of armaments, their cooperation with the Chinese government in facilitating the rapid export of Myanmar's natural resources, and the manner in which they have skimmed off the fruits of an already underachieving economy for their own personal gain, thereby further impoverishing the rest of Myanmar's citizens, there is an understandable tendency to see their actions in support of the *sangha* and *sasana* from a cynical perspective.

On the other hand, Jordt has made the interesting point that "a 'politics of sincerity' has emerged that is validated insofar as the world of internal intentions and cosmological consequences cohere in the same act" (2007, 137–138). I quote Jordt at some great length in what follows in order to articulate in greater detail the complexity of the matters that arise in considering the politics of giving by the military regime in contemporary Myanmar. Jordt argues that

> it appears far from clear even to highly educated and connected Yangonites, among whom I have conducted research most intensively, that the government is engaged in a simple pretense of Buddhist devotion for the purpose of (somehow) maintaining its hold on political power. The lively and nuanced character of the internal debate—always framed in terms of sincerity—suggests that the true meaning behind the government's actions is by no means widely deemed self-evident. But even to confront the question directly in this manner is to inadvertently prefigure the outcome in terms of one or the other two common modes of explanation. One scheme conceives of the military regime as standing in a relation of mystifier to mystified vis a vis the Burmese populace—a kind of Gramscian hegemony. The second scheme also treats the regime as a monolithic agent with conspiratorial intent, but the junta's donation activities are seen less as conspiratorial and more as pragmatic and rational components of its attempt to achieve power and legitimacy in a majority Buddhist country. . . . The unquestioned assumption here is the methodological individualism of formalist economic anthropology, in which strategizing, maximalizing, rational decision-making characterizes economic activity of any kind. But this model cannot account for the *systemic* complexity of donation activities, nor does it benefit us to reduce Buddhist cosmological principles to instrumental plots, economic or soteriological. Dana does have micro— and macroeconomic components. But its perception as a practice leading to purification and nibbana, wherein the goal of donation is to achieve a state of mind in which generosity emerges in the individual's intentions as unprompted volitional acts, is more prominent. It is this native "calculus of intention" that may most beneficially be applied to the regime's donation activities. (2007, 97–98)

Ferreting out the "politics of sincerity" remains difficult precisely because Buddhist cosmology and soteriology remain the dominant discourses by which all evaluations of the generals' ritual behavior are proffered or measured in Myanmar.[32] Jordt insightfully sees the subtleties of awareness that Burmese must perforce entertain in this situation:

> To some degree, it is in the hands of the laity and the sangha to judge the level of sincerity of regime members' actions—or to doubt that sincerity.

> But as long as members of the regime carry out dana with *apparent* sincerity, then, as with the mental state of the monk that can only be guessed at through surface indications, the people must go along. It is not that they believe blindly that the junta is sincere; it is that there is a general acquiescence toward or an acceptance of the conditions set by their adherence to cosmological principles. . . . In accordance with this logic, members of the regime maintain that the basis for their legitimacy is implied in the fact of their ascendance to power. Consequently, their donations and other pious religious acts can be interpreted not as being enacted to gain legitimacy—the manipulation hypothesis—but as evidence of that legitimacy. (2007, 121–122)

It is not only a matter of legitimacy. It is also a question of how the power to give is a reflection of social and political hierarchy, itself an indication of previous *karm*ic accrual. Karma does not produce a democratic distribution of merit. Indeed, *karm*ic action that produces merit necessarily is thought to produce difference, to produce hierarchy. Those who already have, have because of what they have done in the past. This is as true in the political world as it is in the religious.

> One need only observe the government's annual ceremony for presenting titles to scholarly monks and nuns to recognize this logic in action. The highest-ranking official presents the title to the highest-achieving monk and so, down to the lowest ranking official. . . . The indexical ranking of worldly power and status to the accomplishments of world renouncers in ceremonies of this kind are forceful, visual public assertions about who's who in the social, political and religious arena. [Thus, t]he regime's donative activities, whether construed as sincere or manipulative, are both *generative* and *reflective* of social and political hierarchy. (Jordt 2007, 121, 125)[33]

There is some evidence to indicate that Myanmar's generals want to see their meritorious donations in support of the *sangha* as examples for the laity to follow, a perspective, it seems, that if true, only enriches their *karm*ic quests further. While observing at scores of temples in Yangon, Mandalay, Sagaing, Bago, Thaton, and Mawlamyine in 2010, and then in 2014 and 2015 in Mrauk U and Sittwe, I more frequently than not saw military generals and their entourages in the presence of monks and sometimes visiting foreign dignitaries prominently displayed for laity to see, illustrating or reminding viewers of the example of the military's generosity and capacity for giving, and thus earning merit.

There is also evidence to suggest that the military wants to be seen as more than simply an example, that it has had a strategy to encourage support for the *sangha* and *sasana* in ways that are actually quite pragmatically coercive. While having conceded the difficulty of ascertaining the sincerity of volition with regard to the government's *dana* campaigns, Jordt notes that the "dana cliques," which the regime calls upon to "capture moral communities that the would otherwise be donating outside of the influence of the government . . . are a form of control over the religion" (2007, 12). Moreover, in this regard,

> [g]overnment ministries are known to donate to religious organizations as a single group or clique. This is required by the central military government, and it is done in recognition of the fact that patron-client ties emerge from donation societies. In other words, by requiring donations to be organized hierarchically within the officially sanctioned channels of ministries, the government both secures loyalties stretching downward from ministers to their underlings and short circuits the development of relations of loyalties along non-sanctioned social pathways. Put another way, the government that donates together, stays together. This activity is enforced by means of compulsory skimming of bureaucrats' monthly salaries for the purpose of donation. (131)

Jordt describes how various ministries have been given allocations of space at the Shwedagon Pagoda for the construction of small *dhamma* halls where staff can then gather twice monthly on the new and full moons and on other special occasions to listen to sermons and to make offerings to monks. This kind of coercion is rather mild. However, one of the consequences of this type of coercion is that, according to the logic of karma that emphasizes the importance of volition, because the motivation for giving in these instances has its actual source in the government (or with the generals), it is judged as less meritorious for the givers because the element of sincere intention and unprompted giving has been removed from the equation.[34] Indeed, because the request has come from the military, it means that it is the military who would also receive the merit from the donations, since the motivation or intention for the giving has originated with them (Jordt 2007, 104).

Seekins has noted that the military government also takes a very pragmatic approach to the "politics of sincerity," for it "has pressured wealthy business people to donate, in exchange for special privileges such as the granting of export-import licenses or permission to establish joint ventures with foreign companies. In one informant's words, *dana* is a 'matter of policy, not piety,' and another has commented that donations to Buddhist projects are 'good for the next life and for political connections in this life'" (2011, 180).

While it may be difficult to ascertain with precision the religious dimension of the "politics of sincerity" as Jordt argues, Seekins (2011) and Schober (1997) are both thoroughly skeptical of the regime's motives.

Though Schober argues for the conjunction of religion and politics in Myanmar as a major theme in her study (2011), she also, unlike Jordt, sees the state's patronage of Buddhism as an unabashed co-optation of religious sentiments. In an article analyzing the political significance of the state-sponsored series of public cultic exhibitions of the Chinese tooth-relic in the 1990s, she referred to the dynamics of the government's ritual orchestration in this way: "[A] modern, technocratic elite employs traditional ritual patronage to consolidate its hegemony and compel a large segment of its population to participate in the state's veneration of Buddhist relics. The totalizing constructs of the modern nation-state co-opt, for political purposes, the religious sentiments of the Burmese Buddhist majority" (Schober 1997, 243).

Exactly how this was accomplished makes for a fascinating study. In the tradition of great kings of the past and postcolonial politicos who framed their political discourses in Buddhist cosmological terms, the military regime of the 1990s succeeded in no small degree as catalysts for grand generations of merit-making. In a study of the junta's sponsorship of a nationwide exhibition of a "tooth-relic" on loan from China, Schober (1997, 225) has recognized the relevant dots in play and has connected them with analytical precision.

> The Sacred Tooth's procession created fields of merit that mapped a universal Buddhist cosmology onto the territory of the modern nation-state. It placed SLORC [State Law and Order Restoration Council] in a lineage of past kings and obligated to them ritual clients, including contemporary national communities of military, technocratic, business and ethnic elites. . . .
>
> By creating a national cult of relics (*rupakaya*) and sacred sites, the military provided access to merit for the entire nation. National print and television media continually featured ministers and military leaders who, on behalf of the workers' collectives and good citizens of Myanmar, performed merit-making rituals in public contexts. . . . Military generals and politicians officiated at rituals in which lavish donations were given to monks who frequently were also members of the *Sangha Mahanayaka* Council. The merit made was seen as ensuring future prosperity and leading to transcendence of *samsara* and attainment of *nibbana* in time. Large segments of the population were encouraged to participate in the state's elaborate merit-making rituals that evoked Burmese court culture in an attempt to place contemporary celebrations in a lineage of the Buddhist state. (Schober 2011, 159)[35]

Earlier, in her article on the how the military government attempted to capitalize politically on the exhibitions of Chinese tooth-relic of the Buddha, Schober had made the related countervailing salient point that

[v]oices of dissent [can] also emerge from religious donations that circum-
vent the state's collection network. Especially among elites, political opposition is expressed in perfunctory donations to the state's religious
causes, while more generous offerings (*dana*) are made to sources of merit
that reflect a personal choice and are deemed more worthy of support.
Widespread mobilization of donations to the state's religious causes has
reinforced this kind of popular resentment because many Burmese Buddhists see it as a form of taxation. (1997, 239–240)

Seekins, in a similar vein, has also articulated perhaps one of the
shrewdest economic and political analysis of the politics of *dana* in relation to the military government. He asserts,

From the generals' standpoint, the "Buddhist building boom" is a policy
of supreme importance for reasons that illustrate the difficulty of attempting to separate the worldly (Pali *lokiya*) from the world-renouncing (*lokuttara*)[36] spheres of the actual practice of Burmese Buddhism. It is true that
"playing the religion card" puts the junta in good light with many Burmese
Buddhists following the precedent of pagoda-building Mon and Burman
monarchs in centuries past (even if skeptics doubt their sincerity). However, in a society with limited resources, it also prevents the post-1988
class of capitalists (drug-funded or otherwise) from becoming too wealthy,
independent or closely connected with foreign commercial interests.
By expropriating private surplus wealth for purposes that in Burmese society cannot be questioned, the regime not only gets access to these resources and takes credit for their religiously sanctioned use, but also
makes it more difficult for the business class to create an independent
power base that could challenge the state in the future. *Dana*-driven interactions between the SPDC and the business class-donations in exchange
for the state's conferral of special privileges—also keeps the capitalists dependent upon the good will of the junta, or its individual top generals,
since business people, including non-Buddhists—who remain outside the
"*dana* cliques" would find it extremely difficult to survive. (2011, 180–181)

From what has been noted above by these various scholars regarding
the relationship between the government and the *sangha*, it would appear
theoretically, on the surface at least, to be a mutually beneficial relationship. Historically, the ideal model of *sangha* and state relations was one of
the king and his court functioning as the primary patrons and protectors
of the *sangha* on the one hand, with the king, in return, gaining legitimation and prestige for his position of royal power on the other. While this is
a simplification of matters as they have unfolded historically,[37] it is, in general, the type of reciprocity and mutual respect by which the military regime in Myanmar seeks to retain its position of simultaneously gaining

acceptance and sustaining control in the contemporary Myanmar scene. Unfortunately for the military, the *sangha* has a rich history of being the site for Burmese resistance to power that is perceived in the popular mind as being less than morally based or informed. The *sangha*, that is, has often been the moral conscience of the society and a vehicle for political subversion. This was particularly true during the 1920s and 1930s, when the *sangha* was the impetus for various moments of resistance against the British.

TURNING THE BEGGING BOWL UPSIDE DOWN

The *sangha* in general, and the Shwedagon Pagoda in particular as a symbol par excellence of the *sasana,* are the paramount sites that repeatedly have been the locations for resistance to political power in Myanmar that has been deemed illegitimate by a significant element of the laity. That is, the two greatest fields of merit for Buddhists in Myanmar, the *sangha* and its pagodas, especially the Shwedagon, the most highly revered material expression of this Buddhist merit-making economy, are also the two most potent potential sites for rejection of political power, in the same way that they can function positively in terms of the legitimation of power.

There is something to be said for the argument that when either the *sasana,* especially as symbolized by the Shwedagon, or the *sangha* are perceived as having been compromised, a powerful public or political response can be expected to set in. The Shwedagon, lavished upon by a long history of Bamar and Mon rulers for the past several hundred years, has often been a site of resistance, similar to its role in 2007 when the Saffron Revolution of *sangha* demonstrations in Yangon began there and proceeded through the streets to culminate at the downtown Sule Pagoda. Within the British colonial context, Moore et al. point out how the Shwedagon, in the early decades of the twentieth century, was consistently the venue in Rangoon for expressions of resistance to British power by the Young Men's Buddhist Association (YMBA), the General Council of Burmese Associations, and university students (1999, 150–151). Juliane Schober has made the more general point that British attempts to prohibit public political assemblies resulted in religious spaces being utilized for overt political purposes, ensuring that political resistance to the state "unfolded mostly within Buddhist frameworks" (2011, 5–6).

The Shwedagon was not only a place for defiant rallies during the decades-long drive for independence, a drive led in its final stages by General Aung San, but it was also the site where the new national anthem was unveiled for the very first time, and the place chosen by Aung San's daughter, Aung San Suu Kyi, to dramatically make public her pleas for democracy in 1989 and 1990. While the Shwedagon has a long history of association with various Mon and Burman kings, it was Aung San, perhaps, who was most responsible for wedding the Shwedagon to Myanmar's postcolonial identity when he gave what became a famous speech that included these words:

> We have convened at a venue, which, throughout our history has been the quintessence of everything noble and fine and auspicious. So I make a solemn wish for our conference to reflect the nobility and sanctity of the location. The Singuttara Hill is also where the Four-Relic Sacred Shwedagon rests on its crest. The Shwedagon Zedi testified to the nature of our generosity and the noblest of our desires and its golden glimmer is the light of our yearning for the supreme goal, nirvana, where reigns peace and tranquility. If once again we should look at what surrounds us, we will realize that this was where the great movements that fashioned our destiny were born not many years ago. Thus, for us, the peoples of this land, this place is one to be greatly revered. (cited in Moore et al. 1999, 177)

Even before the dramatic appeals of Aung San in post–World War II colonial Burma, and then more recently by his daughter some forty-odd years later, the Shwedagon often has been a site for rallying anticolonial sentiment by groups who were dominated by members of the *sangha*. Schober (2011, 100–102) points out that the *sangha*'s influence in the General Council of Burmese Associations, the umbrella organization that coordinated the nationalist movement among several various constituencies in the 1920s and 1930s, was quite dominant. U Ottama, U Wisara, and Saya San were dynamic and charismatic figures from the *sangha* whose leadership in Buddhist resistance to the British ignited the Burmese drive to independence in the 1920s and 1930s. Saya San had been a monk, disrobed, and then had himself crowned king in a desperate attempt to reestablish an alternative power with cosmological legitimacy. Many Burmese believed that Saya San might be the *setkyamin* (the *cakkavattin* who in various Theravada apocalyptic texts is heralded as an ideal Buddhist king) who will precede and prepare for the coming of the future Buddha Metteyya by establishing a kingdom of righteous concord.[38] Like other nativistic movements in late colonial Southeast Asia, Saya San's movement, though it stubbornly persisted in defiance for two years, was brutally crushed.

Given the history of the *sangha*'s political activism, especially in the leadership vacuum of the post-kingship era of Burmese history, the *sangha*'s repeated challenges to the military regime in 1988, 1990, 1996, 2004, and again in 2007 signal a serious rupture of confidence that no doubt reflects antigovernment sentiments of the broader public. The *sangha* is the only social institution in Burmese history that survived the economic, social, and political transformations wrought by the colonial experience. It remains the only other social institution in the country that can rival the military government regime in terms of size and organization. It certainly continues to eclipse the regime in terms of garnering respect from the populace. Because of this, the military has sought to control the *sangha* at the same time that it has postured, as the kings of old, as the primary patron of the monastic community. Since the *sangha* continues to occupy a position of moral eminence in the perspectives of the vast numbers of masses, its challenges, in the form of refusing to accept *dana* from the military and their families, constituted a very serious and humiliating threat to the military, one that has each time elicited a vigorous and vicious response. The *sangha*'s refusal to be a field of merit for the military is not only humiliating and cuts at the heart of the regime's legitimation in the eyes of most people, but it also threatens the personal spiritual well-being of individuals in the military as well as their families. The *sangha* exercised its socio-cosmological power to thwart the military government's pretensions to be acting in the interests of the people. Juliane Schober explains the unfolding dynamic of tension between the *sangha* and the government in this way:

> Merit is manifested in future spiritual and material prosperity as well as in social status and political power. The ritual exchanges that constitute a Buddhist economy of merit are performed in many contexts and confirm the legitimate status of monks and their lay supporters [here read military government]. Its reversal, namely the refusal of donations from lay donors, requires a formal act of the *sangha* authorized by monastic law. The Burmese *sangha* invoked this provision of monastic law in 1990, 1996, 2004, and most recently in 2007, when this reversal of a Buddhist economy of merit precipitated a political and moral crisis on a national scale. . . . This boycott is tantamount to banning from the Buddhist field of merit any lay supporter who acted to the detriment of the *sasana*. (2011, 120–121)

Jordt points out incisively in this context that by resisting the regime in this way, the *sangha* was further resisting the regime's attempt to control the laity (2007, 123). As mentioned, this included members of the families of military personnel as well. In an economy of merit, with the social and political hierarchy legitimated by the theory of karma retribution, the *sangha* had struck a hard blow, and it seemed for a moment that the monks had knocked the wind out of the karmic sails of the generals. They certainly caught them off-balance, but only temporarily.

The principle that is inherent in these machinations of power—power conceived as based on appeals to an interwoven ethical and cosmological ideology—is purity. Indeed, purification has been the means by which *sangha*, state, and laity have kept each other's power in some balance or check, at least historically (Jordt 2007, 196). In that case, the regime's violent reaction to the monk's refusal to be further co-opted in the economy of merit was rationalized by the military in the same way that Theravada kings historically rationalized their interventions within the *sangha*. The history of Theravada tradition is peppered by royal interventions justified on the basis of declaring that monks have compromised themselves by becoming too involved in society's economic and political concerns. Corresponding on the *sangha*'s side, it has to be noted that Theravada history is also peppered with instances in which the *sangha* quite consciously acted in ways to preserve its position within the milieu of the political economy. Especially in the medieval periods of these respective Theravada civilizations, when the *sangha* constituted the veritably dominant social and economic institution in society, it carefully administrated its holdings in order to parlay its wealth so that it could preserve its robust socioeconomic position.[39] Just as kings benefited from the economy of merit, so did the *sangha*. That is why "[m]any Sangha leaders were suspicious of Ne Win's socialism because they feared it would eliminate private property and make it impossible for lay people to give donations (*dana*) to monks or pagodas; they also opposed his decision to revoke Buddhism's status as the country's official religion" (Seekins 2011, 122).

Thus, relations between the *sangha* and the military regime have been an on again and off again affair. When they have been "off," they have been more than a little bit frayed. The results sometimes have been reprehensible and shocking. I focus here on two moments in particular when a healthy fragment of the *sangha* led national political resistance to the military regime and thereby held out hope that a transition to a less repressive and more democratic political structure could be effected: the uprising of 1988 (and its aftermath in the aborted results of the 1990 elections) and, of course, the so-called Saffron Revolution of 2007, both of which, by all accounts, have been watersheds that portended movements for fundamental change.

The 1988 uprising seemed to have heralded the demise of twenty-six previous years of military rule by General Ne Win, who, at the peak of civil unrest demanding democratic government, had resigned his position and had seemingly withdrawn the military from political rule. Only at the last minute was there a reversal of this apparent withdrawal, occurring on the eve of attempts by Aung San Suu Kyi and U Nu to form a civilian interim government. Instead, the military moved into Rangoon with unprecedented force and targeted the *sangha* for its role in inspiring political change. Schober describes the events as follows:

> The popular uprising of 1988 was a defining moment in Burma's post-independence history. Monks and students again emerged as a political force. Amidst the chaos of the uprising, the *sangha* transformed itself spontaneously into an underground organization aiding the popular uprising. Monks provided logistical support, widespread anti-government mobilization, relayed information through an internal monastic network, and even stepped up to administer some judicial and civil infrastructures in those towns and areas considered "liberated" by the democratic uprising. In the aftermath of the uprising, monasteries became sanctuaries for student protesters military police frequently arrested, particularly at night. As monastic robes offered anonymity to those fleeing from government persecution, the monastic network became a conduit for safe travel to the border and into exile. Unofficial estimates of the state's reprisals against monks range from hundreds killed to thousands missing or imprisoned. . . . As many as 3,000 monks are said to have been jailed. (2011, 107)[40]

In this vein, Seekins depicts how the military government reacted to the major role that the *sangha* had played in leading the mass demonstrations that seemed to have won the day: "In 1988, the army shot members of the *Sangha* in the streets of Rangoon. It became a common practice for the government to defrock protesting monks after they were arrested and then prosecute them for anti-state crimes, despite the principle that expulsion from the order could only be ordered by monastic authorities in accordance with the *vinaya* rules" (2011, 122).

Indeed, the government's repressive response in 1988 signaled the beginning of very strict governmental control over *sangha* affairs.[41] In effect, the *sangha* lost a good deal of its traditional independence (a condition of relative self-rule it has historically enjoyed going back as far as to its very origins in ancient India society when, as its own *samaya,* or "house," it was left alone by the *ksatriya* rulers to govern its own affairs). Schober also describes the retribution that the *sangha* suffered at the hands of the regime in 1988:

> [The *sangha*] suffered severe retribution for its anti-government activities from SLORC [the State Law and Order Restoration Council][42] in the aftermath of the 1988 uprising. The monastic purge recommenced immediately and with great force. Hundreds of monks, including elderly ones, were arrested and imprisoned for extended periods of time. An unknown number of them died in prison. Public sermons that were construed to be critical of the regime in any way engendered serious retaliations. Armed guards

were staged outside major monasteries in Rangoon, Mandalay and other cities to restrict their movements. The Ministry of Religious Affairs imposed tight regulations on the *sangha* through a hierarchy of *vinaya* courts and regional administrations that extended from the center to the local level. (2011, 87)

While these actions constituted the military's short-term response to the intensified politicization of the *sangha*, permanent educational reforms were introduced in which the curricula studied by monks were drastically reformulated, "lay guardians" (basically spies for the government) who supervised some of the more powerful individual monks were assigned, and committees staffed by military officers or appointed by the military were formed to oversee donations to the *sangha*. Donations were encouraged primarily from organized and controlled lay religious associations, rather than from individuals. Moreover, the government "rewarded senior monks who supported its vision. The regime used various efforts to silence and restrain junior monks who might sympathize with the pro-democracy movement, while holding senior monks accountable for the actions of their juniors" (ibid.).

Meanwhile, a national election was held in 1990 in which Aung San Suu Kyi and her National League for Democracy won a landslide victory by polling more than 80 percent of the national vote. The military government apparently simply could not accept or abide by this resounding humiliating repudiation and refused to hand over power. Further repressions ensued, and a climate of hostile estrangement deepened the changed ethos of public Buddhist religious culture profoundly. The state imposed both doctrinal and economic restraints on the *sangha*, concomitantly attempting to prevent the uprising of millenarian movements and charismatic monks who frequently transformed Buddhist social ethics into political rhetoric during the twentieth century. These restrictions wrought renewed tensions. "When 7,000 monks convened in Mandalay in August 1990 to commemorate the uprising [of 1988] and its martyrs, the military dispersed the crowd by force. In a rarely exercised and official act of the *sangha* the monks called for a boycott of donations from members of the military and their families, thereby repudiating their ability to make merit or benefit from religious counsel. This formal boycott symbolized the excommunication of members of the military and their families from the Buddhist field of merit" (Schober 2011, 107–108).[43]

By turning their bowls upside down and refusing any donations from the military government, the *sangha* further incited the wrath of the military.

By means of the control of monks and the reorganization of public culture, the regime went to extreme efforts to reestablish its image as the great protector and patron of the religion. This became the norm throughout the 1990s, and was greeted by widespread and deepening discontent roiling beneath the surface of society throughout Myanmar. In other words, the alienation between the *sangha* and state cut in both directions. Michael Charney has described the dynamics of the scenario from the perspective of the *sangha* and its supporters:

> As promises and continual preparations with no clear end in sight regarding the economy, the transfer of power, and other matters appeared to be no more than delaying tactics, frustrations among the Burmese population simmered for years. Perhaps just as important as the issue of democracy has been the failing economy. International sanctions and other efforts to isolate the regime have hurt the general Burmese population, pushing most [people] further into poverty and sending many now unemployed female workers and others into prostitution.
>
> By contrast, Burma's elite military families have shown incredible resourcefulness in maintaining and expanding their personal wealth. . . . Subordinate officers also benefited from patronage, extensively used by the junta to maintain officer corps solidarity, in the form of business loans, the purchase of land far below its real value, and opportunities to forge highly rewarding connexions with private businesspeople. The growing disparity between the general population and the military families became very difficult to ignore. (2009, 196)

It is somewhat difficult to understand how a regime so unpopular with the public could survive for so long. Seekins argues that the army-state survived both the 1988 and 2007 uprisings because of its "institutional self-sufficiency and *distance* from the people" (2011, 154–155). That is, it retained loyalty from its members largely as a result of the fact that it has become almost a type of caste separate from the rest of society, but one whose attraction continues to be that it controls the country's natural resources and the inflow of capital from foreign sources (now chiefly Chinese). After 2007, in order to ensure loyalty, Than Shwe raised the salaries of five hundred army commanders as much as 1,000 percent (161).

The *tatmadaw* (military government) developed its own institutions to train its officers to run its own various and extensive business enterprises and many government departments. The military government also operated its own educational institutions, not only for its cadres but also for the children of its officers. It ensured that its people received the best health care in the country. It trained its own medical staff. It is not uncommon, therefore, that even families who are politically opposed to the military encourage their children to join, insofar as the military has remained easily the best option for upward social and economic mobility (Steinberg 2010, 102–103).

In this connection, Steinberg has noted various aspects of the extent of military business enterprises including the MEHC (Myanmar Economic Holdings Corporation), which, between 1990 and 2007, wholly owned seventy-seven firms, nine subsidiaries, and seven affiliated companies, with shares available to military units, active-duty and retired military, and veterans groups returning a profit of 30 percent (2010, 163). He notes that "there is another secretive military business enterprise, the Myanmar Economic Corporation that owns many more major industrial types of monopoly businesses" (ibid.). Steinberg framed this situation quite bluntly: "The *tatmadaw* in effect has reversed a Western concept. Instead of the military as a source of support for the civilian population, in Myanmar, the civilians are seen as a source of support for the military" (ibid.). And yet, he also argues that the reason the military has succeeded in sustaining its power is the factor of personal loyalty, and not loyalty to institutions per se. This is why, he asserts, Ne Win and Than Shwe, both enormously unpopular with the masses of people, were able to remain in power. He argues that loyalty to a ruler is what has characterized Burmese politics since the eleventh- through thirteenth-century Pagan period (2010, 150). That is, a kind of charisma, the type that Max Weber famously labeled as "charisma of the office," continues to inform and sustain the ethos of social hierarchy in modern Myanmar. As noted earlier, such "offices" are also rationalized as having been endowed by karmic potency. Indeed, as also noted, the military patterned its profile for public consumption after *dhammaraja* conceptions of Buddhist kingship.

Nevertheless, the monastic challenge to military power in 2007 was explosive for the simple fact that widespread and deepening frustration had been building for so many years. In the face of the military government's continued disregard for general public welfare and its continued self-interested aggrandizement—epitomized by its expensive construction of a new capital located in remote Naypidaw, its growing isolation from the public, and the sustained jailing of pro-democracy leader Aung San Suu Kyi under house arrest on University Avenue in Yangon—deep-seated causes for the ensuing monastic demonstrations were not difficult to identify. In an age of cell-phone cameras and savvy internet usage, the legacy of what happened was significant not only for Myanmar's citizens, but for observers throughout the world. Images proliferated through various media of days of peacefully demonstrating Buddhist monks on the one hand eventually being savagely beaten by armed military personnel on the other. Advances in telecommunications technology effectively internationalized Myanmar's conflict. Myanmar was front-page news and headline material for newspapers and television coverage in the West and in the rest of Asia. The murder of a Japanese journalist by uniformed Myanmar Army personnel was caught on camera for the world to witness.

The actual protests by monks began initially as a reaction to a spectacular rise in fuel prices caused by a withdrawal of subsidies for the public, withdrawals that were declared without any advance warning. This resulted in a price hike so exorbitant that it presented almost impossible economic conditions for anyone dependent on purchasing fuel. Because the government was so well known for insulating itself from the general suffering experienced by the public, outrage was the predictable response.[44] What was not predictable, however, was the extent to which the response would morph into a strategic challenge to the military's very fitness to rule. Charney has aptly portrayed the series of events that followed:

> While the regime remained confident of its ability to suppress the resistance of ordinary citizens, it faced a different kind of opponent in mid-September 2007. In what has become known as the "Saffron Revolution," after the garb of its leaders (numbering some 400,000 in Burma), outraged at what the military had done to the country, protests began in northwestern Burma in support of general protests against new economic policies. When the government physically beat protesting monks on 5 September at Pakokku, where monastic opposition began, monastic protests spread throughout the country. Ultimately, monasteries at Mandalay, the most important monastic centers in the country, called on all monks to refuse donations from the families of the military elite, which effectively meant that they could not earn merit. . . . As the United States and the European Union talked of more sanctions, the military struck on 26 September, beating, shooting and arresting monastic and other protestors. Early the following morning, several monasteries were raided; monks were forcibly (and illegally under Buddhist law) defrocked, beaten, and interrogated, many being killed in the process. Soldiers fired on street protests that ensued. The violence with which the regime suppressed peaceful monastic protests represents, it has been asserted, a historical watershed in relations between the Burmese state and the monastic order. (2009, 196–197)

Charney is right to describe the significance of what happened in 2007 for relations between the Burmese state and the *sangha* as a "watershed." Though the government resumed its posture of patronizing the *sasana*, in fact, it may take a generation of peaceful and less repressive governmental behavior before the scars of 2007 heal.

From another perspective, the early phases the Saffron Revolution can be understood in terms of a collective religious experience. In advancing this interpretive perspective, Juliane Schober underlines the incestuous nature of relations that obtain between religion and politics in Myanmar. Or more accurately, she has argued that religion and politics cannot be understood as intrinsically separated phenomena.

> Protesting monks and their supporters created a national *communitas*, in Victor Turner's sense,[45] whose moral legitimacy transcended the temporal powers of the secular state. Their rallies charted the same routes that had been walked in the protest marches of 1988 and during the colonial era. Their steps retraced a sacred map of public protest that linked sacred sites, such as the Shwedagon Pagoda, Sule Pagoda, and other local repositories of Buddhist power with the reenacted memories of past resistance movements. En route, the monks chanted the *Metta Sutta*, a popular incantation that extols the Buddhist virtues of loving kindness and compassion. A text that formed part of a standard repertoire of *paritta* recitations, the *Metta Sutta* now became a political expression of Buddhist resistance against the regime and was seen as an invocation of Buddhist social engagement, and human rights and democracy." (Schober 2011, 125–126)[46]

Schober is correct in describing the religio-political experience in this way, especially in terms of the way the demonstrations appealed to traditional mappings of *mandala* political power. The Saffron Revolution of 2007 contained within it a portent that the general population could rise again to demand political change and that the *sangha* "represents . . . the only cultural institution to survive, in a much weakened form, the challenges of colonialism and the modern state and constitutes a moral force whose sources of authority transcend the secular power of the military" (Schober 2011, 7).

Since the events of 2007, the government first intensified its relations with a supportive Chinese government in order to maintain a semblance of economic stability. Aside from enriching itself through selling natural resources to the Chinese, it has also reached out to Sri Lanka, which at that time had become another increasingly militaristic "Buddhist inclined" government with a history of violently suppressing dissent and ethnic conflict. Than Shwe and Sri Lanka's president Mahinda Rajapakse exchanged high-profile state visits. Than Shwe had rarely left the country on state visits in the past, so his visit to Sri Lanka, one that was greeted not so warmly by progressive Sri Lankan Buddhist monks, was a clear attempt to show his international statesmanship and acceptance. In turn, Rajapakse's visit to Myanmar occurred exactly during the days of

Aung San Suu Kyii's last trial in 2009, which resulted in her detainment under house arrest until the elections, in November 2010, had been contested. The timing of Rajapakse's visit to Myanmar could not have been accidental. Rather, it was likely designed to show "international" support for the junta in its efforts to control the democratic forces led by Aung San Suu Kyii.

In the meantime, the government advanced a new constitution and held parliamentary polls in November of 2010, just days before it released Aung San Suu Kyi. In commenting critically on the new constitution, in which the military still controls 25 percent of the seats in a parliament that requires 75 percent approval for the passage of laws and constitutional amendment, Steinberg suggests that "[t]he approval of the new constitution in 2008 was likely brought about due to the Saffron Revolution in 2007, even though the constitution had been prepared as early as 1993. That is likely the case because the new constitution contains within it a proviso that no one can be prosecuted for any crimes that have occurred before its promulgation" (2010, 143).

In later developments, the *sangha* has persevered, for now, in not overtly political ways that directly challenge the rule of the military regime. The regime's past violent behavior makes it a dangerous animal, particularly when wounded. In the absence of a groundswell of public support stemming from movements that have their origins from outside the *sangha*, the *sangha* seems headed more in the direction of simply trying to assuage the *dukkha* of the people in a humanitarian fashion. In this regard, Schober (2011, 132–133) has painted a portrait of the contemporary *sangha* in terms of socially engaged Buddhist ideals. While monks used to constitute a class of literati and teachers for the population at large, they have now become active in other social capacities, including the role of healers and purveyors of medicines. Today, they run hospitals and HIV clinics, are active in environmental conservation, and organized vital relief campaigns in the aftermath of Cyclone Nargis in May 2008. As a cultural institution that survived colonial rule, the *sangha* uses its moral authority as political leverage to promote socially engaged Buddhist ideals, human rights, civil society, and democracy in Myanmar.

Further by-elections in 2012 led to the election of Aung San Suu Kyii and some of her supporters to parliamentary positions in the newly formed government. A subsequent visit to Myanmar by President Barack Obama held out the possibility of Myanmar opening up economically on an international basis beyond its ties to China, India, and Thailand, a development that may occur in tandem with the lessening of social control over the populace.

Unfortunately, a darker side of the *sangha*'s social engagement has emerged since 2012 after terrible riots between Arakanese Buddhists and Rohingya Muslims broke out in Rakhine State. A powerful movement among the monks, the Ma Ba Tha, or the Society for the Preservation of Race and Religion, has catalyzed anti-Muslim sentiment nationally and, with the connivance of the central government, still dominated by the military, passed four laws to restrict marriage, religious conversion, citizenship, and childbirth especially among the Muslim population. While incidents of violence against Muslims have abated as of mid-2015, a politically reactionary ethos within the *sangha* now seems to have become dominant.

THE *VIPASSANA* REVIVAL

At first glance, it would seem that the practice of meditation and the ethic of giving lie at two different ends of the spectrum of Buddhist religious practice. Meditation is a practice that requires a tranquil setting for the cultivation of quiet reflection. *Vipassana* meditation leads to contemplative states of awareness beyond discursive thought, a mental abiding beyond the mind-set of perspectival consciousness, an egoless awareness of the relentless flux that characterizes the ceaseless uprising and passing away of all conditioned phenomena. Meditation has been an issue for Buddhist monks who, historically, have been divided on the primary aims of their vocation: some have argued for the path of learning and the giving of service to the village, community, kingdom, or nation, while others have stressed that the path to *nibbana* cannot be won without the solitary and concentrated pursuit of mental discipline, preferably in the context of a forest retreat, or through a continuous homeless wandering from place to place. The argument has hinged on whether wandering in homelessness for the welfare of the people can best be realized through the peregrinations of itinerancy that reflect the egolessness of mental solitude in the forest, or through the selfless devotion of altruistic behavior performed out of compassion for those who suffer in this world.

In Burma, at least in the twentieth century, or roughly since the disestablishment of Burmese kingship in the 1880s, *vipassana* meditation leading to the cultivation of knowledge regarding the many planes of consciousness and beyond that are described meticulously in the *Abhidhammapitaka*[47] seems to have proliferated within the *sangha* and especially within the lay community. In the same spirit in which some Buddhists have argued that the elemental principles of practice (*sila, samadhi,* and *panna*) that underpin the Buddha's noble eightfold path are realized in an integrated fashion rather than in a step-by-step approach, for many Burmese

Buddhists, meditation and politics, and meditation and giving, are not separate aspects of the path, but instead are necessarily united. Several observant scholars in recent years, including E. Michael Mendelson (1975), for instance, have pointed out that the revival of Buddhism in Burma during the early decades of the twentieth century was largely a matter of urbanites taking up the practice of *vipassana* meditation. Many of these same urban middle-class people who became involved in lay Buddhist societies, or *"dana* cliques," were the very class of people who engendered considerable ferment in the politics of seeking freedom from colonial rule. In this regard, Guillaume Rozenberg has opined, "In the history of Burma, all great political reformers tending towards democracy since the second half of the nineteenth century have practiced insight meditation" (2009, 27). In discussing the relationship between religion and politics at the time of Burma's independence from Britain, Rozenberg has also pointed out that General Aung San, leader of Burma's movement for self-rule following the conclusion of World War II, linked the viability of national independence to spiritual aspiration. "In Aung San's conception, the nation was a sacred place founded upon the practice of mental culture whose final goal would be to enable its members to reach nirvana. Symmetrically, Aung San's practice of mental culture determined his political potency, directed towards the achievement by all of the ultimate deliverance" (19).

While in Aung San's approach, there is a reciprocity between meditation and political realization, in the 1950s and early 1960s, Prime Minister U Nu articulated a linkage in terms of how a Buddhist-inspired socialism could create a *lokanibbana* ("nirvana in this world") in which the material needs of society would be fully met in such a way as to create conditions conducive to the undistracted pursuit of *nibbana*.[48] His own practice of meditation was seen publicly as the means to his own achievements of political power.

Ingrid Jordt has argued that the dynamics of power and its relation to society have changed significantly with the spread of *vipassana* meditation as a mass movement. Power is no long simply endowed by social position, as it was in times of kingship when whatever a king did was considered to be his prerogative for instituting and preserving order in society. She says: "I would argue that an important shift was implied when the emphasis became placed on meditation." And with this shift in importance placed on meditation, the soteriological goals of practicing Burmese meditators became much more individually focused. Moreover, she argues that "purification has come to conform more explicitly to a logic of intention and motivation, and it is applied everywhere in the same way: to monks, laity, and most consequentially . . . , to members of the political regime" (2007, 54). As a result,

> [t]he development of vipassana as a movement to create an "enlightened citizenry" has meant that the laity has assumed the responsibility for the welfare of society. It is their sila on which cosmic conditions depend, just as during the time of the kings, the natural and social conditions depended on the king's sila. The nonobservance of dhamma is seen to create calamity within society and nature. Whereas the king used to be the "coordinator" of Nature's and Humanity's orders in society, in the institution of kingship and in the morality of the "head of state," the laity now has undertaken moral purification through "purification of view." In part, this is the gist of the project of verifying empirically the epistemology of Abhidhamma texts through vipassana. (85)[49]

In her studies of the link between *vipassana* and politics, Jordt asserts that intention (*cetana*) is the key factor driving the "politics of sincerity," and at the heart of understanding how merit is generated through ritual acts of giving, epitomized by the charity of so many individuals during the *kathina* season. But with the widespread rise in the practice of *vipassana*, at least among the swelling urban folk, the venue or space of spiritual cultivation has shifted from collective ritual acts in public spaces in which manipulation can occur, to the interior world of contemplative realization. She observes incisively that though public space has been tightly controlled repressively by the military government, Buddhist individuals have "claimed control over *the private space of their intention*" through meditation, in turn creating "a fulcrum of action in the social and political world" (2007, 157). In terms of the importance of cultivating the *brahmaviharas* within the practice of *vipassana*, that is, the development of even-mindedness (*upekkha*), loving-kindness (*metta*), compassion (*karuna*), and sympathetic joy (*mudita*), the practice is not simply solitary, psychological, and a matter of one's private interiority. These are the "wholesome mental states that may be cultivated as the bedrock system of moral purification. These are the mental dispositions leading one to feel motivated to give charity and keep one's sila" (86). Moreover, the practice of *vipassana* can be simultaneously a weapon of resistance:

> [T]hese practices describe the attempt to enclose the world of experience—individual, social, and cosmic, in a framework that encapsulates the whole of reality in a single theory of knowing. That is why the mass lay meditation movement has intrinsically been a political movement because it refutes, out of hand, the primacy of the nation-state as the geospatial boundaries of the Buddha world. It refutes theories for the bureaucratic arrangements

of the state that do not take into consideration ideas about what the sources of truth/power are and how these are morally caused. And it refutes especially Western modernist theories of personhood that do not situate an individual's actions, speech, and intentions in terms of conventional and ultimate contexts for the production of knowledge and being. (2)[50]

The continuing growth of *vipassana* meditation among masses of lay Buddhists in the twentieth century is, indeed, a phenomenon of significant import in the history of Theravada Buddhist practice. Some may see this development as another instance of the laicization of monastic practice, while conversely, others may view it as an aspect of the "monasticization" of lay practice. In either case, meditation is also a specific form of ritual surprisingly related to the realization of power in several different guises: among them, the politics of giving insofar as it relates to the sincerity of intention. As I have mentioned earlier, conceptions of the Theravada religious path have often been divided between those advocating the cultivation of an interior concentration and those who seek to act morally in the public sphere. Moreover, another split has been evident between those who understand the religious path as a step-by-step sequential move through morality to wisdom to meditation, on the one hand, and those who have understood the path as integrated, on the other—that is, meditation enhances moral cultivation and wisdom, wisdom clarified by meditation produces moral action, morality instantiates the affective expression of wisdom and meditation, and so on. Within the context of these ongoing discussions, meditation would seem to provide for the kind of private psychic space conducive to the production of intentions that become affective in public moral awareness. Insofar as the *sangha* and the *sasana* are the preeminent symbols of public space *and* privately cultivated moral awareness, and therefore the undisputed preeminent objects of virtuous giving, the integration of the religious path seems to find its most prominent genuine expression in ritual venues of selfless benevolence, such as *kathina*.

Perhaps it is possible to see this understanding at work in Myanmar among many of its Buddhist laity who, by engaging the ethos of Theravada in such a fashion, have constituted something of a quiet revolution within. And insofar as the moral condition of the king used to be understood as a raison d'être for establishing the well-being of society, so it may be that the moral compasses forged through the meditative diligence of lay *vipassana* practitioners may herald the future of well-being for Buddhist society in Myanmar.

CHAPTER FIVE

Pchum Ben

Caring for the Dead Ritually in Cambodia

Death is an inevitable fact of life. For the religious, its occurrence does not necessarily signal life's end, but rather the beginning of a rite of passage, a transitional experience in which the newly dead leave behind the familiarity of human life for yet another mode of being beyond. We may never know with certainty, but it is possible that thoughtful ruminations about the significance of death, and therefore about the meaning of life, accompanied by ritual practices designed to provide emotional solace in facing the loss that death entails, are seminal to the foundational origins of religious belief and practice. Within the comparative study of religious cultures, rites in relation to the dead are as ancient as they are ubiquitous.

Buddhist interpretations of death, and rites in response to its occurrence, did not originate in an historical or cultural vacuum. Buddhist conceptions of the afterlife, and prescribed rites in relation to the dead, were modified adaptations of prevailing *brahmani*cal patterns of religious culture in ancient India. In this chapter, I demonstrate how Buddhist conceptions, rites, and dispositions regarding the dead have been sustained and transformed in a contemporary annual ritual of rising popularity and importance in Cambodia, *pchum ben*. Moreover, I analyze the ritual in terms of its fundamental importance to the sustenance and coherence of the Khmer family and national identity.

REMEMBERING THE DEAD IN CAMBODIA
AND VIETNAM

Pchum ben is a fifteen-day ritual celebrated in the Khmer month of Potrobot (in September or October, depending on the timing of the lunar calendar), toward the end of the three-month *sangha* (monastic) rain-retreat season (*vassa*). During these fifteen days, Buddhist laity attend ritually to the dead, providing special care for their immediately departed kin and other more recently deceased ancestors. The basic aim of the collective rites constituting *pchum ben* is making a successful transaction of merit-making and karma transfer to one's dead kin, in order to help assuage their experiences of *dukkha* (suffering). *Pchum ben* is now celebrated as the most popular religious occasion of the Khmer Buddhist liturgical calendar year and, in addition to the April New Year celebrations, is one of the two most widely observed holidays throughout Cambodia today.

The proximate catalyst for *pchum ben*'s current popularity is recent social and political history in Southeast Asia, especially the traumatic events that occurred nationally in Cambodia during the early 1970s through the 1980s, when the country experienced a series of convulsions: first, the civil war precipitated by Cambodia's proximity to an unsettled Vietnam, itself completely engulfed in the Second Indochina War;[1] second, as an outcome of Cambodia's concomitant civil war, the establishment of a radical revolutionary government led by the ultra-Maoist Khmer Rouge from April 1975 until early January 1979; and finally, after the Khmer Rouge had baited the Vietnamese into a military conflict along their eastern border—a foolish adventure that ultimately resulted in a countrywide Vietnamese military occupation—the autocratic rule of yet another communist-inspired government, which then controlled an enervated Cambodian society and political economy for the ensuing decade. During the first ten of these twenty years, from 1970 until 1980, close to one-third of Cambodia's population, almost two million people,[2] died from violence and neglect caused by political and military conflicts and economic experiments that turned into mad social misadventures: first from the massive number of American bombs that were dropped in the eastern regions of the country in the early 1970s (an aspect of the escalation of the Second Indochina War that directly precipitated Cambodia's own civil war);[3] second, from the intense military fighting that occurred between the US-supported and rightist Lon Nol (the Republic of Cambodia), which had staged a coup against the longtime neutralist government of Prince Norodom Sihanouk in 1970, on the one hand, and the China-backed Khmer Rouge revolutionary forces, on the other, the latter of which eventually established Democratic Kam-

puchea in 1975; third, and especially, from the insidiously forced reorganization of society and the menacing maltreatment of its own citizens
by the Khmer Rouge for the three years, eight months, and twenty days
that they remained in power; and finally, from the appalling rate of starvation that occurred during the earliest phases of the Vietnamese occupation
in 1980 and thereafter.

The vast majority of Cambodians who died during the intense American bombing campaign, the civil war, the period of Khmer Rouge power,
and the Vietnamese occupation were civilian noncombatants. During the
civil war, especially after May 1970, many innocent people in the countryside, perhaps as many as 150,000,[4] were killed by the devastation brought
about from the intense American bombings dropped on the eastern zones
of the country. Many more innocent people were subsequently killed in
the consequent fighting that broke out between the Lon Nol government
that had come to power with the overthrow of Prince Sihanouk's regime in
1970 and the rising forces of the Khmer Rouge.[5] Another 100,000 were to die
haplessly as refugees while the war dragged on to its conclusion in 1975.[6]
However, the massive number of innocent people who were simply abandoned and left to die, or maltreated in baleful ways that led to their deaths,
or were simply murdered in cold-blooded, systematic fashion during the
period of the Khmer Rouge regime, is staggering.[7] I discuss the nature,
aspirations, and effects of the Khmer Rouge on Cambodian society, especially its impact on the family, in the next section of this chapter, but for
now I want to make the simple but very fundamental point that the vast
majority of those unfortunate people who died in Cambodia during the
1970s amid all of the social and political mayhem died "unnatural deaths."

In popular Khmer Buddhist perspectives, consistent with earlier Indian and Sinhala perspectives, which have been nurtured by Buddhist
tradition as well, those who die a tragic death, whose final moments are
violent, who die unjustly, or who "die in the street" rather than peacefully
at home, are thought to experience grave difficulties in making the transition to the next life beyond or to a new positive rebirth in this world. While
it is a question that has been debated many times throughout the history
of Buddhist thought, what transmigrates from this life to the next, at least
karmically speaking, is the very quality of the mental conditioning process
that is consciously in play at the moment of death. In Pali, this consciousness is known as *vinnana* and more literally means "knowing awareness."
For this reason, Buddhists almost always try to assist their dying family
members to engage death as peacefully as possible. In Theravada tradition, this means attempting to make the dying feel the warmth and love
of *metta* (loving-kindness) and *karuna* (compassion). Chanted, soothing,

gentle, and reassuring words are given to the dying while death impends. Ideally, one's last experiences should be the mirror opposite condition of violent and agitated frightful terror. Moreover, those whose deaths have not been addressed properly through ritual are regarded as not having been "laid to rest," or "put in their place," as it were, and are also thought to be experiencing badly the suffering of *dukkha* in the world beyond. People who die in terrible ways, without benefit of the comfort of their family's care, without benefit of effectively performed ritual, or those who commit questionable moral acts that require retribution, are the very types of people who become lingering ghosts, the *petas*[8] of the Buddhist "Pali imaginaire,"[9] the suffering beings who roam the margins of the world. Hence, *petas* often appear, according to ancient Buddhist literature, especially in the *Petavatthu* (Stories of the Departed) of the *Khuddaka Nikaya*,[10] or in the reports of contemporary Khmer Buddhist folk, in the "betwixt and between" condition of liminality. They often are said to appear to their loved ones in dreams, during twilight hours, at crossroads, at the edges of the temple *sima* (consecrated boundaries), and so on. The rituals constituting *pchum ben* are basically celebrated to help these suffering and wandering beings to become settled ancestors who can garner the respect and karmic patronage of the continuing family.

Shortly after the Vietnamese forced the Khmer Rouge out of their control over Cambodia in 1979, they initiated commemorations of the massive number of Khmer dead in ways reminiscent of how they had commemorated their own dead in Vietnam. That is, they emphasized commemorating the dead as fallen heroes in the war against imperialism or as victims of genocide. The latter strategy is quite understandable, especially in light of the fact that Vietnamese and other ethnicities suffered persecution in even greater percentages than the Khmer under the Khmer Rouge reign in Democratic Kampuchea. In fact, one of the first official acts that the Vietnamese promulgated after they had wrested control of Cambodia from the Khmer Rouge was the establishment of the Tuol Sleng Museum of Genocide (the infamous S-21 interrogation center in Phnom Penh[11]) and what is now the "Killing Fields" memorial at nearby Choeung Ek, both established in an effort to provide heroic commemoration of the dead and to disgrace the Khmer Rouge, simultaneously. Hinton has described the Vietnamese strategy in the following way:

> Memory mixed with politics as the PRK [Peoples' Republic of Kampuchea] regime set out to establish a narrative of the recent past that would buttress their legitimacy both domestically and abroad. Genocide stood at the center of this story. The new political narrative centered around the theme

of a magnificent revolution subverted by a small group of evil doers led by "Pol Pot," "Pol Pot—Ieng Sary," or "Pol Pot-Ieng Sary-Khieu Samphan clique." Inspired by a deviant Maoist strain of socialism, the narrative went, this clique misled or coerced lower-ranking cadre [including by implication, PRK leaders who were former Khmer Rouge] into unwittingly participating in a misdirected campaign of genocide. As a result, most former Khmer Rouge cadres, including, by implication, PRK officials, were not ultimately responsible for the events that transpired during DK. (2008, 68)

The promulgation of this perspective benefited their Cambodian collaborationists, including Heng Samrin and Hun Sen, who had originally been part of the Khmer Rouge but had defected to Vietnam about two years after the fall of Lon Nol's government, when they had felt themselves personally threatened by the Khmer Rouge.[12]

Anthropologist Heonik Kwon has written a remarkable book about how the dead have been memorialized in postwar Vietnam, a subject of great relevance for the situation in neighboring Cambodia, given the Vietnamese "administrative presence" in Cambodia for a decade following the catastrophes inflicted on the population by the Khmer Rouge. Kwon's examination of how the dead have been treated and remembered in postwar Vietnam is complex, subtle, and insightful. Essentially, he argues that the new postcolonial political elite of Vietnam attempted to "shift the focus of festivals and commemoration away from the village and the family and toward the state." In the process, they attempted a "selective redemption of the past" for the purposes of rendering the state as the beneficiary of emotions for the dead (2006, 4). Those who had died heroically against imperialist enemies, who embodied the struggle for freedom in their heroic acts of self-sacrifice, were worthy objects of veneration and commemoration. Such was the initial manner in which the dead who suffered at the hands of the Khmer Rouge were fielded and interpreted for political consumption.

Unwittingly, this interpretation of the dead, casting them as heroic resisters to the evil acts of their inhumane enemies, actually plays out a critical element of the distorted pathology of paranoia that plagued the Khmer Rouge. Documents discovered at the S-21 Tuol Sleng interrogation center, now analyzed in some depth, reveal that the Khmer Rouge leadership suffered gravely from deep obsessions of mistrust and paranoia. They brutally tortured mostly innocent village or middle-class people in their custody in order to extract confessions about alleged collusions with either the CIA or with the Vietnamese. They almost completely fabricated a sustained belief in conspiracy efforts allegedly directed against them by these two supreme enemies.[13] The fact is that those who died at the hands of the Khmer Rouge, either in the detention centers where mass murder was committed or in collectivized agricultural fields of toil and hunger, were not fallen heroes from the battlefields of war. They were simply victims of maltreatment born of a collectively-held sinister psychosis, most of them confused and terrified about why they had been relocated away from their families or singled out for torture.

In his study of postwar Vietnam, Kwon deftly points out the limitations and ultimate failure of the Vietnamese state strategy to co-opt the political significance of the dead through hero commemoration. The Marxist or revolutionary "scientific" doctrine of the Vietnamese state, of course, militated against all types of superstitious acts, including ancestor veneration. The dead were to be regarded as "alive" or functionally useful only to the extent that their commemorations could serve to bolster the enduring moral voice of the party or the state. In their lives and in their deaths, serving the state is what made their lives meaningful. But in such a perspective, there are a vast number of dead whose memories or commemorations simply cannot be accommodated: the dead, for instance, who fought *against* the victorious side in Vietnam;[14] or, the dead who simply died because they got in the way of the fierce fighting between combatants; or, the dead who Kwon writes about at great length in his book, those innocent villagers who were massacred by Korean and American troops in the villages of Ha My and My Lai in central Vietnam. Indeed, Kwon has joined other scholars in asserting that "[a]ncestral rites . . . became a critical locus for a contest of power between the state and family" (Kwon 2006, 5). And as in Cambodia, so in Vietnam, "the demise of the centrally planned socialist economy resulted in the revival of ancestral rituals as a way of strengthening the moral basis of the family—a principal unit in the new economic environment." In his analysis, Kwon describes how the return to privatized agriculture in postwar Vietnam, just as in postwar Cambodia, has led to the growing promotion of various family ritual activities and family memorial renovations "to console the spirits of the tragic dead."[15]

This is precisely the role of *pchum ben* in Cambodia. It has become the repository for the articulation of grief, veneration, and hope for the dead, regardless of the circumstances of their deaths. It has been the arena for the expression of actions that assuage the pains of a collective horror for some, and a way to manage a collective guilt for a few others (those who cooperated with the Khmer Rouge). It is a veritable ritual process reflecting how Cambodians are coming to terms with the tragedy of their recent past, and how some of them are dealing with the unknown facts of their own personal family histories.

It was only after the departure of the Vietnamese in 1989 that some relief came from the official sanctions of the socialist struggle on the cultural front, from the incessant governmental warnings about the wastefulness of religious ritual, and from the official sermons about the antirationality of antiscientific and superstitious backward customs. That is, the hostility toward traditional forms of religious culture finally began to abate, and people were free to publicly venerate the dead in familiar religious and familial fashion.

But there was another reason why the state-sponsored cult of the hero promulgated by the Vietnamese did not prove very effective among the Khmer in Cambodia in the 1980s. During the civil war and the subsequent Khmer Rouge period, the vast majority of those who died unnaturally did so largely at the hands of other Khmer, not against some external imperialist enemy. While it is true that many Vietnamese died at the hands of other Vietnamese during the Second Indochina War, the American presence and role in Vietnam was perceived as the dominant outside and Western colonial power that threatened the future of the nation. The Americans were also understood as successors to the French, as a behemoth military power that needed to be overcome and defeated at all costs. The challenge presented by the American intervention was almost overwhelming. There is no question that the American force constituted the major enemy face and that the American presence lent itself to an oppositional perspective in which the Vietnamese could understand themselves as an oppressed underdog fighting heroically for independence and freedom against an invading imperialist power. Because of this, the end of the fighting in Vietnam signaled a clear victory to be claimed and cherished by that underdog, a victory won against the perception of very long odds. The very same logic obtained in Laos.[16] By comparison, in Cambodia in 1979, the major external aggressors, who styled themselves as liberators of a sort, were the Vietnamese, whose presence, the longer it was sustained after the initial period, was not necessarily warmly welcomed. Nor were their interpretations of the dead.

Kwon has demonstrated how ancestor rites "became a locus for a contest of power between the state and the family" in the Vietnamese context. He also argues that

[the] revived tradition of ancestor worship can help to bring the memory of victims to private and communal places of worship, especially a generation after the tragedy when the victims, the young ones included, become ancestors. . . . If revolutionary doctrine preaches against all superstitious practices, including unauthorized attention to the fate of the dead, the

traditional religious ideals, when revived, may counter it by adopting some elements from the politically dominant hero worship. (2006, 5)

Inadvertently, Kwon's description of the dynamic in Vietnam squares up precisely with the contemporary Cambodian scene, insofar as "modernist" Buddhist monks argue how *pchum ben*, as a practice of ancestor veneration, is not really found in the canonical Pali *Tipitaka*, and therefore is not essentially Buddhist. Nevertheless, they do assert that *pchum ben* should be encouraged because it is such a cardinal expression of Khmer culture, national identity, and custom. This argument itself constitutes a kind of political statement, especially when *pchum ben*'s origins are tied to the kingship of the nineteenth-century Khmer king Ang Duang, whose reign, as we shall see, is not only equated in popular memory with a revival of Khmer culture, but also was the last Cambodian reign of kingship before the French colonial protectorate was established in 1863. I argue that the assessment of *pchum ben*'s origins as a nineteenth-century phenomenon is, in the final analysis, really not historically accurate, that instead its origins are actually rooted deep in the ancient Indian past and probably have been influenced somewhat by the medieval Chinese ghost festival as well. But the fact that *pchum ben* has been construed in this particular cultural manner by many "modernist" Buddhist monks, as a Khmer national pastime, seems quite congruent with what Kwon has asserted in the postwar Vietnamese context:

> [The] revival of ancestor worship in Vietnam, then, is not merely a restoration of traditional social ideals but rather an invention of a countermeasure against dominant political convention. . . . The revived ancestral worship in Vietnam contributes to undoing the legacy of the war by assimilating the historical duality of "this side" and "that side" to the traditional unity of the family. (2006, 161–163)

In Cambodia, *pchum ben* seems to have functioned in exactly this kind of way once the Vietnamese left the country for good in 1989 and the Khmer were left to embrace their own social lives publicly once again: *pchum ben became a major celebration of the family on a national scale, and something of a celebration of the nation on a family scale.* In Vietnam, it seems to be the case that "the popular revival of ancestor worship frustrated the political leaders who saw it as hampering the prospects of an economically prosperous nation. . . . The family worship practices and the popular ritual economy appeared to some officials to be the apparition of an old ghost that would hinder the nation's march forward into the prosperous commodity market economy" (Kwon 2006, 111). Moreover, "[t]he forceful emergence of ancestors and ghosts into the public arena hitherto dominated by war heroes crystallizes the decisive shift in power relations between the state and society. Changes in the social life of the dead, in this context, mirror changes in the political life of the living" (178).

No such kind of state skepticism regarding ancestor veneration has been seen in contemporary Cambodia. Indeed, as Judy Ledgerwood (2008b) has insightfully demonstrated, Cambodia's political leaders after the departure of the Vietnamese, despite the fact that some were one-time Khmer Rouge members themselves, have aligned themselves publicly since 1990 with traditional forms of Buddhist ritual practice, to the extent that Buddhism was declared the country's state religion in 1993. While there may not have been skepticism from the political players about the emergence of *pchum ben,* it is also true that the changes in the public ritual life of the country mirrored corresponding changes in the relationship between state and society. From a political point of view, *pchum ben's* popularity rests on the basis not only that it is a Buddhist practice, but also that it is understood primarily as a Khmer practice.

I think, however, that more than national politics and Khmer identity is at stake in this discussion. *Pchum ben's* popularity has more to do existentially with the fact that it celebrates the health and well-being of the family and the village or community. As Kwon has stated in the final conclusion to his study:

> An ideal place for remembering the victims of mass death, if there is such a place, might be home, where they can be remembered as ancestors. . . . It should be a place where kinship, free from traditional ideologies and political control, reconciles with the universal ethic that all human beings have the right to be remembered. The revitalized memory of mass death relies on this universal norm as well as on the morality of local kinship unity. (2006, 182)[17]

Indeed, sociologically, it was the family unit in Khmer society that suffered the most from the social, economic, and political spasms of the 1970s and 1980s in Cambodia. The current popularity of *pchum ben* seems to be a register of the relative reclaimed health not only of Khmer political fortunes that appeal to the culture of traditional Khmer Buddhist identity, but also of the health of the nuclear and extended family as a social institution in Cambodia. Insofar as villages are often made up of intermarried extended families, the village is also the object of ritual rehabilitation as well.

Within the context of this discussion regarding commemoration of the dead in Vietnam and Cambodia in the aftermath of the 1970s and 1980s, it also needs to be emphasized, if we are going to understand why *pchum ben* is so popular in the Khmer milieu, that Khmer ancestor veneration and Vietnamese ancestor veneration do not exactly correlate. Vietnamese conceptions and practices of ancestor veneration have been much more conditioned by the historical presence of Confucian ideology and practice within Vietnamese society and culture. As a result, the worship of tablets symbolic of ancestral presence on an altar within the home, or the construction of small shrines dedicated exclusively for the worship of a family's lineage, are norms of cultic behavior in the typical Vietnamese household that are not found among the Khmer. Veneration in the Vietnamese family context is a continuous or daily cultic affair. In Khmer society, despite the fact the family is without a doubt the most important social unit in society, the worship of ancestors is much more the by-product of indigenous beliefs in spirits and Theravada Buddhist conceptions of the afterlife, the latter of which I discuss in some depth shortly. A key difference, then, between the Vietnamese and the influence they have derived from Chinese Confucian and Mahayana Buddhists on the one hand, and the Khmer Theravada Buddhists on the other, is that the dead and the living in the Khmer context are not continuously intertwined. In Khmer Buddhist culture, in effect, the dead are given their own place and time, and their contact with the living is therefore limited to those times and places when and where the two are allowed to come together. That place is the Buddhist temple and that time is the *pchum ben* ritual season toward the end of *vassa*. The interaction at these times and places is intense, and it occurs within the context of an annual family reunion.

According to Ang Choulean, the noted Khmer archeologist and anthropologist, *pchum ben* solves a contradiction or paradox that is deep-seated in Mon-Khmer culture. In ancient Mon culture, the dead were dispensed with quickly, or "rejected," as it were, and "kept at bay." Following seven days after death, there was virtually no more exchange between the living and the dead. The dead were, at that time, laid to rest ritually and thereby divorced from the continuing reality of the living world. Ang Choulean believes that this notion of the rejection of the dead, or the separation of the living from the dead, remains unconsciously present among today's Khmer and contrasts sharply with the emphasis placed on revering one's ancestors that has come by way of Indian influence through Buddhism, or by way of Chinese influence through Confucian rites. The contradiction is resolved through the temporary period of fifteen days during *pchum ben* in September/October when the spirits are permitted to gain access to their living descendants in the world.[18] In other words, the dead have been given a limited time and limited space, and that time and that space is perhaps the most spiritually potent that can be imagined in Khmer religious culture: the intensified time period of ascetic religious pursuit among the monks in the Buddhist monastery during the last weeks of the *vassa* rain-retreat and within the continuously sanctified ritual space of the *sima* (boundary) of the *wat* (temple).

FAMILY AND RELIGION IN BUDDHIST CAMBODIA: THE IMPACT OF THE KHMER ROUGE

The great popularity of *pchum ben* in contemporary Cambodia may be generally a by-product of the social, economic, and political upheavals of the 1970s and 1980s that resulted in such a huge spike in the death rate, but its surge in national importance is also due specifically to the manner in which it has abetted the recovery of the nuclear family. In precolonial Khmer culture, it can be argued that the family and the Buddhist *sangha* were not only the two most important social units in society, but they were also essentially the *only* social units constitutive of Khmer society, with perhaps the only other social grouping being military units maintained by the royalty. This was not always viewed positively by outside observers. In the following passage, David Chandler describes how this social fact was fielded, and rather poorly, by some European colonialists:

> French writers in the nineteenth century often denigrated Cambodian society [one of them referred to its institutions as "worm-eaten debris"] and compared it unfavorably with their own "rational," centralized one or with that of the Vietnamese. . . . [I]n Thai and Cambodian villages, in the nineteenth century at least, there were no "durable, functionally important groups" or voluntary associations aside from the family and the Buddhist monastic order, or *sangha*. (2008, 126)

One particular incident, the assassination of the French resident Felix Louis Bardez at Kampong Chhnang in 1925, is quite revealing with regard to the importance of the family and the *sangha* in Khmer society on the one hand, and the kinds of French insensitivities to local cultural norms that often left them held in contempt by the local people on the other. The event has been described in some detail by Chandler (2008, 191–194), but I briefly summarize it here to illustrate the larger point. While collecting taxes in the village of Kraang Laev, the chief monk of the local *wat* had told Bardez that local people simply did not have enough money to pay. Bardez, who even after fifteen years of service in Cambodia could not speak Khmer, would have none of it, and told the chief monk to persuade the villagers that they should pay the requirement by whatever means possible.

He used the rather unconvincing argument that, just as one should honor one's parents, since the French were now the parents of the Cambodian people, the villagers were duty-bound to cough up the money. Bardez also allegedly insulted the villagers by suggesting that if they could afford to build their new Buddhist temple, then they should be able to pay their taxes to the guardian familial French. Subsequently, Bardez and his two assistants were twice attacked, the second time costing him his life. In retrospect, it would seem as if this French administrator could not have played his hand any more poorly. He not only insulted the Khmer concept of family and threatened its well-being and future livelihood by insisting that taxes be paid,[19] but he also badly misjudged the colonial state's importance in Khmer eyes by criticizing the villagers for putting their efforts into constructing a temple rather than "patriotically" supporting the French administration of their country. It would also seem as if Bardez was totally ignorant of how important supporting the *sangha* is to the ideology of merit-making as well.[20]

That the family and *sangha* remained the pillar social units of Khmer society is born out in the landmark ethnography composed by May Ebihara, an anthropologist who produced the only thorough academic ethnography of Khmer village life before the maelstrom of events that swept the country into chaos in 1970 and after. Ebihara's work was wide-angled and dedicated to understanding the totality of Khmer village worldviews. She reported that Khmer villagers, like Sinhalese, Thai, and Burmese Buddhists, "conceive of their religious culture in terms of what is essentially a single religious system" and did not

> segregate various elements of village religious beliefs and practices as deriving from one religious tradition or another, . . . Buddha and ghosts, prayers at the temple and invocations of spirits, monks and mediums are all part of the same religious culture and simply different aspects of which are called into play at different, appropriate times. (1968, 364)

What she goes on to report, then, is commensurate with what many other later ethnographers of Southeast Asian societies would assert: that the *sangha* and the family not only constitute the two social institutions of greatest significance in Theravada-inclined societies, but that the relationship between the two is also of paramount importance. What we shall see, when analyzing *pchum ben* in detail, is that family and *sangha* are understood as mutually interdependent.

It is worth reviewing some of the salient statements that Ebihara provides regarding the nature and importance of the family in Khmer culture and society, for they help to reinforce the thesis that *pchum ben* is the ritual way the family's sustenance has recovered and is now celebrated. She states, for instance, that

> the nuclear family can be considered the most fundamental social group in Khmer society, bound together by a variety of affective, economic moral and legal ties. The strongest and most enduing relationships are found in the bonds between husband and wife, sibling and sibling, and especially parent and child. Even after a family has split into the various families of procreation of the different offspring, members of the former obtain deep affection for and frequent contact with one another. . . . the Nuclear family is often the basic economic unit of production and consumption which cooperates in subsistence activities and shares produce, income and property. It also frequently acts [and is considered by others to be] a single social unit in other endeavors; e.g., in cooperative labor exchanges, the *quid pro quo* is calculated basically in terms of the amount of work owed by one family to another; in contributions to Buddhist and life cycle ceremonies, a gift is often meant to come from the family as a whole; and in community activities each family or household gives a certain amount of money or labor. (1968, 111)

Ebihara goes on to point out that relations between family members are defined, supported and sanctioned by "Buddhist precepts and teachings, by belief in ancestral spirits (*meba*) who oversee their descendants' conduct" (112). This last point about the *meba* or ancestors is of particular importance to the meaning of *pchum ben*, insofar as it indicates something of the reciprocal relationship that obtains between the living and the ancestral dead. The living need ancestors to function as guardians, markers, or symbols of their own moral bases. And so they need to rehabilitate those ancestors about whom they are unsure. The unknown status of one's ancestor(s) is one of the great moments of pathos so frequently encountered at *pchum ben* rites in Cambodia today. Penny Edwards has underscored how important it is that "[a] moral genealogy links current generations to the standard of ancestral behavior: here, ancestors become moral arbitrators, and represent a mythical standard of morality against which contemporary generations can be judged by current elders" (2008b, 221). That is, the bond between the living and the dead is an expression of their moral dependence on each other. This is particularly true when the dead being venerated are one's parents. In Khmer culture, the bond between parents and offspring is perhaps even deeper and stronger than between husband and wife.[21] The importance of this relationship likely has been a staple of Khmer society since the days of the great Angkor civilization, at least from what we know of the ritual and cultural expressions of its elites, particularly within the context of the veneration of parents and Saivite

Hindu adaptations from the ninth through the thirteenth centuries CE.[22] Kings often built temples to honor their parents and identified them with installed images within of Siva and Parvati (or Uma).

Of those commentators who have written about the subject of the family's importance within Khmer society, Erik Davis' reflections are among the most perceptive and comprehensive. He has clearly pointed out how the social experience of the nuclear family becomes paradigmatic for how processes within Khmer society at large are envisaged and then negotiated. He writes:

> The more intimate one's relationship with another, the more hierarchical that relationship, such as in the case of mother and child. The Cambodian family maps larger Cambodian society more flexibly than does the traditional Western family. Family boundaries appear loose, and various types of adoption, god-parenting, and other forms of "fictive kinship" have been documented. One's created family, in addition to one's birth family, produces the known and civilized world that we inhabit. This network of family members defines and delimits the boundaries of the social world, the land in which one may safely travel, the person one may trust and upon, on whom one may rely, and the networks of intimacies that compose our emotional geographies, those spaces where we recognize the emotional landmarks, and where we can navigate with more experience and confidence than with strangers. People say that this is true of family members all the way, potentially, to the "seventh generation." (2008a, 133)

While the penultimate sentence in the quote from Davis constitutes a powerful assessment of how the family functions for the epistemology of Khmer social psychology,[23] the final comment about seven generations of ancestors is also particularly relevant specifically with regard to *pchum ben*. It was commonly believed in medieval China (Teiser 1996, 220–221) that ancestors continued to receive support from their descendants for seven generations before they were reincarnated as members of the family once again. This popular Chinese tradition may have had some influence on the reification of the Khmer conception, for the same belief about the possibility of supporting ancestors for seven generations remains in play during *pchum ben*. Family ancestors of the past seven generations can be assisted and supported by means of karma transfers that occur during *banguskol,* a merit-generating ritual of chanting Pali *suttas* that is performed by Buddhist monks at the behest of family descendants during the final day of the *pchum ben* season.

These views from various scholars writing about the centrality of the nuclear family unit in Khmer society and culture underscore why the revolution orchestrated by Khmer Rouge was so socially and psychologically traumatic, especially for those who managed to survive when the rest of their family members did not. Francois Bizot is a French scholar of Khmer Buddhism whose own intimate experiences with the Khmer Rouge, owing to his own extended incarceration in one of their detention centers, is revealed dramatically in his dialogues with the convicted murderer who was in charge of the notorious S-21 (Tuol Sleng) interrogation center. In this classic confrontation recorded between perhaps the most knowledgeable Western student of Khmer culture and society on the one hand, and one of Pol Pot's chief lieutenants on the other, Bizot has managed to illustrate how the ideology of the Khmer Rouge was completely antithetical to the social and moral norms of traditional Khmer Buddhist society and culture. Because of Bizot's deep knowledge of Khmer language and religious culture,[24] and because of his extensive rich and remarkable years of life experience in Cambodia, I emphasize his perspectives on the Khmer Rouge in what follows, especially as he analyzed what was at stake for the Khmer family and the Buddhist *sangha*.

To begin, this is how Bizot describes in general the ethic of the Khmer Rouge revolutionary cadre: "Denunciation is the first duty of the revolutionary. They quoted the example of some young men who so loved the revolution that they were unafraid to denounce their fathers or their brothers" (Bizot 2003, 54). In place of the traditionally strong kinship bonds of the family, the Khmer Rouge demanded absolute loyalty and, as an organization (*angkar*), jealously guarded its position of authority and brooked no competition from other social forms or groups whatsoever. Chandler's depiction of the young people between fifteen and twenty-five years of age who formed the core of Khmer Rouge cadre is not dissimilar to Bizot's:

> Owing everything to the revolutionary organization, which they referred to as their mother and father, and nothing to the past, it was thought that these young people would lead the way in transforming Cambodia into a socialist state and in moving the people toward independence, mastery, and self-reliance. To the alarm and the confusion of many older people, these often violent Cambodians became the revolution's cutting edge. (2008, 258)

It is not altogether surprising that the ethic of these young Khmer Rouge cadres was antithetical to the cardinal values of traditional Khmer society, for "[i]n every way their behavior validated the arguments of those who had already suggested that the Khmer Rouge had drawn its forces from the most marginal of Cambodia's population. These were men and women, and perhaps above all children, who had dwelt on the outskirts of society, for whom the cities and those who had lived in them were centers of corrupt behavior inhabited by their oppressors" (Osborne 2008, 143). Indeed, according to Bizot, most of the Khmer Rouge cadres were not drawn from the agricultural countryside, which was definitely the case with the cadres constituting the Pathet Lao in Laos, wherein the powerful linkages between Theravada Buddhism and the agricultural way of life, between religion and rice, had been wedded and nurtured for centuries. Rather, these were youth who, ironically, were largely drawn from the city. In putting together a profile of their quixotic yet iconoclastic character, Bizot writes just how far the Khmer Rouge would go to debase the

> traditional system of values. To place letters of Buddhist doctrine in contact with the regions of the body considered "impure" was an absolute sacrilege, one no peasant would risk committing. Only town-dwellers would be capable of such iconoclastic radicalism. The majority [of Khmer Rouge cadres] were poorly integrated Sino-Khmers, the sons of shopkeepers or frustrated employees. Having replaced the traditional village structures with fraternal solidarity, motivated by a sincere idealism, and appalled by the gap between the rich and poor, they shared an existence outside of the rural world, which they knew nothing about. None of them had ever tended rice fields. The way they roamed around the countryside proved they had no respect for crops, gardens, trees or pathways. Nor did they show any deference to sacred images or to anything Buddhism held dear, regarding it all as peasant superstition, cultivated from Angkor by every monarch, to subdue the people. Paradoxically, these city folk, who loathed the plough, the soil, the palm groves and domestic animals, who disliked the open rustic life of the villagers, had an idealized concept of the Khmer peasant as agent of the perpetual revolution, a model of simplicity, endurance and patriotism, the standard against which the new man would be measured, liberated from religious taboos. In this contradictory scenario, Buddhism was replaced by objectives dear to the Angkar, in order to ensure the triumph of equality and justice. The Khmer theorists had substituted Angkar for Dhamma, [as] the personification of Teaching. (2003, 62–63)

Not only did the Khmer Rouge insist on a loyalty that transcended the bonds of family and village relations, but they seemed, at least from Bizot's considered perspective, to function, as he implies toward the end of the statement above, as a kind of surrogate for the Khmer Buddhist monastic *sangha*.[25] In a truly remarkable passage and, as it turns out, a very historically significant one,[26] Bizot writes of his dramatic confrontation with his interrogator, Comrade Douch, while he was being held captive at a remote prison site in the early 1970s. In this long passage at the heart of his personal memoir, he asserts analytically how the Khmer Rouge, with their zealous loyalty to the foundations of *angkar*, had managed to develop a programmatic ideology that was analogous both to the *dhamma* and *sangha* of the Theravada tradition, a view that is scoffed at by Douch in the end. Yet, Douch's comments also belie *angkar*'s suspicion of the family. Bizot's insights are powerful and provocative, and well worth a thorough consideration in determining how the family and the Buddhist *sangha* were the primary social victims of the Khmer Rouge purge. In turn, it is both the family and the *sangha* that are the social entities revived and celebrated within the ritual contexts of *pchum ben*.

"Comrade!" I began, "You speak about Angkar the way that monks speak about Dhamma. So I want to ask you this: is there some ideologist among you, constructing a revolutionary theory based upon the myths and rules of the Buddhist religion?"

Douch was taken back.

"Because, after all," I went on, "are you not defending a new religion? I've followed your educational lessons. They're not unlike courses in Buddhist doctrine: renouncing material possessions, *giving up family ties, which weaken us and prevent us from devoting ourselves entirely to Angkar; leaving our parents and our children in order to serve the revolution.* Submitting to discipline and confessing faults—"

"That has nothing to do with it!" Douch cut in.

"There are ten 'moral commandments' that you call *sila*," I persisted, "that have the same name as the ten Buddhist 'abstentions' [*sila*]. The revolutionary must accept the rules of a *vinaya*, exactly as the monk observes a religious 'discipline' [*vinaya*]. At the start of his instruction, a young soldier is given a pack containing six articles [trousers, shirt, cap, *krama*, sandals, bag], just as the novice monk receives a regulation kit of seven items—"

"These are intellectual ravings!" he broke in.

"That's not all! Wait, comrade," I said, raising my hand. "Look at the facts. In everything you tell me, and in what I have heard myself, one finds religious themes from the past: taking on a new name, for example; enduring hardships, rather like ritual mortification; even the soothing, enticing words of Radio Peking announcing the advent of a regenerated people, born of the revolution. In a word, the Communist leaders to whom you are accountable want to impose an initiatory death on the nation."

My speech was answered by a stubborn silence.

"Comrade Douch!" I continued, raising my voice before he could start speaking again. "The resoluteness of the teachers who speak in the name of the Angkar is unconditional. Sometimes it is even devoid of hatred and purely objective, as if the human aspect of the question did not come into consideration, as if it were an intellectual concept. They mechanically carry out the impersonal, absolute directives of the Angkar, even going to extreme lengths. As to the peasants who come under your control, they are subjected, purely and simply, to a sort of purification rite: new teaching,

new mythology and an amended vocabulary that no-one initially understands. *Then the Angkar is adopted as family, while true kin are rejected.* And
after the population is divided into 'initiates' and 'novices.' The first constitute the true people, that is to say, those who have been won over; others
are those who have not completed the period of preparation and training;
only after that can they be admitted into the former group and acquire the
superior status of an accomplished citizen. Need I go on?"

"That has nothing to do with it!" Douch repeated. "Buddhism benumbs
the peasants, whereas the Angkar seeks to glorify them and build prosperity of the beloved homeland on them! You attribute scholarly ravings
to bogus ideologues when they belong only to yourself. Buddhism is the
opium of the people. And I don't see why we should draw our inspiration
from a capitalist past, which is the very thing that we want to abolish! When
we have rid our country of the vermin that infect people's minds," he went
on, "when we have liberated it from this army of cowards and traitors who
debase the people, then we will rebuild a Cambodia of solidarity, united
by genuine bonds of fraternity and equality. First we must construct our
democracy on healthy foundations that have nothing to do with Buddhism.
Corruption has seeped in everywhere, *even among families. How can you
trust your brother when he accepts the imperialists' wages and employs their
arms against you?* Believe me, Comrade Bizot, our people need to rediscover
moral values that correspond to their deeper aspirations. The revolution
wishes nothing for them besides simple happiness: that of the peasant who
feeds himself from the fruits of his labours, with no need for the Western
products that have made him a dependent consumer. We can manage and
organize ourselves on our own to bring radiant happiness to our beloved
country." (2003, 110–112; italics mine; brackets original)

What Bizot has managed to indicate so adroitly in this incredible passage is not only how the Buddha's *dhamma* and *sangha* could be demonstrably eclipsed and replaced functionally in favor of the *angkar* and its own
substantially similar code of moral discipline, but how the family was regarded by the Khmer Rouge as an impediment to the realization of its
utopian aims for Cambodian society. From the Khmer Rouge perspective,
the primary social institution of the Khmer family was linked to the evils
of private property ownership and capitalistic production, in the same
way that Buddhism was understood as an opiate of the people repressing
a true vision of egalitarian society. Both family and religion (especially
Buddhism), therefore, had to be eliminated in the march forward into a
true socialist society. The social and intellectual functions of the family
and Buddhism could be aptly replaced, and necessarily so, by *angkar*.[27]

Douch's concluding rant against Bizot was no idle threat. What happened to Buddhist monks and Buddhist institutions when the Khmer

Rouge seized control in 1975 is a terrible tale, yet it must be told so that it can never be forgotten. The broadside attack on Buddhism was but a part of a larger process taking place in which the Khmer Rouge sought to dismantle virtually any previously established bases of personal, familial, or religious identity.[28] Skidmore has described this process as an attempt to "restructure personality":

> The major focus of Khmer Rouge personality restructuring was . . . manifested as an attempt to strip Cambodians of their sense of personal individuality and collective identity. In destroying Buddhism in all its forms [disrobing of monks, smashing of effigies, etc.], in uprooting them from their homes, ancestors and guardian spirits; in forcing them to live silently in communal huts; and in removing all personal effects and sentimental items, conformity was enforced, and individualism shattered. The place of a person within a particular cosmological, societal, and familial world was abolished as effectively as the Khmer Rouge could manage. (1997, 6; brackets original)

Others have described what happened during the time of Khmer Rouge hegemony as a consequence of misplaced, zealous, revolutionary fervour. Chandler, for instance, in describing the program inculcated by the clandestine leaders of "the revolutionary organization" (*angkar*), says this:

> They sought to transform Cambodia by replacing what they saw as impediments to national autonomy and social justice with revolutionary energy and incentives. They believed that family, individualism, and an ingrained fondness for what they called feudal institutions, as well as the institutions themselves, stood in the way of the revolution. Cambodia's poor, they said, had always been exploited and enslaved. Liberated by the revolution and empowered by military victory, these men and women would now become the masters of the their lives and, collectively, the masters of their country. (Chandler 2008, 256)

Writing in a somewhat different and more abstract vein, but describing in detail the precise means by which the Khmer Rouge went about systematically attacking the foundations of social memory, Hinton argues:

> [In] their radical experiment in social engineering, the Khmer Rouge launched an assault on the past, seeking to obliterate everything that smacked of capitalism, "privatism," and class oppression. This attack ranged far and wide. The Khmer rouge targeted Buddhism, the family, village structure, economic activity, and public education—key socio-cultural institutions through which memory was ritually, formally and informally

transmitted. More specifically, they assaulted social memory by burning books and destroying libraries, banning popular music, movies, media, and styles, destroying temples, truncating communication, terminating traditional holidays and ritual events, separating family members, homogenizing clothing, and eliminating private property, including photos, memorabilia and other mementos. (2008, 62)

Ian Harris has focused comments about the impact of the Khmer Rouge more specifically on the Buddhist *sangha*, but he has also pointed out how even the less institutionalized dimensions of Khmer religious culture suffered atrophy because of the manner in which the population was uprooted. Virtually all city folk were forced into the countryside, but most villagers were also forced to move to new locations where makeshift communes had been hastily established. Basic living conditions in these new contexts were extremely harsh, as villagers were not allowed to bring hardly any personal accoutrements with them. So while "[i]nformants [say] . . . that they surreptitiously maintained spirit shrines during the Democratic Kampuchea period . . . , the frequent movements of the population after 1975 severed the links between villagers and their ancestors. In consequence, belief in the whole panoply of autochthonous mythological beings, including the tutelary spirits, or *neak ta,* began to disintegrate" (Harris 2005, 176). My point in emphasizing this citation from Harris at this juncture is to underscore how *pchum ben* would eventually become the ritual means by which links with the ancestors would be restored.

While the nuclear family, including links to ancestors, disintegrated under Khmer Rouge policies, institutional Buddhism was practically destroyed. Buddhist monastic leaders of the *sangha* should not have been caught so off guard when the Khmer Rouge finally seized power in April 1975. "Even before the outbreak of the civil war that would end the short-lived Khmer Republic [1970–1975], the CPK [Communist Party of Kampuchea] was pointing to the economic burden that so many unproductive monks place on the country. Not only were they leeches upon society, but they also taught the doctrine of karma, which underpinned the belief in 'natural inequality' and encouraged the laity to passively accept the status quo"[29] (Harris 2005, 163). At the conclusion of the civil war, the attacks ceased to be simply ideological and became institutional and physical instead. The Khmer Rouge leadership may not have been exactly sure about its practical plans for the Buddhist *sangha* in the years immediately leading up to the collapse of the Lon Nol government in April 1975. But a ruthlessly clear policy of eradication of all urban monks became evident from the very first day of their control. Most senior monks in Phnom Penh were killed immediately (Ledgerwood 2008b, 204). Harris describes in painful detail what happened to the *sangharaja*, the chief monk (or *sangha-reach*) of the dominant Mahanikay fraternity, and therefore the leading Buddhist cleric in the country during the first day immediately following the fall of Phnom Penh to the Khmer Rouge:

> After the communists had taken the Information Ministry on April 17, 1975, Ven. Huot That, the Mahanikay *sanghareach*, made a radio broadcast that appealed for a cease-fire and called on commanders to meet with the ousted military High Command, using the words "Now we have peace, put down your guns" [cited in Kiernan 1996, 36–37]. Huot That then returned to Wat Unnalom, where he was falsely accused of having a wife and children in Paris. Evidence brought before the Vietnamese-backed trial of Pol Pot in 1979 affirmed that Huot That was executed at Wat Prang in the old capital of Udong the following day. It is widely believed that he was crushed by a bulldozer. (2005, 175)

The leading monks of the *sangha* were easy targets. Yet, initially, there seems to have been some inconsistency in how the urban monks of Phnom Penh and how the monks of countryside *wat*s would be treated, especially in those areas of the countryside that previously had been nominally under Khmer Rouge control.

In the waning months of the Lon Nol government in the spring of 1975, the ranks of the *sangha* in the capital city had swelled as many frightened young Khmer men sought to avoid conscription from either side of the civil war and managed to find their way to Phnom Penh to seek refuge in the city's major *wat*s as *samanera*s, novice monks. Harris describes how these monks were treated in comparison to established rural monks:

> The Khmer Rouge called these monks "imperialists," "April 17 monks" or "new monks" in comparison to many rural monks who the Khmer Rouge referred to as "base monks." With the fall of Phnom Penh, "new monks" were rapidly laicized, and virtually none remained in robes by the beginning of the 1975 rainy season. In any case, they had no means of support, for the laity were no longer allowed to support the *sangha*. . . . A few monks managed to escape to neighboring countries. Most were sent to work, and if they resisted, they were executed just like everyone else. . . . The so-called "base monks" had a different fate and seem to have been initially tolerated, since many of them had been supportive of Khmer Rouge in the civil war. After the end of the 1975 *vassa* [September/October], we find isolated examples of an "inverted" *kathen* [*kathina*] ceremony . . . when selected monks were presented with revolutionary garb—black trousers, black shirt, and a traditional Khmer scarf [*krama*]—by communist officials, after which they were "invited"[30] to leave the monastic order. Doubtless, few refused. (2005, 177–178)

There is no doubt that ultimately the leadership of the Khmer Rouge decidedly adamantly and thoroughly directed its cadres to the effect that the *sangha* should be totally eliminated. Many temples were converted into interrogation centers and storage facilities. In temple spaces normally associated with the purity of moral behavior, as sanctuaries from the troubles of the routine world, indescribable atrocities occurred as thousands were tortured during the interrogation process. This fact graphically illustrates why Bizot understood the conduct of the Khmer Rouge as a "moral inversion." By the time the Khmer Rouge finished with institutional Buddhism, "it was estimated that five out of every eight monks were executed during Pol Pot's regime. . . . Images of the Buddha were often decapitated or desecrated in other ways; copies of the Buddhist scriptures were burned or thrown into rivers" (Keyes 1994, 56).[31] During the advent of Khmer Rouge hegemony, the *sangha* had already become a weakened, tottering institution during the civil war between 1970 and 1975. In those five years alone, about one-third of the *sangha*'s temples had been destroyed. Thus, the *sangha* was already a crippled and distorted social institution by the time the Khmer Rouge seized power and completely finished it off. In summing up, Charles Keyes has provided perhaps the most apt depiction of the impact of the Khmer Rouge on Theravada Buddhist religious culture in Cambodia during the malignant years of Democratic Kampuchea:

> Without the *sangha*, the Buddhist ritual life of the population had been almost totally eradicated; in its stead, the people were supposed to dedicate themselves to work. In no other Communist society, including even Tibet, was a materialist ideology so radically imposed at the expense of a spiritual tradition. The attack on Cambodian Buddhism went well beyond the Marxist notion that religion serves to disguise class relations. The Khmer Rouge sought, by eliminating the institution that had for so long served as the basic source of Khmer identity, to create a new order with few roots in the past. (1994, 58)

RITUAL AND SOCIO-MORAL REGENERATION

After the Vietnamese armies entered Cambodia and wrested control of the country away from the Khmer Rouge, they gradually relaxed restrictions on the public practice of Buddhism, though it cannot be said that they actually encouraged its practice. Initially, the Vietnamese promulgated a prohibition on the ordination of monks who were under the age of fifty years old, and established a quota for the total number of men who could be in robes at one time. Monks from the Khmer-dominant region of the Mekong delta in Vietnam were brought to Phnom Penh to reconstitute the ordination process, but the reform-minded and discipline-conscious Thammayut order, "because of its connections to Thai royalty," was not allowed to return. "It was not until after they [the Vietnamese] left and [the Khmer] royalty was re-established in Thailand that the Thommayut [*sic*] was again re-introduced" (Osborne 2008, 185).

Descriptions of life in Cambodia in 1979 and 1980 paint a very grim picture. There are many lurid descriptions composed during the past thirty years about the almost complete devastation of Khmer society, but those offered by Chandler (2008) and Osborne are among the most informative and vivid. Osborne writes:

> We now know that upwards of two million people had died while the Khmer rouge ruled Cambodia. The country was shattered physically and the number of those who remained alive and who possessed the skills required to make the country work had been drastically reduced. Only a tenth of the doctors who had been in the country in 1975 were still alive in 1979. There were even fewer teachers, proportionately, who had survived. Malnutrition was endemic among children, and within six months of the Vietnamese invasion the whole country was on the brink of starvation." (2008, 180)

Osborne also says that no more than 15 percent of the entire Khmer middle class survived, including the country's civil servants, its technically qualified people, and the business or commercial class (182). This meant that restarting the economy, the government, and the educational system was almost a matter of complete reinvention that would require perhaps a generation of training. The situation was further complicated by the fact that as the post–Khmer Rouge years wore on, the Vietnamese were increasingly hard-pressed to devote the resources necessary to revive the beleaguered economy and battered social structures, owing in part to the decreasing amounts of assistance that they, in turn, were receiving from the Soviet Union, itself on a course of decline that would lead to its implosion in 1989.[32] Assistance from Western countries was not forthcoming during the years of Vietnamese occupation in the 1980s because the United States, under the administration of Ronald Reagan, together with its allies, actually supported continuing Khmer Rouge claims in the United Nations to be the legitimate legal representative of the Cambodian people. This resulted in both government and private assistance from the West to Cambodia being largely precluded, though the sorry events of what had transpired in Cambodia in the 1970s, originally precipitated by the American military campaign, became increasingly known throughout the world in the early 1980s. Moreover, models for the government and economy that were initially launched by the Vietnamese and their Khmer collaborationists were models that were eventually jettisoned in the early 1990s. Suffice it to say that life in the 1980s was exceedingly grim, though without the immediate threats of terror, forced labor, torture, and violence that were the hallmarks of the Khmer Rouge.

Chandler's description complements the statistics provided by Osborne by giving us a more intimate view of the conditions of social process that were then in play. I have selected Chandler's description because he emphasizes the broken condition of the nuclear family in the aftermath of Khmer Rouge rule and the context in which the celebration of the *pchum ben* ritual season was restarted after a hiatus of about five years:

> Throughout 1979, and for most of 1980, hundreds of thousands of Cambodians crisscrossed the country looking for relatives returning to their homes. . . . As the PRK struggled to its feet, many prerevolutionary institutions, including markets, Buddhism and family farming, came back to life. Buddhists *wats* and schools opened soon afterward. . . . Villages had been abandoned or torn down, tools, seed, and fertilizer were nonexistent; hundreds of thousands of people had emigrated or been killed; and in most areas the survivors suffered from malaria, shock, or malnutrition. So many men died or disappeared in DK that in some districts more than 60 per cent of the families were headed by widows. Thousands of widows raised their families alone and with difficulty. (2008, 278–279)

As families were reunited and the violence of life under the Khmer Rouge became a painful memory of recent history, the extent of which only became more clear with the passage of time, many traditional ritual practices of Khmer Buddhist religious culture began to resurface, including weddings, funerals, and other annual rites in addition to *pchum ben*. Hayashi notes that "[t]he repairing of temples preceded all other activities in restoring Buddhism around Phnom Penh . . . [because] . . . temples were urgently required as the 'stages' to hold annual collective rites, e.g. *pachum bon*, the biggest and longest [15 days] merit transference ritual for the dead among the Khmer" (2003, 208). Hayashi also reports that it was the fall of 1980 before *pchum ben*, which he refers to as "the most important . . . among the annual rites," was performed again (214).

It is extraordinarily difficult, well-nigh impossible, to measure the degree of human suffering of a mental, physical, or social nature experienced by the Cambodian people for nearly twenty years, from 1970 until 1990. Indeed, the legacy of those twenty years is still being played out by the both older and younger generations today. Back in 1990, while problems of restarting the economy and the government were problematic, the problem of reinventing the family was even more acute.

Pchum ben is a ritual process that regenerates family cohesion among the living through pilgrimage, and family reunion through compassion, and thus merit-transfer, for the dead. In establishing ritual links to the dead, a kind of moral order is reestablished unconsciously. While moral order may be in part reestablished through a linking or re-union with the dead, the possible cases of dealing with immorality on the part of some ancestors can also be confronted within this ritual context as well. This is an especially difficult issue for those families with members who were active members of the Khmer Rouge or who publicly collaborated with them extensively. Zucker insightfully reflects on this issue:

> The loss of elders creates an obstacle to the restoration of moral order by impeding the transmission of traditional knowledge and practice and therefore creating a disjunction with the past and the ancestors. This limits the resources that may be excavated from the past to create society anew and curtails access to the ancestors' generative power. . . . [A]though villagers are restoring order by turning either towards tradition or towards what they consider "modern" ideologies and practices,[33] there is [also] the problem of the perceived immorality of the actions of elders and ancestors in the past. I suggest that this perception contributes to the sense of disorder and obstructs the remaking of order because these immoral elders and ancestors then present the negation of the narrative of the moral past, and they undermine people's vision of the original moral order as a whole. (2008, 197)

Yet, it is precisely because the moral condition of so many ancestors from the recent violent past is simply unknown that surviving kin feel compelled to undertake ritual actions specifically on their behalf. The fact that the dead are envisaged as *pretas* by those who attend the *pchum ben* rites means that the ritual is being undertaken by some as a kind of insurance policy against the possible deleterious fate of their kin. Zucker seems to understand this clearly herself. She states, "Order, then, is restored by honoring ancestors and then maintained through the predictable transmission of stories, rituals and customs that are drawn from the ancestral past" (2008, 196). That is, moral order is affirmed by the family, reestablished within the context of ancestor veneration. Troubled ancestors may be rehabilitated by the righteous actions of their living kin. This reassertion of a moral order through the rehabilitation of ancestors makes it possible for living kin to abide in a lineage whose past symbolizes the ideals of moral order. In the semiotics of ritual theory that was articulated so clearly by Mircea Eliade in his many works, ancestors ideally represent the qualities of *in illo tempore*, a past or origin that was ideal or normative before the problematic nature of the present existence was introduced.[34] In this vein, ancestors are regarded as paradigmatic forces of the primordial past who establish fundamental patterns of being to be emulated by the living in the present. Venerating what ancestors stand for, or what they symbolize, is a way of simultaneously recovering the qualities of that past, of transcending a problematic present, and of overcoming the condition of alienation by reestablishing the link between past and present. As we shall see, the engine driving this process of recovery is karma and its transfer.

It is within this purview that we can field Skidmore's comments about the power of ritual. In focusing her study on the *dhammayietra*, an annual public pilgrimage articulating a progressive agenda of social engagement led by the activist monk Mahaghosananda,[35] she emphasizes

> the potential healing abilities of the performance of ritual and its possible function as a resistance strategy to terror and violence. The total field of Khmer religion includes belief in ancestor spirits, pagan demons, and the spirits that inhabit the heavens and hells of Buddhist cosmology, as well as the Buddha Himself. This worldview also allows Cambodians access to different levels of reality such as the world of dreams, the world of ancestors, and the world of spirits. Cambodians draw upon this worldview to both comprehend violence and to provide an idiom for their experience of a culture of terror and the space of death. Psychiatrists have documented Cambodian attempts to express distress and rework their life-world epistemologies from within this cultural frame. Some respondents reported having dreamed of relatives, some alive, some dead, only to have the relatives step out of the dream and appear to the dreamer in waking life. Other refugees suffering from extreme emotional distress reported being visited by ancestors' disembodied female skulls with entrails dangling behind, sorcerers, and vengeful spirits. (1997, 11–12)

Indeed, dreams have been an important venue for the communication of the dead with the living within Buddhist religious culture since the early centuries of Buddhist tradition in ancient India. The stories that make up the Pali *Tipitaka's Petavatthu* almost always include an episode wherein the dead appear to speak with the living within a dream to inform the living of their current condition of suffering. Many of the people I interviewed at *pchum ben* rites in Cambodia in 2010 reported communications with their dead ancestors within the context of dreams. Ritual, then, becomes a means of acting upon the sense of imperative that derives from a dream of this kind.

While the place of dreams is an important detail, the larger issue here is how the ritual process helps to reconstitute and re-enchant the family.

The reconstitution of the family, within the context of Khmer culture, is necessarily the predicate for the reconstitution of society. Wounds may never completely heal, as memories may never be completely erased. But the reinstatement of ritual culture in the immediate aftermath of social devastation, a process that was allowed to accelerate after the exodus of Marxist-inclined Vietnamese ideologues, has abetted the ability to at least cope and, just as importantly, to at least hope. The hope that is expressed within *pchum ben* rites is an especially precious quality insofar as, as Osborne notes, there is a very "high rate of mental illness among those who were adults when Pol Pot was in power" (2008, 200).[36] Not only is hope a quality cultivated within *pchum ben*, but extensive interviews among hundreds of refugees in camps on the Thai side of the border with Cambodia in 1992, thirteen years after the transition to Vietnamese rule, indicated not only high levels of post-traumatic stress disorder, but also that "Cambodian survivors wish they would have given deceased family members more of their own food, or speak of feeling badly about taking the clothing of a deceased relative. Many describe guilt feelings for not having been able to perform a proper funeral ceremony for their loved ones" (Savin and Robinson 2000). Concern for a proper funeral is among the basic material and psychological matters addressed within *pchum ben*.

CELEBRATING *PCHUM BEN*

In early October 2010, the *Cambodia Daily* ran a series of articles on how spending during *pchum ben* seemed to be down that year. Its reporters had interviewed traders in the central market and monks from Wat Langka. But there was a sudden burst of spending in the final days of the season as many Phnom Penh people prepared for their pilgrimages back to home villages and *wat*s. The monks at Wat Langka said that perhaps the next phase of building and remodeling would have been put on hold unless donations had recovered, which they did. *Pchum ben* is clearly a major economic moment during the year, not only for the donations made to the temples, but also in the feasts prepared and in the gifts to parents that children provide. It is likely about as important to the fledgling Cambodian economy as Christmas is to the American. Certainly, the transportation industry receives its biggest boost of the year as hundreds of thousands leave Phnom Penh for the provinces, a pilgrimage home to honor parents and ancestors. Thus, *pchum ben* is not only a festival season aimed at establishing the well-being of the dead, it is a marker of the well-being of the living as well.

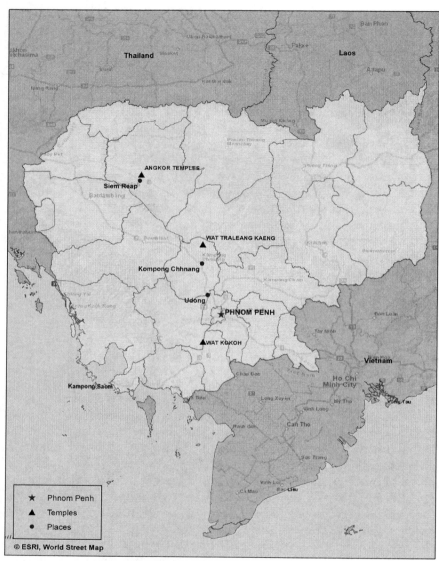

Figure 5.01. Map of Cambodia

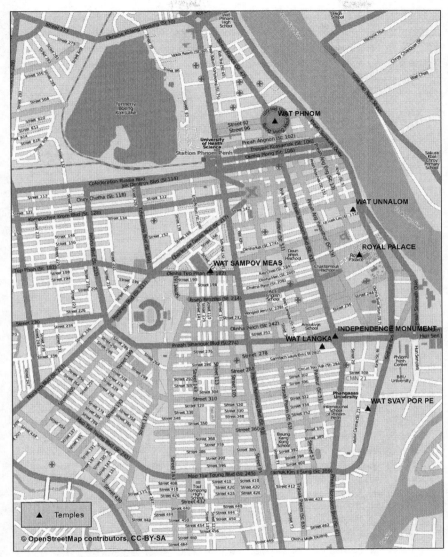

Figure 5.02. Map of Phnom Penh

I rely on Davis to introduce the salient cultural and religious issues in play within the rites constitutive of *pchum ben*. His descriptive statements provide for an insightful introductory summary of *pchum ben*'s general religious and socioeconomic significance in contemporary Khmer society:

> Once a year during the fifteen-day festival of Bhjum Pinda [*pchum ben*], the king of hell, Yamaraja, allows the *preta* to travel back to the villages where they previously lived as humans. During this "dark fortnight" of the waning moon, the *preta* search for gifts of food that their living relatives and descendants are suppose to leave them at Buddhist temples. They are supposed to search in at least seven temples during this period; if they find food, they will give their blessings. If on the other hand, they find nothing and return to hell as hungry when they left, they may choose to curse their descendants, so that they will share in the ghost's hunger and desperation. If they cannot eat together, the ghosts will ensure that they at least starve together. [. . .] [While] [p]reta embark on epic journeys during the festival period, from hell to the villages of their relatives . . . , they are not the only ones going on pilgrimages. Khmer assert that they too should return to the villages of their birth for Bhjum Pinda, or at least for the final day of Bhjum, the day of gathering. Since Bhjum should be celebrated in one's home village, the holiday involves massive evacuations of cities to agricultural birth villages. Although the vast majority of Cambodia's monetized wealth is concentrated in the cities, over eighty per cent of the population remains in the countryside. Families from the city make great efforts to give to the limits of their ability when they journey back to the villages. They don't come empty-handed: they bring food, treats, bread and rice. If they are indeed wealthy, they will often arrange for the temple ceremonies, and will hire a tent for a catered meal for themselves and a few of their country relatives on the temple grounds after the ceremony. In return, they occupy the major roles in communally performed rituals, sit in the best places, receive more attention from the high ranking monks, and eat delicious food in catered tents, around which children and hungry adults wait for left overs. These human pilgrimages back and forth between city and village are undertaken in a spirit of generosity, in order to serve one's poor dead relatives and one's home village, but the economic and social distinctions between the city and the villagers are also points of contention. The generous gifts to the countryside's dead from the city are highly symbolic. They return the countryside's wealth without acknowledging it. [. . .] Their food and gifts do go a long way to help create a sense of solidarity, familial love, and trust, which might otherwise be strained by the tyranny of distance, the length of absence and the gulf in lifestyles. During the two weeks of Bhjum Pinda, the direction of wealth is reversed. (2009, 175, 188, 189)

In September and October of 2010, I attended as many ritual occasions during the fifteen-day season of *pchum ben* as I possibly could. I selected

Figure 5.03. Wat Unnalom

five Buddhist *wat*s located within the city of Phnom Penh according to pro-files of the clientele they served: Wat Langka, Wat Unnalom, Wat Sampov Meas, Wat Svay Por Pe, and Wat Phnom. The first three *wat*s belong to the traditional and still dominant Mahanikay order and are arguably the larg-est and most well known of all of Phnom Penh's many Buddhist temples. Wat Unnalom is the home temple of the *sangharaja* (or *sanghareach*) of the Mahanikay order and is located in close proximity to the royal palace. It is here that the Buddhist *sangha* was first regenerated following the disper-sal of the Khmer Rouge. It remains an unofficial headquarters of the *sangha* in Cambodia.

Wat Langka is probably the second most important *wat* institutionally in Phnom Penh. It has been described by Davis as "catholic in its acceptance and performance of rites considered by modernist or reformist monks as brahmanist—such as *poh paya pinda* [the early morning *pinda* offerings during *pchum ben*]—and had a largely middle and upper class congrega-tion on its normal morality day [*thnai sila*] celebrations" (2009, 18). Indeed, it is a very well-endowed temple located just opposite Phnom Penh's Inde-pendence Monument and the prime minister's official residence.

Wat Sampov Meas is a very large *wat* located in a more working-class and traditional business section of Phnom Penh and is also home to some

Figure 5.04. Independence Monument

of the most socially and politically progressive monks in Cambodia, including the activist Mahaghosananda, who was nominated for a Nobel Prize for Peace in 1994 and 1996. Wat Svay Por Pe is a smaller and rather nondescript Thammayut temple located across from the sprawling Russian embassy in a middle-class section of town. It enjoys a reputation for having monks of a more intellectual bent who are connected to some of the Buddhist universities in Phnom Penh. Wat Phnom, of course, has become iconic for the city. It is the legendary site of the city's origins (see appendix 3). Despite the fact that it has an elaborate image hall and an adjacent royally endowed stupa, no monks live at Wat Phnom, so it doesn't have a regular congregation, nor does it observe the regular liturgy of Buddhist rites on monthly *sila* days, *pchum ben,* and so on. In addition, there are popular Chinese and Vietnamese deity shrines located to one side of the Buddha image hall, and an active cultic site for "Madam Penh" or "Grandma Penh" on the other.[37] It is, therefore, not a "normal" Buddhist temple. In repeated visits, the only Buddhist cultic activity I observed there were prostrations to the central Buddha image. I also observed a ritual gathering of the royal family sending off their ancestral spirits on the eve of the final day of *pchum ben* at an auspicious ford located along the Tonle Sap River just opposite the royal palace in Phnom Penh.

Since *pchum ben* is so robustly celebrated in the countryside, I observed *bay ben* rites at two very important rural *wats*, each located about forty kilometers outside of Phnom Penh, and I made sure that I was at a rural venue for the final day of *pchum ben,* the day that serves quintessentially as a time for family reunion. The first rural venue, located to the southwest, was Wat Kokos a temple that had been turned into an interrogation center and prison by the Khmer Rouge for the duration of their time in power. My visit there was an especially grim reminder of the crimes committed in the late 1970s. The second venue, Wat Traleaeng Kaeng in Kompong Chhnang, is northwest of Phnom Penh near the old capital of Udong. This particular *wat* is famous for its four-faced Buddha image that in popular lore is believed to be the image of the four-faced king mother, who is also thought to be the reincarnated mother of the Buddha.[38] It is also the site of a temple dedicated to Preah Ko Preah Keo, whose well-known myth reflects late-medieval tensions with the invading Thai in the eighteenth and nineteenth centuries. The spirits of these two mythic figures, who represent important aspects of Khmer culture, are thought to reside in this *wat.* Wat Traleaeng Kaeng, therefore, is a site of considerable nationalistic sentiments.

In my observations at these venues, I was ably assisted and supported by two outstanding Khmer graduate students, one male and one female, both of whom are Buddhist by background and fully fluent in English and Khmer. They readily handled all translation issues that arose and interviewed many individuals on each occasion at my behest. My notes indicate that, collectively, we interviewed scores of people from all age brackets and both genders. In addition, we participated in and observed for the duration of ritual activities, as they were held at these locations on each of several early mornings.[39] As such, we were able to assemble, by means of comparison, a somewhat typical liturgy by noting which elements appeared as constants and which elements proved to be idiosyncratic or variables.

What follows is an analytical account based on our efforts to understand what occurred at each *wat.* The knowledge we gained about *pchum ben* was cumulative, and that is how my discussion proceeds. That is, the discussion is guided by the sequence of our observations. My descriptions and analyses begin with the first venue we visited, Wat Langka, and proceed serially through to the last occasion, on *pchum ben* day itself, at Wat Trale-aeng Kaeng in Kompong Chnang. The discussions occurring in relation to each *wat* become progressively focused as we continue. We learned more that was new to us, of course, at the first sites. The information we gained as we proceeded day to day from *wat* to *wat* became increasingly redundant, although it often confirmed and sometimes contradicted what we had learned earlier. In any case, I discuss the many issues in what follows as they surfaced. Progressively, the picture that is painted is completed.

THE *KAN BEN* LITURGY AT WAT LANGKA

The first fourteen days of the *pchum ben* season are known as *kan ben*. *Kan* in Khmer means "to hold or to adhere," while *ben* is Khmer for Pali and Sanskrit *pinda*, referring to the ball of sticky rice offered ritually to ances-tors to appease their hungry conditions. Determining the symbolic signifi-cance of *pinda* figures heavily in ascertaining the cardinal religious meaning of this entire ritual season. *Pchum* means "collection," and so *pchum ben* is the "gathering or collecting/making of *pinda*." During *kan ben*, the ritual of *bay ben*, or "tossing" the *pinda*, is performed every morning between 4 a.m. and 6 a.m., depending on the ritual schedule of each of the *wats*.

At 3:45 a.m. on the first day of the *pchum ben* season, laity began to ar-rive at Wat Langka with trays filled with *pinda*s, incense, candy, water, and small white spirit flags known in Khmer as *tung proleung* (literally, spirit flag).[40] These flags, of course, are symbols of their deceased kin, their ancestors to whom the laity will be offering their trays of food. Some of the trays that have been sold by hawkers on-site just beyond the gates of the temple compound contain *pinda*s that have been shaped into the form of a cone by means of a banana leaf wrap.

This form is the traditional way of offering *pinda*s to one's ancestors. That rice is the primary offering to the ancestors, as it is the primary offer-ing to the Buddhist monks when they go on their morning alms rounds (Pali: *pindapata*), reflects the vital centrality of this food as the byproduct of agricultural labor, the predominant form of "value-producing activity" (Davis 2009, 31) in Khmer culture and society. That is, "Cambodian soci-ety, so thoroughly agricultural, finds its dominant image of value and value-creation, in the production, distribution and consumption of food" (110). The giving of rice, therefore, is symbolic of the giving of life, its nur-turance, its sustenance.

Rice is life's vital principle, and so the giving of rice to ancestors, which is precisely what occurs during the *bay ben* of *kan ben*, is not only symbolic

Figure 5.05. Spirit effigy
on offering plate

of regenerating the life of the lineage or family, but it also a fundamental mark of respect.[41] With regard to previous discussions about the creation of moral order as a by-product of ancestor veneration, what should be stressed, then, is that the gift of rice to one's ancestors seems to generate a sentiment of reverence for life in the disposition of the donor. Thus, the gift is emblematic of sacrifice to what has been deemed worthy. It is a ritual act of worship indicating the "worthship" of the enduring family. It is also an act of thanksgiving and, as clearly seen in the pages that follow, an act of compassion. Finally, I would add that the generation of a sentiment that gives rise to acts of compassion, acts that reflect an ethical intention, signals the way ritual is often the context in which ethical consciousness is forged.

Figure 5.06. Traditional banana leaf rice cone offering

When the central image hall at Wat Langka finally opened, approximately five hundred laity entered first,[42] before about a hundred monks entered in stately, composed fashion to sit quietly and observantly in neat rows of about ten each behind the chief monk and his most senior fellow monks.[43] A rather distinguished family of high rank—as it turns out, the family of an air force officer who serves as the chief bodyguard of the current prime minister—were designated as the primary lay patrons of the occasion.[44] The ritual then began with the family patrons offering lit incense and making prostrations before the main Buddha image in the sermon hall. Following the prostrations, the chief monk led all monks in chanting the *Namassaka* in Pali, followed by a Khmer translation of the same. The text is simply an homage, a praise of the virtues of the *triratna:* Buddha, *dhamma,* and *sangha.* During this monastic chanting, laity, in turn, lit their incense and candles and some poured a little water onto their trays. Following the invocation, the chief monk told everyone to concentrate on the next *dhamma,* which consisted of the recitation of the *pancasila,* the five basic moral precepts: not to kill, not to steal, not to engage in sexual misconduct, not to lie, and not to take intoxicants. This taking and avowal established the conditions of moral purity, or at least the moral intentions driving the performance of the rite. The chanting of the five precepts was followed by the head temple *achar* (lay ritual specialist) leading the chanting in Pali of the *Namotassa,* again basically a respectful invocation of the Buddha's name.

To this point in the ritual, the elements of the liturgy had been generic and not unique to the *pchum ben* season or to *kan ben.* But after the *Namotassa,* the chief monk chanted the *Tirokudda Sutta,* an ancient Pali text found in the *Petavatthu* that actually forms a song or chant originally attributed to the Buddha within the mythic story he tells that establishes the basis for the rite of *bay ben,* the giving of *pindas* to ancestors. Davis has aptly translated the short text of the *Tirokudda Sutta* as follows:

> They stand at crossroads and outside the walls
> Returning to their old homes, they wait at thresholds
> Because of karma, no one remembers them
> When an abundant feast of food and water is served.
>
> Those who feel pity, therefore, at the right time
> Give truly pure food and drink to their relatives, rejoicing
> "This is for you; may our relatives be happy."
>
> Spectral relations gather and assemble.
> Thoroughly pleased with the food and water, they reply
> "May our relatives who provide for us have long lives.
> We are honored; giving is not without benefits."
>
> There is no plowing in that place, and cow-herding is unknown;
> No trading, no buying, no selling with gold;
> Dead *preta* survive there on what is given from here.
>
> Just as water poured on a hill
> flows down and around it, sustaining the land all around,
> so a gift from here benefits ghosts in precisely the same way.
>
> "He gave to me, he worked for me,
> he was my friend, relative and companion."
> Give properly to the ghosts, remembering past deeds.
>
> The weeping, mourning, and laments of relatives are useless
> To those who remain in such a way.
> But proper gifts dedicated to the sangha become useful to them
> Immediately and for a long time.

> The duties toward relatives have thus been shown:
> Veneration for the ghosts,
> Strength for the monks
> And no small merit for you. (2009, 167)

The *Tirokudda Sutta* is recited on virtually every *kan ben* occasion during the fifteen-day *pchum ben* season. Along with the *Parabhava Sutta* (see below), it is one of the two primary texts consistently invoked or recited within *pchum ben* ritual liturgies that we observed wherever we went. These texts are unique to the observance of *pchum ben*. According to Gombrich (1971a, 218), the *Tirokudda Sutta* forms one of the most ancient strands of the *Petavatthu*, a Pali text that is likely to be more than two thousand years old at least.[45] Within this text, we find the beginnings of a rationalization for the practice of merit transfer, especially in the third-to-the-last verse, which emphasizes what departed kin have provided on behalf of the living. In fact, this *sutta* is none other than a notice of the Buddhist observance of *dhamma* in relation to honoring ancestors. Though regarded as *Buddhavacana* (words of the Buddha), it signals how the early Buddhist community initially understood and transformed the ancient Indian *brahmanical* practice of venerating the familial dead.[46] In *brahmanical* traditions, paying one's debt to one's family ancestors, including one's parents, is one dimension of the triple debt that all devout people owe, the other two being to one's teachers and the gods.

In the *Petavatthu* story titled "The Petas Outside the Wall,"[47] the Buddha recites the *Tirokudda Sutta* verses to explain to King Bimbisara why the duty of honoring one's familial dead is an act that is morally incumbent on all. Since this particular story is also very often referred to in sermons preached by Khmer monks on *bay ben* occasions, and since it is therefore known by most Khmer laity as the authorized beginnings of *pchum ben* traditions, I summarize it here.

Ninety-two cycles ago, a king by the name of Jayasena ruled over Kasipura (Benares). His queen, Sirima, gave birth to a prince who became a buddha. The king resolved to keep the Buddha, *dhamma,* and *sangha* only for his sole edification and gave no one else the opportunity to take refuge. The Buddha's three younger brothers, born to a different mother, knew that *buddha*s are awakened for the benefit of the whole world, and not for the selfish ambitions of society's elite. As a strategy, they created a disturbance in one of the kingdom's borderlands and were sent by the king to quell the problem. When they returned, the king offered them a boon to which they replied that they wished to venerate the Buddha. The king denied them. The brothers then approached the Buddha directly and the Buddha agreed to spend the rain-retreat season with his brothers in his attendance, offering them the chance to make great merit. During the rain-retreat season, the local provincial ruler and the royal treasurer also took refuge in the *triratna,* along with the three brothers. The provincial ruler and treasurer then made magnificent gifts to the Buddha and *sangha,* but other people in the province became jealous of their charity, consumed their gifts of food, and set fire to the refectory of the monastery that they had built for the Buddha and his *sangha.* In time, all the major players in this episode died and were reborn: the brothers, the provincial ruler, and the treasurer were reborn in splendid heavens, while those who had been jealous and had burnt the monastery were reborn in hell. After ninety-two cycles of rebirths in heavens and hells, during the time of the Buddha Kassapa, those reborn in hell were finally reborn as *peta*s, who noticed how some surviving kinfolk provided gifts on behalf of their deceased relations to help assuage their suffering conditions. They asked Kassapa when this might happen for them. Kassapa told them that they had to await the appearance of the future Buddha, Gotama, and the rebirth of the provincial ruler as King Bimbisara. Bimbisara would provide relief through dedicating the merit of his benevolence to Gotama to them. Eventually, Gotama was born, set the *dhamma* wheel rolling, converted thousands, and made his way to Rajagaha, where he established King Bimbisara on the path of *dhamma.* The *peta*s waited, but Bimbisara did not assign credit for his gifts to the Buddha and his *sangha* to them. One night, now without hope, the *peta*s howled dreadful cries heard throughout the palace. In the morning, an alarmed Bimbisara expressed his fears to the Buddha that something sinister might happen to him soon. Then the Buddha told him the story and how the *peta*s, his ancestral kinsmen, were waiting for a transfer of merit. Bimbisara then prepared a generous bounty while the *peta*s waited outside the walls. When the merit for Bimbisara's generosity was transferred to them, they found themselves newly ensconced in lotus ponds, their thirsts slaked with sweet nectars, eating delicious soft food, wearing beautiful divine clothes, living in grand mansions, sleeping on comfortable couches, being adorned with jewel-studded ornaments, and so on. All of this remarkable scene was made manifest by the Buddha for a delighted Bimbisara to see the benefits of his merit transference. In conclusion, the Buddha then recited the verses of the *Tirokudda Sutta.*

After the chanting of the *Tirokudda Sutta,* the *achar* in Wat Langka recited a Pali *gatha* or verse indicating *anumodana,* the moment when all beings, alive and dead, are invited to share in the joy of what is now to be given. Both Gombrich (1971a, 206–207) and Malalasekera (1967, 85–86) argue that it is precisely this ability to rejoice in the action of another's good actions, or the quality of "empathy in joy" that signals how the change in disposition in the *peta*s is what allows them to benefit from the transferred merit. Their *cetana*, or intentions, have been transformed. I was genuinely surprised that this somewhat sophisticated aspect of Buddhist philosophy was known to several of the older laity that we interviewed during *pchum ben*. *Cetana* is actually how the Buddha defined karma within the early Buddhist Pali texts. In other words, the karma of the *peta*s had been changed, as evidenced by the fact that they could now rejoice in the good works of others. They now enjoyed an awareness of what constitutes morally wholesome action. As such, they could share in the merit generated.

Following the *anumodana* invitation, everyone inside the temple responded with "Sadhu Sadhu Sadhu." Then the temple bell rang three times signaling that the moment had come for everyone to go outside into the dark and begin circumambulating the image hall clockwise three times, in the process distributing *pinda* to their deceased kin, their departed ancestors. Solemnly, all the laity joined in this procession and began to quietly distribute the contents of their *"pinda* plates" into metal pails or buckets that had been placed at intervals around the temple. Younger monks were stationed at various intervals to supervise outside the sermon hall.

In popular Khmer lore about *preta*s, it is important that each layperson recite the name of his or her deceased relation while making their donations. As Davis noted in the introductory comments to this section, it is believed that the deceased will frequent up to seven temples searching for donations made by their descendants on their behalf. At the same time, it is believed that seven generations of ancestors can benefit from the donations provided by their descendants. What is interesting about the *Petavatthu* story of the *peta*s "outside the walls" is that not only do they benefit from the karma of merit transfer, but also they physically receive the benefits from material offerings. That is why, for many Khmer traditional laity, it is important to actually make physical gifts and why the gift of rice is so significant. Moreover, in the *Petavatthu* stories, the types of punishments suffered by *peta*s are physically reflective of the nature of the moral offence that they committed as human beings. For instance, liars are born with worms in their mouths. Bullies are reborn with severe bruises or broken limbs. The greedy are continuously hungry.

Yet, the physical act of giving *pinda*s has recently become a popular controversy in Cambodia. Buth Savong, a famous Khmer Buddhist *dhamma* preacher, has mounted a vigorous campaign against the practice of *bay ben* by arguing that *"pinda* throwing" is not sanctioned in the *Tipitaka* and not prescribed by the Buddha. Other monks have complained about how the practice of *bay ben* dirties the temple environment and attracts stray animals and vermin. Consequently, some temples have abandoned the practice of *bay ben*. In temples where *bay ben* is observed, I did hear sermons by monks to the laity regarding the importance of keeping the temple neat, along with warnings, especially to the youth, not to throw *pinda*s indiscriminately. Other temples, like Wat Langka, try to contain the practice of throwing *pinda*s by placing pails or canisters around the temple as receptacles and posting monastic "guards" intermittently to make sure that the fun does not get out of hand.

In any case, one of the questions my assistants and I asked of the laity we met was how one knows for sure whether or not their offerings during *bay ben* made any difference to their ancestors. Several times, we were told that ancestors would appear in dreams, and from those appearances in dreams, it would be clear that they were wearing nice clothes, were no longer hungry or suffering from thirst, and so on, and had, therefore, received merit. This is a very curious explanation, because in most of the stories of the *Petavatthu*, the manner through which the dead communicate with the living is through dreams. Consistently in our interviews with Buddhist laity during *bay ben*, we were told about how the dead appeared to their surviving kin in dreams. Later, I argue that dreaming is one of the conditions of liminality that is so characteristic of *pchum ben*.

During the ritual circumambulation of the temple and the ritual distribution of *pinda*, the second ritual text of primary importance to the *pchum ben* proceedings, the Pali *Parabhava Sutta*, was then intoned by the chief monk over the loudspeaker system. The *sutta* can be translated as follows:

Thus have I heard:
On one occasion the Blessed One was living near Savatthi, at Jetavana,
    at Anathapindika's monastery. Now when the night was far advanced,
    a certain deity, whose surpassing radiance illuminated the whole of
    Jetavana, came to the presence of the Blessed One, respectfully saluted
    him, and stood beside him. Standing thus he addressed the Blessed
    One in verse:
[The Deity:]
About the causes of the fall of men we ask, Gotama, O Blessed One: What
    is the cause of his fall?
[The Buddha:]
It is easy to know the ascending one, and easy to know the falling one.
    The lover of the *dhamma* ascends. The despiser of the *dhamma* wanes.
We understand this as the first cause of his decline. Tell us the second,
    O Blessed One. What is the cause of decline?[48]
The ruthless are kin to him. He despises the worthy; he approves of the
    teachings of the bad tempered.

The declining include the man who is fond of sleep and the slothful,
   who is lazy and easy to anger.
Whoever is well-to-do and does not support his parents who are old,
   and past their prime.
Whoever deceives a Brahmin or recluse.
Whoever is wealthy, who has much gold, and who has an abundance
   of food, but enjoys it all by himself.
Whoever is proud of his lineage, of his wealth, and yet despises
   his relations.
Whoever is addicted to women, alcohol, gambling, and loses his
   wages because of these vices.
Whoever is not satisfied with only his own wife and seeks others.
Whoever becomes old and yet takes as his wife a girl in her teens.
Whoever delegates authority to a woman given to drink and squandering,
   or a man of the same sort.
Whoever has few possessions but colossal greed, is born of the *ksatrya*
   [warrior] lineage birth and aspires selfishly to royalty.
Fully realizing these (twelve) causes of decline in the world, the wise,
   with *aryan* [worthy or noble] insight, realizes the security of *nibbana*.[49]

The *Parabhava Sutta* is obviously an explanation of how *preta*s become
*preta*s. It is a ritual chant that is shorthand for the content of karma stories
of the *Petavatthu* that illustrate how immoral actions result in a suffering
rebirth and how the fruit of meritorious actions, or moral actions, can benefit those who have made mistakes in the past. It is clearly an attempt to
explain why it is necessary to rehabilitate one's ancestors, to return them
to a moral status that symbolizes the continued healthy well-being of the
family. We asked many laity how they knew whether or not their ancestors
had become *preta*s owing to their past actions. Again, some indicated that
they knew this through dreams, while others said they knew because their
relatives were known to have done bad things during the Khmer Rouge
period. Others said they simply did not know. The latter were performing
bay ben just in case their familial ancestors needed them. In this instance,
pchum ben functions as insurance. When the *Parabhava Sutta* was concluded, *tumnouy prêt,* or "the moan of the *preta*," was heard dramatically
over the microphone in Khmer. It was a heartrending moaning cry for help
and added significantly to the rather somber ambience of the occasion.
   Following the rite, we asked people why they came for *bay ben* at Wat
Langka. It was clear that people prioritize some pagodas because of where
the relics of their deceased relatives have been deposited or where they were
cremated. Some will go to the temple nearest the site where their departed
one died, especially if the death was accidental or violent. Others prefer to
go where their departed kin preferred to go while they were still living. Liv-

ing relatives might remember also which sect, Mahanikay or Thammayut, the deceased preferred when he or she was alive. This sense of honoring the preferences of the dead sometimes carried over to what was included on the "*pinda* plate." Often favorite sweets and fruits were added to the *pinda*.

As we were preparing to leave, one elderly woman reminded us that Cambodian people not only bring food to the pagoda for their deceased relatives, but they also bring food, money, or clothes to their living parents or relatives at home. They are well aware that much of the money they give to parents will be used to prepare food for the monks at the pagoda during this season. Food for the monks translates into merit for the family. Therefore, *pchum ben* should be seen as a cycle of family caring: from the children to their living parents and relatives and then to their deceased grandparents and other deceased relatives. These transactions signal a threefold type of relationality: the living venerate the dead in return for their blessing through support of the *sangha*. In this way, the living, the dead, and the *sangha* are entwined. Elsewhere (Holt 1981a, 20–21), I have argued that in the transformation of ancient *brahman*ical ancestor rites, it is the Buddhist *sangha* that replaced the ancestors and the *brahman*ical family as the primary social entity of importance in connection with actions performed on behalf of the dead. That is, the *pinda*s of *brahman*ical funeral rites, or balls of rice constituting symbolic bodies made for transitions of the dead from this world to the worlds beyond,[50] became the food given to Buddhist monks. The monks, in turn, on their rounds of *pindapata* every morning, came to represent the new morally virtuous presence that was "dead to the world," a presence worthy of entering into a mutually beneficial or reciprocal relation.[51]

CONSOLING THE *PRETAS* AT WAT SAMPOV MEAS

On the third morning of *pchum ben,* amid a drizzle following several hours of thunderous downpour, laity began to arrive at Wat Sampov Meas around 4 a.m., although the *bay ben* rite did not commence until 4:30. Wat Sampov Meas is hardly upscale in comparison with Wat Langka or Wat Unnalom. The smell of rot came from garbage overflowing the garbage cans lining one of the lanes leading to the main entrance of the temple. While some of the monks here are quite socially progressive, the temple grounds are much more pedestrian. The ritual service was also decidedly much more informal. There was no grand entry by a hundred monks, no traditional orchestra, and no appointed lay patrons for the rite. Indeed, when the laity were summoned to begin the rite, we all assembled in a

courtyard opposite the sermon hall while a single monk took up a microphone on the steps to the hall and began to chant first the *Namassaka* and
then the *Parabhava Sutta*. This was the one venue where we did not hear
the *Tirokudda Sutta* recited. Following the chant, the monk launched into
what seemed to be an impromptu sermon, the first part of which was
about the proper and improper ways to toss the *pinda*. He stressed that
*pinda*s should not be thrown at someone else's head, or fired around in fun.
It was improper to throw *pinda*s on to the cement walkways and court-
yards as well. Instead, *pinda*s should be gently deposited where there is
dirt or ground in which bushes grow. In that way, *preta*s can get to them. By
not following this method, people could find themselves reborn as *preta*s!
This drew some muffled laughter from some of those in attendance.

The monk then proceeded to tell a story. Once a monk in Sri Lanka was
traveling to his temple when he heard the sound of two *preta* children calling him. He asked of their identity, and they replied that they were *preta*
children and that their mother had gone to the temple in search of food
but had not returned. They pleaded with the monk to tell their mother to
please return quickly. The monk responded by saying that he could not
do this because he did not have the ability to see *preta*s. The *preta* children
gave him a black magic root. When he reached the temple, he saw several
preta and one of them was the children's mother. He approached her and
told her how her children were in her need. Surprised, the mother *preta*
wanted to know how she could be seen by the monk. When told, she
grabbed the black magic root from the monk and disappeared. Henceforth, *preta*s cannot be seen by human beings. Ironically, just as the monk
finished his story, a power cut occurred and the premises were pitched
into darkness. A few flashlights eventually broke the darkness and the
monk announced that it was now time for *bay ben*.

An elaborate display of the Buddha meditating peacefully above a row
ten *preta*s dominated the courtyard where the monk had chanted and
preached. Below the depictions of each suffering *preta*, a summary of their
actions that led to their sorry rebirths was written in Khmer. I was able to
identify about half of these portrayals with stories in the *Petavatthu*. During the early morning festivities, canisters were set up to receive monetary
donations. As we circumambulated the sermon hall three times in the
dark, most of the people followed the advice of the monk by deposited
their *pinda*s gently in the bushes and not on the cement walkways.

It was at Wat Sampov Meas that we were able to chat with many laity
with the greatest ease. We met some people who said that they came to
Wat Sampov Meas because here *bay ben* was celebrated without a lot of restrictions. One young man said he came because his *wat* did not allow the

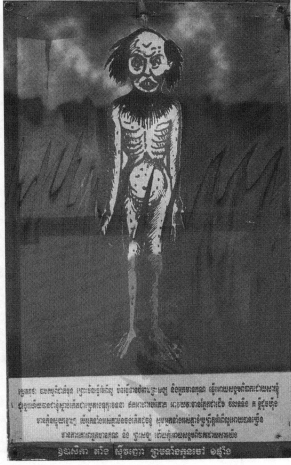

Figures 5.07a and 5.07b.
*Preta*s portrayed at Wat
Sampov Meas

practice. Here, we also met a sixty-three-year-old woman intent on performing *bay ben* at as many *wat*s as possible during *kan ben* because it made her happy to know that she could be of help to her deceased kin in this modest way. We met an especially candid seventy-two-year-old woman who admitted that she couldn't be sure that her merit transfers would actually benefit her deceased relatives. She said it all depended on whether they had developed morally wholesome dispositions, which is the doctrinally correct position, as we have seen, articulated by scholars Gombrich and Malalasekera. She mentioned that she had celebrated *pchum ben* religiously after she encountered many ghosts while hiking in the mountains following the Pol Pot era. She had also dreamed about some of her dead relations who had appeared to her with swollen bodies. She says that they have not reappeared since she dedicated merit to them. She said she lost a lot of relatives during the Pol Pot regime. She didn't tell us how or why, but she mentioned that her two children were also dead. She had a lot of motivation for assisting the dead. We also met a middle-aged man who broke down and sobbed uncontrollably when we asked why he came to perform *bay ben*. He stammered that his father had fallen out of a palm tree during the Pol Pot years and had died as a result of his fall. We gathered that he had witnessed this unfortunate event. He said that he had a lot of relatives, including brothers and sisters, who had died during the time of Pol Pot as well. While he is a person of not many resources, during every *pchum ben* season he performs *bay ben* and merit transfer for the deceased members of his nuclear family. He says he feels closer to them during this time, although he knows that his life will never be the same without them.

We left Wat Sampov Meas somewhat sobered by our encounters with people who clearly were emotionally affected during the *bay ben* rite. It was clear to us that one of the functions of this rite, at least for many Buddhist laity, is that it provides emotional compensation for the experiences of great family losses that they have endured.

BORAN AND *SAMAY* AT WAT UNNALOM

On the sixth morning of *kan ben*, we attended the *bay ben* rite at Wat Unnalom, which, as mentioned, is regarded as the leading *wat* or headquarters of the Mahanikay sect. Just opposite the front entrance of the *wat*, in a small garden plot of its own, stands a sculpture of Yama, king of the dead. In many years of visiting Buddhist temples in Sri Lanka and throughout Southeast Asia, I had never before seen a sculpture of Yama, and certainly not one that was alive in cultic terms. I had to remind myself that *pchum*

Figure 5.08. Yama (Lord of Death) in front of Wat Unnalom

ben is perhaps the most important ritual time of the year religiously in Cambodia, and that Wat Unnalom is arguably one of the most sanctified spaces in the country.

Given the important role played by Yama in the mythology of *pchum ben,* and the specter of death that has haunted Cambodia during its recent history, it is not so surprising that we should find Yama's likeness prominently displayed. Sometimes it seems that Buddhism has made a pact with death to ensure its popularity. Davis puts the matter this way:

> In the historic spread of Buddhism, it has been in the care of the dead that Buddhism most successfully established itself, and death continues to be a major part of the *sangha*'s economic and social reproduction, via temple's income generating funeral rituals, and the donations they receive on behalf of the dead. (2009, 132)[52]

The laity at the crowded image hall at Wat Unnalom were an extremely interesting mix. As at Wat Langka, many monks were ceremoniously present, the liturgy was long and full (including all the texts that had been chanted at Wat Langka), *pin peat* complemented the chanting, and the general decorum inspired a palpable ambience of "high church" symbol and rite. Yet, though many of the laity were well heeled indeed, many were clearly drawn from the commercial and entertainment districts of Phnom Penh located just to the north of the temple. I recognized a couple of "tuk tuk" drivers who had harassed me for rides on a daily basis during my stay, as well as some waitresses from the neighborhood restaurants. And it was clear from the skimpy outfits that drew stares from many others present that some of the young women in attendance had just finished their night shifts as hostesses in some of the local nightclubs. These denizens of Phnom Penh's business and tourist culture mixed in with families of obvious upper-class backgrounds and reminded us that participation in *pchum ben* canvasses from all classes of people in Cambodia. In a few days, most of these people would temporarily shed their "urbanity" when they return to their native villages and *wats*.

From talking to many of the laity present, it was clear that Wat Unnalom attracted a lot of people who could not otherwise make it to their home temples. In that sense, it was both everyone's and yet no one's "home temple." One young man said he had come to Wat Unnalom because people in his family take turns going to the temples so that every night at least one family member transfers merit at a temple on behalf of the family ancestors. When asked why he came to this temple rather than others, his answer was that some temples were *boran* (traditional) and others *samay* (modern), so the former would provide *bay ben* while the latter might not.

In fact, this middle-aged layman had identified a critically important marker delineating different emphases within monastic Buddhism and lay practice in Cambodia during the twentieth century. The Japanese anthropologist Satoru Kobayashi spent a year and a half conducting fieldwork focusing on two rural temples in Kompong Say district, located east of Tonle Sap Lake, noting how these two temples were sites of "conflicts and compromises in local people's lives" (2005, 493). More specifically, Kobayashi was concerned with understanding Buddhist practices as these were interpreted as either *samay* (modern) or *boran* (traditional—from the Sanskrit *purana*, meaning "of old"). One of the best illustrations of the tension between *boran* and *samay* centers on the question of whether or not to provide one's deceased kin with rice directly (499–502). With reference to *bay ben*, Kobayashi quotes one of the local *achars* as saying, "If one wants to transfer merit to the dead, rice should be offered to a monk as a source of merit. In the Buddha's sacred words in the *Tripitaka*, we could not find any explanations about *bah baybin*. Such practice is really meaningless, because merit must be transferred through Buddhist monks. Dogs eating rice on the field can't help anything" (501).

Kobayashi goes on to describe other minor differences and ends this section of his article by noting how *samay* and *boran* become differences in

attitudes, chiefly between those who stress an understanding of the absolute consequences of karma from a more rational perspective. His article
concludes by showing how the periods of the civil war, the Khmer Rouge
regime, and the Vietnamese intervention all disrupted the ways in which
younger monks came to understand the practice of the monastic vocation
insofar as the more *boran*-oriented practices had become somewhat otiose.
As a result, the previous legacy of these *boran* practices learned through
observation had been interrupted in favor of a more doctrinally oriented
religion. I think that in this Kobayashi is largely correct, insofar as reconstruction was abetted by conceptions of religion that ultimately informed
modern nation-state understandings that, in turn, were derived somewhat
from Westernized understandings of religion.[53] Both Penny Edwards
(2007) and especially Anne Hansen (2007) have thoroughly sketched out
how French conceptions of religion and the reform of Buddhism in the
first half of the twentieth century were characterized by an emphasis on
rationalism and criticisms of superstition.

Harris (2005, 221–224) provides an effective overview of *boran*-oriented
monks and their reestablished presence in the 1990s. He notes moments
of conflict with *samay*-oriented monks over the practice of *parivasa*—the
boran performing various types of ascetic practices aimed at generating
magical power, rather than simply practicing the rite as a form of peni-
tence for wrongdoings. More specifically, he telescopes the discussion of
boran and *samay* rightly on the figure who was perhaps the leading reform-
minded monk of the twentieth century, Venerable Chuon Nath who

> [i]n 1944, . . . became chief monk of Wat Unnalom. . . . [I]t is clear that
> Chuon Nath's views held sway for some time before his official elevation
> [to *sanghareach* or *sangharaja*] was confirmed. Controversy had, for exam-
> ple, blown up over the use of the *Tirokudda Sutta* as a protective chant
> [*paritta*] during the ceremony of merit making for dead ancestors [*pchum
> ben*] in September—modernizers were attempting to rewrite the text to
> eliminate its non-Buddhist elements. The suppression of the traditional
> New Year festivities by a royal decree of July 17, 1944, also appears to be
> related to the dispute over the presence of extraneous and superstitious
> features in popular ritual. (121)

What *boran* and *samay* mean, therefore, in relation to *pchum ben* is a
matter of emphasis. The more *boran*-oriented disposition focuses on efficacy of *bay ben* and the provisions of *pinda* for the ancestors, while the more
samay-oriented disposition focuses efficacy on the merit made by providing gifts for the monks and the consequent merit that can be transferred
to the dead. Keeping in mind the deep *brahman*ical roots of the *pinda* as

Figure 5.09. Chuon Nath sculpture

symbolic of the corporeal form of the departed in the time of their transition from this world to the next, the *boran* disposition is definitely *brahman*-ist in orientation. Its relative popularity in the post–Khmer Rouge period also signals the attempt on the part of many Khmer to reconnect to the traditions of the past.

Kobayashi's comment about the *samay* orientation of most monks since the 1990s period of reestablishing the *sangha* is accurate and very significant, at least corresponding to my own limited experiences. I interviewed several monks outside the context of *pchum ben* rites and every one of them could have been categorized comfortably as *samay* in disposition and orientation. While this should not be so surprising, given the fact that all of these interviews took place in Phnom Penh or its suburbs, with monks who were comparatively young (in their twenties or early thirties), it did drive home a position that has become increasingly popular within the *sangha* as well: that *pchum ben* is more of a Khmer national custom reflecting Khmer identity than it is a Buddhist ritual. I heard this point of view articulated in a few of the sermons as well. It struck me as quite odd that monks would take this position when they continued to ritually envelope *bay ben* rites with unabashedly Buddhist substance—that is, chanting the moral precepts, the invocations to the *triratna*, the *Tirokudda Sutta*, the *Parabhava Sutta,* and so on. It may be that it has now become quite well known that *pchum ben* is a rite that is unique to Cambodia within the Theravada Buddhist world, so its "Khmerness" must be understood as its raison d'être rather than the Buddhistic teachings embodied within the ancient *Petavatthu* source. It also occurred to me that this assertion was simply inconceivable in pre-independence or perhaps precolonial Cambodia insofar as the separation between religion and ethnic identity was impossible to conceptualize then. The traditional, or *boran,* worldview was simply more integrated. There was no distinction, as it were, between the sacred and secular, between religion and custom. To be Khmer *was* to be Buddhist in an integrated socio-cosmos. With the introduction of modern conceptions of the "nation" and "religion," sacred and secular, especially as these had been demarcated by the colonial French and imbibed by the educated elite, such a division was now possible. On the other hand, the consistent description of *pchum ben* as a national custom adds a dimension of discourse about the rite that transcends the focus on the family per se, one that embraces the nation as a whole. Consistently, older people informed us about how the popularity of *pchum ben* had soared since its reinstitution following the Khmer Rouge. It may well be that, while its rising popularity is primarily about the recovery of the family, it includes the sense of a nation reasserting itself also.

ANG DUANG AND NATIONALIST SENTIMENTS OF *PCHUM BEN*

On several occasions, at least three of them during monastic sermons (one being at Wat Unnalom), but also in newspaper and magazine articles, I heard how King Ang Duang (r. 1848–1860) was responsible for the establishment of *pchum ben,* that his own practice of the rite had become paradigmatic for Khmer Buddhists today.[54] It is said that he condensed the period of venerating ancestors—which previously had been coextensive with the three-month rain-retreat season for monks—to just fifteen days, in effect intensifying the practice. Ang Duang does provide a good fit for explaining the origins of *pchum ben,* especially its identification as a national Khmer custom, for he is widely regarded as a symbol of the regeneration of Khmer national culture. It is worth providing a brief resume of his significance, drawn from a variety of scholarly commentators, in order to see how this figure's association with *pchum ben* aggrandizes the rite in the eyes of many Khmer people, both traditional and modern.

Ang Duang's reign lasted for only twelve years, from 1848 to 1860. He had been groomed in Bangkok by the Thai court for the Khmer throne. In the face of a growing Thai military threat in 1847, the Vietnamese had tactfully returned the Khmer royal regalia that they had hijacked earlier in the century and then released several members of the Khmer royal family before withdrawing their forces from Cambodia. Harris describes the political and historical context on the advent of Ang Duang's ascension to the throne in this way:

> From the Thai perspective, Vietnamese political control of Cambodia meant that Buddhism was without a royal sponsor. But the crowning of a new king was problematic because the royal regalia had been taken off to Saigon in 1812 and was not returned until the end of 1847. Ang Duang's coronation finally took place in Udong on April 8, 1848. When Duang returned to Udong from Bangkok, he found a culture on the brink of extinction. As a contemporary chronicler, Ta Mas, noted "[The novices] and priests suffered because the *viharas* had been plundered. The gold and silver buddhas had been taken from them and the soldiers had set fire to many *viharas*. In many places the *wats* that remained often did not have roofs. The roofs had sunken down and broken apart and the rain came down on the monks. Those who remained in robes were largely ignorant of the Buddha's teachings, and very few sacred writings remained intact." Ta Mas could easily have been describing the situation immediately after the Pol Pot period. Duang refurbished the royal funerary monuments and reinvigorated surrounding monasteries, by recasting Buddha images, encouraging the people to pay respect to the monks once again, and ordering a census of monks and *wats*. (2008 46)

The amelioration of these conditions made Ang Duang something of a national savior, at least in the manner in which history has been remembered in Cambodia. His association with *pchum ben* makes the revival of the ritual also, part and parcel, a piece of national cultural regeneration, especially when Ang Duang is identified with other Buddhist kings of a paradigmatic nature who are remembered historically as being responsible for moral regeneration:

> [The] chronicles tell us that Duang indefatigably encouraged the Buddhist virtues. He forbade his ministers to consume alcohol; toured the country, discouraging drinking and opium smoking; condemned hunting and the ill treatment of animals; and laid down guidelines on the proper size for fishing nets. He personally prepared food for monks, taught them liturgical chanting, and urged them to provide accommodations for the homeless. Acting on a model already established by Asoka and Jayavarman VII, Duang had rest houses built along the principal roads of the kingdom. (Harris 2008, 47)

Complementing this perspective, Chandler adds to the more general social and political significance of Duang's royal profile in this way:

> Duang reenacted the restoration of Thai-sponsored kingship that had been eclipsed for so many years. It would be a mistake to mistake these ceremonial actions as mere protocol because Duang, like most Southeast Asian rulers at the time, did not disentangle what we would call the religious and political strands of his thinking, duties and behavior. Kingly behavior . . . was thought to have political results, and political actions were thought to enhance or diminish a monarch's fund of merit. Many of these ceremonies had to do with restoration of Theravada Buddhism. . . . The chronicles of his reign emphasize its restorative aspects. A wide range of institutions and relationships was involved. The chronicle points to linguistic reforms, public works, sumptuary laws and new sets of royal titles. . . . Chroniclers of the 1880s and 1930s, looking back to those few years of Cambodian independence prior to French control, seem to have considered Duang's reign to be a kind of golden age. (2008, 162–164)

More than half of the chronicle passages dealing with Ang Duang describe the ritual dimension of his reign. Chandler argues that he set into motion a kind of "narrative performance." Ledgerwood specifies the content of this "narrative performance":

> We can see Ang Duang desperately trying to orchestrate a set of relationships with Hindu deities, local spirits, the Buddhist *sangha* and, of course, ancestors. In other words, he was trying to reset the order of the cosmos. This is seen not only in the ritual procedures that he enacted, but in his attempts to recast linguistic etiquette and to rename the titles of people and places. (2008b, 198)

While it is clear that Ang Duang is now seen in retrospect as a powerful king fulfilling the traditional model of Buddhist kingship, it also needs to be pointed out that "he also acted as a patron of the Thommayut sect" (Osborne 2008, 52). His years in Bangkok with the prince who eventually became Thailand's "Westernizing" and "modernizing" symbol, the king (Mongkut) who established the reform-minded, discipline-conscious, doctrinally focused, and academically competent Thammayut Nikaya, made him more than simply a "past-conscious" king. In Ang Duang we can see the intriguing figure of a culture hero who was simultaneously also regarded as modernizer. A perfect example of this combination is illustrated by the fact that he imported a coin-minting machine from Birmingham, England, and proceeded to mint coins with the stylized façade of Angkor Wat (ibid., 52). He therefore appealed to Buddhists, lay and monastic, of both the *boran* and *samay* dispositions. He was, and is, the perfect historical figure of the Khmer past to associate with the championing of *pchum ben*.

THE THAMMAYUT DISPOSITION
AT WAT SVAY POR PE

Having observed the rites of *bay ben* at three of Phnom Penh's largest and most well-known pagodas, all of them belonging to the Mahanikay order, we arrived at the closed gates of Wat Svay Por Pe, a Thammayut Nikaya pagoda, at a very dark and quiet 3:45 a.m., in the early morning hours of the eighth night of *pchum ben*. Since its founding by King Mongkut in Bangkok in the mid-nineteenth century, the Thammayut Nikaya has embodied what is now meant by *samay*: it claims to represent the reformed, enlightened, rational, modern, educated, discipline-conscious, and doctrinally oriented sect of Theravada monasticism. While this self-image is generally accurate, it should not be forgotten that most of the monks of the Mahanikay, as Kobayashi indicated earlier, also could be categorized as *samay*. Historically, however, it has been the Thammayut who have been identified as such. The Thammayut has also been associated, of course, with Thai Buddhism and Thai national interests, owing to the origins of its impetus within mid-nineteenth century Thai royalty. For this reason, at various times in the twentieth century, beginning in the 1920s and 1930s with the French colonialists and continuing with the Cambodian and Lao communists of the 1960s through 1980s, those politicos who have worried about the power of Bangkok becoming an encroachment in Cambodia and Laos have cast an especially jaundiced eye on the Thammayut, primarily out of concern that these monks could be used by the Thai to extend their spheres of political influence. Following the departure of the Vietnamese and the holding of UN-sponsored elections in the early 1990s, the Thammayut had been allowed to return to Cambodia. Indeed, in many quarters, they were encouraged.

I wouldn't say that I was delighted that early morning to discover that the temple was shut up tight with no signs of life, especially given the effort required to be prepared for field work at 2:30 in the morning, but I was not surprised and actually a little delighted to find that this pagoda did not observe *bay ben*. We found our way to a twenty-four-hour coffee shop located in a nearby hotel and whiled away the time until morning twilight, when we returned to the temple and found some stirrings afoot.

The first laypeople that we came across told us that this pagoda does not allow its people to perform *bah baay ben* because it is Thammayut, an answer that we expected precisely. When we subsequently put this matter to the *achar* who had shown up for the regular early morning chanting of *sutta*s, he became a little defensive and asserted that it was really not the decision of the pagoda to do the ritual or not. Rather, he argued that it depended on whether or not the laity wanted to hold the ritual. Betraying his *samay* disposition, he asserted that Vat Svay Por Pe's laity simply found no need to perform this rite. I suspected that the *achar* was being a bit disingenuous. My suspicions were deemed correct when, after a rather unsuccessful attempt to interview an elderly woman who was preoccupied with cooking the monks' breakfasts in the refectory, we encountered a well-spoken layman who was an ex-monk at this *wat*. He told us that, when he was in the monkhood, he and the other monks of the *wat* had agreed to hold *bah baay ben* and provided for the ritual from 1998 until 2002, when they stopped. The reason they had decided to "allow" *bay ben* back then was that they wanted the people to have a ritual in which to express their "solidarity" at the pagoda. Unfortunately, he said, not many people showed up for the ritual because everybody knew that this is a Thammayut pagoda and they simply did not expect *bay ben* to be held there. He went on to add that one of the other reasons that this pagoda no longer allows people to perform *baay ben* is that some youths used this ritual as a time and place where they could be involved in some "love related" activities.

The ex-monk-now-turned-layman seemed to have a lot of opinions about different types of *preta*s and which types could really be helped by *bay ben*. He insisted that *preta*s could receive merit only from living relatives via monks. He said that *bay ben* could physically benefit only those beings who had been reborn as animals. He did not seem to be aware of the philosophically more nuanced view that it is actually only the *vinnana* (consciousness) on whose behalf merit can be transferred. In writing specifically about this very point, Davis says that

> [m]erit is never made on behalf of the *bralin* or *khmoc*, but only on behalf of the Buddhist *vinnana*, that which travels through death and takes rebirth. The Abhidhammic perspective that prevails during the funeral rites emphasizes that all conditioned and compounded things . . . must decay and break up again. The *vinnana* will take rebirth as a result of its karma, which can be positively affected by the making of merit. But the *vinnana* is not the whole of the self. The amoral vital spirits must also be channeled and dealt with. Indeed, while death provides an opportunity for merit-making

and an improved rebirth in the figure of the *vinnana*, it represents a danger in the release of other vital spirits. (2009, 141–142)

This metaphysical discussion begins to indicate why it is the case that the *pretas* are regarded ambivalently, as figures in need of compassion and generosity, on the one hand, but also figures to be feared for their potential threats, on the other, if their calls for help are not heeded. Merit transfer is thus not only an attempt to turn *pretas* into proper ancestors and exemplary moral standards, it is also a way to control the potential negative fallout of the disintegration of the dead, that is, when the *vinnana* separates from the rest of the psycho-physical compounded being.

Fortunately, enough laity came to the pagoda that early morning as a matter of course that we were able to garner other opinions about why the non-performance of *bay ben* was not problematic. According to a laywoman, who was about forty-five years old and had come to Phnom Penh from Prey Veng province, she had bought some clothes and given some money to her parents at the beginning of *kan ben*. She had gone home in order to make these gifts to her parents and to meet her relatives, but she had not gone to the pagoda in her village. She said that as long as her parents are still alive, they will go to pagoda, make merit, and assist the dead family relations; she just offers them some money now to help them make merit but does not feel obligated to go to the pagoda herself. Asked if she was afraid of being cursed by deceased relatives, *pretas* who might be expecting her to transfer merit at the pagoda, she replied that her parents had taken care of the matter by dedicating merit to them already, so her deceased relations would not curse her. When her parents died, then she would assume responsibility. Her comments were very interesting in that they underscored how the making of merit for deceased relations is primarily a family affair. In the same way that some families attempt to send a family member every night during *kan ben* to perform *bay ben*, other families delegate the responsibility to perhaps only the parents. In either case, the process of assisting dead kin remains a collective effort. This woman also reflected a view that we often heard: a confession of agnosticism in relation to whether or not *bay ben* or merit transfer actually directly affects their deceased kin. This agnosticism, however, does not lead to a decision not to perform the rites. The rites are performed anyway. For they foster a degree of moral consciousness.

Finally, we interviewed an elderly woman, one of the assistant cooks in the refectory, who added another important perspective. She said that she felt that the question of whether or not that merit reached deceased relatives depends on the moral conditions of the monks at the *wat*. She said that she strongly believed in the moral goodness of the monks at Wat Svay Por Pe, and she felt confident that she could transfer merit to her deceased relatives because the monks are so well disciplined. That is, she believed that these monks were most worthy objects of good intentions. What was so significant about her remark was that, though the monks of the Thammayut Nikaya are generally not enthusiastic about rites such as *pchum ben*, their moral integrity, owing to their commitment to the monastic discipline of the *Vinaya*, establishes them as very efficacious objects of support. They are, ironically, the best catalysts for the power of merit transfer, despite the fact that many are skeptical of the practice and don't necessarily encourage it among their supporters.

MEMORIALIZING THE DEAD AT WAT KOKOS

Forty kilometers southwest of Phnom Penh, Wat Kokos was an interrogation center and prison where the bones of approximately eight thousand Cambodians were discovered after the Khmer Rouge had been dislodged. We arrived a little after 3 a.m. on the eleventh day of *pchum ben* to a completely empty and darkened temple, except for a solitary man standing in front of what is normally the refectory for the fourteen monks of residence. He told us that he would be the patron for the morning rite and that villagers would begin to arrive around 4 a.m. Our arrival had awakened his wife and two old women who were sleeping under mosquito-netted tents on the floor. One of the old women came to peer at us out of curiosity. We gradually found a verandah away from the others who had been sleeping, and the old woman joined us and the chief lay patron for a chat. She told us that she had come to Wat Kokos for seven nights, and so it seemed that the practice of visiting pagodas seven times has been concentrated here at this one place. We soon learned why: her husband and one of her sons were murdered here, her husband, she said, for simply complaining that he was hungry, interpreted as a sign of resistance to the *angkar*. The merit she earns each year for her annual pilgrimage to Wat Kokos she hopes will alleviate the suffering of her husband and son in the other world, though she is not sure about their rebirth destinies. Soon she was interrupted by the boisterous *achar*, who seemed to crave attention and yet, at the same time, offered us only evasive answers to our questions except one: he agreed that the social disaster inflicted by the Pol Pot regime has definitely had an effect on the rising popularity of *pchum ben*.

At 5 a.m., rather than 4 a.m., some villagers arrived, perhaps forty to fifty, who joined the other twenty or so others who had been sleeping and who were now moving about. Incense was lit, and about seventy-five or eighty people moved over to the *vihara* and began to circumambulate the building in proper clockwise *pradaksina* fashion. This group of laity was a younger set than usual and, of course, entirely rural. During their circum-ambulation, they stopped at the spirit shrines located at the four points (NE, SE, SW, and NW) on the platform, where they briefly sat in quiet meditation, remembering the names of those to whom they offered *pin-da*s. Their *pinda* plates were almost entirely rice balls, though some had wrapped candy. None had the white paper spirit effigies we had seen at each *wat* in Phnom Penh. Moreover, no receptacles had been put into place to receive the *pinda*. Instead, they were gently placed at either the base of the six spirit shrines lining the platform, or tossed over the three-foot-high decorative railing surrounding the *vihara*'s platform. Following the three circumambulations, the liturgical service began inside the sermon hall, a service that lasted roughly half an hour and included the chanting of the *Namassaka*, the *Namotassa*, the *pancasila* (five moral precepts), the *Parabhava Sutta*, the *Tirokudda Sutta,* and the *anumodana*. What was done differently at this temple was that the *bay ben pradakshina* was performed first, and the liturgical chanting followed.

Following the monks' liturgical chanting, we met with one of the *wat*'s lay patrons who was instrumental in reestablishing the *wat* back in 1981, about a year and a half after the Vietnamese had chased the Khmer Rouge to the northwest. He told us that, over the years, many people had come to the *wat* knowing that their relatives had been taken here and that this was the last place in which they had breathed. He spoke of the practice of grabbing a handful of dirt from the temple grounds to become a surro-gate for their relations' ash to be interred into a family stupa. Indeed, an inordinate number of votive stupas seem to have been built on the temple's premises, many, we learned, by Khmer-American refugees re-turning to memorialize their dead. This pattern was rather spectacularly illustrated by a stupa erected by a surviving wife who had built a shrine containing hundreds, if not a thousand or more, skulls, placed within a glass-enclosed room. The room measured about five meters by five meters, and the pile of skulls was about four to five feet high, the legacy of three years, eight months and twenty days.

We learned that the temple would be thronged on the final day of *pchum ben,* as hundreds would make their ways from Phnom Penh to this shrine to express their care and affection for the dead. We also learned about the cultic activities of a Sino-Khmer laywoman whose

Figure 5.10. Human skulls within votive stupas at Wat Kokos

father had been killed at this center. She also built a stupa filled with bones of those exhumed for commemoration. She not only transferred merit during *pchum ben,* but she also performed the *cheng meng* Chinese rite as well.

CHINESE INFLUENCE ON *PCHUM BEN?*

There are some *samay*-oriented intellectuals in Phnom Penh who argue that the practice of *pchum ben* owes its origins to Chinese influence and that this explains why the rite is not found in any other Theravada country. It is worth exploring briefly this possibility if, for nothing else, we can arrive at a comparative understanding of ancestor rites and, concomitantly, an understanding about what is unique about Khmer ritual practice. It is undeniable that, in general, the medieval Chinese ghost festival functioned somewhat analogously to *pchum ben.* It was likely the most important festival for Chinese Buddhists during the liturgical year. Moreover, it was through proving its relevance to the family that Buddhism was able to gain a foothold in China. This was not altogether easily done, since the story of the Gotama Buddha's quest for enlightenment included his renunciation of family and society. Another Buddhistic logic had to be invented or introduced in the Chinese context, and it is this logic that bears a fundamental similarity to the logic of *pchum ben.*

The Chinese ghost festival was held on the fifteenth day of the seventh month in medieval China (Teiser 1996, xii). Teiser begins his masterful study of the medieval ghost festival in China by introducing the Buddhist religious logic of this rite in this way:

> Offerings to monks were especially efficacious on the full moon of the seventh month, since this was the day when the Sangha ended its three-month summer retreat. During this period monks abstained from contact with lay society and pursued an intensified regimen of meditation completed with monastic ritual [that] Ennin refers to as "releasing themselves," confession and repentance of their transgressions in front of other monks. Having accumulated ascetic energy in retreat, monks released it in communion with householders. Moreover, the festival was held just at the time of the autumn harvest. Thus, the ghost festival not only marked the symbolic passage of monks and ancestors to new forms of existence, it also ushered in the completion of a cycle of plant life. Coming at the juncture of the full moon, the new season, the fall harvest, the peak of monastic asceticism, the rebirth of ancestors, and the assembly of the local community, the ghost festival was celebrated on a broad scale by all classes of people throughout medieval Chinese society. (4)

While the timing of *pchum ben* in Cambodia is not literally at the same time as the performance of the "ghost festival" in medieval China, it does come within fifteen days of the end of *vassa,* the rain-retreat season celebrated by Theravada monks. The power of the *sangha,* or better, the purity of the *sangha,* reaches its apogee at the conclusion of the rain-retreat. That is precisely why the monks are regarded as such efficient conduits for merit transfer during *pchum ben*: their conditions of purity render the charitable acts of which they function as objects all the more efficacious.[55] If, for a moment, we shift this discussion from time to space, we gain insights into how the pagoda has become an intensified pure space during the *vassa* rain-retreat season, owing to the monks' ascetic religious pursuits and, as such, becomes the most auspicious venue for interactions between the living and the dead.[56] The monastery is precisely the place where the dead, who, in the form of *pretas*, represent a suffering yet potentially dangerous presence for the living, may be safely encountered. The *pretas*, condemned as they are to suffering in the abode of *pretaloka*, or hell, as a result of their immoral behavior while among the living, are here offered a chance for rehabilitation in the space that has been morally sanctified/purified. They must come to temples to gain some relief from their conditions of suffering. They can search for help in seven different temples, but it is only within temple space that any transformations in their plights may occur. Moreover, the sanctified space of the temple provides the laity with a safe space to interact with the potentially dangerous dead.

Like the medieval ghost festival in China, *pchum ben* occurs temporally amid a liminality of various conditions, in times of transition. *Bay ben* must be performed in the early morning hours just before or during the breaking of the day, in twilight. *Pchum ben* season is celebrated during the end of the raining season, at the end of *vassa*, just before a new season of planting occurs. *Preta*s almost always make their presence known to their surviving kin, as in the *Petavatthu* stories, in dreams, a condition of consciousness that is neither fully awake nor fully unconscious. *Preta*s are, themselves, constitutive of a form of "betweenness," waiting and aspiring to be reborn as humans or as *devata*s in the heavens.

What Teiser has described in the Chinese context is also ever so the case among the Khmer in terms of the presence of liminality and how the merit transfer rites of *pchum ben* are thought to affect the dead. He points out that the rituals of the medieval Chinese ghost festival helped

> to effect the passage of the dead from the status of a recently deceased threatening ghost to that of a stable, pure and venerated ancestor. Although it is observed on a yearly schedule not synchronized with the death of a single person, the ghost festival marks an important transition in the life of the family, which is composed of members both living and dead. Like mortuary rites performed in many other cultures, the festival subsumes the potentially shattering consequences of the death of individuals under the perpetually regenerating forces of the community and the cosmos. (1996, 13–14)

This seems to be precisely the function of *pchum ben* among the Khmer.

Returning to these themes in the conclusion of his study, Teiser further unpacks the significance of liminality as a condition that the recently deceased must negotiate and argues that this liminality serves as the primary reason for why dispositions toward the dead among the living are necessarily ambivalent. What he writes about the medieval Chinese context resonates again vibrantly with the Khmer in this instance as well: how ancestors of the past seven generations can be positively affected by these rites.

> The celebration of the seventh moon marks the passage of the dead from the liminal stage, where they are troublesome, threatening, and feared as ghosts, to the stage of incorporation, in which they assume a place of honor within the family. In this liminal phase the dead lack clothes, they have subhuman bodies, they have difficulty eating, they are constantly in motion. Ghosts are a species in transition. . . . Ghost festival offerings are frequently dedicated to this dangerously shifting: "all sinners in the six paths of rebirth." But offerings are also made to the dead in the phase of incorporation, after they have joined the group of ancestors stretching back seven generations. As ancestors they have successfully completed the journey from life, through death, to rebirth. They are welcomed back into the

family as its immortal progenitors, creators and maintainers of the values
necessary to sustain the life of the kinship group.

Far from indicating a confusion of categories or an accident of history,
the coupling of apprehension about ghosts with the propitiation of kin represents a necessary ambivalence about the dead. The ghost festival articulates
the fear that the dead have not been resettled and might continue to haunt the
community as strangers, at the same time that it expresses the hope that the
dead be reincorporated at the head of the family line. (1996, 220–221)

Finally, what Teiser has to say about the centrality of the ghost festival to the ethos of family religion, and how the centrality of the Buddhist monks' role in the ghost festival made them indispensable to the
family-oriented religion of the Chinese, also resounds loudly within the
Khmer Buddhist social and religious world too.

While it did mark an important event in the yearly cycle of life for monks,
[the ghost festival] was even more firmly anchored in the dominant social
institution of China, the family. Its rituals became part of the system of
observances that united living and ancestral members of the family, rein-
forcing their reciprocal obligations and harmonizing the rhythms of family
and monastic life with agricultural schedule. (1996, 17)

While the ghost festival articulated the heart of family religion, it also became the means by which Buddhism secured its place within Chinese
society.

The spread of the ghost festival in medieval China signals the movement
of the Buddhist monkhood into the very heart of family religion, monks
were not simply accessories to the continued health of the kinship group;
their role was nothing less than essential for the well-being of the family.
[How] Buddhism was domesticated in China [is] particularly clear in the
ghost festival—through the inclusion of monks as an essential party in the
cycle of exchange linking ancestors and descendants. (Teiser 1996, 196–197)

It is quite clear from Teiser's considerations that the general social function of the ghost festival and *pchum ben* is that both rites unite the family
and the *sangha* as the principal players of these respective (Chinese and
Khmer) religious cultures. That is precisely why this particular ritual
has become so functionally important in the post–Khmer Rouge era in
Cambodia during a time of recovery and rehabilitation. *Pchum ben* functions as a primary means of effecting the recovery and prosperity of the
family. It also emphasizes how the *sangha* has become a necessity for a
family-dominated Khmer religious culture.

Having been impressed by striking parallels in the respective functions of the Chinese ghost festival and *pchum ben,* it is more than simply
interesting to note that during Ang Duang's reign, the very time when
pchum ben was purportedly established in Khmer culture by this ritually
minded Buddhist king, that "[a]t a rough estimate, it seems we should envisage Phnom Penh's population in the late 1860s as being upwards of
half composed of Chinese, with Cambodians at most a quarter of the total
and the remainder made up of . . . diverse ethnic groups" (Osborne 2008,
57). This demographic fact would seem to constitute circumstantial evidence supporting the thesis that *pchum ben* owes its recent existence
among the Khmer to the influence of Chinese culture.

While this discussion about the Chinese ghost festival yields fundamental insights into the parallel function of these rites for the well-being
and maintenance of the family in China as well as in Cambodia, it is another matter to attribute the sole existence of *pchum ben* in Cambodia to a
matter of Chinese influence, demographics notwithstanding. Davis has
noted the great functional similarities that exist between the Chinese
ghost festival and *pchum ben,* yet he stakes out a position in juxtaposition
to the thesis that *pchum ben* derives from Chinese influence. He refers to
pchum ben as "the most important ritual within the Buddhist calendar. It is
uncommon in the Theravada Buddhist world: while Chinese Buddhists
perform a well known similar ritual on behalf of hungry ghost ancestors,
the rituals appear to possess divergent textual warrants and histories"
(2009, 160). Davis' point is correct insofar as the Buddhist textual warrants
for *pchum ben* are clearly Pali sources, especially the *Petavatthu.* But this
does not dislodge the similar chartering importance of the Buddhist
sangha in the ritual transactions concerned with advancing the dead to
ancestor status in both contexts. What may be at some variance, however,
is the relative historical importance of rites for the ancestral dead in establishing a legitimate presence for the *sangha* in both societies. One of the
great strengths of Teiser's study is that it brilliantly supports the thesis
that the way Buddhism became assimilated and anchored in Chinese culture was through its adaptation to the centrality of Chinese familial religion. While Theravada Buddhism's presence in Khmer culture was no
doubt assisted by its relevance to the overriding importance attached to
the family, there may have been other compelling reasons for its grassroots adoption in fourteenth- and fifteenth-century Cambodia.

It is well known how the legacy of Angkor's high cultural achieve-
ments lived on for centuries among the Thai.[57] It was not just the legacy of
Angkor that inspired royalty within the river civilizations of mainland
Southeast Asia. It was also the Theravada ideology of kingship found

within the Pali *Tipitaka,* centering on the figures of the *cakkavattin* and the paradigmatic figure of Asoka, as these had been embodied in Sinhala forms of kingship, especially during the reigns of the Polonnaruva kings, Parakramabahu I being the best example. Forest has suggested that "Thai princes found in reformed Theravada a powerful means of making the societies over which they gained control cohere around their own person" (2008, 18). He goes on to suggest that a good measure of dynamism existed in the relations between monastic communities in neighboring *mandala*s (Lanna, Sukhotai, Ayutthaya, and Lang Xang). Because Jayavarman VII's son was one of those Khmer monks who traveled to Polonnaruva, Sri Lanka, in the thirteenth century to receive ordination in the newly re-formed *sangha,* intimate monastic relations between Theravada Khmer and Thai monk communities may have also been obtained. He further notes the involvement of Khmer monks in the fifteenth-century *sangha* del-egation, who went to Lanka to be reordained before returning to Chiang Mai to take up residence. In any case, he speculates that "[s]uccessive de-feats by the Siamese together with enormous demographic losses suffered by the Angkorean empire prompted the last Angkorean kings to adopt the religious system that seemed to have provided so much power to the Thai princes" (19). While such an argument leaves room for identifying other reasons for Theravada's wholesale adoption at the level of Khmer villages and Khmer families, it does underscore the intimate relations that ob-tained between kingship and political rule that solidified Theravada's po-sition as the ideological umbrella providing legitimation of power within Khmer religious culture in the post-Angkor era.

Beyond this concern, there remains the fact that some archeological evidence suggests that *pchum ben* existed far earlier than either Ang Duang's nineteenth-century reign or during the time of Theravada's intro-duction to grassroots Khmer village culture in the fourteenth and fifteenth centuries.

> The earliest reference we possess to Bjhum Pinda [*pchum ben*] is an inscrip-tion on the East Bray, the enormous, now dry reservoir to the east of the ancient city now called Angkor Dham, in which the East Mebon temple was later constructed. King Yasovarman built the East Baray around 900 CE, and inscribed the wall with references to Bhjum Pinda. The ritual de-scribed differs from the contemporary celebration as it was oriented to dead soldiers rather than familial ancestors. (Davis 2009, 162)

If this inscriptional evidence from material culture is taken into account, then it would seem to be the case the origins of the *pchum ben* are to be found in Angkor, or even possibly among the more ancient strands of Mon culture, and that it transcended the family in its object of concern.

In a conversation about the possibility of Chinese influence on *pchum ben*, Ang Choulean stressed the major differences, in his view, that separate the Chinese practice of venerating ancestors from the Khmer and therefore render it unlikely that a Chinese source is responsible for *pchum ben*. He notes that Chinese do not seek to keep their ancestors at bay for fifty out of fifty-two weeks a year.[58] Moreover, their festival is clearly to transform and liberate for the purpose of ancestors ultimately gaining nirvana, as in the famous story of Mu-lien traversing the hells in search of rescuing his suffering mother. That story, which became so central to the ethos of Chinese Buddhism, clearly reflects the Mahayana bodhisattva ethic.

We may never resolve this issue entirely. What complicates it is that both the Chinese and Khmer traditions of familial religion have been influenced by Buddhist thought and practice. It may be that this shared history of Buddhism, especially as it relates to how the *sangha* functioned in both social contexts, is what accounts for such remarkable parallels. That the traditions were inflected by different textual sources is obvious, and no doubt further inflected by antecedent cultural histories that include Taoist and Confucian trajectories on the Chinese side, and the legacy of Mon culture for the Khmer.

PCHUM BEN PROPER AND *BANGSUKOL* AT WAT TRALAENG KAENG

On the final *pchum ben* day proper, Phnom Penh, except for its colorful pagodas brimming with people dressed in their best finery and carrying their sumptuous festival foods to be offered to the monks for breakfast or lunch on behalf of their departed kin, is, indeed, something of a genuine ghost town. The evening before, on the fourteenth night, the royal family has briefly processed from their palace grounds across Sisowath Quay to the Tonle Sap River bank accompanying a festooned, *naga*-shaped boat with its *wat*-shaped canopy for the protection of its passengers, seven generations of royal ancestors. The boat is laden with food—ripening bananas, rice cakes in banana leaves, fruits, and vegetables—to ease their ancestors' return to the abode of the dead. The boat is carried by twelve ceremonial-clad *brahman*s, preceded by a flute-playing orchestra of four and protected by an honor guard of eight. About thirty relatives of the royal family clad in white finery, mostly men, constitute the procession

Figure 5.11. Ritual boat to ferry spirits home on *bangsukol*

that follows, a procession led by four pairs of prepubescent girls and boys. The boat is lowered from a canopied platform onto a bamboo raft that is waiting in the river, and then towed to a rented yacht, *Paris One*. Some of the family members board the rented yacht and accompany their ancestors downriver into the night. While this marks the official close of interaction with the ancestors, the rite of sending the ancestors home is carried out in the afternoon or evening at pagodas throughout Phnom Penh and in the rural provinces on the final *pchum ben* day in the afternoon. It is one of two primary rites observed on the final festive day and officially marks the conclusion of the *pchum ben* season. The ancestors and *pretas* are sent back to their proper abodes.

At the same time that Phnom Penh is a shell of its normal bustling self, the countryside has come alive with family reunions, the hallmark of which is a family visit to the family pagoda on *pchum ben* day. I wanted to make sure that I spent *pchum ben* day at a village pagoda, so we decided to spend the morning at Wat Tralaeng Kaeng in Kompong Chhnang, just north of the old capital of Udong.

The centrifugal force of *pchum ben* in calling the family home was also a matter of methodological concern for me, owing to the fact that my research assistants were often telephoned during that morning by their family members, who were asking why they were not where they needed to be. We had decided on Wat Tralaeng Kaeng for several reasons, one of which was its proximity to the native home of one of my research assistants. Trying to do fieldwork on *pchum ben* day was a bit like trying to work on Thanksgiving or Christmas in the United States. The compelling call of the family needed to be heeded, so our work involved only an early to midmorning stint. But it proved well worth the effort.

In addition to sending one's ancestors back to their proper places and feasting the monks at their two morning meals, the other important rite to observe on the final day of *pchum ben* is *bangsukol*.[59] *Bangsukol* is a simple rite of merit transfer normally solicited by an extended family for its departed kin. It is probably the most important Buddhist ritual for the laity regularly performed during the year, with the exception of a funeral or a monastic ordination of a family member. Special gifts for monastic comfort and care are presented to monks, who then chant Pali *gatha*s on behalf of the family dead of the past seven generations, and also for the benefit of surviving parents as well. *Bangsukol*, in effect, is a ritual that is designed to promote the health and longevity of the lineage. The rite is often held in front of a votive stupa containing the ashes of the family dead.

Since the construction of votive stupas is a costly affair well beyond the means of most villagers or even many in the middle class, some of the stupas in the *wat* are accessible to any Buddhist family for their use in making merit-transfer offerings. Reciting the specific names of the dead for meritorious benefit of the departed is a sine qua non. There seems to be some variation with regard to which Pali *sutta*s are chanted for the family by the monks. The monk who chanted at Wat Tralaeng Kaeng and another monk from a suburban Phnom Penh *wat* both mentioned portions of the *Dhammapada* as essential. What was also essential, the Wat Tralaeng Kaeng *achar* insisted, was that the texts articulate the fact of *anicca*, the transitoriness of existence. From the *achar*, we also learned that the *Vessantara Jataka* used to be chanted at this *wat* each day during the fifteen-day observance before the time of the Khmer Rouge. Now, the monks no longer do this because they do not have the knowledge of the text, according to the *achar*. The interruption of this tradition seemed another example of what Kobayashi had pointed out: that the civil war, the Khmer Rouge era, and the Vietnamese occupation had resulted in the elimination of many so-called *boran* or traditional practices. In any case, the fact that the *Vessantara* used to be chanted in conjunction with *pchum ben* reflects the fact that, like *bun phravet* in Lao religious culture, *pchum ben* is the primary merit-making rite of the year.

Figure 5.12. Temple spirit streamers

CONCLUSION

Observing *kan ben* and *pchum ben* in the rural areas of Cambodia provides something of a contrast with the manner in which it is observed in Phnom Penh's Buddhist *wat*s. The social religious experience in the countryside is far more intimate in nature for most of the participants, owing to the fact that it is shared primarily with family members. It is a family homecoming affair, as members of the family, both the living and the dead, are reconnected through solemn observance within a village context. One might say that the village also reassembles in a unified revivification. At the large and major temples of Phnom Penh, the experience is considerably more anonymous, given the large throngs in attendance and despite the attempts of monastic and temple officials to foster a type of congregational social experience. While those who attend in Phnom Penh certainly retain a motivation to assist the familial dead, they come from a broad cross-section of socioeconomic backgrounds and are united by only a common ritual purpose, and not the shared intimacy of village life and history. Not surprisingly, overt ties to the interests of the state were clearly in evidence in Phnom Penh, especially at Wat Langka and Wat Unnalom. In these instances, a sense of celebrating the nation certainly did not eclipse the importance of the familial orientation, but its presence could not be denied either.

It remains, in conclusion, to specify the Buddhistic logic of *pchum ben*, to underscore its religious significance in addition to its profound associations with familial ancestor veneration and family solidarity. That is, while there is an intrinsic religious conceptuality to ancestor veneration, there is also an accompanying spirit of Buddhist rationality to *pchum ben*. What makes the ritual performances of *bay ben* and *bangsukol* specifically Buddhist in the religious sense is that they both foster the fundamental act of taking refuge in the Buddha, the *dhamma,* and the *sangha.* Or, to put the matter in even more specific terms, these rites stress the importance of recognizing the Buddha's *dhamma* as preserved by the *sangha,* a recognition clearly articulated in the ancient chartering stories of the rite found within the *Petavatthu.* Merit produced is merit produced not because it is simply a mechanical transference of karmic power from one family member to another. Merit is merit because it is morally generated, and therefore has the power to morally regenerate in turn. Merit is morally generated because it comes from essentially *self-less* actions, actions generated by intentions that are not self-centered. Gifts made by the refuge-seeking laity to virtuous monks are basically sacrifices with "no strings attached." That is, gifts are not given to generate merit for oneself. They are given for the benefit of others, be it the monks who need gifts practically or the ancestors who may need the consequent merit because of their previous absence of moral consciousness. Thus, it is this ability to give, and the ability to rejoice (*anumodana*) in the intrinsic moral goodness of these ritual acts, that constitutes the Buddhistic religious quality of *pchum ben*. Far from being simply a mechanistic ritual of maintenance, *pchum ben* rites foster a moral awareness that transcends concern for the self, a moral awareness that seems to be the realization of *anatta*. It is precisely this realization in the mode of merit transfer that was parlayed in Mahayana schools where it became the means by which bodhisattvas such as Ksitigarbha (Japanese: Jizo) and Amitabha were thought to rescue suffering sentient beings from the rounds of *samsara*. In the Theravada contexts, merit transfer remains the chief means of articulating an individual altruism that finds its object in the care and compassion one feels for the familial dead. In Cambodia, it has become the ritual venue for restoring the vitality of family and nation.

APPENDIX 1

The *Dalada Sirita*

An Extract[1]

Further, this King (Sri Parakramabahu)[2] caused to construct, within the royal court, a mansion consisting of rows of pillars, walls and stairs, decorated with beautiful murals. It had high domes as brilliant as the rows of Himalayan peaks and flags with gilded poles jutting out from the cornices of domed windows which shone like divine rainbows; these flags visible through the clouds of scented smoke appeared like golden cranes. With gilded doorjambs, the mansion was as brilliant as one that had descended from heaven. (Then) he had cotton and silk canopies spread from which were suspended gold and silver flowers; right around, the hall was covered with broad cloths and on the floor, creeper designed lamps of gold and silver kept along with full water-pots of gold and silver in an orderly manner. Seats were set up covered with decorated cloths and the Tooth Relic and the Bowl Relic were deposited on them. Then, so as to increase his own delight and merit, he donated to the Tooth Relic palace service villages fertile with plantations such as banana, sugar cane, ironwood, *jak,* and coconut, along with service men and cattle. In order that ceremonies be perpetually performed, he appointed musicians who were experts in playing instruments including *sak-panca, vaddaru, dalahan, maddala, mahumakudarn, pana-bera, Mihingu-bera, damaru, dakki, udakki, talappara, virandam, viramorosu, kamsutalam, Sinnam, Tammata, nisana, timbilivu, rodiebera, bombilli, mabera, kudabera, gatapahatu, ekasbera, dahara, kahala, sirivili, tantiripata, vijayadhvani, gavarahan, vangi, vasdandu, vaskulal, tantiri,* and *dandi;* he also arranged for dancing girls of divine beauty, well versed in the thirty-six *raga*s and Bharata dance, and provided them with extremely beautiful costumes;

(he also) employed groups of actors and dancers who were exponents of performances such as *kolavandam, godeli, niyali, pevali,* and *bahurupa.* He then laid down many enactments including the following:

1. No one other than those who spread altar covers should be allowed to enter the scented chamber beyond the third inner gilded doorframe.
2. No one other than monks, royal personages, those entering the crown chamber, guards of the Tooth Relic house and *dharma-dhara*s should be allowed to cross beyond the second gilded doorframe.
3. The circle of ministers should be allowed to cross the third gilded doorframe.
4. Others who wished to take *darsan* should pay obeisance, staying outside the gilded doorframe.
5. Offerings brought ceremoniously should be accompanied [by persons holding] canopies with star designs, bowls held in knitted cloth bags, mouth bands [worn by bearers to maintain purity], service drumming of *sak-panca, vaddaru, dalahan,* and *kahala;* on ceremonial occasions elaborate services should be performed.
6. When the (golden *pingo* of) *chatties* is brought everyone should stay standing.
7. When meal offerings are served cooks should wear mouth bands, wash tooth picks in strained water and empty that water into a spittoon, spread table cloths, set the plates on trays with peacock shaped legs, serve food within eight hours[3] in the morning, accompanied by service (drumming and incantation).
8. [The rest of the] rice on the cloth spread (*pavada*) should be distributed among the service persons and musicians.
9. The virtuous kings of Sri Lanka after assuming kingship should desire to visit the Tooth Relic house once a day for worship; they should leave their retinue behind, purify themselves and enter the chamber with honor and respect, sweep the floor with a broom, wash their hands, offer gold [coins] and flowers, and pay obeisance reflecting on the nine virtues of the Buddha and take the five precepts.
10. Kings should offer a *poya*-plate on every *poya* day.[4]
11. Each of the ministers, according to their status, should offer a plate of food including the plate for regional chiefs, on a one-person-per-day basis.

12. A daily offering of a plate of rice should be made to Mahasup Thera[5] and his relic.

13. On the occasion of *nanumura* [ritual bathing] at the Tooth Relic house, offerings and due rituals should be performed to Mahasup Thera twice a month.

14. On the occasion of kings going into to occupy palaces, the Tooth and Bowl relics should first be conducted there ceremonially, and the monks should be made to recite *pirith* and, after providing protection by sprinkling of *pirith* water, they [the royal personages] should enter [the palace] after performing due rituals to the Triple Gem.

15. Those on guard's duty of the Tooth-Relic house, namely persons from Ganavasi clan, *kapurala*s (4), and *gebalanna*s, should wear jackets and turbans.[6]

16. Further, on an auspicious astrological conjunction, the Tooth Relic house should be cleaned, canopies hung and delicately decorated with silk cloths; after that, the royal personages, those in the harem, ministers and city dwellers should gather in a procession and conduct ceremonies for seven days offering flowers, lamps and food. Then on the morning of the seventh day, flowers and lamps should be offered and in the evening the city should be adorned like the heavens. After that, the Relic Casket should be taken out from the scented chamber by the head and the resident monks of the Uttaramula and authorized persons from the Ganavasi and Kiling clans[7] and (the casket) should be placed on an exalted seat of the elegantly decorated carriage. Two persons from Ganavasi and Kiling clans should ascend the carriage to conduct the casket.

17. An elegant tusker with auspicious marks should be harnessed to the carriage and well-robed monks should follow it in a line chanting *pirith* and holding the *paritta* thread.

18. A suitable person from the clan of Doranavasi[8] should be entrusted to sprinkle *pirith* water in the city from the silver pot.

19. On the two sides of the carriage services of oxtail fans and parasols should be provided.

20. Musicians and singers of the Tooth Relic house should accompany the carriage from the front.

21. After them should proceed the group of musicians and singers of the royal house providing their services.

22. After them should proceed the batch of ministers with the four-fold army providing protection.

23. After circumambulating the city in this manner it (the casket) should be conducted back, whereupon the king, the head and resident monks of Uttaramula, two persons from Ganavasi and Kiling, and house guards (Gebalannam) should come together, remove the seals, and take out the Tooth-Relic. Then the head and the resident monk of Uttaramula should be made to raise the relic and show it to the community of monks and hand it over to the king. They in turn should carry it in a procession accompanied with yak-tail whisks, parasols and conches; with great honor and respect conduct it to an elevated position, and in the assembly of the head and the resident monks of the Uttaramula, monks, members of the Ganavasi and Kiling clans, and the ministers, should exhibit the relic to the multitude.

24. To the strangers it should be exhibited from a distance to be ensured of protection.

25. After the exhibition it should be carried back to the Tooth-Relic house with the participation of the king. The Lord (relic) should then be placed back in the casket that should then be sealed with the three seals, namely that of the store room for vessels [tatukassa] of the royal treasury [pamul pettiya] and that of the temple [gana].

26. Those who make offerings of pandura [coins] should be anointed with a prasad of scented paste.

27. Dues for the Tooth-Relic should be collected from (state) taxes and gifts.

28. Seven or five monks should be employed for the regular chant of pirith.

29. Annual rituals should be performed in the aforesaid manner.

30. When the rains fail, Tooth-Relic rituals should be performed in the above manner.

31. When exhibiting Lord Mahasup [image or relic], arches should be erected and shown to the proper persons.

32. On the birthday rituals and coronation day rituals of the kings, a permanent gift of land to the Tooth-Relic house [dalada pamunu] should be given.

33. [State] taxes due from different services for the New Year [April] and Karti [November] offerings should first be made to the Tooth-Relic and subsequently to the king.

34. In case of any danger to the Tooth-Relic house, ministers appointed by the royal house and the head and the resident monks should get together to resolve it, and failing that, it

should be resolved with the participation of the community of monks.

35. Not even a single *kahapana* coin from the Tooth-Relic house should be appropriated by the royal house.
36. If borrowed during difficult times, twice the amount should be returned within six months.
37. Those who seek refuge in the Tooth-Relic house through fear should not be harassed.
38. Of the residents of Sri Lanka, *panduru* [gifts] offerings should be made by holders of *pamunu* lands, wicks and oil by holders of *divel* [service] lands, and per capita levies [*isran*], monthly levies [*mas-ran*], and day levies [*davas-ran*] by the others.

These and other diverse enactments were laid down for the Tooth-Relic house. The kings, crown princes, and ministers in the future will, by violation of these customs laid down by this noble King Parakramabahu, enter the hells; but those virtuous kings, heirs, and assemblies of ministers who are of the disposition to honor and respect the Three Jewels and follow them correctly, they will enjoy the pleasures of the six heavens, meet with Mete [Maitreya] Budu [Buddha] and, having listened to His discourse, will cross over the ocean of samsara and enjoy the pleasures of nibbana.

These customary laws were laid down in the one thousand two hundred and forty seventh year of the Saka Era on the suggestion of King Parakramabahu, the Gem of Kings, the king of this prosperous island of Sri Lanka.

This set of enactments was written down by Devrada, the Minister of Religious Matters [*daham pasakna*], mindful of the compassion of the leading *thera* of Parakumba *pirivena*, exponent of Sanskrit, Magadhi, Sinhala and poetics and drama.

Randoli Perahara

Date: 29th of July 2012 Time: 8:15 p.m. to 10:25 p.m.
Venue: Media Block in Maligava Premises

Items (in order)	Items (in detail)	Number of dancers/ performers	Number of supporting members to the dancers/ performers
Pilot Vehicle	Police car with a police officer and a driver		
Maligava *Perahara*			
1. Whip Crackers		10	
2. Fire Workers	Fire workers who carried fire balls with a rope attached to their hair	22	06
	Fire workers with fire ball bangles	28	
	Fire workers on artificial legs with fire ball bangles	03	
3. Man with a Sri Lanka National Flag		01	
4. Men with Buddhist Flags		30	
5. Men with Traditional Sri Lankan Provincial Flags		22	

(*continued*)

Items (in order)	Items (in detail)	Number of dancers/ performers	Number of supporting members to the dancers/ performers
6. Men with Brassware Flags		22	
7. Boys with Swords		24	
8. Elephant 1	With the Peramune Rala (front walker)		
9. Drummers	Including double drummers and tom-tom beaters	60	
10. Elephant 2			
11. Bulath Padaya Dance	Dance with betel leaves on the hands	18	11
12. Elephant 3			
13. Chamara Dance	Dance with traditional fans	20	09
14. Elephant 4			
15. Kotala Padaya Dance	Dance with a small gold pot on the hands	21	14
16. Elephant 5			
17. Mal Padaya Dance	Dance with coconut flowers on the hands	20	10
18. Elephant 6			
19. Pantheru Dance	Dance with brassware bangles with small cymbals attached	14	13
20. Elephant 7			
21. Lee Keli Dance	Dance with two sticks in hands	16	13
22. Elephant 8			
23. Kandyan Dance (ves)		16	12
24. Elephant 9			
25. Pathuru Dance	Dance with an instrument made with pieces of wood attached like a fan	16	12

Items (in order)	Items (in detail)	Number of dancers/ performers	Number of supporting members to the dancers/ performers
26. Elephants 10 and 11	Two baby elephants		
27. Dance with Tambourine	Dance with a small tambourine placed on the top of a curved thin bamboo	15	09
28. Elephant 12			
29. Cane Dance	Dance that creates weavings from cane	22	10
30. Savaran Dance	Dance with two sticks in hands with bunch of crape attached both ends of the sticks	20	09
31. Elephant 13			
32. Traditional Kandyan Dance		22	07
33. Elephant 14			
34. Drummers	Dance by double drummers	30	
35. Kadu Dance	Dance with swords and shields	16	15
36. Elephant 15			
37. Pantheru Dance	Dance with brassware bangles with small cymbals attached	20	
38. Elephants 16 and 17			
39. Reaping Dance	Paddy Reaping Dance with half-curved knives in the hands	16	15
40. Elephant 18			
41. Traditional Kandyan Dance		20	08
42. Elephant 19	Baby elephant		

(*continued*)

Items (in order)	Items (in detail)	Number of dancers/ performers	Number of supporting members to the dancers/ performers
43. Dance with Tambourine	Dance with a small tambourine placed on the top of a curved thin bamboo	14	
44. Elephants 20 and 21	Two small elephants		
45. Udakki Dance	Dance with narrow drums	32	
46. Elephants 22 and 23			
47. Traditional Kandyan Dance	Ves dancers	44	18
48. Nilame		01	
49. Elephants 24, 25, and 26	Elephant with Dalada in casket on middle elephant		
50. Sesath Carriers		05	
51. Small Boys	Boys with white flowers and oil lamps	12	
52. Traditional Kandyan Dance	Ves Dancers	50	10
53. Diyavadana Nilame		01	

Summary of Maligava *Perahara*
  Total Number of Dancers: 442
  Total Number of Drummers: 90 (excluding supporting drummers in the items)
  Total Number of Elephants: 26

Natha *Devalaya Perahara*

54. Peramune Rala		01	
55. Men with Buddhist Flags		10	
56. Drummers	Tom-tom beaters and double drummers	20	
57. Elephant 27			
58. Pantheru Dance	Dance with brassware bangles with small cymbals attached	18	05

Items (in order)	Items (in detail)	Number of dancers/ performers	Number of supporting members to the dancers/ performers
59. Elephant 28			
60. Lee Keli Dance	Dance with two sticks in hands	24	08
61. Elephant 29			
62. Savaran Dance	Dance with two sticks in hands with bunch of crape attached both ends of the sticks	18	03
63. Udakki Dance	Dance with narrow drums	12	04
64. Elephant 30			
65. Kandyan Dance		12	04
66. Kandyan Dance		12	04
67. Elephants 31, 32 and 33	Elephant with golden palanquin on the middle elephant with Natha's insignia		
68. Traditional Kandyan Dance	*Ves* dancers	42	08
69. Basnayaka Nilame	Basnayaka Nilame with two other nilames from village *devalaya*s	03	
70. Sesath Carriers		02	

Summary of Natha *Devalaya Perahara*
   Total Number of Dancers: 138
   Total Number of Drummers: 20 (excluding supporting drummers in the items)
   Total Number of Elephants: 7

Vishnu *Devalaya Perahara*

71. Men with Flags	Traditional flags	28	
72. Drummers	Tom-tom beaters and double drummers	24	

(continued)

Items (in order)	Items (in detail)	Number of dancers/ performers	Number of supporting members to the dancers/ performers
73. Elephant 34			
74. Lee Keli Dance	Dance with two sticks in hands	18	08
75. Elephant 35			
76. Dance with Drums	Dance by tom-tom beaters	18	
77. Elephant 36	Baby elephant		
78. Traditional Kandyan Dance	*Ves* dancers	26	08
79. Elephant 37			
80. Savaran Dance	Dance with two sticks in hands with bunch of crape attached both ends of the sticks	15	10
81. Elephant 38			
82. Pantheru Dance	Dance with brassware bangles with small cymbals attached	26	08
83. Elephants 39 and 40			
84. Traditional Kandyan Dance	*Ves* dancers	20	09
85. Elephants 41, 42, and 43	Elephant with golden palanquin on the middle elephant with Vishnu's insignia		
86. Traditional Kandyan Dance	*Ves* dancers	28	08
87. Basnayaka Nilame	Four Nilame from village *devalayas* wearing white dresses walked along with the Basnayaka Nilame	05	

Summary of Vishnu *Devalaya Perahara*
 Total Number of Dancers: 133
 Total Number of Drummers: 42 (excluding supporting drummers in the items)
 Total Number of Elephants: 10

Items (in order)	Items (in detail)	Number of dancers/ performers	Number of supporting members to the dancers/ performers
Kataragama *Devalaya Perahara*			
88. Man with a Sri Lanka National Flag		01	
89. Men with Buddhist Flags		09	
90. Men with Traditional Sri Lanka Flags		09	
91. Drummers	Including tom-tom beaters and double drummers	32	06 (trumpeters)
92. Elephant 44			
93. Pantheru Dance	Dance with brassware bangles with small cymbals attached	10	04
94. Elephant 45			
95. Savaran Dance	Dance with two sticks in hands with bunch of crape attached both ends of the sticks	16	05
96. Elephant 46			
97. Lee Keli Dance	Dance with two sticks in hands	16	06
98. Elephant 47			
99. Drummers	With south Indian drums	02	
100. Elephants 48, 49, and 50	Elephant with golden palanquin on the middle elephant with Kataragama's insignia		
101. Traditional Kandyan Dance	*Ves* dancers	46	10
102. Basnayaka Nilame		01	

Summary of Kataragama *Devalaya Perahara*
   Total Number of Dancers: 88
   **Total Number of Drummers: 34 (excluding
   supporting drummers in the items)**
   Total Number of Elephants: 7

(continued)

Items (in order)	Items (in detail)	Number of dancers/ performers	Number of supporting members to the dancers/ performers
Pattini *Devalaya Perahara*			
103. Men with Buddhist Flags		24	
104. Sesath Carriers		02	
105. Drummers	Tom-tom beaters with trumpeters and conch shell blowers	28	
106. Elephant 51			
107. Lee Keli Dance	Dance with two sticks in hands and creating weavings from the ropes attached to a column— Lanu Havadi Dangaya	20	05
108. Elephant 52			
109. Kulu Dance	Dance with winnowing fans (by girls)	16	06
110. Elephant 53			
111. Pantheru Dance	Dance with brassware bangles with small cymbals attached	15	05
112. Elephant 55			
113. Traditional Kandyan Dance	By girls	20	05
114. Elephants 56 and 57			
115. Traditional Kandyan Dance	*Ves* dancers	26	06
116. Elephants 58, 59, and 60	Elephant with golden palanquin in the middle elephant with Pattini's insignia		
117. Traditional Kandyan Dance	*Ves* dancers	30	08

Items (in order)	Items (in detail)	Number of dancers/ performers	Number of supporting members to the dancers/ performers
118. Basnayaka Nilame	Basnayaka Nilame walked along with other four Nilame from village Pattinin *devalaya*s	05	

Summary of Pattini *Devalaya Perahara*
   Total Number of Dancers: 127
   Total Number of Drummers: 28 (excluding supporting drummers in the items)
   Total Number of Elephants: 10

119. Dola Carriers (*Randoli*s)	Dola carriers of four *devalaya*s	08	

Summary of *Randoli Perahara*
   Total Number of Dancers: 928
   Total Number of Drummers: 214 (excluding supporting drummers in the items)
   Total Number of Elephants: 60

APPENDIX 3

———◆———

Wat Phnom

A MICROCOSM OF POPULAR RELIGION
IN PHNOM PENH

Wat Phnom, thanks to the *Lonely Planet* tourist guide, sees its fair share of
curious Westerners, but it is also a popular venue for the practice of contemporary urban religion in Cambodia. Its various associations cut across
the gamut of religious orientations, or layers of religious culture, in part
because of the absence of the *sangha* at this site, which otherwise would
demand a more specifically Buddhist rationale for the cultic activities that
occur here. There were no rites of *bay ben* during *kan ben* or *pchum ben* offered here during the two-week festival for the dead, precisely because of
the absence of monks, the holy men who are needed to organize temple
ritual liturgies and to receive the merit-making gifts of the laity, the power
of which is then transferred to the deceased. Nevertheless, Wat Phnom is
a local site of great power, a rather "extra-canonical" or heterodox example of the wider popular religious culture in play. It is thoroughly eclectic
and predominantly this-worldly in ethos.

The main foci within the complex consist of an imposing and elevated
stupa containing the ashes of King Bana Yat (r. 1405–1467) on top of the
forested hill that can be seen in a rather grand vista when the complex is
approached from the south on Norodom Boulevard. This is the king who
allegedly consecrated the *wat* by overseeing the establishment of its *sima*
(boundaries) and by investing the *vihara* with sacred images brought from
Angkor. Thus, the *vihara* proper contains a veritable welter of assorted
Buddha images, old and new, as well as images of Nang Thoranee (the

325

earth goddess who witnessed the Buddha's enlightenment and protected him from Mara's army while he was trying to attain it), Nandi (Siva's *vahana*, or vehicle), and various other figures of popular supernatural repute. Yet the main traditional focus of the image house is the four-Buddha constellation roughly constructed in the shape of a stupa that, nowadays, is rather shrouded by a new and more modern colossal Buddha image blocking its front. The four-Buddha bronze constellation figures prominently in the *shtalapurana*, or myth of origins of Phnom Penh, insofar as Madame or Lady or Grandma Penh, who now seems to function as an original euhemeristic guardian spirit of the space, in the same manner as village deities throughout Khmer and Thai-Lao culture areas purportedly discovered the Buddha images in a log that was floating down the river, along with an image of Visnu. This type of constellation of Buddha images is often associated with the cult of Maitreya, the future Buddha, who is the fifth and yet-to-appear Buddha implied by the presence of the previous four (Thompson 2004, 13–39). What this may indicate is that the presence of such an icon signals that the orientation of Buddhist worship here was, perhaps at one time if not now, apocalyptic or millennial in orientation. Or more simply, a place to articulate the spiritual hope that as a result of one's karmic actions, one might be reborn during the auspicious future of Maitreya's time.

The most active cultic activities, however, center around a little shrine between the *vihara* and *stupa* associated with the bespectacled and plump Lady Penh herself, who seems to be well known for adding her positive blessing or negative reaction to petitions set forth by her Khmer devotees seeking a boost of some kind in their daily lives, usually having to do with personal relationships or the want of material well-being. She reveals fortunes, for good or ill. To the north of the *vihara* are small shrines associated with a *neak ta* spirit who serves as the local guardian or power associated with the forested hill. Spirits are almost always particularly identified with the forest, and so the presence of this *neak ta* is actually rather matter-of-fact, which dovetails with the fact that he is usually rather perfunctorily acknowledged by the mostly Chinese and Vietnamese devotees who make their ways to the more substantial shrines where the minor deities Thang Cheng and Thang Thay, as well as Preah Chau, are venerated, respectively, for traditional wants of health, success in education, marriage, fertility, and so on. An adjacent eight-armed Visnu image also commands the attention of some Khmer devotees, although its presence, I think, is now more of an afterthought connected to its place in the discovery myth associated with Grandma Penh.

Wat Phnom has been rebuilt at least four times, as recently as 1926. But it was "renovated and landscaped by *resident superiur* de Verneville in 1894 so it might be transformed into a 'national pagoda'" (Harris 2008, 111). It would not be an exaggeration to say that Wat Phnom continues to retain many important elements constitutive of Cambodia's contemporary urban religious landscape: royal legitimation of Buddhism; the cult of the Buddha in its Maitreya inflection; an outstanding natural landmark—the only hill in Phnom Penh—which is therefore associated with sacrality; the presence of guardian deities, or spirits of the place, in the figures of Grandma Penh, whose power continues to be tapped, and the *neak ta* of the local forest, whose powers continue to be acknowledged. Within the context of Khmer religious culture, these activities articulate the so-called Buddhist, *brahman*ist, and animistic orientations. They are also reflective of an urban religious landscape that is even broader in scope, insofar as the presence of shrines that the Vietnamese and Chinese can tap their this-worldly desires is pronounced. In that sense, it remains a kind of "national pagoda" that transcends simply Khmer interest and is, therefore, a rather inclusive example of the types of sources of power tapped by contemporary Phnom Penh religieux. Moreover, it helps to locate the contemporary practice of venerating the ancestors during *pchum ben* more squarely within the orbit of Buddhist cultic practice and belief.

The Feast of the Offering to the Dead

BY ADHEMARD LECLERE

(Translated by Annelle Curulla[1])

It was the *thvoeu-bon pchum-boent sammnen,* the feast of the reunion for the offering of nourishment for the ancestors and spirits of the land, a type of festival of the dead. The court of the monastery was full and the gong that was struck vigorously by a swarthy strong man was still ringing to call the late-comers to tell them to hurry. The monks, dressed in yellow, with heads that had been shaved the night before, were seated in the conference hall talking among themselves before going to the temple. It was the last day of the lunar month of *photrobot,* the sixth month of the Cambodian year, fifteen days before the end of the ritual season of the rains and thus the annual retreat during which no monk, without serious cause, is able to leave the monastery and sleep elsewhere.

The night before, around 8:00, the monks gathered in the temple before the altar of the "saint" that was brilliantly illuminated [229; pages in brackets indicate pages in Leclere's original text] by many candles of beeswax in the middle of which were smoking sticks of incense made of resin and sandalwood powder. The monks recited the *Sampidher,* the *Yiersanta,* and the *Mahasomay,* religious verses that recall the path that the Buddhas had followed. They also recited a ritual prayer of exorcism in order to cast off evil, another text addressing boon-conferring deities, a formula for the aspersing of holy water on the faithful, and yet another chant to instill well-being on those attending. Before the three principal monks, there was lain next to the priest four indispensible items: three bowls of scented water, a bowl of water in which there were three sticks of cassia bark, three little packets of woven cotton that were knotted according to a ritual manner and were called the *amboh-thlol.* These packets of cotton were used to sprinkle water or were given to three of the faithful who immediately put them on their right ears; and finally there were three *sla-thor,* which are palm flowers and simple emblematic offerings.

It was at that time 9:30 in the morning; the air was wet and humid and the rays of the sun were barely coming through the clouds of the last winds of the southwest monsoon that were pushing their way to the north. Not a single leaf stirred atop the great trees and [230] not one shadow was made on the ground by the sun which remained invisible and betrayed only by a white glow. It had rained during the night in such quantity that the ground had remained wet everywhere and muddy in several places, and all around the monastery, beyond the fort enclosure and its high boundary walls of unequal size, there was something of a swamp. The frogs were croaking and twenty types of insects were singing. In the shrubs, the grasshoppers were chirping and there, near the entrance to the temple, there were two thin dogs threatening each other, their heads lifted up bearing their teeth and their wild fir standing on end. In every moment, women in great numbers, and men and children arrived, some women carrying a bowl of copper, a shallow bowl containing white cooked rice as an offering to the monks. Atop it was a great spoon made of roughly hewn wood, or a flat-handled thin copper ornate spoon of Chinese origin, or another copper spoon of ornate nature topped with a stylized lotus embossed in silver, sometimes quite intricate. Other women were carrying with their two hands bowls with cooked rice that were decorated with ceremonial cloths to be offered to the ancestors, to the spirits of the land [230], to the *thewada,* either auspicious or inauspicious, who have left their habitual dwellings in either paradise or hell in order to accept the invitation that was made to them yesterday to come find "in this monastery where they had come so many times while they were living that had come to pray" to see those of the living upon whom they keep watch. Men were carrying their little children who were set astride their hips. The eldest boys soberly followed their mothers who in turn followed their husbands and all the children followed in order of age, which was further indicated by their clothes of the boys and girls, the *chpap pros* and the *chbap srey.* Some of the women carried young children in their arms who were wrapped in white fabric. These people wore their most beautiful clothes spun of beautiful fabric which both sexes lifted up between their legs to form bell-shaped shorts. The same silk fabric was used for the white vests worn by the men, and the elegant tunics worn by the women which were very colorful and yet revealing [232] their waists and chests. They also wore beautiful long scarves which were folded into pleats, wrapped around one armpit to the shoulder, and hung down the back. The hair styles of the women were of three types: a pony-tail flowing behind the neck, a bun gathered atop the head worn by women of mixed race (Chinese), and another style in which the hair was held in a bun by an ornate pin. The hair of the children is shorn the night before and their heads are topped with a ring of hair that is knotted and held together by a black and white quill. Some of the little girls with hair on top of their hair wore a small garland of flowers on their heads. Others wore their hair on their shoulders. Many children had silver rings on their feet and golden bracelets on their arms and golden rings on their hands. The women are covered with jewels and beads strung in bracelets and necklaces that drape their torsos . . . [233].

All of these people arrive and enter into the temple, press in, chat, laugh, and exchange pleasantries.

In the temple, the head monk/teacher, the literate one who presides over the ceremonies, invites the monks to come in in the name of the faithful and recites the Pali formulas, dressed in white, sitting in the presence of the governor, and in front of the enormous statue of the Buddha. Both the governor and the teacher are wearing white scarves and behind the governor are his wives and the ladies in waiting of his wives, his children, and all of his family.

The gong rang out its last call and hereupon the faithful entered. The women grouped themselves to the left of the altar on the lower side and the men placed themselves on the right. Then they take off their white scarves and like the women, governor, and teacher, put the scarf around their bodies. All of these people sitting on the ground, on mats have their two legs folded as they laugh and smoke, chewing and spitting betel juice into dirty vases that one would believe had never been washed since their creation [234].

The monks enter the temple "Indian file" by the door that opens behind the altar on the right. They salute the statue of the Buddha three times by putting their foreheads in the dust and come to take their places on mats on the ground like the others with their legs folded on the left. There are a dozen of them, serious and without any showing any affect. All of them are young. Even their elder mentor who is the chief of the monastery sits with the same affect. They look without curiosity at the women who are facing them behind a double cue of *patra* or *batr*. They also look at the men who are surrounding them. The faithful on their knees pull on the feet of the monks to get their attention to give them presents of betel. The women get up and they leave bowls of rice and go to light candles of beeswax that are as large as a finger and also to light the incense that they place on the altar. And then they join hands, make a gesture, and go back to their places and again sit down with hands joined as if to pray [235]. The men carry bowls of the *bay-boent* that carries candles of incense and little white banners. They leave all of these things at the foot of the altar and light incense sticks. The altar is all afire and the smoke of incense rises to the face of the deity and spreads in the air.

The *achar* salutes the Buddha thrice and puts his head thrice in the dust and then salutes the head of the monastery but a bit less low. All of the hands are linked and open at the height of the face. All heads are inclined. The head monk says three times: *namo tassa bhagavato, arahato samma sambuddhassa*, and to all those gathered there. All repeat the invitation of the priest in one long murmur of devotion. The sky has darkened, the air is heavier, hotter, the frogs croak, the insects sing, scream, and whistle. The grasshoppers chirp and the voice of the priest, strong and well-timbered rises up to the heavens where the fortunate delight in their deserved happiness. And the response of the assembly is hummed like a flock of bees or hornets [236].

The priest, once the salutation is finished, speaking a bit louder and a bit more slowly, invites the monks to recite for the assembly of the faithful the five sacred precepts, the three sacred refuges. The faith agree with one word: *sadhu*, which is the amen or the so-be-it of the Buddhists, what is said on the day of coronation of their kings.

The monks repeat three times the salutation to the Buddha and then recite the five precepts: do not kill, do not steal, do not commit impurities, do not lie, and do not drink alcohol. That said, they lean forward and recite the three *paramita*s or three verses in which they ask that all evils and misfortunes be kept away from the faithful.

The assembly responds: *sadhu*, and bows to the statue of the Buddha, hands joined in front.

Then the priest takes the floor and asks the monks to recite the *Dhammakusalakusala*, the eight *Chanararas*, and the four other recitations that they follow. The faithful say: *sadhu*. The monks raise their screens and again their voices to recite the stanzas that they do not understand and that they say through their [237] noses empty of meaning for them. They know vaguely, the most instructed and eldest among them, what the point is and that's all. The others content themselves with what was told to them that morning by a brother or by the priest reciting from memory with the others, reciting from memory with a fan before their faces in order not to be distracted by the women seated in front of them and to not be distracted by anything that might happen in the assembly. The laymen, with their hands joined, hear without listening and the children, with their little fingers, trace out figures in the sand on the ground.

As soon as they've finished, a man reveals the *patra*, and the priest takes a bowl of rice and a spoon with his face turned toward the monks taking the offering of cooked rice or *reap batr*. He puts a large spoonful of rice in each of the *patra*, and after the last offering has been made, puts the bowl on the ground and salutes the monks by bowing his head and bringing his two hands to the height of his forehead. The governor [238] follows him with another bowl and follows the same routine, then the wives of the governor, his daughters, who altogether in Indian file with the great wife at the head, each one in their hierarchical order of rank, each one with a bowl in the left hand and a spoon in the right, drag themselves on their knees all along the *patra*. The other women of the land come next, pressing themselves ahead, one after another, pressing their spoons always full from one vase to another, never losing their attention. The offering is made, without saluting the monks who by their very presence have given them the opportunity to complete a pious act. After the women come the men, who are less ritualistic in their movements, who do not kneel but stand bowed forward and hunching to salute. When the *patra* are full, a man empties them, but only half way "because a monk must not ritualistically receive more than his *patra* can contain." And he empties the extra into baskets and puts these back on their stands. Now that the baskets are filled, the *reap batr* continues [239]. Finally the last man, an old man, painfully drags himself, and given his last spoonful, salutes humbly and with the last effort goes back to his place with his plate, his hands shaking so much that the copper spoon slides off.

A little girl comes to him, takes his bowl from him, and the poor old man who dreams of a better existence in his next incarnation supports himself on the shoulder of an adjacent young man and takes his place next to him, happy to have made an offering himself with his poor old hands.

The monks repeat a Pali recitation, the gong rings, and almost all of the assembly arises, gathers the bowl that still contains the *bay-boent*, topped with little flags in which candles and incense still burn. They go out organizing themselves into a ceremonial procession and repeat three times a *pradaksina* around the temple. They go from the east to the south (*dakshina* in Sanskrit), from the south to the west, from the west to the north, and from the north to the east, three times with the right shoulder turned to the temple in order to honor it. And while the gong rings setting a rhythm to their paces, they throw to the ancestors the spirits of the land, and to the *thewadas* small balls of rice prepared for the occasion along with small cakes also especially prepared [249]. They also throw sweets prepared the night before and they lay out these offerings on the palms of young *borasus*, a sugar tree, on the stems of the branches of the tree, at the foot of the *simas*, or the sacred boundaries that lay out the reserved space of the temple, or on the small houses [phi shrines] constructed on posts around the temple for the gods of the Buddhist paradise.

The last round completed, the person beating the gong strikes one final time and the faithful return to the temple with their bowls half empty. The frogs croak, insects sing, dogs run, and in the grass the spirits find the offerings that have been rejected and find the leftovers. They lift themselves up on their hind legs to find on the palms of the *borasus* all these good things and they jump up and shake down these offerings to the ground so that they can eat them.

Inside, men with their hands full of bowls with *bay boent*, approach the monks from behind touching their feet in order to attract their attention and receive their blessing [241]. A monk turns, takes a leaf of betel placed inside a glass of perfumed cocoa water in which has been thrown a bit of rice flour. Then the monk recites a Pali stanza of well wishing and shakes the betel leaf with rice on the flowers that decorate the bowl. Then he recites once more the *sappa putthea*.

The monks recite stanzas inviting the ancestors to go back to paradise or their hells, and the priest, taking a bowl of *bay boent* reserved for them, salutes the happy ones, the *thewada*, and he makes them an offering in Cambodian. The assembly responds: *sadhu sadhu* and then retires to go throw into the shadows the food that has been blessed by the disciples of the Buddha.

The monks name all of the deities who have come in order to thank them, the mantra of *pohou tevea*; then a few of them throw a little a branch, still having leaves on it taken from a *kantuot* [tree?], a *sambuor*, bamboo, or a banana leaf, and sprinkle holy water on the priest or on the faithful who have approached for lustrations.

It's finished, the temple slowly empties [242], a few old women and old men remain, during which time the monks recite the *gatha* of blessing, the final prayer, a last request. And they throw a few in order to take Preah Thorni (Dharani) [Nan Thoranee] as a witness to the requests that have been initiated. She is a goddess of the earth and a great revenger of the oppressed. What are these old people asking for who are going to die soon from those who are already dead? They ask that the young make for them the *pchum bun* as they have just celebrated for their ancestors. They ask that the future does not forget them no more than they have forgotten the past.

The recitations of this occasion of the feat of the death number 12 [*Parabhava Sutta*].

They are preceded by a reading from the *kusalakusala dhamma* [doctrine of merit], unfortunately in Pali that the faithful do not understand at all.

Among them there are three parts. The first part, called the *kusala dhamma*, recalls the efforts the Buddha has made in order to attain the Buddhist truth and what he practiced over the course of his lives as he advanced on the path of salvation [243]. The second part, called the *akusula dhamma* [doctrine of demerits], speaks of the passions that the Buddha repressed, and in imitation of him, is necessary to vanquish if one wishes to avoid the pains of hell. Thus it is necessary to rise above it like a light piece of wood. Like him, it is necessary to avoid throwing oneself into the abyss. The third part, called *apiyakatha* [conclusions], explains that if many of the beings who are dead come back, it is because they were not able to avoid sin.

The twelve recitations that come afterward are also in Pali and, as a result, incomprehensible to the faithful as the excerpt that I have just analyzed.

The first seven recitations are the *Chana-varas* [the *Tripitaka*], or the extracts having to do with the seven books of *Abhidhamma* . . . (*pamsukula?*)

The eighth recitation is a prayer for the dead. Its title begins with the word *Tirokkaro* which means "disrespectful" [244]. This prayer was recited for the members of the family of the King of Rajagrha, Bimbisara, who ate one part of the sweets he had had prepared for the Buddha and the *sangha* because these people expiated the *pretas* and, except for these actions of our prayers and the coming of the future Buddha, could not have been saved.

The ninth recitation, called *pohou devamanusa cha mangala* speaks of the occasions by which salvation is provided by the Buddha, *dhamma* and *sangha*.

The tenth recitation, called the *Sakatvabuddharatanam*, teaches that the three blessed ones are a remedy for the healing of sins.

The eleventh recitation, called the *Sabbabouddha nuphavena* appears to speak to the wishes of the shadow of the three gems and engages those present to make these wishes.

The twelfth recitation, and the last, is called the *Yathavarivaha*. It says that virtues lead to nirvana and that sins, no less naturally, lead to hell and to successive rebirths in the same way that the current leads to the sea.

Such are the twelve recitations that the monks of the Buddha chant in the Pali language without really understanding what these phrases mean, the phrases they are chanting in the presence of the faithful who are listening, hands joined to the height of their foreheads but with their ears closed. Faith saves them and who knows if they don't obtain the things that they are not aware that they have asked, or the things they have asked from their mouths or the things they have asked from their heart and understanding?

At the palace, or more exactly in the *ho preah* of the palace, the *bakhou*s celebrate this festival of the dead that has been forgotten by the masses of Khmer people, of the cult that they had once designated to the Brahmin divinities.

About fifty of them (Brahmins) gather in the last of their temples [to perform *pujas* to the Siva, Visnu, Ganesa, Kajjayana, and Khvam for the benefit of their ancestors. . . .]

That done, they next invoke the deities, ancestors, and *devata*s and pray to protect the kingdom and its prosperity [247].

Notes

Introduction

1. Steven Collins, *Nirvana and Other Buddhist Felicities* (Cambridge: Cambridge University Press, 1997), 48.
2. The phrase has been suggested by Justin McDaniel.
3. Particularly the Pali *Dipavamsa* and *Mahavamsa*.
4. *The Visuddhimagga* by Buddhaghosa. Bhikkhu Nyanamoli, trans., *The Path of Purification*, 2 vols. (Boulder/London: Shambhala, 1976).
5. See especially Prapod Assavavirulhakarn, *The Ascendancy of Theravada Buddhism in Southeast Asia* (2010).
6. More precisely, Skilling elaborates:

> All that can be said is that a school that used Pali as a scriptural language was prominent in the Chao Phraya Basin and in lower Burma, and that the school, or more probably schools, were likely to have been descendants of the Theriya lineage. It is simplistic to say that this Buddhism "came from Ceylon." Trade and political relations were complex; the many communication routes from India and Sri Lanka to Southeast Asia allowed diverse cultural contacts. Given (I believe) complete silence of extant Mahavihara literature on relations with Southeast Asia before the Polonnaruwa period, it does not seem likely that the dominant *Vinaya* lineage in the Chao Phraya basin was that of the Mahavihara. Nor is there compelling evidence (at least for the mainland) for an affiliation with the Abhayagiri. I tentatively conclude that a Theriya lineage, or Theriya lineages, were introduced at an early date, that is, in the early centuries CE from India—at several times and in several places, and that these lineages developed into a regional lineage or regional lineages it is or their own right, with their own architecture, iconography, and (now lost) literature (2009, 74).

This is also largely the view of Assavavirulhakarn (2010), who seeks to establish this by a perusal of the remains of material culture in Thailand that precedes the Chiang Mai and Sukhothai periods.

7. Bell is quite conscious of the political ramifications of her theorizing. She notes that "[r]eligion and ritual do not just serve the status quo; they can also articulate major upheavals of it" (1997, 136). Moreover, "[p]olitical rituals . . . indicate the ways in which ritual as a medium of communication and interaction does not simply express or transmit values and messages, but also actually creates situations. That is, rites of subordination to royal power, from bowing to the passing entourage of the Javanese king to watching the formal torture and execution of a convicted criminal, are not secondary reflections of the relationships of authority and deference that are structuring interactions between rulers and ruled. They create these relations; they create power in the very tangible exercise of it" (ibid.).

8. Gananath Obeyesekere, "Religious Symbolism Political Change in Ceylon" (1972). Yet, see my critique of this understanding in "Protestant Buddhism? "*Religious Studies Review* 17 (1991): 307–312.

9. While Emile Durkheim, in his *Elementary Forms of Religious Life*, lends credence to this characterization, the formulation and emphasis on the atheistic or nontheistic nature of Buddhist practice lies in the perception articulated by a long line of Euro-American admirers who were simultaneously disenchanted with the theistic religions of the West.

Chapter 1: Phra Bang

1. Susan Huntington (1990), however, argues that iconic anthropomorphic images of the Buddha may date as early as the first sculpted expressions of Buddhist art.

2. But see Jacob Kinnard's (2008, 81–103) argument that Amaravati relief sculptures depict ritual scenes of cultic activity in which stupas, bodhi trees, or footprints venerated by attendant laity are not necessarily symbols of the Buddha.

3. The principal exceptions to this are the "grandmother" and "grandfather" guardian *phi* of Luang Phrabang, whose cartoonish figures form an important presence in the annual New Year (*pi mai*) rites during the month of April. Yet, they too are not fashioned anthropomorphically at their central shrine within Vat Aham in Luang Phrabang. Nang Thoranee, the earth goddess (and therefore not quite a *phi*) is another exception.

4. Swearer and Premchit (1995) and Keyes (2002) have provided fascinating studies in the Thai context in which local female deities with some historical bases have been transformed into heroic Buddhist guardian deities of larger urban areas or cities. In these contexts, images have been crafted for their public representations. Moreover, one can also find in both Thai and Lao contexts public images of the earth goddess Nang Thoranee (in Sri Lanka, Bhu Devi). While the inspiration of the former originally may have been motivated by beliefs in the *phi* cult, the latter is a Thai-Lao adaptation of an ancient Indian Buddhist cult. For a comprehensive study of Nang Thoranee, see Guthrie (2004). In any case, none of these goddesses would be now popularly regarded primarily as *phi*. That is probably why they are anthropomorphically represented.

5. *Devalaya*s or deity shrines in Sri Lanka are usually open to the public at least twice a week on Wednesday and Saturday mornings, although the larger and most famous shrines that cater to a national clientele, such as Kataragama or Alutnuvara, may be open every day of the week.

6. Condominas (1973, 254) agrees: "In general the phi do not require any substantial public ritual structures comparable to the Buddhist monastery."

7. In some ways, the cult of Nang Thoranee, though not a *phi* per se, functions as a protective cult for the Buddhasasana. See Elizabeth Guthrie (2004).

8. Harris also agrees: "[T]he *phiban* [village deities of Laos] are geographically more specific and functionally less well-defined" (2008, 257). Indeed, the fact that they are more "geographically specific" is a key insight in recognizing their archaic yet continuing function for Lao religious culture, as we shall see.

9. This observation would seem to argue against, or perhaps constitute an exception to, Stewart Guthrie's argument about anthropomorphism as a theory of religion advanced in his *Faces in the Clouds* (1993). Here, Guthrie makes the case that apparent images in cloud formations were construed as the presence of deities.

10. The French scholar Condominas also saw the relationship in this very same way: "[T]his common religious core [of the spirit cults] has been penetrated only superficially by exogenous world religions, and has been less than profoundly affected by other cultural elements taken over seemingly *in toto* by the peoples of Southeast Asia" (1973, 272).

11. The art historian Robert DeCaroli (2004) has also recently argued cogently that the rise of Buddhism, at least insofar as it can be understood through a study of sculpture and popular literature (especially the *jatakas*), needs to be understood within the context of a religious culture dominated by spirit cults.

12. In commenting on Mus' argument some forty years later, Condominas relates it more specifically to the Chinese context: "The cult of territorial spirits is common to the T'ai peoples of Southeast Asia, whether Buddhist or not, and bears some resemblance to the Chinese veneration of the earth god" (1973, 255). I think that Mus' argument has to be kept separate from the theory of "soul stuff" and "men of prowess" that Wolters (1982 and 1999) has attributed to "pre-Indianized" Southeast cultures. Wolters' theory misses the correspondences of power between the supernatural and the human, and then makes some questionable links to Hindu conceptuality by identifying *sakti* with this "soul stuff." More likely, it is linked to the kind of "rule by ritual" described by Lucien Pye (1985, 39–46) and the "bureaucratic cosmology" described by Bell (1992, 128–129) and McMullen (1987, 181–236) clearly evident in Chinese culture.

13. See Bechert (1966–1973), Southwold (1983), and Obeyesekere and Gombrich (1988) for a thoroughgoing discussion of these respective terms that refer to a reform-minded and rationally composed understanding of Buddhism. See also my "Protestant Buddhism?" (1991b), for a critique of this nomenclature.

14. Tambiah (1970), Hayashi (2003), Terweil (1978a and 1978b), Condominas (1968, 1973), Tiyavanich (1997), Davis (1984), and Zago (1972 and 1976).

15. Harris (2008), Edwards (2007), and Marston and Guthrie (2004) for the Khmer, and Spiro (1967) for the Burmese.

16. For a more elaborate summary of these points, plus the manner in which Mus understood them as relevant to the Vietnamese struggle against the French, see Susan Bayly (2000).

17. See Eliade, *Patterns in Comparative Religion* (1996).

18. This principle can also be observed in relation to how the lineage of clans were later understood as protected by *phi ka* or *phi dam*, the "clan spirit." See Davis' (1984, 54–65) extensive discussion.

19. As Mus asserts:

The correspondence between the two wings of monsoon Asia extends to practices of remarkable complexity. You are aware that in China, with the strengthening and expansion of the social order, the ancient cults of the soil finally produced a magic duplication of the map of the country. To each one of its rural or urban centres there came to be attached peculiar genies among whom was instituted a hierarchy that reproduced on the supernatural plane the administrative divisions of the country. The genie of the district centre would give orders to those of the townships and take them from the genie of the capital. The emperor and his dynastic earth-god stood at the head of this "government of the beyond," divided among ministers. The emperor even appointed and dismissed local genies.

Indology, preoccupied with its classical reminiscences and its Indo-European interests, has, as far as I know, almost completely neglected to use the scattered but ancient and specific documents which would attest, on the Indian side, [to] very similar beliefs. In the *Jataka*, the *Sutta* and the *Atthakatha* of the Pali tradition may be found all the elements of the government of the beyond: the family genie is responsible to the genie of the town, and he in turn to the gods presiding over the four quarters: these, finally, obey Indra whose divine city is represented on earth by the capital of the kingdom, in a sense its material "double." (1975, 19)

20. Davis (1984) notes that "[u]ninhabited territory is not conceived as being part of any particular *muang*, and the mountain wilderness which is the border between two *muang* is like an empty space. Conceptually, a forest is the opposite of a *muang* in that it is uninhabited." Justin McDaniel notes that it is from the forest that many holy men and sorcerers emerge, precisely because their powers have not been domesticated (personal communication).

21. I use the term "ritualization" in Bell's sense of referring "to the way certain social actions strategically distinguish themselves in relation to other actions . . . , for creating and privileging a qualitative distinction between the 'sacred' and the 'profane,' and for ascribing such distinctions to realities thought to transcend the powers of human actors" (1992, 74).

22. Wolters prefers to refer to individuals like the *chao muang* as "men of prowess" (1982, 1999). This manner of characterization is helpful insofar as the "prowess" in question is understood as a consequence of what Mus means by "doubling."

23. But Michel Lorrillard, a leading historian of ancient and medieval Lao material culture, remains skeptical on this point (private communication, June 2007). Moreover, Davis (1984, 29–30), citing Coedes, asserts that the style of kingship in Angkor was much more autocratic and hierarchical in nature than the conceptions of chiefdoms found among the Muang of Northern Thailand and possibly the Lao.

24. Later known as Xieng Thong Xieng Dong and, later than that, as Luang Phrabang.

25. Michael Vickery, in closely analyzing two nineteenth-century Lao texts—one with relevance to a *muang* in Isan (Northeast Thailand) and another to Xam Neua during the time of the early nineteenth century rule of Vientiane's Anu—has tried to mitigate what he calls the "mantrification" of *mandala* discourse in Lao historical inquiry. He seeks to readdress the primary issue of "whether the political economy of early Southeast Asia resulted in rulers being more concerned with control of land or control of people" (2003, 3). In this wide-ranging and carefully argued article, he makes a strong case that economic circumstances sometimes made various kingdoms "land hungry" or that founding myths, such as the foundation myth for Ayutthaya, imply a search for land, and not just for people (5). Vickery's argument can stand as a corrective to those studies that simply reduce all dynamics between center and periphery as a matter of *mandala* ideology when, in fact, the specifics of a given context of political economy were usually far more complex in nature.

26. "These forms of legitimation rested on an animist worldview that owed nothing to Buddhism, a worldview similar in many respects to that still held by the tribal upland Tai of northeastern Laos" (Stuart-Fox 1998, 51).

27. This is a very unfortunate choice of phrase, as it relegates the understanding of *dukkha* ("unsatisfactoriness"), the problematic nature of *samsara*, and the Buddhist quest to overcome it by means of the Noble Eight-Fold Path, to a thoroughgoing Christian idiom. "Sin" is not a good translation for *dukkha* and "saved" connotes a means of "grace" acquired from a divine power without.

28. Again, "redemption" is not quite the right word here for the path leading to *nibbana*, since for most Buddhists progress on the path is a matter of karma or merit derived from self-effort. Moreover, I think what Stuart-Fox actually has in mind here would be better expressed in the phrase "universal history of the Buddhasasana."

29. See notes 27 and 28.

30. Jayavarman VII styled himself as a bodhisattva reflection of Avalokitesvara.

31. Evans writes incisively on this point: "Sacred centers, and not sacred territories and boundaries, were the preoccupation of these polities, which were made up of personal networks focused on the king rather than territorial units. The king's innate spiritual power attracted followers, and had to be shown to attract even greater numbers of followers, as expansion in the known world demonstrated prowess and spiritual potency. This spiritual prowess was not automatically transmitted to sons, however, thus the death of a king threatened to unravel the structure of personal loyalties making up any particular mandala" (2002, 7).

32. The *Mahavamsa* (18–19, 122–135) contains an account of how a cutting from the original bodhi tree from what is now Buddha Gaya in Bihar was brought to Anuradhapura by Sangamitta, the daughter of Emperor Asoka, who establishes the *bhikkhunisangha* on the island. A later Pali text, the *Mahabodhivamsa*, is an account of how saplings from the tree have been distributed to sacred places throughout Sri Lanka. The practice of planting saplings taken from the original tree is thus an ancient practice, symbolizing the dispensation of the Buddha's *dhamma*.

33. Stuart-Fox notes the political significance of the establishment of *vats* at the village level: "At the village level, the cultural focus is the village monastery, just as at the level of the *mandala* the center is the royal palace and the royal monastery, where the symbolic ceremonial is enacted that underpins the office of the rule as the keystone holding the whole political edifice together" (2002, 10).

34. Referring to the precolonial context in general Pholsena says, "Contacts between the ethnic Lao and these upland populations were primarily economic, and studies have demonstrated that there has always been a tradition of interdependence between the various ethnics groups, mostly through exchange" (2006, 21).

35. For a detailed study of Lan Na's Pali literary culture during the time of its own fifteenth and sixteenth century "golden age," see Veidlinger's *Spreading the Dhamma* (2007). We can assume that Veidlinger's observations on writing, orality, and textual transmission in contemporary Lan Na are, in general, an accurate reflection of similar dynamics in sixteenth century Lan Xang.

36. Lorrillard (2003, 190), in commenting on this stele, says that Lan Xang epigraphy seems to be directly related to La Na epigraphy and to the *tham* alphabet used for the writing of Pali as well.

37. Here I am intentionally invoking "Buddhist-mindedness" to associate Pho-thisarath's dispositions with what Clifford Geertz (1971, 60–62, 102–107, 114–117) has termed "religious-mindedness." By "religious-mindedness," Geertz meant to draw the distinction between individuals who "hold truths" rather than experience "being held" by them. "Religious-mindedness celebrates belief itself rather than what belief asserts. That is, the difference between "religious-mindedness" and "being religious" is that "religious-mindedness" is an intolerant scripted orthodoxy that imposes a divinely attributed design on to reality, while "religiousness," on the contrary, encounters the reality or quality of the sacred that is present within experience itself.

38. Martin Stuart-Fox notes that the "best example [of this] is Vat Si Meuang in Vientane, where the *lak meuang* is in the centre of the temple" (private communication).

39. See chapter 3 for a discussion of the *vinaya*'s significance.

40. Because the Siamese believed that it was bad luck to have both the Phra Bang and Phra Keo in the same city (Stuart-Fox, private communication).

41. Even before "revolutionary history" was written, one can observe the importance of Anu to the memory of the Lao in the grand glass murals on the parlor walls of the Luang Phrabang palace, where Anu's revolt is depicted in a splendid display dating to the early twentieth century.

42. For exceptionally perceptive analyses of contemporary Thai and Lao readings of the Anuvong rebellion, see Keyes (2002) and Grabowsky (1997).

43. "Men of prowess" is a phrase first coined by Wolters (1982, 1999) to further characterize his "big man" political theory in which "soul stuff" accounts for power. I much prefer Mus' explanation, for reasons made clear earlier.

44. Volker Grabowsky (1997, 148) points out that That Prince Damrong Rachanuphap, an inveterate Thai nationalist scholar of the early twentieth century, has argued that the Thai had completely trusted Anu before he launched his military move. This interpretation, no doubt, assists the interpretation that Anu's "rebellion" was traitorous.

45. Grabowsky reviews the various motives attributed to Anu's decision to invade the Khorat Plateau: to restore the status quo ante before 1778 or even 1709; "to liberate the numerous Lao war captives whom the later Rama I had deported from Vientiane in 1778 and resettled in Saraburi, Suphanburi and other provinces"; or as "a preventive war against a lingering Thai aggression," and so on (1997, 148–150).

46. According to Grabowsky, "By conservative estimates, in the first three decades following the conquest of Vientane, at least 100,000 Lao were forced to leave the eastern bank of the Mekong and resettle in territories on the western bank of the river or in the interior of the Khorat Plateau" (1997, 150).

47. Grabowsky suggests that the depopulating of the Lao from the upper Mekong may be one of the reasons why Ho invaders of the late nineteenth century were "able to shake the Lao states like Luang Phrabang and Siang Khwang so effectively. . . . In this light, the continuous immigration of the 'Lao Sung' [almost entirely Hmong from southern China] can be interpreted as an indirect result of the forced resettlements of Lao populations into Isan and Central Thailand" (1997, 151).

48. See my *Spirits of the Place: Buddhism in Lao Religion Culture* (2009, 76–185) for a historical overview of the relationship between religion and political power in Laos during the nineteenth century until the contemporary period.

49. Lior Bear, private communication, January 28, 2007.

50. "The World Travel and Tourism Council (WTTC) estimated that in 2003 the employment generated by the travel and tourism industry nationally in the Lao PDR was 145,000 jobs or 6 per cent of total employment. By 2013, it is estimated that tourism created 269,000 jobs or 9 per cent of total employment. . . . While official figures record the number of persons with salaried jobs in tourism agencies and related services, they do not, for example, take into account persons earning a living from handicraft production and restaurants or from construction jobs created by new tourist hotels or the expansion of airport or other forms of transportation. Staff employed in new business ventures, such as internet cafes and souvenir shops that have opened recently in response to increased numbers of visitors, are also missing from the figures" (UNESCO 2004, 61).

51. "While tourism is not the only causal factor, tourism and associated development have definitely intensified environmental problems. [Specifically], landowners have filled in ponds to extend or construct new buildings thereby jeopardizing fragile eco-systems. . . . [W]etlands and waterways are also being seriously damaged due to the dumping of raw sewage and other waste products, which in part can be traced to tourism. Guesthouses, restaurants and laundries generate substantial amounts of wastewater, which is not currently being adequately managed. . . . [T]here is no doubt that without adequate and en-

forceable regulations dealing with waste, the transportation system and wetland and waterway issues, the environmental conditions in Luang Prabang will be seriously threatened in the future. . . . Many residents of Luang Prabang link the increase in crime and drug abuse to the rise of tourism in the town and perceive that these will increase as tourism numbers grow" (UNESCO 2004, 66–70).

52. On the authenticity of the Phra Bang image now in Luang Phrabang, Evans writes,

> Around this time of year in Luang Prabang a story has circulated every year since the disappearance of King Sisavang Vatthana, and one can hear it further afield. The story speculates about whether the Prabang today is real or just a copy. Rumor has it that the communist government removed the real one and placed it in a vault somewhere. I have heard this story many times, and this time in Luang Prabang one person assured me she had heard it from an official in the Ministry of Information and Culture in Luang Prabang, and therefore it had to be correct. Perhaps even more astonishingly, during an interview with me in May 1996, the vice president of the Lao sangha said, yes the Prabang in Luang Prabang is a fake. He claimed that in 1976 Sali Vongkhamsao, then attached to Prime Minister Kaysone's office, went to Luang Prabang with an entourage and brought the Prabang back to Vientiane, the seat of government. This story was obviously formed around the assumptions of traditional cosmology which assumed that now that the communists had taken over they were the heirs of its powers. Of course, I have no way of confirming the rumors one way or another. But what is important about this story from an anthropological point of view is that it suggests that people somehow feel that the ritual since 1975 has become debased and is even "fake," too. The fact that the person telling you the story of the Prabang being a fake will go and pay homage to the Prabang during the New Year ritual confirms this interpretation, showing that the rumor reflects on the ritual as a whole rather than the object itself. It is also a comment on the collapse of the monarchy, on the pressure that Buddhism came under in the early years of revolution, and perhaps even a comment on the illegitimacy of the Lao government. For possession of the Prabang historically has been an objectification of the legitimacy of the Lao monarchy. The idea of it being a fake therefore withdraws this legitimacy from the communist regime." (1998, 139–140)

In fact, the genuine Phra Bang image was brought from Vientiane and finally installed in a newly constructed image house in 2013.

53. Evans provides a detailed account of the Phra Bang's lustration from his observations in the mid- to late 1990s:

> The parade of the Prabang from the old palace to Vat May remains one of the central religious activities of the New Year in Luang Prabang. This holy relic, the palladium of the former kingdom, after appropriate rituals by leading members of the sangha, is carried down the steps by museum attendants . . . , and placed in its palanquin, at which point scores of tourists with their cameras converge on the statue to photograph it, while older Luang Prabangese in traditional dress watch the spectacle non-plussed. Just before the descent of the Prabang, the foreign minister, Lengsavad and the *chao khouang* of Luang Prabang line up on the steps of the palace, also dressed in traditional *sampots*. Previously it would have been the king who followed the Prabang to Vat May, and begun its purification. Now a high official in the LPDR fills his shoes. . . . Over the next few days almost every family in Luang Prabang has at least one

person go to pour water over the Prabang, despite the fact that the official New Year celebrations are over, and on the final night there is a veritably orgy of merit-making. But at the side of the temple as traditional orchestra strains to be heard over taped music, and attempts at traditional singing founder, to the disappointment of one older Luang Prabang man who lamented that older styles of singing rounds between men and women were being lost. The Prabang is then returned to the old palace on 18 April. Just inside the grounds, a new resting place for the Prabang, begun under the old regime, is being built with its main sponsor being the Lao government and business. (1998, 138–139)

54. The valorization of women in Southeast Asian Theravada Buddhism has received some recent attention in the works of Leedom Lefferts (1999) and others. In the conclusion to his "Women's Power and Theravada Buddhism," Lefferts has written: "Women also (re)produce the means by which all Lao and Thai Buddhist laypeople—men as well as women—obtain salvation." That is, the very commonly held view in the West that women play only a highly subordinated and largely excluded role in the religious cultures of Southeast Asia is now being contested. As I observed throughout my fieldwork, the entire ritual system obtaining between the laity and the monks is completely dependent upon women.

Chapter 2: Asala Perahara

1. To Ptolemy and the Mediterranean world, it was the gem-bearing island known as Taprobane. In Mahayana Buddhist Sanskrit literature, such as the *Avalokitesvara-Guna-Karandavyuha Sutra,* it was known as Simhaladvipa (the island of the Sinhalas). For the Theravada Buddhist monks of the Mahavihara monastery in the Lankan royal capital of Anuradhapura who wrote and read the *Dipavamsa* and *Mahavamsa,* chronicles dating to the fourth and fifth centuries CE, it was Dhammadipa (the island of the Buddhist teaching). To Tamils throughout history, it has been known as Eelam. For the Sinhala people, it has always been Lanka. For the Arabs, the island was Serendib, from which in English we derive the term "serendipity." For the Portuguese, it was Ceilao. It was also known to the British colonial world as Ceylon, which remained its official name until the Sinhala-dominated government formally changed it to Sri Lanka in 1972.

2. See Gunawardana (1979) for a thorough analysis of how the monastery dominated virtually all forms of social, cultural, and economic life in medieval Sri Lanka.

3. See my own study of the cult of Avalokitesvara and its transformations in Sri Lanka from the eighth century to the present in my *Buddha in the Crown* (1991).

4. In fact, the *bhikkhunisangha* was reestablished in Sri Lanka in the 1990s. For further inquiry, see Bartholomeusz (1994), Semmens (2011), Salgado (2013), and Crosby (2014).

5. For an overview of classical Sinhala literature written during this period, see Hallisey (2003, 689–746).

6. Following the increase in Sinhala Buddhist nationalism in the 1950s, many of the Dutch Burghers emigrated, many to Australia and some to Canada.

7. For a reprise of the public career and impact of Ven. Gagodawila Soma, see my *The Buddhist Visnu* (2004, 331–350) and Berkwitz (2008).

8. See my *The Religious World of Kirti Sri* (1996) for a study of how this king appealed to various discourses of Buddhist kingship, reestablished the Buddhist monastic *sangha,* and sponsored an effervescent revival of artistic expression in the forms of temple wall paintings of the monasteries that he rehabilitated.

9. Walshe's precise translation of this important passage is as follows: "Now, monks, I declare to you: all conditioned things are of a nature to decay—strive on untiringly."

10. This reading would seem to be consonant with the ramifications of how biographies of the Buddha depict the birth of the Buddha with his auspicious marks indicating that he would become either a great *cakravartin* (wheel-turning king) or a buddha. It is also commensurate with the discussions presented by Frank Reynolds in his seminal essay, "The Two Wheels of Dhamma" (1972), and S. J. Tambiah's monumental study, *World Conqueror, World Renouncer* (1976).

11. Underlining this point, Seneviratne points out that "[w]hen in the rebellion of 1818 the British captured the Dalada, the people gave up resistance, acceding that since they have the Dalada, they are indeed the masters of the country. . . . In the more spectacular of the Dalada rituals [e.g., the *asala perahara*], the British governor was referred to sometimes as the 'king' and his wife as the 'queen,' and his residence as the 'the king's house' (*raja-gedera*)" (1978, 19).

12. For this and Fa Hien's entire description of ritual activities he observed in Anuradhapura, see my *The Sri Lanka Reader* (2011, 44–49).

13. This image conjured up by the *Dalada Sirita* prescriptions is not at all unlike the manner, and certainly the function, of how consecrated images from Hindu temples are taken out of the sanctum sanctorum each year and circulated ceremoniously through the streets of the city, usually on a massive and magnificent cart, for all to see.

14. For a more detailed account of this century of political imbroglio, see my *Buddha in the Crown* (1991, 118–122); an especially revealing personal profile of Vimaladharmasurya I was written by the Dutch emissary, Sebald de Weert, in 1602. For his account, see my *The Sri Lanka Reader* (2011, 191–200); the *Culavamsa*'s account of Vimaladharmasurya I is also found in the same source (2011, 297–298).

15. The *Culavamsa* (96; 2, 234–238) reports that Senarat had divided up the inheritance of the kingdom through a practice of divination—he placed three leaves in front of the Dalada, which had temporarily been moved to nearby Dumbura to the northeast of Kandy owing to Portuguese attacks on Kandy—and that the regions around Kandy fell to his own biological son who became Rajasimha II. The two others, Dona Catherina's sons by Vimaladharmasurya, drew outlying regions. After initial harmony, the three brothers quarreled, and eventually Rajasimha established himself as the sole king of all regions not under control by the Portuguese.

16. It is quite possible that Knox's account, a best seller in its day, provided the inspiration for Daniel Dafoe's classic, *Robinson Crusoe*.

17. For a detailed analysis of the cult of Dadimunda (aka Devata Bandara) in Sri Lanka, see my *The Buddhist Visnu* (2004, 247–330).

18. According to local lore recorded on a public sign posted in the middle of the Alutnuvara Devalaya complex today, the shift to Kandy was made by King Senarat (1604–1635 CE), but erroneously gives the date as 1714. Bhikkhu Thalgaspitiye Thero, incumbent of the Kirti Sri Rajamahaviharaya opposite the Alutnuvara *devalaya*, told me that Senarat made the move in 1643, again a problematic date. The dating of the move from Aluthnuvara to Kandy is a difficult problem to resolve with any certainty. Duncan says, "In 1748 Kirti Sri had the image of the god Visnu brought from Alutnuvara to Kandy. A temple for Visnu was built to the northwest of the palace where a temple for the local godling, Devata Bandara, had been. The image of Devata Bandara was removed to Alutnuvara and a small *devale* for a smaller image of Devata Bandara was built next to the new one for Visnu in Kandy. Devata Bandara, who was also known as Dedimunda, remained in Kandy as Visnu's chief *adikar* and commander in chief" (72). H. L. Seneviratne says this: "According to the Sinhalese work of the Kandyan period, the *Lanka Puvata*, it was in the early seventeenth century that he [Visnu] was brought to Kandy, and Robert Knox (1681) refers to him as 'the god of Alutnuvara,' an allusion to the town where to this day the most famous shrine dedicated to him is located and from where he was ceremonially brought to Kandy" (1978, 12). Neither Duncan's

nor Seneviratne's statements are exactly correct. With regard to Duncan's statement, the *devalaya sannasa* clearly indicates the presence of the Visnu *devalaya* in Kandy in 1709. With regard to the uncharacteristic mistakes in Seneviratne's statement, the *Lanka Puvata* actually refers to the insignia of the four warrant gods being brought to Kandy during the reign of Vimaladharmasurya II (1687–1707 CE), which makes the dating of that text at least late seventeenth century or early eighteenth century. And further, Alutnuvara is not known "to this day" as the location of the most famous shrine to Visnu. Rather, it is known as the cultic seat of Dadimunda instead, who is also now known as "Alutnuvara Deviyo." There is a rather newly constructed Visnu *devalaya* now located within the Kirti Sri Rajamahavi-haraya located nearby the present Alutnuvara Devalaya, but it was built in 1985, seven years after the publication of Seneviratne's study, and therefore its presence cannot account for Seneviratne's confusion.

19. Another less well known but significant example is Ridigama Deviyo.

20. In his own note to this passage, Geiger (*Culavamsa* 1953, vol. 2: 261n1) says that the reference is undoubtedly to the Dalada.

21. Natha, originally the Mahayana Bodhisattva Avalokitesvara, whose main shrine is located directly across from the Dalada Maligava and is regarded as the oldest building structure in the city of Kandy (dating to the fourteenth century), was regarded as the tutelary deity of the Kandyan kings, the next Buddha-to-be (Sinhala, Maitri; Sanskrit, Maitreya; and Pali, Metteyya) from whom Kandyan kings received their formal names upon consecration.

22. Lily de Silva (1981, 57–78) has written an extensive essay on the significance of the Indra *khila* within the context of the *paritta* (*pirit*) ceremony and in Pali literature in general.

23. See my *Buddha in the Crown* (1991, 179–183) for a more detailed discussion and a list of the sacred places and correspondent shares of rice, medicine, and oil that are received by each.

24. In the seventeenth and eighteenth centuries, the Dutch coveted the king's monopoly on the sale of elephants to various regions of India.

25. I have written extensively about the *perahara* in Devinuvara while researching *The Buddhist Visnu* (2004, 351–370) and in researching *Buddha in the Crown* (1991, 176–201).

26. Michael Ondaatje, *Anil's Ghost* (New York: Vintage, 2001); see also Jean Arasanayagam's gripping short story, "Search My Mind," in my *The Sri Lanka Reader* (2011, 656–663).

27. Hexagonal or octagonal panels of framed, almost cartooned, pictures encircled by variegated flashing electric bulbs forming a rather spectacular marketplace display.

28. Seneviratne notes (1978, 148) that these seats sold for Rs.25 in 1969 (~US$3).

29. This arrangement began during the 1990s. Security was further enhanced after the 1997 truck bomb attack by the LTTE weeks before Sri Lanka was to celebrate its fifty years of independence, in Kandy, to be attended by the United Kingdom's Prince Charles. As a result of the bombing, the venue for the chief public celebrations was shifted to Colombo. Subsequently, a tall iron fence was constructed on the south side of Dalada Vidiya along with the installation of iron gates defended by a robust contingent of well-armed soldiers from the Sri Lanka Army.

30. For a further description of this behavior, see my *The Buddhist Visnu* (2004, 362–365).

31. Invented by the American theosophist Henry Steel Olcott in the late nineteenth century, the flag consists of five colors symbolizing the moral virtues of the *pancasila:* to abstain from killing, lying, stealing, improper sex, and intoxicants.

32. See also Seneviratne's (1978, 108–110) detailed listing of the various sections constituting the *perahara* procession as he observed them in the late 1960s.

33. This interview was conducted in Sinhala on August 10, 2012. Because of the sensitivity of some of the information, I have left the identity of the dancer anonymous.

34. Reed provides a photo of one of these sketches. See Susan Reed, *Dance and the Nation* (2010, 102).

35. The equating of "Sinhala" with "national" was pervasive in the field of dance. Sinhala dances were referred to as "national dances." "National" dance troupes, such as the Ceylon National Dancers, were made up only of Sinhalas performing Sinhala dances. An unself-conscious use of the word "national" or Ceylonese to denote "Sinhala" is found in many of the books and articles on dance that were written in the 1950s and 1960s, and the equation of "Ceylon" with "Sinhala" was reproduced in a variety of media, including dance performances, programs, posters, and speeches. See Reed (2010, 128–150) for her thorough discussion in a chapter titled "Dance, Ethnicity and the State."

36. Here she is following the hermeneutical suggestion offered by Daniel (1996, 62–66).

37. The *goyigama* is the "rice cultivation" caste, the highest caste in the Sinhala social hierarchy, to which approximately 60 percent of the Sinhalese belong. *Radala* refers to the small subcaste of Kandyan *goyigama* who dominated the court and higher echelons of the traditional political economy.

38. For an especially insightful analysis of these issues leading up to the appearance of Dharmapala, see Kitsiri Malalgoda, *Buddhism in Sinhalese Society, 1750–1900* (1976); for a comprehensive study on how Dharmapala has been understood, see Steven Kemper, *Rescued from the Nation* (2015); an extract of Dharmapala's antagonistic perspective on Christianity and his nationalistic understanding of Buddhism can be found in my *The Sri Lanka Reader* (2011, 350–355).

39. *Kemmura* days refers to Wednesdays and Saturdays, the days when, because they are generally inauspicious, devotees will most likely find a need to make requests to the deities for assistance. Attendance is up because of perceptions in the village that various types of problems are increasing. Again, the problems associated with the civil war made many people anxious, particularly because the armed services were overwhelmingly drawn from youth from the village. In response to so many deaths, "funeral societies" emerged in many rural villages, a pattern that anticipates the topic in the chapter 5, "Caring for the Dead Ritually in Cambodia."

40. See my *Buddha in the Crown* (1991, 151–175) for accounts of these myths.

41. See my essay, "The Persistence of Political Buddhism" in Bartholomeusz and de Silva (1998, 186–196).

Chapter 3: Upasampada *and* Pabbajja

1. van Gennep (1972, 3); italics mine.

2. In Thailand, as I shall explain in some depth, the monastic ordinations of sons are especially important to their mothers, as the merit derived from these occasions is thought to redound primarily to them.

3. In doing so, I am returning to a consideration of the *Mahavagga* portion of the *Vinayapitaka* some forty years after analyzing this text while preparing my doctoral dissertation, a work that was subsequently rewritten into a book and published as *Discipline: The Canonical Buddhism of the Vinayapitaka* (Delhi: Motilal Banarsidass, 1981). Pages 106–124 contain an earlier analysis of *upasampada* as contained in the Pali account of the *Vinaya*.

4. According to the second chapter of the *Mahavagga* (II: 1–5; *Book of Discipline* 4: 130–137), King Bimbisara requested that members of the early *sangha* preach their *dharma* on *uposatha* days, a custom shared by other *sramana* (non-*Brahmanical* or heterodox) religious communities. The Buddha obliged on the ensuing *uposatha* day, but on following days, when his *bhikkhus* were silent and then criticized by laity for being "like the dumb, or like hogs," the Buddha declared that henceforth the *patimokkha* would be recited by the entire community

on *uposatha* days. This is a clear equation between a public profession of *dhamma* and the substance of the disciplinary rules, or that the *patimokkha* rules, at least in this instance, were regarded as both expressive of *dhamma* and leading to its realization.

5. For a discussion of the various historical issues considered in relation to the timing and substance of the Second Great Buddhist Council, see Erich Frauwallner, *The Earliest Vinaya and the Beginnings of Buddhist Literature* (Rome: Instituto Italiano per il Medio ed Estremo Oriente, 1956), and Charles Prebish, "A Review of the Scholarship on the Buddhist Councils," *Journal of Asian Studies* 33 (1974): 239–254.

6. Mara, as embodiment of death, is the cosmic enemy of the Buddha who tries to prevent the Buddha from gaining enlightenment.

7. I am not sure what to make of the fact that volition (*cetana*), usually identified as the fourth aggregate (*sankhara*), is not addressed in this sermon as impermanent, as with the other four.

8. Wells' book was first published in 1940, then updated in 1960 before being reprinted in 1977 and 1982.

9. For a translation of a *sukhwan* liturgy, see my *Spirits of the Place* (2009, 271–274).

10. In Thailand, the *sangha* is not only administered by a government department, but it is also organized in a mirror image of the hierarchical administration of the state.

11. In Bunnag's discussion of ordination, written about twenty years after Wells', she indicates that literacy was a requirement for *pabbajja*, but that it was not stringently enforced, such that even the inability to recite Pali formulae did not appear to be a serious obstacle. She notes that it used to be that several weeks of preparation in the monastery was the norm, but that this was not happening very often in most contexts. Formal training in the recitation of relevant Pali texts that constitute the liturgies for *pabbajja* and *upasampada* is found more likely in urban contexts (Bunnag 1973, 40).

12. For a profile of *samaneras* in Luang Phrabang based on one hundred interviews conducted in 2006–2007, see my *Spirits of the Place* (2009, 193–210).

13. For a discussion of Phra Keo or the Holy Emerald Buddha, see Reynolds (1978).

14. Was he at least twenty years old? Was he indeed a man? Did he have his parents' permission? Was he a criminal? Free of debt? Free of disease? and so on. The full list of "disqualifications" is found in the *Vinaya*. See my *Discipline* (1981, 116–122) for a discussion of these "disqualifications." For a photo of the "disqualifications" being formally asked of a monk during an *upasampada* rite at Wat Phra Dhammkaya in Bangkok.

15. In Luang Phrabang in 2007, I was told by a Thai monk leading a group of lay Bangkok Buddhists to attend Bun Phravet that some Thai laity undertake pilgrimages to Laos and remote regions of Thailand to gain merit from monks that they believe are more virtuous objects of veneration, or monks who are innocent of the widely publicized types of corruptions reported in the Thai media about some urban monks.

16. See my *Spirits of the Place* (2009), especially 15–28 and 232–255, for discussions about how understandings derived from the indigenous spirit cults inflect the perspectives intrinsic to what is often dubbed "popular Buddhist religious culture."

17. By "temple sleeper," Eberhardt is referring to elderly *upasaka*s and *upasika*s who spend a good deal of their "retirement" at the temple attending whatever rituals that transpire in an effort to increase the bounty of their merit.

18. At Wat Phra Dhammakaya in suburban Bangkok, I observed *pabbajja* candidates as young as five years old.

19. This claim is only true if Thailand's monarchy is not understood as an essentially "Buddhist institution," a label that I would argue is not inappropriate, since traditionally Thai kings, the present not excepted, have postured as the lead patrons and exemplary lay practitioners of the Buddhasasana; the royal Thai family is exceedingly wealthy, among the very richest families in the world, with assets of over $64 billion as of 2015.

20. For an effective overview of critiques of this nature, see Scott (2009, 129–156). There are numerous other reasons why Wat Phra Dhammakaya has become so controversial. In addition to its very positive valorization of the acquisition of wealth (based on its argument that it is not wealth per se that is problematic, but what one does with it; e.g., to use it for the spread of the *dhamma* is virtuous), the lead abbot (Phra Dhammachayo) has been accused of promoting himself esoterically as a bodhisattva or even "creator deity" (according to Laohavanich 2012), and he has been repeatedly accused in a widely publicized embezzlement scandal that began in 1998 and continued into 2015, when he was finally acquitted. Moreover, Dhammakaya's doctrinal position that *"nibbana* is an essential self" has drawn fire from a number of Thai Buddhism's leading monastic apologists and academic observers.

21. This very accomplished and articulate Wat Dhammakaya monk was ordained as a novice at age twelve, spent eight years as a *samanera* before taking *upasampada* at the minimum age of twenty, and has attained the highest level of distinction in the study of Pali on Thailand's national exams. He also holds a bachelor's degree in political science.

22. For a detailed history of the successive leaders of Wat Phra Dhammakaya beginning with Luang Pho, see Scott (2009, 66–78).

23. Scott (2009, 78–86) provides details of the Dhammakaya theory and practice of meditation.

24. For a series of essays comparatively focused on the problem of modernization in contemporary Theravada societies, see Juliana Schober and Steven Collins (forthcoming).

25. See especially cogent analyses of the *dasa sil mata* movement in Sri Lanka in Bartholomeusz (1994) and Salgado (2013).

26. This is the same assertion made by conservative monks in Sri Lanka to the prospect of *bhikkhuni* ordinations.

27. For a detailed study of the process with regard to Buddha images, see Swearer (2004).

28. For an analysis of spirit "ontology" following Paul Mus, see my *Spirits of the Place* (2009, 15–28).

29. http://www.bangkokpost.com/learning/learning-from-news/420819/lung -kamnan-to-phra-suthep.

Chapter 4: Kathina

1. Mahayana sculptures have been recovered at Sri Ksetra, a first- through fifth-century CE Pyu archaeological site that is located midway between Pagan and Yangon in central Myanmar (Moore et al. 1999, 114).

2. 69 percent of the population is Bamar (Burman), of which almost all are Buddhists. Shan, Mon, Arakanese, and Karen peoples are also preponderantly Buddhist. A former director of religious affairs for the government told me in 2010 that there are about 400,000 Buddhist monks in the country. About 175,000 of these have taken the full *upasampada* monastic ordination. But David Steinberg, without citing sources, reports that as of 2008, there were only 56,840 fully ordained monks; 246,000 novices; and 43,000 *thila shins* (or precept-observing and robe-wearing lay women "nuns") (2010, xxv). Despite the fact that some 85 percent of Myanmar's population is Buddhist, there are still some three thousand mosques and four thousand churches in the country, according to the Department of Religious Affairs. In addition to Yangon, especially its downtown area, some cities are quite multireligious in orientation. Mawlamyine (aka Moulmein), for instance, boasts many mosques and churches, as the British used this coastal city in what is now the Mon state from 1825 until 1852 as their colonial "capital" before shifting to Sittwe. Mawlamyine also became the chief seat of the aggressive and successful American Baptist mission to Burma: two large churches and a very substantial high school were founded there by Adoniram

Judson, the American Baptist missionary who later became famous for his Burmese/ English dictionary.

3. As noted in the introduction, the *Visuddhimagga*, or the "Path of Purification," is the Pali title of the celebrated fifth-century CE commentary on the religious path written by the orthodox-minded Buddhaghosa in the Mahavihara monastic complex in Anuradhapura, Sri Lanka. Heim (2014) is an excellent analytical study of this venerable text.

4. This formula is also embedded in much of *Vinaya* literature, especially the stories that lead up to the proclamation of a disciplinary rule wherein in it is possible to identify one of the *asava*s as responsible for the errant behavior admonished by the Buddha. See my *Discipline* (1981).

5. A variety of terms are used to designate Buddhist temples in English and in the vernacular languages of Southeast Asia. For instance, in Sri Lanka, the preferred English term is "temple," while Pali *vihara* and Sinhala *pansala* are also normally heard. In Thailand, Laos, and Cambodia, the Pali term *vat* (from *vatthu*) is universally used and the preferred English term is also "temple." But in Myanmar, the preferred term is *pagoda*, a term with its own odd history as an English misreading or poorly rendered attempt at *dagaba*, itself a compressed version of the Sanskrit *dhatu + garbha* (essence + presence or womb) that designates a reliquary or stupa, sometimes containing a relic of the Buddha.

6. See Sukumar Dutt (2008, 35–97; originally published in 1962) for what is still the most cogent account of the origins of ritual life in the *sangha*.

7. Here we encounter the curious relationship that obtains between the *Patimokkha Sutta* and the *Vinayapitaka*. While it is certain that the *Vinaya* is an elaboration of the *Patimokkha*, the *Vinaya* contains within it a story about how the *Patimokkha* was originally recited! The texts seem to engage in a relationship of mutual legitimation.

8. I am quite consciously deploying this hermeneutical construct advanced by Steven Collins, who writes "the 'Pali imaginaire' is a mental universe created by and within Pali texts, which remained remarkably stable in content and throughout the traditional period, but which moved, as a developing whole, through various times and places within the premodern material-historical world" (1997, 41).

9. Those excluded are either morally culpable or derelict in some fashion. See *Book of Discipline* (4: 137–181), and Holt, *Discipline* (1981, 126–127). In addition, there are carefully delineated means for determining and maintaining *sima*s or local monastic boundaries that designate purified ritual spaces. Thus, when the local *sangha* declares its collective purity, it is also declaring that the space within which they dwell is also ritually and morally purified.

10. Some scholars, such as Prebish (1975, 4), have argued that concerns for *ahimsa*, for inadvertently injuring any form of life, were a matter of primary concern that led to a suspension in the monastic eremitic lifestyle.

11. Found in Horner, *Book of Discipline* (4: 353); the entire section about robe allowances, generally regarded by I. B. Horner, the editor and translator, as legalistic literary material later added to the core *patimokkha* corpus of the *Vinaya*, continues to 4: 357.

12. "Rag-wearing" signifies that these are *dhutanga* or *thudong* monks, "forest monks" of an ascetic orientation.

13. For a brief discussion, see Schober (2011, 26).

14. Exactly how the robe is worn may also signify sectarian loyalty.

15. Horner provides a rather arcane, yet interesting, explanation for *siveyakka*. It can mean either a cloth that is used to cover dead bodies in cemeteries, in which case it could symbolize the Buddha's presence as being "dead to the world," or it could signify a renunciant of the world. Or, it could refer to the fine cloth woven in the Sivi kingdom (Horner, *Book of Discipline* 4: 393n4).

16. *Ancient Myanmar Inscriptions* (in Burmese) (1: 99). Translated privately for me by Than Zaw; brackets inserted into text by Than Zaw. This is a line-by-line translation. The inscription is important in establishing that monks, as well as laity, were involved in making gifts and engendering merit during *kathina* ritual occasions

17. Ibid., 71–73.

18. Ibid., 2: 246–247.

19. My assistant/guide was a young faculty member, a newly minted PhD from a nearby Buddhist university. Graciously welcomed by a very courteous, good-natured, and knowledgeable chief monk, congenially given the run of the extensive grounds of the temple for the day's duration, and cordially informed about the various proceedings as they unwound during the day, I was afforded an intimate view of contemporary monastic-lay relations in this impressive urban monastic setting. I was embarrassed by the generosity of my hosts and made to feel far more important than I deserved.

20. A lakh is 100,000. In a conversation over lunch I learned that the chief donor owned an extremely lucrative auto parts business. Given that there were virtually no new vehicles in Myanmar at that time, it was an essential and thereby thriving trade.

21. The flowerpot has been a symbol of fertility and prosperity in use since before the beginnings of Buddhist art in ancient India. See Sree Padma (2013, 84–97).

22. Alicia Turner's *Saving Buddhism* (2014) is an excellent recent study of the rise and significance of lay associations during the period between 1890 and 1920.

23. Nash indicates how this was true in his village in the early 1960s. He provides an elaborate description of how about thirty young girls from thirteen to twenty years of age worked on spinning wheels throughout the night to finish at least five yards of cloth before daylight and that their purity and innocence is thought to add to the merit produced (1965, 135).

24. In Sri Lanka, the phrase "man in robes" is sometimes juxtaposed *hamaduruwo* (the Sinhala term used when addressing a monk) to indicate that the individual is a spiritual imposter.

25. Perhaps "beyond sexuality" is a better way of putting the issue.

26. Nash (1965), Spiro (1970), Tambiah (1970), Gombrich (1971b), Southwold (1983). Mendelson (1975), Terweil (1975), Condominas (1968), Ebihara (1968), Zago (1972), among others.

27. Made from pounding the soft bark of the Thanaka tree. It has a color and consistency similar to sandalwood.

28. Indeed, the changes I observed between 2014 and 2016 were palpable in Yangon. Thousands of reconditioned Japanese vehicles were now clogging the traffic of Yangon, stores filled with new electronics goods, refrigerators, generators, and the like were ubiquitous, along with the construction of new hotels and high-rise apartment buildings. Tourists now flocked in large numbers to the Shwedagon Pagoda. Prices had soared.

29. *Anguttara Nikaya* 3: 295. Cetanaham bhikkhave kammam vadami; cetayitva kammam karoti kayena vacaya manasa; for a discussion, see my *Discipline* (1981, 75–76), and Heim (2004, 42–43).

30. Jordt puts it this way: "For the Burmese Buddhist laity, the 'free will act of giving' . . . is considered the foundational practice on which other practices, in pursuit of the final soteriological goal of nibbana, can develop. Through repetitive acts of giving, the donor is understood to be cultivating a mental disposition toward the world characterized by a lessening of attachment to material wants. In the native cosmology, donations motivated by the desire to receive material sustenance and abundance are considered inferior to those acts motivated by the aspiration to cultivate a proper disposition toward material circumstances. One should cultivate a disposition in which loss of material wealth and pleasant

circumstances can be accepted without attachment and therefore without sorrow and suffering" (2007, 100).

31. For an excellent comparative and theoretical study of "the gift" in Buddhist, Hindu, and Jain literary contexts, see Maria Heim (2004).

32. A similar dilemma was faced by Sinhala Buddhists in the late 1980s and 1990s when they were faced with almost nightly television news broadcasts portraying President Ranasinghe Premadasa performing merit-making donations in support of the *sasana* at Buddhist temples throughout the country while his government was systematically engaged in a ruthless suppression of a rural Sinhala rebellion on the one hand and a violent confrontation as the result of an ethnic conflict with the Liberation Tigers of Tamil Eelam (LTTE) on the other.

33. The Burmese are aware of the quest for legitimacy that underlies the government's actions. But they are no less impressed by the regime's projects, which are for them an indication of veritable power. The renovation of the country's great pagodas in particular has made an impact on the population and conferred on "the generals" an aura of power. This renovation and construction program for pagodas is not only a way of marking territory and ensuring one's symbolical control of it; in the Burmese's opinion, it is part and parcel of a necessary process of Buddhicizing the environment favoring spiritual practice (Rozenberg 2009, 25).

34. Jordt makes the very interesting point that other coercive actions by the military government have inadvertently prompted large-scale merit-making donations to the *sangha*. "The regime's attempts to nationalize properties and relocate large segments of the urban populace were met with massive land donations. Some donors explicitly explained to me that they felt it was better to make merit by donating the land to the religion rather than having them confiscated by the military government. According to statistics provided by the Ministry of the Interior, religious landholdings grew from 43% to 57% of the total inhabitable land between 1989 and 1994. . . . Taking title to the land, the monks nevertheless permitted donors to continue living on and enjoying sustenance from the donated land" (2007, 130). Moreover, "these donations are classified as sacred property and hence are exempt from taxation. In aggregate, these tax shelter-like arrangements also underpin a territorial competition between the regime and the sangha" (129).

35. The affinity that the generals seek to establish between themselves and the great Buddhist kings of the past who patronized the *sangha* and *sasana* is seen vividly in the manner that both General Ne Win in the 1990s and Than Shwe in the 2000s have built massive and expensive stupas. Ne Win's stupa was built adjacent to the Shwedagon in Yangon and Than Shwe's in the new capital city of Naypidaw (the name of the new capital meaning literally "the abode of the king").

36. I completely agree with Seekins on this point. I have argued explicitly that in Sinhala Buddhist religious culture, these terms should not be interpreted as "this-worldly" and "other-worldly," which is how they have been often construed by some Westerners and Buddhists alike. Instead, *lokuttara* (in Sinhala *lokottara*) has the meaning of "pre-eminent in the world" and, as such, *lokiya* and *lokuttara* should be understood as two terms marking the ends of a continuum, understood more in temporal rather than in spatial terms, with *lokiya* referring to what is more immediate and *lokuttara* as what is more ultimate. See my *Buddha in the Crown* (1991, 19–26).

37. For classic studies of the *sangha* and state relations in Theravada-inclined societies, see Sarkisyanz (1965) Tambiah (1976), Mendelson (1975), Smith (1978), Chandler (2008), and Holt (2009).

38. See E. Sarkisyanz (1965, 120–166) for an extended discussion of these monastic politicos who challenged British colonial authority by appealing to Buddhist cosmological conceptions of time and space.

39. In the case of medieval Sri Lanka, see Gunawardana (1979); for Burma, see Aung-Twin (1979); for Thailand, see Tambiah (1976), for Laos, see Holt (2009); for Cambodia, see Harris (2005).

40. While economic and political frustrations with the government were building between 1962 and 1988, especially in 1974, when the funeral and burial of U Thant, the revered former secretary-general of the United Nations and confidant of U Nu, was manipulated in an insulting fashion by a jealous Ne Win and his military cronies. But the spark that set off the 1988 riots that led to Ne Win's resignation was the manner in which a university student, and then other students, had been killed by riot police at Rangoon University. Steinberg suggests, with some credibility, that the government actually fomented some of the riots that ensued throughout the country as a pretext for rationalizing a new military crackdown that then occurred subsequently (Steinberg 2010, 77–80).

41. Steinberg describes the progressively reactionary steps taken in the last thirty years by the government to control the *sangha*.

> In 1980, the state finally placed controls on the *sangha*. In 1979, the military formed the Sangha Maha Nayaka—the centralized Supreme Council of 33 monks—and a group of 1,219 monk representatives of the *sangha* as a whole, as well as local councils at all levels. The hierarchy of the monkhood was established, and all monks were registered with the state by 1980. The educational activities of the *sangha* were controlled and monitored. The state also placed the monastic educational system, which went through the university level, under scrutiny. Military officers were placed within the hierarchy but control at the local level was not completely absolute. Chief monks at individual temples, including large temples, continued to exercise their authority. It was not until after 1988 that an even more thorough attempt was made to put the *sangha* even more tightly under the control of the military command. The "Saffron Revolution," however, demonstrated the volatility of the *sangha* even within a Buddhist hierarchy tightly under government command. (2010, 72)

42. This is the name that the military government gave to itself as it reemerged from General Ne Win's shadow in 1988 following Ne Win's resignation. In the late 1990s it would rename itself again as the State Peace and Development Council.

43. Jordt also reports how, in the aftermath of the 1990 elections, when the military refused to hand power over to the National League for Democracy, many monks turned their bowls down to the military. Four were found shot dead, others were arrested and stripped of their robes before being sentenced to imprisonment. This actually emboldened more monks to change their morning *pindapata* routes to avoid the military, moves that, in turn, angered the wives of key military personnel who reportedly then refused to cook for their husbands! (2007, 134)

44. Charney discusses what has become a serious problem in many South and Southeast Asia countries when he notes that "most of the post-independence regimes sacrificed the wellbeing of the country for the economic benefit of the ruling minority. One of the main underlying reasons for this is the association of wealth with political power, perhaps inherited from pre-colonial times, but certainly strengthened by the colonial period, in that there is an expectation that political power should bring with it personal wealth. Complaints during the colonial period that Burmese politicians were enriching themselves through their offices at the expense of the general population appear no less relevant when one views the control over the economy exerted by the families of prominent SPDC officers today" (2009, 203). Schober concurs: "The military and its supporters [are] seen as internal colonizers who extracted the country's resources at the cost of economic development" (2011, 119).

45. "Communitas" has enjoyed a long life of reference since it was initially deployed to characterize the "social mysticism" of collective ritual pilgrimage experiences wherein a new social community is born of common experience that transcends the normal world of social routine. See Turner's classic article "The Center Out There: Pilgrim's Goal," *History of Religions* 12 (1973): 191–230.

46. Schober's general description of the main events of 2007 are as vivid as Charney's:

> For several weeks, the regime had permitted the protest to gain momentum throughout the nation without intervening, but it began a brutal reprisal on September 26 and 27, 2007. *The New Light of Myanmar*, a government-run English language newspaper, predicted that "national traitors will soon meet their tragic ends," as fear, terror, and doom replaced the earlier hopes attached to the events of September 2007. Police and military troops armed with automatic weapons and tear gas had been put into place to squash the protests. A curfew was imposed in major cities. In Yangon, police trucks equipped with loudspeakers announced that "We have your pictures and we will come to arrest you!" . . . According to reports by the Human Rights Council of the United Nations and Human Rights Watch, the estimated number of deaths in the aftermath of the protests ranged from 31 to 200. . . . As many as 6,000 people may have been arrested initially, although the regime claims that the number was closer to 3,000 and that many were eventually released. Prominent participants in the protests were eventually arrested and received life long prison terms. The armed reprisals against unarmed protesters ended public opposition to the regime, although isolated acts of resistance, such as the self-immolation of a monk at the Shwedagon Pagoda in March, 2008. (2011, 127–129).

Steinberg adds an additional observation to what happened during the demonstrations: "The monks demonstrated in 2007, marching peacefully through the streets of Rangoon. . . . When these religious . . . but quiescent political marches were infiltrated by political opponents of the regime and political slogans against the junta were seen and heard, the military violently cracked down on both the monks and the general population involved. At least thirty-one people were killed and many injured. . . . [I]f one were to point to a single act that undermined the prestige of the *tatmadaw's* leaders, it was the violent suppression of the Saffron Revolution" (2010, 136–137).

47. See Jason Carbine's (2011, 144–152) analysis of the importance of *Abhidhamma*, for instance, among the Shwegyin order of monks.

48. Sarkisyanz (1965). The logic is very similar to Buddhist apocalyptic thought in such texts as the *Anagatavamsa Desana*, in which the heralding of the future Buddha Metteyya is determined by the appearance of a future *cakkavattin* who establishes norms of righteousness paralleled by conditions of material splendor. See Holt (1993).

49. Jordt puts this matter another way in the opening paragraphs of her book: "[M]editation is seen not only as the technique leading the individual to true experiences and ultimate reality but also as a core, reliable source of knowledge verifying what the goals of society are, what the obligations and rights of the state are, and how the individual is situated in relation to state, society and soteriology. Monks, laity and state draw on these epistemological and concrete resources (sometimes cynically, sometimes sincerely) in order to make claims and assert limits in terms that are highly moralized and in reference to a variety of phenomena that together reflect and validate normative and emergent social practices" (2007, 3).

50. Jordt also stresses how the meditation movement has empowered women by providing them with an additional space in which they can also pursue the soteriological aim

of the religion for themselves (2007, 161). Therefore, Spiro's arguments about how women have been subordinated to men in the context of Burmese religious culture now needs to be reexamined, especially in the urban context (162). A woman may now have other means for progressing beyond the monastic ordination of her son (163).

Chapter 5: Pchum Ben

1. Better known in the United States as the Vietnam War.

2. Chandler (2008, 15).

3. "Richard Nixon's May 1970 invasion of Cambodia (undertaken without informing Lon Nol's new government) [the very military government that the CIA had helped to overthrow Prince Sihanouk's neutralist government] followed simultaneous invasions by Saigon and Vietnamese communist forces. It created 130,000 new Khmer refugees, according to the Pentagon. By 1971, 60 per cent of refugees surveyed in Cambodia's towns gave U.S. bombing as the main reason of their displacement. The U.S. bombardment of the Cambodian countryside continued well into 1973, when Congress imposed a halt. Nearly half of the 540,000 tons of bombs were dropped in the last six months. From the ashes of rural Cambodia arose Pol Pot's Communist Party of Kampuchea. It used the bombing's devastation and massacre of civilians as recruitment propaganda and as an excuse for its brutal, radical policies and its purge of moderate communists and Sihanoukists" (Kiernan 2002, 19).

4. Kiernan (2002, 24); perhaps only Laos suffered more casualties from these intense American bombing campaigns.

5. On the American responsibility for the breakdown of order that led to Khmer Rouge's rise and eventual control of the country, Ben Kiernan, who has written the definitive study of Pol Pot's rise to power and its subsequent policies of genocide, says: "Although it was indigenous, Pol Pot's revolution would not have won power without U.S. economic and military destabilization of Cambodia which began in 1966 after American escalation in next-door Vietnam and peaked in 1969–1973 [under President Richard Nixon] with the carpet bombing of Cambodia's countryside by American b-52s. This was probably the most important single factor in Pol Pot's rise" (2002, 16). David Chandler, perhaps the foremost American student of Cambodian history, writes similarly: "The Vietnam War destabilized the Cambodian economy and eventually drove Sihanouk from office. Otherwise he probably would not have been overthrown, and Cambodia's Communists would not have come to power" (2008, 236).

6. About the desperate conditions of the country on the eve of the Khmer Rouge takeover in 1975, Keyes writes: "The refugee population [in Phnom Penh] could not be supported on food produced within the country since so much land had been abandoned or had fallen under Khmer Rouge control, while transportation had come to a near standstill. Despite a massive airlift by the United States of food into the country, starvation became a fact of life—or rather a fact of death—to perhaps tens of thousands of Khmer in 1974 and 1975. Starvation accelerated after the fall of the country to the Khmer Rouge and the concomitant ending of the airlift of food supplies by the Americans. The new government was incapable of feeding its large refugee population even if it had been willing to do so. While it is impossible to calculate the number of deaths from starvation between 1973 and the end of 1975, they could not have been fewer than a hundred thousand" (1994, 54).

7. The most recent estimates put the figure of dead under the Khmer Rouge at 1.75 million, though Chandler continues to use the approximate figure of two million in his most recently revised *A History of Cambodia* (2008, 25).

8. As in the vernaculars of other Theravada-inclined cultures, Sanskrit *preta* has been adopted in common use rather than the Pali *peta*. I will use *peta* only within the context of Pali literature and *preta* on all other occasions.

9. The phrase belongs to Steven Collins, who introduced it as his chief hermeneutical device in his *Nibbana and Other Buddhist Felicities* (1997). See especially his "General Introduction."

10. This the fifth, last, and most recent of the collections of *sutras* that make up the *Suttapitaka* section of the *Tripitaka*, those texts are regarded as *Buddhavacana*, "words of the Buddha," according to Theravada tradition.

11. For a careful and thorough analysis of this torture chamber, see Chandler (1999).

12. Both Heng Samrin and Hun Sen would become key political players in the formation of a new government following the fall of the Khmer Rouge. Hun Sen eventually parlayed his position as prime minister within the context of the United Nations–sponsored elections of 1993. Though his party, Cambodian Peoples' Party (CPP), did not enjoy an outright victory, Hun Sen has remained as Cambodia's prime minister until the time of this writing (2016).

13. The journalist Elizabeth Becker (2010) has culled and compiled the pathetic yet compelling story of one young woman, Hout Bophana, from letters and documents of her "interviews" while she was being tortured to death at Tuol Sleng. A documentary film made by a European filmmaker about Bophana is currently shown twice daily at Tuol Sleng in Phnom Penh.

14. Kwon points out how "fallen soldiers who also fought for national independence, but who happened to have done so on the wrong side of 'the puppet regime,' have absolutely no right to the space of the virtuous war dead" (2006, 21).

15. John Marston makes a similar argument. In trying to account for the popularity of the practice of not cremating monks immediately following their deaths, he muses that among the reasons may be the fact that "there is now a far greater circulation of money in Cambodia that there was during the socialist period, a development that has often favoured new religious projects and, logically, has opened up the possibility of conspicuous expense in the funerary expenses of monks as well." He goes on to say that all of the monks involved in this practice were monks who can be identified with building up the religious community following the demise of the Pol Pot era (2006, 503–504).

16. For a detailed discussion of this scenario, see my *Spirits of the Place* (2009, 116–127).

17. Moreover, "[t]he memory of tragic death is left in a void in the monument of heroes, whereas in ancestor worship it becomes an essential part of the spatial structure of worship, representing a generalized anonymity worthy of a particular kind of respect" (Kwon 2006, 154–155). He continues by stating that further differences between hero commemoration and ancestor veneration, aside from the state and familial bases, respectively, are this: that in the state hero cult, the "politically challenged" and those who died unproductively in relation to the cause are excluded. In ancestor veneration, it is true that genealogy leads to exclusion, but almost everyone has a family to belong to.

18. Personal interview with Ang Choulean, Reyum Institute, Phnom Penh, October 13, 2010.

19. As in Laos, the French were notorious in Cambodia for giving very little in return for the taxes they exacted, especially in the countryside.

20. A further example of French colonial arrogance has been noted by Chandler. He describes the efforts of the French resident, Georges Gautier, in 1943, who announced "his intention to replace Cambodia's forty-seven-letter alphabet, derived from medieval Indian models, with the Roman one. . . . Gautier and his colleagues viewed the reform as a step toward modernization, which in turn was seen unequivocally as a good thing. In a pamphlet devoted to explaining the reform, Gautier attacked the 'Cambodian attitude to the world,'

as 'out of date' and compared the Cambodian language to a 'badly tailored suit.' The addition of a supposedly more rational French vocabulary to Romanized Khmer, Gautier thought, would somehow improve Cambodian thought processes. Citing the example of Romanization in Turkey, while remaining diplomatically silent about the Romanization of Vietnamese, Gautier seems to have believed that the virtues of the reform were as self-evident as what he thought of as the primitiveness of the Cambodian mind" (2008, 207).

21. As Ebihara reported: "In general, the bond between parents and children is perhaps the strongest and most enduring relationships in village life. Even when an individual marries and establishes a family of procreation that comes to take precedence over the family of orientation, deep-rooted sentiments and feelings of obligation persist toward parents and are manifest in mutual visiting, aid in times of need, and abiding concern. . . . Affection and loyalty among siblings are encouraged, and serious discord among family members both siblings and parents and children is thought to be punished by ancestral spirits" (1968, 119–120).

22. For studies of ancient Khmer society, political structures, and religious culture, see Hermann Kulke (1978), Ian Mabbett (1978), and Alexis Sanderson (2003–2004).

23. Zucker succinctly reiterates what Davis has stated more elaborately: "The language of social thought was limited and did not travel far beyond the use of family relationships as metaphors for broader political and social occurrences" (2008, 202–203). This language is seen expressly in the manner that King Sihanouk referred to his subjects as "his children" and himself as a "father" in relation to them (Chandler and Kent 2008, 6).

24. Bizot was arguably the most knowledgeable Western student of Khmer Buddhist culture and society of his generation. His studies concentrated not only on inscriptions, textual interpretations, and sculpture of the Khmer elite, but also on the ritual, mythic, and symbolic expressions of popular Khmer religion. See Harris (2008, 311–312) for a representative list of his long bibliography of contributions to the study of Khmer culture. For a more precise study of the significance of Bizot's scholarly work, see Kate Crosby (2000).

25. As Bizot has asserted that the Khmer Rouge constituted a kind of quasi-religion of their own, Keyes discusses how it is that they viewed their own Communist Party members as engaged in more perfect behavior than monks. Quoting Yang Sam, another scholar with intimate knowledge of the situation in Cambodia during Khmer Rouge hegemony, the ideal party member was described in this way: "He/she persevered in improving his/her personality by loving and respecting people, being honest, protecting people's interests, confessing his/her misdeeds, using modest and polite words, and avoiding adultery and polygamy, avoiding drinking, avoiding gambling, avoiding thievery." Keyes goes on to add: "Although many rural people appear to have been impressed by the similarity between the disciplined moral authority of the Khmer Rouge cadre and that of members of the *sangha*, the Khmer Rouge sought to create a world that was the moral inversion of that of Buddhism" (1994, 57).

26. Douch was convicted by a United Nations–sponsored war crimes court in the summer of 2010 for his direct role in the deaths of some seventeen thousand people who passed through the S-21 interrogation center that came under his administrative purview.

27. Harris has an especially poignant section in his book (2008, 182–189) that is focused on the "internalization of Buddhist symbolism and language" into the mind-set of the Khmer Rouge. He writes that "there can be little doubt that internalization of aspects of an older religiously inspired thought universe was pervasive during the period" (184). Specifically, he examines the similarity between *sila* and the ten basic "moral rules" that the Khmer Rouge inculcated, the penchant for and practice of self-sacrifice and the life of self-examination exhorted in the *Vinaya*, how the term *paticcasamuppada* ("dependent or conditioned origination") was employed to translate "dialectical materialism," and so on. In the same vein, Chandler and Kent (2008) describe how "[t]he concealed leaders of the party, or

Angkar [the 'Organization'], envisioned themselves as the new, moral substitute for the *sangha*. Alternate, pre-revolutionary sources of domestic or community-based power—the *sangha*, older family members, and local spirits—were discredited. The moral order was now rendered as the imposed, historically inevitable egalitarianism of the impoverished population, supposedly liberated from the shackles of the past and from a wide range of dominations" (7).

28. Skidmore put the matter rather succinctly when she wrote: "The destruction of 'traditional' social structure and the inculcation of a sense of collectivity as opposed to individuality took a myriad of forms. The concept of family was abolished, and people lived in large shelters on the collective farms" (1997, 5).

29. This is the classic Marxist critique of karma, one that ignores the fact that it is not only an explanation for how and why events and situations of the present unfold, but it is a forward-looking and empowering concept owing to the fact that it emphasizes the present: the quality of one's inward dispositions gives rise to behavioral actions that become part of the conditioning process, thereby determining what will become later.

30. The use of the term "invited" here is doubly significant insofar as it also refers to the meaning of the *pavarana* monastic rite usually held in Cambodia during the night before the celebration of *kathina*. In the context of *pavarana* (which literally means "invitation") all monks are *invited* to critically examine the behavior of their fellow monks, an invitation that, in turn, leads to a confession of shortcomings that have occurred during the *vassa* rain-retreat season. At the conclusion of the rite, the *sangha*'s collective *parisuddhi*, or "complete purity" is declared. This status is what renders the *sangha* especially worthy receivers of gifts, particularly robes, from the laity during the *kathina* rite on the following day.

31. Ledgerwood has noted that "the devastation was so effective that an estimated ninety per cent of Cambodia's Buddhist literary heritage was lost in that span of less than four years" (2008b, 204).

32. Osborne says that during the Vietnamese occupation, life in Phnom Penh was mostly a matter of survival tactics, very difficult indeed. Usually one partner of the marriage engaged in some form of petty commerce. "Supplies of all kinds were limited, with aid from the socialist bloc, and in particular the Soviet Union, insufficient to overcome the constant shortages that hindered a full economic recovery. Rubber plantations were only slowly being brought back into production, and in Phnom Penh those factories that were operating had to contend with frequent power outages," with most factories only being able to operate three days a week owing to electricity shortages (2008, 189).

33. Chandler and Kent are stressing the same point: "[T]he regeneration of the ritual life of a community may also offer a way for people to formulate and relate to their collective stories through a symbolism that recalls a shared cultural origins. . . . [I]t is therefore important to explore the processes by which a community like Cambodia is attempting to recover moral order after violent conflict both in relation to indigenous values and experience, as embedded in social relations and history" (2008, 2).

34. See especially Eliade's *Myth of the Eternal Return*.

35. Mahaghosananda founded more than thirty *wats* for Cambodians in Canada and the United States in the 1980s and has been a major force, along with ex-Jesuits and Japanese Nichiren monks, as well as Christian and ecumenical NGOs, in holding annual *dhammayietra* peace marches designed to "wash away" memories of the Khmer Rouge (Harris 2008, 208). Mahaghosananda was nominated for the Nobel Prize for Peace in both 1994 and 1996.

36. In Dan Savin and Shalom Robinson, "Holocaust Survivors and Survivors of the Cambodian Tragedy: Similarities and Differences," in *Echoes of the Holocaust* 3 (2000), the results of hundreds of interviews with Khmer survivors have been published as a way of

understanding, comparatively, the continuing, long-term psychological impact of having witnessed mass murder. Their findings are summarized as follows:

> The stories of the interviewees presented here illustrate the terrible suffering of millions of Cambodians during the Khmer Rouge regime, as well as the psychological late effects caused by this suffering. . . . The first author has found posttraumatic stress symptoms in hundreds of Cambodians whom he examined during his two-and-a-half-year stay in Cambodia. In a group of 100 Cambodian child survivors interviewed in a refugee camp near the Thai border 13 years after the end of the Pol Pot regime, 46% met full DSMIII-R criteria for PTSD [post traumatic stress disorder], and an additional 40% met the lesser criteria for a diagnosis of PTSD not otherwise specified (NOS). In another group of Cambodian child survivors who made it to the United States and were interviewed around the same time, 28% met full criteria for PTSD, and an additional 20% for PTSD NOS. . . . By talking with Cambodian survivors in more detail, however, it becomes clear that guilt is a major issue for them as for Holocaust survivors.

37. The purported beginnings of Phnom Penh as a center for the Khmer are now a matter of mythic articulation and connected directly to Wat Phnom. Osborne retells the story: "As for the city's more familiar name, there is a romantic legend accounting for its existence. Sometime in the fourteenth century, the legend recounts, and not long before the Cambodian court left the great city of Angkor with its magnificent temples, a woman named Penh lived beside a small hillock close to the river bank and a little above the point where the Mekong and its tributary came together. One day, when the rivers were in flood, she saw a huge *koki* tree—a type traditionally planted only by royalty or Buddhist monks—floating in the current. When she pulled it to the shore, hoping to use it for firewood, she found to her amazement that wedged in the tree's branches were four statues of the Buddha and one of the Hindu god Vishnu. Penh recognized this as a sign that the gods had decided to leave the holy city of Angkor and to give their blessing to a new Cambodian capital. Like women in contemporary Cambodia, Penh was energetic and determined. Calling on the people who lived nearby to carry the images to her home, she then organized them to pile earth on the hillock close to her home, so transforming it into a feature that could legitimately be called a hill, a *phnom* in Cambodian. When this was done, she built a temple on the top of the hill to house the images of the Buddha and a stupa for other holy relics, while the statue of Vishnu was placed in a separate chapel. In memory of these events, the city took the name as Phnom Penh, the 'Hill of lady Penh.'" Osborne continues: "[C]harming though the story is, the record is clear that the settlement did not acquire its modern name until after the Cambodian court, led by King Ponhea Yat, left Angkor to settle briefly at the site of modern Phnom Penh. Despite some assertions to the contrary, we do not know exactly when this profoundly important event took place, although it occurred sometime after 1431, possibly in the same decade. It was a final act in a long drawn out drama of the decline of the Angkorian empire's power in the face of a century of attacks by the emerging Siamese [Thai] principalities on Cambodia's western frontier" (2008, 21–22).

38. Though the "king mother" is currently living in hell, it is believed that she comes to this *wat* to respond to those who call on her for help.

39. Given the fact that our usual meeting time ranged between 2:30 a.m. and 3:30 a.m., we developed something of a healthy, albeit ascetic, esprit de corps.

40. These simple paper "cutouts" seem to be inspired by the elaborate hand-sewn cloth hangings one finds decorating some village temples during the *pchum ben* season, the making of which is regarded as highly meritorious. See photo 5.12 from Wat Traleaeng Kaeng.

41. On this point Davis has quoted Maria Heim: "When the recipient is someone whom one can esteem, the feelings of *sraddha*, respect, and joy, naturally arise. These are among the most noble feelings one can have, and thus it is perfectly appropriate to value these gifts above others" (Heim 2004, 81–82).

42. The majority of people coming to the early morning ritual were women. They were mothers and daughters, grandmothers and granddaughters, nieces, wives, and teenagers. Perhaps a third of those in attendance were males. In terms of age, virtually all age groups were equally represented, but the preponderance seemed youthful. At Wat Langka, a decidedly upper-middle-class clientele predominated.

43. The opening scene of parading monks, at the time, made me recall the description of *pchum ben* offered a hundred years ago by Adhemard Leclere. See appendix 4.

44. As in the countryside, each night of *kan ben* requires a different chief sponsor or lay patron for the ritual whose responsibility is to pay for all expenses incurred, including not only the cost of providing breakfast to all of the monks, but also the payment of musicians (*pin peat*) and any other costs associated with the ritual performance. The cost, by local standards, can be very considerable. At major *wats* in Phnom Penh, only the very well-to-do may be able to afford playing this role. At most rural *wats*, families take turns meeting the responsibility and earning the merit that accrues. Often, the chief patron is a person of some means who has returned from the city.

45. Winternitz (1927, 2: 99) assigned the *Petavatthu* to the latest strata of literature assembled in the *Tipitaka*. In the fifth-century CE *Mahavamsa's* account (14.58: 96) of the transmission of Buddhism to Sri Lanka in the third century BCE, it is referred to as the second text preached by Asoka's monastic missionary son, Mahinda, who establishes the *sangha* and then converts the court and Lankan king who is then recrowned as Devanampiya Tissa.

46. I have traced the roots of the early Buddhist transformation of ancestor veneration in my article "Assisting the Dead by Venerating the Living" (1981).

47. *Petavatthu* (7–11).

48. This verse is repeated after each stanza. Though it adds to the cadence of the chanted during the ritual, I have omitted it here for the sake of brevity.

49. My translation.

50. For a study of these rites historically, as well as their contemporary observance, see David Knipe (1977).

51. On the efficacy of gifts to the ancestors during *pchum ben* and the intermediary role that is performed by the monks that creates this tripartite set of relations, Davis notes: "These gifts, furthermore, must be given via a specific ritual of transfer. Merely mourning their loss, mere remembrance—will not help the dead. Nor will giving gifts directly to the dead assist them properly. . . . Instead, the dead must be given their gifts by offering them to Buddhist monks 'at the right time.' And these gifts have the result—the fruit—of benefiting every member of the three-way transaction which creates this gift economy: the monks receive strength from the food they receive and eat, the ghosts receive new bodies and an alleviation of their suffering, and the donors receive blessings from their pleased ancestors and merit from their gifts to the monks" (2009, 168–169).

52. On the further significance of death for the function of Buddhism among the laity, Davis argues, "[W]e can see a Buddhist insistence on the control of death as the ongoing reproduction of morally authorized power and value for the living. It is the ancestors who, properly controlled and approached (both, via the agency or technique of Buddhist monks), are the source of worldly blessings, such as 'health and happiness, wealth, and status.' . . . [D]uring the largest communal celebration for the dead, Bhjum Pinda [*pchum ben*], gifts are given to the dead twice—once directly by the family, and without monks as mediators, and again via the monks. Although monks insist that the former offerings are not efficient . . . ,

direct offerings are at least as popular during this period as indirect offerings, and laypeople seem to have no doubts about their efficacy" (2009, 114).

53. In the introduction to their volume on crises of authority in East and Southeast Asia, Kendall, Keyes, and Hardacre have detailed the matter this way:

> In pursuit of "progress" free from primordial attachments (which is what most experts believed was inhibiting the modernization of Asian nation-states), the rulers of the modern states in East and Southeast Asia all have instituted policies toward religious institutions. These policies have been predicated on the adoption of official definitions of "religion," definitions that again have tended to be derived from the West. Indeed, in most Asian cultures prior to the modern period, there was no indigenous terminology corresponding to ideas of "religion" held by Christians or Jews [and, I would add, Islam]. Complex dispositions about the nature of religion—the primacy of texts; creeds pledging exclusive allegiance to a single deity, all originating in the theologically unadorned varieties of Protestantism—were brought to Asia by missionaries in the nineteenth century. When these predispositions came to inform official discourse on religion, they were often used to devalue other aspects of religious life such as festival, ritual and communal observances—precisely those aspects that were at the heart of popular religious life in East and Southeast Asia. And as Western notions about religion were incorporated into law and custom, they also came to exercise a great influence on popular religious life in Asia as well. (1994, 4–5)

The introduction of modernization, albeit at different times for different Asian states, always accompanied an attack on traditional rites as superstitious.

54. Davis says: "King Ang Duong . . . is supposed to have refounded the festival, by shortening the period of its celebration" (2009, 169).

55. Teiser points out that in the Yu-lan-p'en Sutra, "[t]he Buddha instructs Mu-lien and all other devoted sons to make offerings to the assembly of monks as they emerge from their summer retreat. Rather than sending gifts directly to their ancestors, people should henceforth use the Sangha as a medium: benefits will pass through monks to the inhabitants of the other world. In fact, monks possess the distinctive ability to multiply the blessings that reach the ancestors in hell. Having renounced the bonds of kinship, Buddhist ascetics generated a store of power made even greater over the course of the summer meditation retreat. For the price of a small offering during the ghost festival families may tap that power, directing its benefits to their less fortunate members" (1996, 202).

56. In explaining how the power of monks reached its zenith after the *pavarana* and *kathina* rites, Teiser explains: "Themes of renewal and regeneration are evident in this culminating ritual." Monks "released themselves: in several ways: they loosened the rules of discipline, they unleashed ascetic energies built up during the retreat, they submitted to criticism from other monks, and through their repentance they let loose the positive forces of purification and renewal" (1996, 205).

57. See, for example, the fact that, into the late nineteenth century, Pali texts in central Thai monasteries were still being written in the *khom* (Khmer) script.

58. Personal communication, October 13, 2010, Reyum Institute, Phnom Penh.

59. *Bangsukol* is the Khmer rendering of Sanskrit and Pali *pamsakula,* which has two primary meanings within the Buddhist context: (1) it refers to the robe made out of rags worn by the ascetic *dhutanga* wandering monks; and (2) at least in Sri Lanka, it refers to the Buddhist funeral ceremony in which the body is cremated and turned to ashes. In both instances, there is a clear association with what is "dead to the world."

Appendix 1: The Dalada Sirita

1. Welivitiye Suratha Thero, ed., *Dalada Sirita,* 2nd ed. (Colombo, Sri Lanka: M. D. Gunasena, 1970), 48–54; translated privately from the Sinhala into English by P. B. Meegaskumbura.

2. The passage ends with a dating of 1247 of the Saka era which, conventionally, since there is a sixty-one-year discrepancy according to *Culavamsa* (2–4), corresponds to 1186 CE, the last year of Parakramabahu I's reign. However, Berkwitz (2007, 11) assigns the dating of the *Dalada Sirita* to the reign of Parakramabahu IV in the early years of the fourteenth century.

3. Eight Sinhala hours is about three hours and twelve minutes after sunrise, that is, around 9:15 a.m. Morning service for the Dalada is done at 9:30 a.m. now.

4. The four quarters of the lunar cycle.

5. Mahasup refers to Ven. Mahakassapa, one of the chief disciples of the Buddha, who was foremost among ascetic practices. His Tooth-Relic was also an object of worship.

6. Ganavasi are descendants of the Lambabakarana clan who came with the Mahabodhi from India to Sri Lanka. *Kapurala*s are the officiating priests of deity shrines. *Gebalanna* is a house guard presently called *gebarala*.

7. Kiling clans were Kalingas (from what is modern-day Orissa in India) of royal descent.

8. *Dorana* refers to the chief of gatekeepers.

Appendix 4: The Feast of the Offering to the Dead

1. Translation of Adhemard Leclere, *Cambodge: Fetes Et Religieuses* (Paris: Imprimerie Nationale, 1916), 228–247.

Bibliography

Aluvihara, Sir Richard. 1952. "The Kandy Esala Perahera." Colombo, Sri Lanka: *Ceylon Daily News.*

Ancient Myanmar Inscriptions (in Burmese). 1972 and 1982. Vols. 1 and 2. Yangon: Department of Archeology.

Archaimbault, Charles. 1959. "La naissance du monde selon les traditions Lao: le mythe de Khun Belom." In *La naissance du monde* (Sources orient. I). Paris: Editions du Seuil.

Ariyapala, M. B. 1956. *Society in Mediaeval Ceylon.* Colombo, Sri Lanka: Department of Cultural Affairs.

Assavavirulhakarn, Prapod. 2010. *The Ascendancy of Theravada Buddhism in Southeast Asia.* Chiang Mai: Silkworm Books.

Aung-Thwin, Michael. 1979. "The Role of *Sasana* Reform in Burmese History: Economic Dimensions of a Religious Purification." *Journal of Asian Studies* 38:671–678.

Bartholomeusz, Tessa. 1994. *Women under the Bo Tree.* Cambridge: Cambridge University Press.

Bayly, Susan. 2000. "French Anthropology and the Durkheimians in Colonial Indochina. *Modern Asian Studies* 34:581–622.

Bechert, Heinz. 1966–1973. *Buddhismus, Staat und Gesellschaft.* 3 vols. Frankfurt: Institut fuer Asienkunde in Hamburg.

Becker, Elizabeth. 2010. *Bophana.* Phnom Penh: Cambodia Daily Press.

Bell, Catherine. 1992. *Ritual Theory, Ritual Practice.* New York: Oxford University Press.

———. 1997. *Ritual: Perspectives and Dimensions.* New York: Oxford University Press.

Berkwitz, Stephen. 2007. *The History of the Buddha's Relic Shrine: A Translation of the Sinhala Thupavamsa.* New York: Oxford University Press.

———. 2008. "Resisting the Global in Buddhist Nationalism: Venerable Soma's Discourse on Decline and Reform." *Journal of Asian Studies* 67:73–106.

Bizot, Francois. 1994. "La consecration des statues et la culte des morts." In *Recherches nouvelles sur le Cambodge,* edited by Francois Bizot. Paris: EFEO.

———. 2003. *The Gate.* London: Random House.

Book of Discipline. 5 vols. 1938–1952. Sacred Books of the Buddhists, vols. 10, 11, 13, 14, and 20. Edited and translated by I. B. Horner. London: Luzac and Company for the Pali Text Society.

Bunnag, Jane. 1973. *Buddhist Monk Buddhist Layman: A Study of Urban Monastic Organization in Central Thailand*. Cambridge: Cambridge University Press.

Carbine, Jason. 2011. *Sons of the Buddha: Continuities and Ruptures in a Buddhist Monastic Tradition*. Berlin: Walter de Gruyter.

Chandler, David. 1999. *Voices from S-21: Terror and History in Pol Pot's Secret Prison*. Berkeley: University of California Press.

———. 2008. *A History of Cambodia*. 4th ed. Boulder, CO: Westview Press.

Chandler, David, and Alexandra Kent, eds. 2008. *People of Virtue: Reconfiguring Religion, Power and Moral Order in Cambodia Today*. Copenhagen: Nordic Institute of Asian Studies.

Charney, Michael. 2009. *A History of Modern Burma*. Cambridge: Cambridge University Press.

Cholean, Ang. 1988. "The Place of Animism within Popular Buddhism in Cambodia: The Example of the Monastery." *Asian Folklore Studies* 47:35–41.

Coedes, G. 1972. *The Making of Southeast Asia*. 4th ed. Berkeley: University of California Press.

Collins, Steven. 1997. *Nibbana and Other Buddhist Felicities*. Cambridge: Cambridge University Press.

Comaroff, Jean. 1994. "Defying Disenchantment: Reflections on Ritual, Power and History." In *Asian Visions of Authority: Religion and the Modern States of East and Southeast Asia*, edited by Laurel Kendall, Charles Keyes, and Helen Hardacre, 301–314. Honolulu: University of Hawai'i Press.

Condominas, Georges. 1968. "Notes sur le bouddhisme populaire en milieu rural Lao." *Archives de sociologie des religions* 25–26:81–150.

———. 1973. "Phiban Cults in Rural Laos." In *Change and Persistence in Thai Society*, edited by William Skinner and A. Thomas Kirsch, 252–273. Ithaca, NY: Cornell University press.

Coomaraswamy, Ananda K. 1956. *Mediaeval Sinhalese Art*. 3rd ed. New York: Pantheon Books.

Crosby, Kate. 2000. "Tantric Theravada: A Bibliographic Essay on the Writings of Francois Bizot and Other Literature on the Yogavacara Tradition." *Contemporary Buddhism* 2:141–198.

———. 2014. *Theravada Buddhism: Continuity, Diversity and Identity*. West Sussex: Wiley-Blackwell.

Daniel, E. Valentine. 1996. *Charred Lullabies*. Princeton, NJ: Princeton University Press.

Darlington, Susan. 2013. *The Ordination of a Tree*. Albany: State University of New York Press.

Davis, Erik. 2008a. "Between Forests and Families: Death, Desire, and Order in Cambodia." In *People of Virtue: Reconfiguring Religion, Power, and Moral Order in Today's Cambodia*, edited by Alexandra Kent and David P. Chandler, 128–144. Honolulu: University of Hawai'i Press, NIAS Studies in Asian Topics.

———. 2008b. "Imaginary Conversations with Mothers about Death." In *At the Edge of the Forest: Essays in Honor of David Chandler*, edited by Anne R. Hansen and Judy Ledgerwood. Ithaca, NY: Cornell University Press.

————. 2009. *Treasures of the Buddha: Imagining Death and Life in Contemporary Cambodia.* PhD diss., University of Chicago Divinity School.

Davis, Richard. 1984. *Muang Metaphysics: A Study in Northern Thai Myth and Ritual.* Bangkok: Pandora.

Davy, John. 1983. *An Account of the Interior of Ceylon and Its Inhabitants with Travels in That Island.* Dehiwala, Sri Lanka: Tisara Prakasakayo (reprint).

de Bernon, Olivier. 2000. "Le rituel de la 'grande probation annuell' (*mahapraivasakamma*) des religieux du Cambodge." *Bulletin de l'ecole francaise d'extreme orient (BEFEO)* 87 (2): 473–510.

DeCaroli, Robert. 2004. *Haunting the Buddha: Indian Popular Religions and the Formation of Buddhism.* New York: Oxford University Press.

De Silva, Lily. 1981. *Paritta: The Buddhist Ceremony for Peace and Prosperity in Sri Lanka.* Colombo: National Museums of Sri Lanka.

Duncan, James. *The City as Text.* Cambridge: Cambridge University Press, 1990.

Dutt, Sukumar. 2008. *Buddhist Monks and Monasteries of India: Their History and Their Contribution to Indian Culture.* Delhi: Motilal Banarsidass (originally published in 1962).

Eberhardt, Nancy. 2006. *Imagining the Course of Life: Self-Transformation in a Shan Buddhist Community.* Honolulu: University of Hawai'i Press.

Ebihara, May. 1968. *Svay: A Khmer Village in Cambodia.* PhD diss., Columbia University.

Ebihara, May M., Carol A. Mortland, and Judy Ledgerwood, eds. 1994. *Cambodia Culture since 1975: Homeland and Exile.* Ithaca, NY: Cornell University Press.

Edwards, Penny. 2007. *Cambodge: The Cultivation of a Nation, 1860–1945.* Honolulu: University of Hawai'i Press.

————. 2008a. "Between a Song and a *Prei*: Tracking Cambodian History and Cosmology through the Forest." In *At the Edge of the Forest,* edited by Anne Hansen and Judy Ledgerwood, 137–162. Ithaca, NY: Cornell Southeast Asia Program Publications.

————. 2008b. "The Moral Geology of the Present: Structuring Morality, Menace and Merit." In *People of Virtue: Reconfiguring Religion. Power and Moral Order in Cambodia Today,* edited by David Chandler and Alexandra Kent, 213–237. Copenhagen: Nordic Institute of Asian Studies.

Eliade, Mircea. 1996. *Patterns in Comparative Religion.* Translated by Rosemary Sheed. Introduction by John Clifford Holt. Lincoln: University of Nebraska Press; originally published in 1958 by Sheed and Ward, Inc.

————. 2005. *The Myth of the Eternal Return or, Cosmos and History.* Translated by Willard Trask. Princeton, NJ: Princeton University Press; originally published 1954.

Evans, Grant. 1998. *The Politics of Ritual Memory: Laos since 1975.* Honolulu: University of Hawai'i Press.

————. 2002. *A Short History of Laos.* Chiang Mai: Silkworm Books.

Forest, Alain. 2008. "Buddhism and Reform: Imposed Reforms and Popular Aspirations." In *People of Virtue: Reconfiguring Religion. Power and Moral Order in Cambodia Today,* edited by David Chandler and Alexandra Kent, 16–34. Copenhagen: Nordic Institute of Asian Studies.

Frauwallner, Erich. 1956. *The Earliest Vinaya and the Beginnings of Buddhist Literature.* Rome: Instituto Italiano per il Medio ed Estremo Oriente.

Freeman, Michael. 1997. *Phimai.* Bangkok: River Books.

Geertz, Clifford. 1966. "Religion as a Cultural System." In *Anthropological Approaches to the Study of Religion,* edited by M. Banton. New York: Praeger.

————. 1971. *Islam Observed: Religious Developments in Morocco and Indonesia*. Chicago: University of Chicago Press.

————. 1981. *Negara: The Theater State in Nineteenth Century Bali*. Princeton, NJ: Princeton University Press.

Gehman, H. S., trans. 1942. *Petavatthu: Stories of the Departed*. In *Minor Anthologies of the Pali Canon, Part IV*. Sacred Books of the Buddhists, vol. 30. London: The Pali Text Society.

Gethin, Rupert. 2012. "Was Buddhaghosa a Theravadin? Buddhist Identity in the Pali Commentaries and Chronicles." In *How Theravada is Theravada: Exploring Buddhist Identities*, edited by Peter Skilling, Jason Carbine, Claudio Cicuzza, and Santi Pakdeekham, 1–63. Chiang Mai: Silkworm Books.

Godakumbura, G. C. 1970. "Sinhalese Festivals: Their Symbolism, Origins and Proceedings." *Journal of the Royal Asiatic Society (Ceylon Branch)* n.s. 14:91–34.

Goloubew, Victor. 1933. "Le Temple de la Dent a Kandy." *Bulletin de l'Ecole Francaise D'Extreme-orient (Hanoi)* 32:441–474.

Gombrich, Richard. 1971a. "'Merit Transference' in Sinhalese Buddhism: A Case Study of the Interaction between Doctrine and Behavior." *History of Religions* 11:203–219.

————. 1971b. *Precept and Practice: Traditional Buddhism in the Rural Highlands of Ceylon*. Oxford: Clarendon Press.

Gombrich, Richard, and Margaret Cone. 1977. *The Perfect Generosity of Prince Vessantara*. Oxford: Oxford University Press.

Gombrich, Richard, and Gananath Obeyesekere. 1988. *Buddhism Transformed*. Princeton, NJ: Princeton University Press.

Grabowsky, Volker. 1997. "Origins of Lao and Khmer National Identity: The Legacy of the early Nineteenth Century." In *Nationalism and Cultural Revival in Southeast Asia: Perspectives from the Centre and the Region*, edited by Sri Kuhnt-Saptodewo, Volker Grabowsky, and M. Grossheim, 145–167. Wiesbaden: Harrassowitz Verlag.

Gunawardana, R. A. L. H. 1979. *Robe and Plough*. Tucson: University of Arizona Press.

Guthrie, Elizabeth. 2004. "A Study of the History and Cult of the Buddhist Earth Deity in Mainland Southeast Asia." PhD diss., University of Canterbury (Christchurch, NZ).

Guthrie, Stewart Elliot. 1993. *Faces in the Clouds: A New Theory of Religion*. New York: Oxford University Press.

Hallisey, Charles. 2003. "Works and Persons in Sinhala Literary Culture." In *Literary Cultures in History: Reconstructions from South Asia*, edited by Sheldon Pollock, 689–746. Berkeley: University of California Press.

Handley, Paul. 2007. *The King Never Smiles: A Biography of Thailand's Bhumibol Adulyadej*. New Haven, CT: Yale University Press.

Hansen, Anne. 2007. *How to Behave: Buddhism and Modernity in Colonial Cambodia*. Honolulu: University of Hawai'i Press.

————. 2008. "Modernism and Morality in the Colonial Era." In *People of Virtue: Reconfiguring Religion. Power and Moral Order in Cambodia Today*, edited by David Chandler and Alexandra Kent, 35–61. Copenhagen: Nordic Institute of Asian Studies.

Hansen, Anne, and Judy Ledgerwood, eds. 2008. *Songs at the Edge of the Forest*. Ithaca, NY: Cornell Southeast Asia Program Publications.

Harris, Ian. 2008. *Cambodian Buddhism: History and Practice*. Honolulu: University of Hawai'i Press.

Hayashi, Yukio. 2003. *Practical Buddhism among the Thai-Lao: A Regional Study of Religion in the Making.* Kyoto: Kyoto University Press.

Heim, Maria. 2004. *Theories of the Gift in South Asia.* New York: Routledge.

———. 2013. *The Forerunner of All Things: Buddhaghosa on Mind, Intention and Agency.* New York: Oxford University Press.

Hinton, Alex L. 2008. "Truth, Representation and the Politics of Memory after Genocide." In *People of Virtue: Reconfiguring Religion. Power and Moral Order in Cambodia Today,* David Chandler and Alexandra Kent, 62–81. Copenhagen: Nordic Institute of Asian Studies.

Hocart, A. M. 1931. *The Temple of the Tooth Relic in Kandy.* Memoirs of the Archaeological Survey of Ceylon. Vol. 4. London: Luzac and Company.

Holt, John Clifford. 1981a. "Assisting the Dead by Venerating the Living: Merit Transfer in the Early Buddhist Tradition." *Numen* 28:1–28.

———. 1981b. *Discipline: The Canonical Buddhism of the Vinayapitaka.* Delhi: Motilal Banarsidass.

———. 1991a. *Buddha in the Crown: Avalokitesvara in the Buddhist Traditions of Sri Lanka.* New York: Oxford University Press.

———. 1991b. "Protestant Buddhism?" *Religious Studies Review* 17:307–312.

———, ed. 1993. *Anagatavamsa Desana: The Sermon of the Chronicle-To-Be.* Translated by Udaya Meddegama. Delhi: Motilal Banarsidass.

———. 1996. *The Religious World of Kirti Sri: Buddhism, Art and Politics in Late Medieval Sri Lanka.* New York: Oxford University Press.

———. 2004. *The Buddhist Visnu.* New York: Columbia University Press.

———. 2007. "Gone but Not Departed: The Dead among the Living in Contemporary Buddhist Sri Lanka." In *The Buddhist Dead: Practices, Discourses, Representations,* edited by Bryan Cuevas and Jacqueline Stone, 326–344. Honolulu: University of Hawai'i Press.

———. 2009. *Spirits of the Place: Buddhism and Lao Religious Culture.* Honolulu: University of Hawai'i Press.

———. 2011. *The Sri Lanka Reader.* Durham: Duke University Press.

Huntington, Susan L. 1990. "Early Buddhist Art and the Theory of Aniconism." *Art Journal* 49:401–408.

Jordt, Ingrid. 2007. *Burma's Mass Lay Meditation Movement: Buddhism and the Cultural Construction of Power.* Athens: Ohio University Press.

Kabilsingh, Chatsumarn. 1991. *Thai Women in Buddhism.* Berkeley, CA: Parallax Press.

Kemper, Steven. 2015. *Rescued from the Nation: Anagarika Dharmapala and the Buddhist World.* Chicago: University of Chicago Press.

Kendall, Laurel, Charles Keyes, and Helen Hardacre, eds. 1994. *Asian Visions of Authority: Religion and the Modern States of East and Southeast Asia.* Honolulu: University of Hawai'i Press.

Kent, Alexandra. 2008. "The Recovery of the King." In *People of Virtue: Reconfiguring Religion. Power and Moral Order in Cambodia Today,* edited by David Chandler and Alexandra Kent, 109–127. Copenhagen: Nordic Institute of Asian Studies.

Keyes, Charles. 1994. "Communist Revolution and the Buddhist Past in Cambodia." In *Asian Visions of Authority: Religion and the Modern States of East and Southeast Asia,* edited by Charles Keyes and Helen Hardacre, 43–73. Honolulu: University of Hawai'i Press.

―――. 2002. "National Heroine or Local Spirit?: The Struggle over Memory in the Case of Thao Suranari of Nakhon Ratchasima." In *Cultural Crisis and Social Memory: Modernity and Identity in Thailand and Laos,* edited by Shigeharu Tanabe and Charles F. Keyes, 113–136. Honolulu: University of Hawai'i Press.

Kiernan, Ben. 2002. *The Pol Pot Regime.* 2nd ed. New Haven, CT: Yale University Press.

Kinnard, Jacob. 2008. "Amaravati as Lens: Envisioning Buddhism in the Ruins of the Great *Stupa.*" In *Buddhism in the Krishna River Valley,* edited by Sree Padma and Anthony Barber, 81–103. Albany: State University of New York Press.

Knipe, David. 1977. *"Sapindikarana:* The Hindu Rite of Entry into Heaven." In *Religious Encounters with Death: Insights from the History and Anthropology of Religion,* edited by Frank R. Reynolds and Earl Waugh. University Park: Pennsylvania State University Press.

Knox, Robert. 1984. *Historical Relation of the Island Ceylon.* Introduction by H. A. I. Goonetileke. New Delhi: Navrang (originally published, London: Robert Chiswell, 1681).

Kobayashi Satoru. 2005. "An Ethnographic Study on the Reconstruction of Buddhist Practice in Two Cambodian Temples: With Special Reference to Buddhist *Samay* and *Boran." Southeast Asian Studies (Kyoto)* 42:489–518.

―――. 2008. "Reconstructing Buddhist Temples: An Analysis of Village Buddhism after the Era of Turmoil." In *People of Virtue: Reconfiguring Religion. Power and Moral Order in Cambodia Today,* edited by David Chandler and Alexandra Kent, 169–194. Copenhagen: Nordic Institute of Asian Studies.

Kulke, Hermann. 1978. *The Devaraja Cult.* Ithaca, NY: Cornell University Southeast Asia Program Data Paper No. 18.

Kwon, Heonik. 2006. *After the Massacre: Commemoration and Consolation in Ha My and My Lai.* Berkeley: University of California Press.

Laohavanich, Mano Mettananda. 2012. "Esoteric Teachings of Wat Dhammakaya." *Journal of Buddhist Ethics* 19:483–513.

Leclere, Adhemmad. 1916. *Cambodge: Fetes et Religieuses.* Paris: Imprimerie Nationale.

Ledgerwood, Judy. 2008a. "Buddhist Practice in Rural Kandal Province: An Essay in Honor of May Ebihara." In *People of Virtue: Reconfiguring Religion. Power and Moral Order in Cambodia Today,* edited by David Chandler and Alexandra Kent, 147–168. Copenhagen: Nordic Institute of Asian Studies.

―――. 2008b. "Ritual in 1990 Cambodian Political Theatre: New Songs at the Edge of the Forest." In *At the Edge of the Forest: Essays on Cambodia, History, and Narrative in Honor of David Chandler,* edited by Anne Ruth Hansen and Judy Ledgerwood. Ithaca, NY: Cornell Southeast Asia Program Publications.

Lefferts, Leedom. 1999. "Women's Power and Theravada Buddhism: A Paradox from Xieng Khouang." In *Laos, Culture and Society,* edited by Grant Evans, 215–225. Chiang Mai: Silkworm Books.

Lorrillard, Michel. 2003. "The Earliest Lao Buddhist Monasteries According to Philological and Epigraphic Sources." In *The Buddhist Monastery: A Cross-cultural Survey,* 139–148. Paris: Ecole Franciaise d'Extreme Orient.

Loschmann, Heike. 2006–2007. "Buddhism and Social Development in Cambodia since the Overthrow of the Pol Pot Regime in 1979." *Journal of the Center for Khmer Studies* 8–9:98–110.

Mabbett, Ian. 1978. "Kingship in Angkor." *Journal of the Siam Society* 66:1–58.

Mabbett, I. W., and D. P. Chandler. 1975. "Introduction." In *India as Seen from the East: Indian and Indigenous Cults in Champa*, edited by I.W. Mabbett and D. P. Chandler. Monash: Monash University Centre for Southeast Asian Studies; Monash papers on Southeast Asia, No. 3. Originally published as "Cultes indiens et indigenes au Champa." *Bulletin de l'Ecole Francaise d"Extreme Orient* 33 (1933): 367–410.

Mahavamsa. 1912. Edited and translated by Wilhelm Geiger. London: Luzac and Co. for the Pali Text Society.

Malalasekera, G. P. 1967. "'Transference of Merit' in Ceylonese Buddhism." *Philosophy East and West* 17:85–90.

Malalgoda, Kitsiri. 1976. *Buddhism and Sinhalese Society: 1750–1900*. Berkeley: University of California Press.

Marston, John. 1994. "Metaphors of the Khmer Rouge." In *Cambodia Culture since 1975: Homeland and Exile*, edited by May M. Ebihara, Carol A. Mortland, and Judy Ledgerwood, 105–118. Ithaca, NY: Cornell University Press.

———. 2006. "Death, Memory and Building: The Non-Cremation of a Cambodian Monk." *Journal of Southeast Asian Studies* 37:491–505.

Marston, John, and Elizabeth Guthrie, eds. 2004. *History, Buddhism, and New Religious Movements in Cambodia*. Honolulu: University of Hawai'i Press.

Masefield, Peter. 1986. *Divine Revelation in Pali Buddhism*. Boston: George Allen and Unwin.

McMullen, David. 1987. "Bureaucrats and Cosmology: The Ritual Code of Tang China." In *Rituals of Royalty and Ceremonial Traditional Society*, edited by David Cannadine and Simon Price, 181–236. Cambridge: Cambridge University Press.

Meegahakumbura, K. 2011. *Heritage of the Sacred Tooth Relic and the Temple of the Tooth Relic*. Translated from the Sinhala by Mahindadasa Ratnapala. Padukka, Sri Lanka: Government Printing Corporation.

Men, Chean R. 1999. *Lien Arak: A Study of Khmer Healing Ritual Performance*. Master's thesis, Northern Illinois University Department of Anthropology.

Mendelson, E. Michael. 1975. *Sangha and State in Burma*, edited by John Ferguson. Ithaca, NY: Cornell University Press.

Moore, Elizabeth, Hansjorg Mayer, and Pe Win U. 1999. *Shwedagon: Golden Pagoda of Myanmar*. London: Thames and Hudson.

Mus, Paul. 1975. "India Seen from the East: Indian and Indigenous Cults in Champa." Translated from the French by I. W. Mabbett and D. P. Chandler. Monash: Monash University Centre of Southeast Asian Studies; Monash Papers on Southeast Asia No. 3 (originally published as "Cultes indiens et indigenes au Champa," *Bulletin d'Ecole Francaise d'Extreme Orient* 33 (1933): 367–410).

Nash, Manning. 1965. *The Golden Road to Modernity: Village Life in Contemporary Burma*. Chicago: University of Chicago Press.

Obeyesekere, Gananath. 1972. "Religious Symbolism and Political Change in Ceylon." In *The Two Wheels of Dhamma*, edited by Bardwell L. Smith. Chambersburg, PA: American Academy of Religion; AAR Studies in Religion, no. 3.

Osborne, Milton. 2008. *Phnom Penh: A Cultural and Literary History*. Oxford: Signal Books.

Overland, G. 1999. "The Role of Funeral Rites in Healing the Wounds of War among Cambodian Holocaust Survivors." Paper presented at the 20th Nordic Sociological Congress, Bergen, June 17–19.

Padma, Sree. 2013. *Vicissitudes of the Goddess*. New York: Oxford University Press.

Perreira, Todd Leroy. 2012. "Whence Theravada? The Modern Genealogy of an Ancient Term." In *How Theravada Is Theravada?*, edited by Peter Skilling, Jason Carbine, Claudio Cicuzza, and Santi Pakdeekham. Chiang Mai: Silkworm Books.

Petavatthu. 1942. Translated by Henry Gehman. In *Minor Anthologies of the Pali Canon, Part IV*, edited by I. B. Horner. London: The Pali Text Society.

Pholsena, Vatthana. 2006. *Post-War Laos: The Politics of Culture, History and Identity.* Ithaca, NY: Cornell University Press.

Prebish, Charles. 1974. "A Review of the Scholarship on the Buddhist Councils." *Journal of Asian Studies* 33:239–254.

———. 1975. *Buddhist Monastic Discipline.* University Park: Pennsylvania State University Press.

Pye, Lucien. 1985. *Asian Power and Politics: The Cultural Dimensions of Authority.* Cambridge, MA: Harvard University Press.

Reed, Susan A. 2010. *Dance and the Nation: Performance, Ritual and Politics in Sri Lanka.* Madison: University of Wisconsin Press.

Reynolds, Frank. 1969. "Ritual and Social Hierarchy: Traditional Religion in Buddhist Laos." *History of Religions* 9:78–89.

———. 1972. "The Two Wheels of Dhamma: A Study in Early Buddhism." In *AAR Studies in Religion,* no. 3, edited by Bardwell L. Smith. Chambersburg, PA: American Academy of Religion.

———. 1978. "The Holy Emerald Jewel." In *Religion and Legitimation of Power in Thailand, Laos and Burma,* edited by Bardwell L. Smith. Chambersburg, PA: Anima Books.

Rozenberg, Guillaume. 2009. "How Generals Think." *Aseanie* 24 (December): 11–31.

———. 2010. *Renunciation and Power: The Quest for Sainthood in Contemporary Burma.* Translated by Jessica Hackett. New Haven, CT: Yale Southeast Asia Studies Monograph 59.

Salgado, Nirmala. 2013. *Buddhist Nuns and Gendered Practice: In Search of the Female Renunciant.* New York: Oxford University Press.

Sanderson, Alexis. 2003–2004. "The Shaivite Religion among the Khmers." *BEFEO* 90–91:345–462.

Sarkisyanz, Emmanuel. 1965. *Buddhist Backgrounds of the Burmese Revolution.* The Hague: Martinus Nijoff.

Satha-Anand, Suwanna. 2001. "Truth over Convention: Feminist Interpretations of Buddhism." In *Religious Fundamentalism and the Human Rights of Women,* edited by Courtney W. Howland, 281–291. New York: Palgrave.

Savin, Dan, and Shalom Robinson. 2000. "Holocaust Survivors and Survivors of the Cambodian Tragedy: Similarities and Differences." *Echoes of the Holocaust* 3.

Schober, Juliane. 1997. "Buddhist Just Rule and Burmese National Culture: State Patronage of the Chinese Tooth Relic in Myanma." *History of Religions* 36:218–243.

———. 2007. "Buddhism, Violence and the State in Burma (Myanmar) and Sri Lanka." In *Religion and Conflict in South and Southeast Asia: Disrupting Violence,* edited by Linell E. Cady and Sheldon W. Simon. New York: Routledge.

———. 2011. *Modern Buddhist Conjunctures in Myanmar.* Honolulu: University of Hawai'i Press.

Schober, Juliane, and Steven Collins, eds. Forthcoming. *Theravada Buddhist Encounters with Modernity.* New York: Routledge.

Scott, Rachel M. 2009. *Nirvana for Sale? Buddhism, Wealth and the Dhammakaya Temple in Contemporary Thailand.* Albany: State University of New York Press.

Seeger, Martin. 2006. "The Bhikkhuni-Ordination Controversy in Thailand." *Journal of the International Association of Buddhist Studies* 29:155–184.

Seekins, Donald. 2011. *State and Society in Modern Rangoon.* London: Routledge.

Semmens, Justine. 2011. "Ten-Precept Mothers in the Buddhist Revival of Sri Lanka." In *The Sri Lanka Reader,* edited by John Clifford Holt, 364–375. Durham, NC: Duke University Press.

Seneviratne, H. L. 1978. *Rituals of the Kandyan State.* Cambridge: Cambridge University Press.

———. 1999. *The Work of Kings: The New Buddhism in Sri Lanka.* Chicago: University of Chicago Press.

Sizemore, Russell F., and Donald K. Swearer. 1990. *Ethics, Wealth and Salvation.* Columbia: University of South Carolina Press.

Skidmore, Monique. 1997. "In the Shade of the Bo Tree: *Dhammayietra* and the Reawakening of Community in Cambodia." *Crossroads: An Interdisciplinary Journal of Southeast Asian Studies* 10:1–32.

———. 2004. *Karaoke Fascism: Burma and the Politics of Fear.* Philadelphia: University of Pennsylvania Press.

———. 2005. *Burma at the Turn of the 21st Century.* Honolulu: University of Hawai'i Press.

Skilling, Peter. 2009. "Theravada in History." *Pacific World* 3 (11): 61–94.

Skilling, Peter, Jason A. Carbine, Claudio Cicuzza, and Santi Pakdeekham, eds. 2012. *How Theravada Is Theravada? Exploring Buddhist Identities.* Chiang Mai: Silkworm Books.

Smith, Bardwell. 1978. *Religion and the Legitimation of Power in Thailand, Laos and Burma.* Chambersburg, PA.: Anima Books

Smith, Jonathan Z. 1987. *To Take Place: Toward Theory in Ritual.* Chicago: University of Chicago Press.

Sombo, Lin. 2006–2007. "Threads of Continuity: Buddhism and Conflict in Cambodia, 1953 to 1979." *Journal of the Center for Khmer Studies* 8–9:82–97.

Southwold, Martin. 1983. *Buddhism in Life: The Anthropological Study of Religion and the Practice of Sinhalese Buddhism.* Manchester: Manchester University Press.

Spiro, Melford. 1970. *Buddhism and Society: A Great Tradition and Its Burmese Vicissitudes.* Berkeley: University of California Press.

Steinberg, David I. 2010. *Burma/Myanmar: What Everybody Needs to Know.* New York: Oxford University Press.

Strong, John S. 1987. "Images." In *Encyclopedia of Religion,* edited by Mircea Eliade, vol. 7, 97–104.

———. 1992. *The Legend and Cult of Upagupta: Sanskrit Buddhism in North India and Southeast Asia.* Princeton, NJ: Princeton University Press.

———. 2004. *Relics of the Buddha.* Princeton, NJ: Princeton University Press.

Stuart-Fox, Martin. 1998. *The Lao Kingdom of Lan Xang: Rise and Decline.* Bangkok: White Lotus Press.

———. 2002. "Historiographuy, Power and Identity: History and Legitimisation in Laos." In *Contesting Visions of the Lao Past: Lao Historiography at the Crossroads,* edited by Christopher Goscha and Soren Ivarsson. Copenhagen: Nordic Institute of Asian Studies.

Swearer, Donald K. 2004. *Becoming the Buddha: The Ritual of Image Consecration in Thailand.* Princeton, NJ: Princeton University Press.

Swearer, Donald K., and Somai Premchit. 1995. *The Legend of Queen Camadevi.* Albany: State University of New York Press.

Tambiah, S. J. 1970. *Buddhism and the Spirit Cults of North-East Thailand.* Cambridge: Cambridge University Press.

———. 1976. *World Conqueror, World Renouncer.* Cambridge: Cambridge University Press.

———. 1985. *Culture, Thought and Action.* Cambridge, MA: Harvard University Press.

Tannenbaum, Nicola. 1992. *Who Can Compete against the World?* Ann Arbor, MI: Association for Asian Studies.

———. 2000. "Protest, Tree Ordination, and the Changing Context of Political Ritual." *Ethnology* 39:109–127.

Teiser, Stephen F. 1996. *The Ghost Festival in Medieval China.* Princeton, NJ: Princeton University Press.

Terweil, B. J. 1975. *Monks and Magic: An Analysis of Religious Ceremonies in Central Thailand.* London: Curzon Press.

———. 1978a. "The Origin and Meaning of the Tai City Pillar." *Journal of the Siam Society* 66:159–171.

———. 1978b. "The Tais and Their Belief in Khwans: Towards Establishing an Aspect of Proto-Tai Culture." *The Southeast Asian Review* 3:1–16.

Thant Myint-U. 2007. *The River of Lost Footsteps: A Personal History of Burma.* New York: Farrar, Straus and Giroux.

Thompson, Ashley. 2004. "The Future of Cambodia's Past: A Messianic Middle-Period Cambodian Royal Cult." In *History, Buddhism, and New Religious Movements in Cambodia,* edited by John Marston and Janet Guthrie. Honolulu: University of Hawai'i Press.

Tilakaratne, Asanga. 2012. *Theravada Buddhism: The Way of the Elders.* Honolulu: University of Hawai'i Press.

Tiyavanich, Kamala. 1997. *Forest Recollections.* Honolulu: University of Hawai'i Press.

Trainor, Kevin. 1997. *Relics, Ritual and Representation in Buddhism.* Cambridge: Cambridge University Press

Trankell, Ing-Britt. 1999. "Royal Relics: Ritual and Social Memory in Louang Prabang." In *Laos: Culture and Society,* edited by Grant Evans, 191–213. Chiang Mai: Silkworm Books.

Turner, Alicia. 2014. *Saving Buddhism: The Impermanence of Religion in Colonial Burma.* Honolulu: University of Hawai'i Press.

Turner, Victor. 1973. "The Center Out There: Pilgrim's Goal." *History of Religions* 12:191–230.

UNESCO. 2004. *Impact: The Effects of Tourism on Culture and the Environment in Asia and the Pacific. Tourism and Heritage Site Management in Luang Prabang, Lao PDR.* Bangkok: Office of the Regional Advisor for Culture in Asia and the Pacific, UNESCO, Bangkok, and the School of Travel Industry Management, University of Hawai'i.

van Gennep, Arnold. 1972. *The Rites of Passage.* Translated from the French by Monika Vizedom and Gabrielle Caffee. Chicago: University of Chicago Press, 1973 (originally published as *Les rites des passage,* 1908).

Veidlinger, Daniel M. 2007. *Spreading the Dhamma: Writing, Orality and Textual Transmission in Northern Thailand.* Honolulu: University of Hawai'i Press.

Vickery, Michael. 1998. *Society, Economics and Politics in Pre-Angkor Cambodia: The Seventh–Eighth Centuries.* Tokyo: Centre for East Asia Cultural Studies for UNESCO, Toyo Bunko.

————. 2003. "Two Historical Records of the Kingdom of Vientiane." In *Contesting Visions of the Lao Past: Lao Historiography at the Crossroads,* edited by Christopher Goscha and Soren Ivarsson. Copenhagen: Nordic Institute of Asian Studies.

Wales, H. G. Quaritch. 1992. *Siamese State Ceremonies.* Richmond, VA: Curzon.

Walshe, Maurice, trans. 1987. *The Long Discourses of the Buddha: A Translation of the* Digha Nikaya. Boston: Wisdom Books.

Welivitiye Suratha Thero, ed. 1970. *Dalada Sirita.* 2nd ed. Colombo, Sri Lanka: M. D. Gunasena.

Wells, Kenneth E. 1982. *Thai Buddhism: Its Rites and Activities.* New York: AMS Press.

Wickremesinghe, Nira. 2006. *Sri Lanka in the Modern Age.* Honolulu: University of Hawai'i Press.

Winternitz, Maurice. 1927. *History of Indian Literature.* 2 vols. Calcutta: University of Calcutta.

Wolters, O. W. 1982 and 1999. *History Culture and Region in Southeast Asian Perspectives.* Singapore: Institute of Southeast Asian Studies. Revised edition, Ithaca, NY: Southeast Asia Publications, Southeast Asia Program, Cornell University.

Zago, Marcello. 1972. *Rites et Ceremonies en Milieu Bouddhiste Lao.* Roma: Universita Gregoriana Editrice.

————. 1976. "Buddhism in Contemporary Laos." In *Buddhism in the Modern World,* edited by Heinrich Dumoulin and John C. Maraldo, 120–129. London: Collier Macmillan Publishers.

Zucker, Eve. 2008. "The Absence of Elders: Chaos and Moral Order in the Aftermath of the Khmer Rouge." In *People of Virtue: Reconfiguring Religion. Power and Moral Order in Cambodia Today,* edited by David Chandler and Alexandra Kent, 195–212. Copenhagen: Nordic Institute of Asian Studies.

Index

"soul stuff," 339n12, 342n43
Southeast Asia, xii*map*, 2, 3
Southwold, Martin, 8, 9
Soviet Union, and Vietnamese, 261
spirit cults, 14–15, 339n10; ancestor
  veneration and, 21–40, 248; Buddhism
  replacing, 37–40, 339n11; Lao, 12, 13–40;
  ontology, 14–22, 38–41; *phi muang*, 23, 26,
  39, 40; territorial, 18–22, 27, 32–33
spirit effigy, offering plate, 273*fig*
spirit flags, 272, 306*fig*
spirit houses, 14–15
spirit streamers, 306*fig*
Spiro, Melford, 213, 355n50
sponsors: *kan ben*, 360n44; ordination,
  159–163, 178, 186
sramanas (non-*brahman*ical or heterodox
  religious communities), 137, 145, 193,
  347n4
Sri Ksetra, Mahayana sculptures, 349n1
Sri Lanka, 3, 67–130, 344n1; Anuradhapura,
  2, 68–69, 78, 83, 179, 344n1, 350n3;
  bhikkhunisangha (order of nuns), 1–2, 179,
  344n4, 349n26; bodhi tree plantings,
  341n32; Buddha images, 11–12, 72;
  Buddhism, 2, 11–12, 68–130, 360n45;
  Buddhist nationalism, 72–78, 108,
  122–130, 344n6; *devalayas*, 93–105, 94*fig*,
  99*fig*, 116–119, 119*fig*, 121, 127–129, 338n5;
  economy, 133; education and health
  care system, 74; European colonization,
  71–76, 82, 87, 88–89, 122, 123, 125,
  344nn1,6, 345nn10,15; *hamaduruwo*,
  351n24; independence, 74, 346n29; "JVP
  insurrection," 106–107, 130; kingship,
  69–71, 81–93, 103, 105, 302, 345nn15,18,
  346n21; modernization, 133; monasteries,
  2, 68–70, 90, 135, 344nn1,2,8; Myanmar
  government relations with, 233–234;
  Nissanka Mala, 69; ordination, 135,
  157–158, 302; political unrest, 73–78,
  106–108, 130, 133, 179, 346n29, 352n32;
  Polonnaruva, 69–71, 84–86, 302; President
  Rajapaksa, 73, 77, 109, 233–234; society, 67,
  68, 74–76, 124–127, 347n37; spirit cults,
  15–16; terms for temple, 350n5;
  Theravada lineage, 1–2, 337n6;
  "upcountry" and "low country"
  distinction, 124–127; urban migration,
  128. See also *asala peraharas*; Kandy
Sri Vijaya (modern Malaysia/Sumatra), 70

State Law and Order Restoration Council
  (SLORC), Myanmar, 192, 222, 228
State Peace and Development Council
  (SPDC), Myanmar, 192, 218, 353nn42,44
Steele Olcott, Henry, 6
Steinberg, David I., 231, 234, 349n2,
  353nn40,41, 354n46
sthalapuranas (mythic stories of origins),
  128–129
Sthaviravadin sect, 181
Strong, John, 79, 80, 84
Stuart-Fox, Martin, 29, 31, 37, 44,
  341nn28,33,38
stupas, 79, 350n5; Lao, 34, 41, 53*fig*, 54; merit
  transfer, 305; Myanmar military giving
  and, 352n35; robing of, 183; Sri Lanka, 68.
  See also temples
sukhwan rite, 146–147
Surasena, Peter, 115*fig*, 122
Surinyavongsa, Lao King, 41–42
Suthep Thaugsuban, 187
Suttapitaka, 190–191
suttas (sermons), 70, 191, 203, 252, 305. *See
  also individual suttas*
Suttavibhanga, 136–137
Swearer, Donald, 13, 33, 185, 338n4
symbols, 4–5; *asala perahara*, 92–105;
  custodians of the relic, 82; flowerpot, 211,
  351n21; *jak* tree, 96; not Buddha images,
  338n2; *pinda*, 272–273, 278–281; robing,
  213. *See also* images; relics

Taiwan, nuns, 179, 181–182
Taksin-based populist movement,
  Thailand, 188
Tambiah, S. J., 8–9, 17, 30, 50, 105, 159
Tamils, 70–71, 87, 344n1; Nayakkar kings,
  92; Sinhala conflict with, 73–78, 106–108,
  130, 133, 179, 346n29, 352n32
Tannenbaum, Nicola, 9, 186
Taoist, 303
tatmadaw (military government), Myanmar,
  192, 217–232, 352–354
taxes: French in Cambodia, 249–250,
  356n19; Myanmar land donations,
  352n34
Teiser, Stephen F., 298–301, 361n55
temples: Angkor, 32, 49, 291; for
  Cambodians in Canada and the US,
  358n35; Gadaladeniya and Lankatilaka
  temple complexes, 70; Lao Buddhist, 13,

whip-cracking, *asala perahara*, 110*fig*, 112–113
Wickramasinghe, Nira, 71, 72
Winternitz, Maurice, 360n45
Wolters, O. W., 339n12, 340n22
women: *asala perahara*, 97, 103, 116; "dana
   cliques," 217–218; Fa Ngum and, 34; "lady
   boys," 61; Lao femininity ideal, 65–66;
   meditation movement, 354–355n50; and
   ordination, 152, 161–163, 170–171, 178–183,
   186, 347n2, 355n50; *pchum ben*, 360n42;
   prostitution as life choice, 180–181; role
   in Theravada Buddhism, 161, 179, 344n54;
   sexually harassed in public, 110; *upasikas*
   (female lay disciples), 141, 153, 164, 170,
   199, 348n17; Wat Phra Dhammakaya,
   170–171. *See also* beauty pageants;
   goddesses; nuns
World Conqueror, World Renouncer
   (Tambiah), 17
World Fellowship of Buddhists, 3

World Travel and Tourism Council
   (WTTC), 342n50
World War II, 74, 225, 236

Xetthathirat, Lao king, 38, 39, 41, 43

yaksa (malevolent spirit), 16
Yama, 284–285, 285*fig*
Yang Sam, 357n25
Yangon (formerly Rangoon): economics,
   351n28; *kathina*, 189–190, 196, 198,
   201–213, 215; multireligious, 349n2;
   Saffron Revolution (2007), 224, 227,
   232–233, 353n41, 354n46; Shwedagon
   Pagoda, 211–213, 217, 221, 224–225, 351n28,
   352n35, 354n46
Yasa, 141–142

Zago, Marcello, 8, 12–13, 50, 52
Zucker, Eve, 263, 357n23

About the Author

John Clifford Holt is William R. Kenan Jr., Professor of Humanities in Religion and Asian Studies at Bowdoin College in Brunswick, Maine. He is the author of many books, including *Discipline: The Canonical Buddhism of the Vinayapitaka* (1981), *Buddha in the Crown: Avalokitesvara in the Buddhist Traditions of Sri Lanka* (1991), for which he was awarded an American Academy Book Award for Excellence, *The Religious World of Kirti Sri: Buddhist Art and Politics in Late Medieval Sri Lanka* (1996), *The Buddhist Visnu* (2004), and *Spirits of the Place: Buddhism and Lao Religious Culture* (2009). He has edited *The Sri Lanka Reader: History, Politics and Culture* (2011) and *Buddhist Extremists and Muslim Minorities* (2016). He was awarded an honorary Doctor of Letters from the University of Peradeniya in 2002, and selected as University of Chicago Divinity School Alumnus of the Year in 2007. He received a John Simon Guggenheim Foundation fellowship in 2014–2015 to begin research and writing on Buddhist/Muslim conflicts in Sri Lanka, Myanmar, and Thailand.